Site Development Associate
Academic Student Guide

Certification
PARTNERS

President/Chief Certification Architect

James Stanger, Ph.D.

Vice President, Operations

Todd Hopkins

Senior Content Developer

Kenneth A. Kozakis

Managing Editor

Susan M. Lane

Editor

Sarah Skodak

Project Manager/Publisher

Tina Strong

Customer Service   Certification Partners, LLC
1230 W. Washington St., Ste. 201
Tempe, AZ 85281
(602) 275-7700

Site Development Associate

Developer

Patrick T. Lane

Contributors

DeAnne Bowersock, James Stanger, Ph.D., and Kenneth A. Kozakis

Editor

Sarah Skodak

Project Manager/Publisher

Tina Strong

Trademarks

Disclaimer

Copyright Information

Table of Contents

List of Labs

List of Tables

Course Description

Site Development Associate teaches you essential Web page development skills. You will learn to develop Web sites using Hypertext Markup Language version 5 (HTML5) and Cascading Style Sheets (CSS). You will learn to write code manually, as well as use graphical user interface (GUI) authoring tools. You will also learn to insert images, create hyperlinks, and add tables, forms, video, and audio to your Web pages.

In addition to learning about HTML5 and CSS coding, you will learn how to use HTML5 Application Programming Interfaces (APIs) to extend the functionality of Web pages, such as geolocation, drag-and-drop, canvas, and offline Web applications. Other topics include validating your HTML code, recognizing the importance of search engine optimization (SEO), using style sheets extensively to format Web page content, and implementing fundamental design concepts. Throughout the course, you will learn how Web sites are developed as managed projects. You will also identify e-commerce solutions and relate Web site development to business goals.

Site Development Associate provides an introduction to tasks, job roles and careers in Web development. This course will teach you to work as a productive part of a Web site development team. Hands-on labs include real-world scenarios based on a previously live version of the Habitat for Humanity site. Note that students will build prototype pages using Habitat for Humanity content. This content is provided by Habitat for Humanity with permission to use it in labs teaching site development skills. The prototype pages that students build do not necessarily represent, duplicate or simulate the current live Habitat for Humanity Web site, which can be visited at *www.habitat.org*.

All CIW Web Foundations courses offer Case Studies for class discussion about real-world skills applications, and job-related topics such as project management and the relationship between technology and business operations. Guided, step-by-step labs provide opportunities to practice new skills. You can challenge yourself and review your skills after each lesson in the Lesson Summary and Lesson Review sections. Additional skill reinforcement is provided in Activities, Optional Labs, Lesson Quizzes and a Course Assessment that are available from your instructor.

This coursebook includes supplemental material located on CIW Online. To practice the skills presented in class or to perform any labs that were not completed, refer to the Classroom Setup section for information about system requirements and using the lab files.

The CIW Web Foundations courses prepare students to take the CIW Web Foundations Associate certification exam.

Series

Site Development Associate is the second course in the CIW Web Foundations series:

- Internet Business Associate
- *Site Development Associate*
- Network Technology Associate

Prerequisites

No prior experience using the Internet, developing Web pages or configuring networks is necessary. However, students should be familiar with an operating system such as Microsoft Windows 7 before taking this course. The CIW Web Foundations courseware does not provide entry-level computer literacy. Rather, it builds upon computer literacy training and certifications such as Microsoft Office Specialist (*www.microsoft.com*).

Certification

The CIW Web Foundations series of courses prepares students to take the high-stakes CIW Web Foundations Associate certification exam (1D0-610*). Those who pass the CIW Web Foundations Associate exam earn the highly respected CIW Web Foundations Associate certification, which is recognized throughout the industry as validating essential Internet skills for the workplace. The CIW Web Foundations Associate certification proves that an individual has evolved from being an Internet consumer to an Internet producer, capable of producing real-world Internet applications. A CIW Web Foundations Associate certificant can use common Internet-ready applications, can create properly formed HTML5 documents, knows database essentials, understands project management concepts and can troubleshoot networks.

Candidates also have the option to take any or all of the three modular CIW Associate exams, each of which earns the candidate a modular subject certification if passed:

- Internet Business Associate (exam 1D0-61A*)

- Site Development Associate (exam 1D0-61B*)

- Network Technology Associate (exam 1D0-61C*)

Candidates who pass all three modular certification exams also earn the comprehensive CIW Web Foundations Associate certification.

For information about taking any CIW Associate exams, visit *www.CIWcertified.com*.

* Please note that these updated exams will be live Dec. 1, 2012. Prior to Dec. 1, exams 1D0-510, 1D0-51A, 1D0-51B and 1D0-51C are available.

Target audience

Students and professionals who are interested in Web site development can benefit from the CIW *Site Development Associate* course and/or certification:

- IT professionals

- Marketing professionals

- Graphic artists

- Web site designers

Courseware

This coursebook was developed for instructor-led training and will assist you during class. Along with comprehensive instructional text and objectives checklists, this coursebook provides easy-to-follow hands-on labs and a glossary of course-specific terms. It also provides Internet addresses needed to complete some labs, although due to the constantly changing nature of the Internet, some addresses may no longer be valid.

The student learning materials include the following:

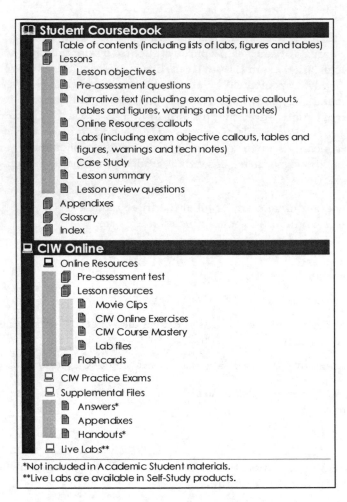

Student Coursebook
- Table of contents (including lists of labs, figures and tables)
- Lessons
  - Lesson objectives
  - Pre-assessment questions
  - Narrative text (including exam objective callouts, tables and figures, warnings and tech notes)
  - Online Resources callouts
  - Labs (including exam objective callouts, tables and figures, warnings and tech notes)
  - Case Study
  - Lesson summary
  - Lesson review questions
- Appendixes
- Glossary
- Index

CIW Online
- Online Resources
  - Pre-assessment test
  - Lesson resources
    - Movie Clips
    - CIW Online Exercises
    - CIW Course Mastery
    - Lab files
  - Flashcards
- CIW Practice Exams
- Supplemental Files
  - Answers*
  - Appendixes
  - Handouts*
- Live Labs**

*Not included in Academic Student materials.
**Live Labs are available in Self-Study products.

When you return to your home or office, you will find this coursebook to be a valuable resource for reviewing labs and applying the skills you have learned. Each lesson concludes with questions that review the material. Lesson review questions are provided as a study resource only and in no way guarantee a passing score on the CIW Web Foundations Associate certification exam.

Coursebook versions

The CIW Web Foundations courseware is designed for various classroom environments: academic, learning center and corporate. These coursebooks are available in both instructor and student versions. Student versions are available for both the academic environment and the learning center/corporate environment. Check your book to verify which version you have.

- **Instructor (Academic, Learning Center and Corporate)** — Example syllabi for 10-week, 16-week and 32-week instruction periods are included with the instructor supplemental files available on CIW Online. Learning centers can teach this series at an accelerated pace; consult the implementation tables that can be found on CIW Online. The supplemental files also include an appendix listing the CIW Web Foundations Associate certification exam objectives and locations of corresponding material in the coursebook. The instructor version of this book includes Instructor Notes in the margin, which provide additional tips and commentary for the instructor to supplement course narrative. Margin callouts also direct instructors to material that relates directly to specified CIW Web Foundations objectives. The instructor book and supplemental online files contain all answers to Activities (pen-and-paper-based), Optional Labs (computer-based), Lesson Quizzes and the Course Assessment. The supplemental online files also include handout versions of all Activities, Optional Labs, Lesson Quizzes and the Course Assessment, which the instructor can print and assign during class or as homework. Lesson Quizzes and Course Assessments are provided as study and course-grading resources only; success on these materials in no way guarantees a passing score on the CIW Web Foundations Associate certification exam. The movies provide supplementary instruction in a multimedia format, and enhance the coursebook narrative and labs. However, movie content does not comprehensively address CIW Web Foundations Associate exam objectives and is not intended to replace coursebook content.

- **Student (Academic)** — The student book and supplemental online files include Pre-Assessment and Lesson Review questions for each lesson. However, the student book does not provide answers to these questions. It also does not include any Activities, Optional Labs, Quizzes or the Course Assessment. Students can obtain these elements and answers only from the instructor. The student supplemental materials include appendixes and files used to perform many of the labs in the coursebook. The supplemental files also include an appendix listing the CIW Web Foundations Associate certification exam objectives and locations of corresponding material in the coursebook. Lesson Quizzes and Course Assessments are provided as study and course-grading resources only; success on these materials in no way guarantees a passing score on the CIW Web Foundations Associate certification exam. The movies provide supplementary instruction in a multimedia format, and enhance the coursebook narrative and labs. However, movie content does not comprehensively address CIW Web Foundations Associate exam objectives and is not intended to replace coursebook content.

- **Student (Learning Center/Corporate)** — Designed for the learning center/corporate environment, this student book includes Pre-Assessment and Lesson Review questions. The student supplemental online materials include appendixes; files used to perform many of the labs in the coursebook; and answers to the Pre-Assessment Questions, Lesson Review Questions, Course Assessment, Activities, Optional Labs and Lesson Quizzes. The supplemental files also include an appendix listing the CIW Web Foundations Associate certification exam objectives and locations of corresponding material in the coursebook. Lesson Quizzes and Course Assessments are provided as study and course-grading resources only; success on these materials in no way guarantees a passing score on the CIW Web Foundations Associate certification exam. The movies provide supplementary instruction in a multimedia format, and enhance the coursebook narrative and labs. However, movie content does not comprehensively address CIW Web Foundations Associate exam objectives and is not intended to replace coursebook content.

Online resources

You can visit CIW Online at *http://education.certification-partners.com/ciw/* to access supplemental course materials and to get help in preparing for the CIW Web Foundations Associate certification exam. CIW Online provides a variety of online tools you can use to supplement the Official CIW Courseware.

CIW courseware supplemental files

This coursebook includes supplemental material that can be accessed from CIW Online. Online materials are provided for both instructors and students, and include some elements required to complete the coursework and other optional elements that are provided for your interest or further study. Student materials include lab files used to complete the course labs, answers to student exercises and quizzes, and appendixes with related information (including the CIW Web Foundations Objectives And Locations Appendix). Instructor materials include course syllabi and implementation tables, answers to students exercises and quizzes, and appendixes with related information (including the CIW Web Foundations Objectives And Locations Appendix). See the CIW Supplemental Files section under Classroom Setup for information about accessing these files.

CIW Movies

CIW Web Foundations courses offer movie clips that provide supplementary instruction in a multimedia format, and enhance the coursebook narrative and labs. However, movie content does not comprehensively address CIW Web Foundations certification exam objectives and is not intended to replace coursebook content.

Instructors in a classroom environment are strongly encouraged to present movies to the entire class using a computer screen projector. Group presentations enable instructors to present and discuss movie content when appropriate. Controlling the presentation of movies also minimizes distractions from course material and essential lecture or lab time.

Students are strongly encouraged to watch the movie clips on their own if they are unable to view them in class. Each student is provided access to CIW Online to view the movies.

CIW Online Exercises

These interactive activities are instructional supplements to the official print and online books, designed to offer a blended-learning approach. Mapped directly to the Official CIW Courseware, the CIW Online Exercises enable you to review important concepts from the Web Foundations courses and measure your proficiency on content relevant to the CIW Web Foundations Associate certification exam. CIW Online Exercises challenge you with a wide range of activities, including glossary flashcards, matching exercises, fill-in-the-blank exercises, crossword puzzles and true/false questions — all providing immediate feedback.

CIW Course Mastery

CIW Course Mastery is designed to assess your knowledge of the concepts, skills and best practices of Web technology taught in the Official CIW Courseware. The CIW Course Mastery assesses lesson knowledge, reinforces classroom learning and enhances instruction. This online review program contains multiple-choice questions that cover CIW Web Foundations courseware content lesson by lesson. The Course Mastery program is based on a unique method that maximizes knowledge retention.

CIW Certification Practice Exams

After you have mastered the Web Foundations course material, you are ready to prepare for the high-stakes CIW Web Foundations Associate certification exam. The online CIW Certification Practice Exams program helps you build confidence with your knowledge of the CIW exam objectives. This program provides you with:

- Timed practice exams that simulate the high-stakes testing environment and help predict actual performance on CIW certification exams.

- A feedback review mode that allows you to check answers while taking the practice exam and gain valuable feedback that relates each question to a CIW exam objective and a lesson in the Official CIW Courseware.

- Exam results that report on your mastery of each CIW exam objective.

- Personalized performance reports and study plans to track individual progress and view overall class trends.

Course Objectives

After completing this course, you will be able to:

- Discuss the importance of a business Web site that complements your organization.

- Identify front-end and back-end Web page design issues, demonstrate knowledge of Web site development principles, and define the concepts of creative design and branding standards.

- Discuss the history of markup languages, and identify markup language standards and the organizations that define them.

- Define markup and document structure elements, and use Cascading Style Sheets (CSS) to apply formatting to Web pages.

- Use both a text editor and a GUI markup language editor to create HTML5 pages.

- Create HTML5 pages with horizontal rules, images, browser-safe colors, hyperlinks, tables, Web forms, client-side image maps, audio and video.

- Test processing of Web forms using a public test engine, and validate your HTML5 code to W3C standards.

- Identify requirements for Web site publishing, identify uses for client-side and server-side Web technologies and languages, and demonstrate HTML5 Application Programming Interfaces (APIs).

- Identify the benefits of Dynamic HTML (DHTML) and the Document Object Model (DOM).

- Identify Web page development techniques for mobile devices, and use Web application frameworks to create and manage dynamic Web sites.

- Use Web 2.0 technologies to customize your Web pages.

- Compare using a service provider to hosting your own Web server.

- Discuss Internet marketing issues and search engine optimization (SEO), and their effects on the content and performance of your Web site.

- Identify issues related to working in a global environment.

Classroom Setup

Your instructor has probably set up the classroom computers based on the system requirements listed in the following sections. Most software configurations on your computer are identical to those on your instructor's computer. However, your instructor may use additional software to demonstrate network interaction or related technologies.

System Requirements

This section lists the hardware, software and connectivity requirements to implement this course.

Hardware

Each classroom should be equipped with an individual computer workstation for each student and the instructor. The following table summarizes the hardware requirements for all courses in the CIW program.

Note: The CIW hardware requirements are similar to the minimum system requirements for Microsoft Windows 7 implementation.

Hardware Specifications	Minimum Requirements
Processor	1 GHz 32-bit (x86) or 64-bit (x64) processor
Hard disk	16 GB available hard disk space (32-bit) or 20 GB available hard disk space (64-bit) for Windows 7 installation. 16 GB of additional space must be available for course applications and files.
RAM	1 GB RAM (32-bit) or 2 GB RAM (64-bit)
Network interface card (NIC)	Wireless, 10/100 Ethernet, or Gigabit Ethernet
Wireless router (AP)	Wireless-G, Wireless-N, or Wireless-AC router with built-in 4-port Ethernet switch to connect wired network PCs and devices. Wireless NICs must support the wireless router (G, N or AC).
Sound card/speakers	Required
Video adapter	DirectX 9 graphics device with WDDM 1.0 driver
Network connectivity	Enough wireless nodes, hubs or switches to allow classroom computers to communicate and access the Internet.
Monitor	1024 x 768 screen resolution using a VGA, DVI or HDMI connector
Web camera (Webcam)	Any type of Web camera. Some monitors include an internal Webcam. USB Webcams are a good choice.

Software

The CIW Web Foundations series is intended to be largely operating system- and browser-independent. Provided you use Hypertext Markup Language version 5 (HTML5)-compliant browsers, the labs should function properly. HTML5-compliant browsers include Windows Internet Explorer 9, Google Chrome (any version) and Mozilla Firefox (version 10 or higher).

Each school's network is configured differently. You should test each lab to ensure the ports are open on the firewall before presenting the lab to the class. You may have to talk to your network administrator to open the ports.

WARNING! If you are unable to upgrade to Microsoft Windows 7, you will be unable to use Windows Internet Explorer 9 (IE9). Unfortunately, IE9 is the only IE browser that supports HTML5 without modifications. Windows XP and Vista only support up to IE8. If your classroom must use a Windows XP or Vista installation, please use the latest version of Google Chrome or Mozilla Firefox instead of IE8 or previous for the labs. If you are required to use IE8 or previous, then the Site Development Associate course will require you to include JavaScript into each Web page for the HTML5 coding to render properly. Instructions for adding the JavaScript code is included in the Classroom Setup Guide.

If you are teaching all three CIW Web Foundations courses sequentially, there is no need to reformat your computers for each course. The recommended software configurations for computers used to complete the labs in this book series are as follows.

Internet Business Associate

To be installed before class:

- **Microsoft Windows 7 Professional** (typical installation)

- **Windows Internet Explorer 9** (typical installation)

To be registered by students during class:

- **Google account** (*www.google.com*) — necessary for students to access online cloud services and resources, such as Google Drive, Google Docs, Gmail, Google+ and Blogger. Students are responsible for their own account registration.

- **Windows Live account** (*explore.live.com*) — necessary for students to access online cloud services and resources, such as SkyDrive, Hotmail, Essentials and Messenger. Students are responsible for their own account registration.

To be installed by students during course labs:

- **Firefox 10 or higher** (binary provided in the C:\CIW\Internet\Lab Files\Lesson04 folder)

- **Google Chrome — any version** (binary provided in the C:\CIW\Internet\Lab Files\Lesson04 folder)

- **Ogg Codecs** (binary provided in the C:\CIW\Internet\Lab Files\Lesson05 folder)

- **Thunderbird 2.0** (binary provided in the C:\CIW\Internet\Lab Files\Lesson07 folder)

- **TightVNC, Bzip2 and Bunzip2** (binaries provided in the C:\CIW\Internet\Lab Files\Lesson09 folder)

- **Windows Live Messenger** (binaries provided in the C:\CIW\Internet\Lab Files\Lesson02 folder)

- **Ad-AwareAE** (binary provided in the C:\CIW\Internet\Lab Files\Lesson08 folder)

- **GanttProject** (binary provided in the C:\CIW\Internet\Lab Files\Lesson10 folder)

Site Development Associate

To be installed before class:

- **Microsoft Windows 7 Professional** (typical installation)

- **Windows Internet Explorer 9** (typical installation)

- **Google Chrome — any version** (typical installation)

- **Firefox 10 or higher** (typical installation)

- **Windows Live Movie Maker** (typical installation)

To be installed by students during course labs:

- **Lynx** (binary provided in the C:\CIW\Site_Dev\Lab Files\Lesson01\Lab_1-3\Lynx folder)

- **FormMail** (binary provided in the C:\CIW\Site_Dev\Lab Files\Lesson06\Lab_6-1\FormMail folder)

- **KompoZer** (binary provided in the C:\CIW\Site_Dev\Lab Files\Lesson09\Lab_9-1 folder)

- **Free Video Converter Factory** (binary provided in the C:\CIW\Site_Dev\Lab Files\Lesson07\Lab_7-2 folder)

To be installed by instructor for instructor-led demonstration in Optional Lab 8-1:

- **XAMPP** (binary provided in the C:\CIW\Site_Dev\Lab Files\Lesson08\Optional_Lab_8-1\XAMPP folder)

Network Technology Associate

To be installed before class:

- **Microsoft Windows 7 Professional** (typical installation)

- **Windows Internet Explorer 9** (typical installation)

- **Firefox 10 or later** (typical installation)

- **Chrome — any version** (typical installation)

To be registered by students during class:

- **Google account** (*www.google.com*) — necessary for students to access online cloud services and resources, such as Google Drive, Google Docs, Gmail, Google+ and Blogger. Students are responsible for their own account registration.

- **Windows Live account** (*explore.live.com*) — necessary for students to access online cloud services and resources, such as SkyDrive, Hotmail, Essentials and Messenger. Students are responsible for their own account registration.

To be installed by students during course labs:

- **uTorrent** (binary provided in the C:\CIW\Network\Lab Files\Lesson01 folder)
- **FileZilla_v3.0.2.1** (torrent file provided in the C:\CIW\Network\Lab Files\Lesson01 folder)
- **7-Zip** (binary provided in the C:\CIW\Network\Lab Files\Lesson01 folder)
- **TruCrypt 7 or higher** (binary provided in the C:\CIW\Network\Lab Files\Lesson06 folder)
- **VirtualBox** (binary provided in the C:\CIW\Network\Lab Files\Lesson02 folder)
- **Porteus Linux** (binary provided in the C:\CIW\Network\Lab Files\Lesson02 folder)

Connectivity

Internet connectivity is required for this course. You will experience optimal performance with a dedicated Internet connection (e.g., a cable/DSL modem or a T1 line). However, you can teach the course using slower connections (e.g., 56-Kbps modem).

CIW supplemental files

Each coursebook includes supplemental materials that are referenced and used throughout the course. These supplemental materials are provided online at *http://education.certification-partners.com/ciw/*.

You will need to create a directory for all supplemental materials for the course. The default location is *C:\CIW\[Course_Title]*. To view or download the materials, go to CIW Online, click the link for each file and save to this directory. You can then create a shortcut to this directory on your Desktop. As you conduct the course labs, you can use this shortcut to quickly access your lab files.

Conventions and Graphics Used in This Book

The following conventions are used in these coursebooks.

Terms
Technology terms defined in the margins are indicated in **bold type** the first time they appear in the text. However, not every word in bold type is a term requiring definition.

Lab Text
Text that you enter during a lab appears in ***italic bold type***. Names of components that you access or change in a lab appear in **bold type**.

Notations
Notations or comments regarding screenshots, labs or other text are indicated in italic type.

Program Code or Commands
Text used in program code or operating system commands appears in the Lucida Sans Typewriter font.

The following graphics are used in these coursebooks.

Tech Notes point out exceptions or special circumstances that you may find when working with a particular procedure. Tech Notes that occur within a lab are displayed without the graphic.

Tech Tips offer special-interest information about the current subject.

Warnings alert you about cautions to observe or actions to avoid.

This graphic signals the start of a lab or other hands-on activity.

The *CIW Online* graphic signals appropriate points in the course at which to view additional online resources, available at *http://education.certification-partners.com/ciw/*.

Each lesson summary includes an *Application Project*. This project is designed to provoke interest and apply the skills taught in the lesson to your daily activities.

Each lesson concludes with a summary of the skills and objectives taught in that lesson. You can use the *Skills Review* checklist to evaluate what you have learned.

This graphic indicates a line of code that is completed on the following line.

Lesson 1:
Markup Language and Site Development Essentials

Objectives

By the end of this lesson, you will be able to:

↪ 2.1.1: Relate the history of markup languages to current techniques and technologies, including Standard Generalized Markup Language (SGML), previous versions of Hypertext Markup Language (HTML).

↪ 2.1.2: Identify the format and various versions of HTML, including HTML 4.01, Extensible HTML (XHTML), HTML5.

↪ 2.1.8: Explain the importance of consistently developing to a single W3C standard (e.g., HTML5).

↪ 2.6.1: Describe the functionality of XML.

↪ 2.7.1: Obtain input from stakeholders about acceptable technologies and color combinations.

↪ 2.7.2: Create an initial Web site diagram (i.e., a story board or prototype), and translate it into a site map.

↪ 2.7.3: Verify compliance with government and industry accessibility standards, including W3C Web Accessibility Initiative (WAI), U.S. Government Section 508, Americans with Disabilities Act (ADA).

↪ 2.7.4: Validate Web page design according to technical and audience standards adopted by employers.

↪ 2.7.5: Verify Web site usability, viewability and browser compatibility.

↪ 2.12.1: Test and validate Web documents.

↪ 2.12.3: Test Web pages in multiple browsers.

↪ 2.13.1: Work as a team member to develop pages and sites.

↻ 2.13.2: Collaborate with technical (e.g., IT) and non-technical (e.g., marketing) members of the organization to ensure sites meet requirements.

↻ 2.13.3: Determine information and audience requirements for a site, including stakeholders such as customers, employees, shareholders, suppliers.

↻ 2.13.4: Document a Web site plan.

↻ 2.13.5: Communicate the Web site plan effectively, both orally and in writing.

↻ 2.13.6: Obtain and document feedback, then improve the site, including working closely with sales and marketing to evaluate site effectiveness.

↻ 2.14.1: Define legal issues related to a Web site, including trademarking, licensing, copyrighting, licensing copyrighted materials, scope of copyright, reach of copyright, copyrighting process, copyright infringement and consequences.

↻ 2.14.2: Identify fundamentals of project management, including major stages of a Web design/development project cycle.

↻ 2.14.3: Identify processes of pre-launch site/application functionality testing, including checking links, testing with various browsers, testing against corruption of your e-commerce site, load testing, access to the site, testing with various speed connections.

↻ 2.14.4: Manage existing sites (e.g., remove dead links and/or upgrade connectivity when necessary).

↻ 2.14.5: Remove old sites and pages.

↻ 2.15.1: Identify ways to elicit useful feedback from management and customers.

↻ 2.15.2: Use presentation aids and support material, including charts, tables, figures, written content, overhead projection.

↻ 2.15.3: Use presentation software (e.g., slide-based software).

↻ 2.15.4: Clarify technical concepts for a non-technical audience, and use strategies to retain listener interest.

↻ 2.15.5: Interpret verbal, non-verbal and written feedback.

↻ 2.15.6: Address diversity and corporate/organizational culture when communicating your message by customizing meeting and message delivery, and listening for responses.

↻ 2.15.7: Identify ways to lead meetings (e.g., make introductions, invite questions, set time frames, set action times, monitor time, ensure proper discussion focus, publish minutes).

↻ 2.18.1: Investigate costs associated with placing and developing your own server.

↻ 2.18.2: Identify costs associated with using a cloud service provider.

↻ 2.18.3: Distinguish among dedicated hosting, co-location and virtual servers.

↻ 2.18.5: Manage information relevant to a site (e.g., account information, passwords, IP addresses).

↻ 2.19.3: Consider corporate/organizational culture when designing page layout.

↻ 2.19.4: Demonstrate sensitivity to ethnic and cultural issues in page layout and design.

↻ 2.20.1: Obtain proper permissions from developers when repurposing content (e.g., other developers' code, images, concepts).

↻ 2.20.2: Create and sign a Non-Disclosure Agreement (NDA) when necessary.

↻ 2.20.3: Identify situations in which it is necessary to consult with a legal team.

↻ 2.20.4: Identify ethical concerns when developing a Web site.

Pre-Assessment Questions

1. Which of the following establishes nationally recognized rules meant to protect the rights of a Web site's author?

   a. Ethics
   b. Copyright
   c. Trademark
   d. Trade secrets

2. Which of the following is an example of an HTML markup interpreter?

   a. Bluetooth device
   b. Proxy server
   c. Text editor
   d. E-mail application on a mobile device

3. What is the latest version of HTML?

   _____

Creating Web Pages

The skills of Web page creation have become vital to many careers. You are likely to need skills with Web-based technologies for various job-related tasks, including:

- Informing colleagues about progress on team projects.

- Using or contributing to the company intranet.

- Working with customers online.

- Posting or retrieving résumés.

- Gathering information from customers or community members about their interests.

- Obtaining information from social networking activities.

You may also want to work as a Web developer or site designer, with responsibility for the Web pages of an entire company or organization. Whatever job role you choose, this course will teach you how to create Web pages using text editors and graphical development applications. Each tool creates similar pages, but the creation processes are quite different.

markup language
A series of commands used to format, organize and describe information on a Web page.

It is important to understand that Web pages are no longer viewed only through standard Web browsers. Your smartphone, tablet, smart TV and gaming console are all capable of reading **markup languages**. In fact, many Web design professionals refer to HTML as "markup," simply because many of their pages will be viewed using applications other than Web browsers. Because markup languages are becoming more common in the workplace, it is important for you to understand how to use them.

Hypertext Markup Language (HTML)

Hypertext Markup Language (HTML)
The traditional authoring language used to develop Web pages for many applications.

Web page creation by any method requires a working knowledge of **Hypertext Markup Language (HTML)**. It is the standard markup language on the Web, and in other settings. HTML is standardized by an organization called the World Wide Web Consortium (W3C). You can learn more about the W3C at *www.w3.org*.

HTML is the markup language that defines page structure, hyperlinks, graphics and more to enable pages to render in Web browsers and other devices. You will learn about HTML in detail throughout this course. You can type HTML code manually into a text editor, use a graphical user interface (GUI) editor program to create the code automatically (by pointing and clicking your mouse), or combine both methods.

Cascading Style Sheets (CSS)

Cascading Style Sheets (CSS)
A technology that allows greater style definition and formatting control of HTML elements. Formatting can be placed within the HTML or called remotely from an external style sheet.

Cascading Style Sheets (CSS) are rules in an external text file that determine how to display HTML elements in your Web pages. CSS contain formatting instructions that can define the font, color and phrase elements used on a particular markup page.

If all pages on your site are linked to the same external style sheet, then one simple change to the style sheet will change all elements across the site. If you then want to change those instructions (for example, the size of a document heading), you need not change every page manually. You need only change a line in the style sheet file, then all your headings will change their appearance to conform to the style sheet. This technology can save a great deal of development and maintenance time, as well as make a more consistent, accessible interface.

Additional Web page elements

Web pages can incorporate more than just HTML and CSS. You can use other languages to enhance a page, such as JavaScript, Jscript and VBScript. You can also enhance Web pages by inserting specialized content created with programs and technologies such as Java (*www.java.com*), ActiveX (*www.microsoft.com*), Microsoft Silverlight (*www.microsoft.com/silverlight/*) and Flash (*www.adobe.com/products/flash/*). You will learn about all these technologies throughout this course.

CIW Online Resources – Movie Clips

Visit CIW Online at http://education.Certification-Partners.com/CIW to watch a movie clip about this topic.

Lesson 1: Markup Language and Site Development Essentials

Mobile and Cloud Issues

Web site development has been impacted by smartphones, tablets and other mobile devices. Smaller screens are used to view Web pages previously viewed only on much larger PC monitors. This limited screen size has caused Web site designers to modify their existing sites or create alternative sites for these mobile devices.

cloud computing
Software, infrastructure and platform services that are hosted by a remote data center and provided to organizations or individuals over the Internet.

Cloud computing has also impacted Web design. Cloud computing is software services that are provided over the Internet, rather than at a company site. For instance, in the past, companies had to have a server room with Web, e-mail, file and database servers. These servers can now be located in the "cloud" (i.e., a remote data center that is accessed over the Internet).

Cloud services include social networks and blogging sites. These sites do not require knowledge of HTML to create Web pages. Users simply "point and click" the available Web site tools to design a personalized page.

You will learn how to create both mobile and cloud Web pages (as well as traditional Web sites) in this course. These methods will demonstrate how Web designers must design their sites and Web pages for users who will view them on different types of devices.

Text Editors and Markup Languages

You do not need to use a special editor application to create HTML. You can use a simple text editor. A text editor is any program that allows you to type simple text and edit it, such as Microsoft Notepad and WordPad, or UNIX-based programs such as Vi and Pico. However, you must save your code files as plaintext. Any formatting instructions embedded in a file by a word-processing program, for example, can prevent the file from functioning properly.

Multipurpose Internet Mail Extensions (MIME)
A protocol that enables operating systems to map file name extensions to corresponding applications. Also used by applications to automatically process files downloaded from the Internet.

After you save the Web page code as a text file, you should save it with the .htm or .html file name extension. Many operating systems and Web browsers are configured with **Multipurpose Internet Mail Extensions (MIME)** to automatically process files with these extensions. Figure 1-1 shows a text editor with HTML code. You will use Notepad as your HTML text editor in the first part of this course. You will then use a simple GUI-based editor application later in the course.

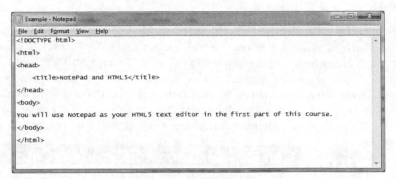

Figure 1-1: HTML code in text editor

Many text editors exist, all with more capability than Microsoft Notepad. Open-source examples you may want to use include:

- Notepad++ (http://*notepad-plus.sourceforge.net*).

- jEdit (*www.jedit.org*).

- Vim (*www.vim.org*).

- Cream (http://*cream.sourceforge.net*).

- Emacs (*www.gnu.org/software/emacs*).

Most of these products have versions that will run on multiple operating systems.

Graphical User Interface (GUI) Editors

graphical user interface (GUI)
A program that provides visual navigation with menus and screen icons, and performs automated functions when users click command buttons.

Graphical user interface (GUI) markup editor applications place markup instructions into files for you; you do not need to know HTML to use GUI editors. Many GUI HTML editors still do not produce valid HTML. Nevertheless, such editors provide a graphical user interface   that makes it easy for you to create HTML pages without writing any code manually. You simply point and click with your mouse, and the code is generated by the program. Commands are displayed on the graphical user interface as they will appear in a browser, thus the programs are often called WYSIWYG (What You See Is What You Get) editors. Some developers feel that using a GUI editor application saves time. Others feel that GUI editors create confused HTML code and do not provide true flexibility.

Popular GUI HTML editors include Adobe Dreamweaver, Microsoft Expression Web, Mozilla SeaMonkey and Adobe GoLive. The KompoZer GUI editor is shown as an example in Figure 1-2. In this course, you will use the Bluefish GUI editor.

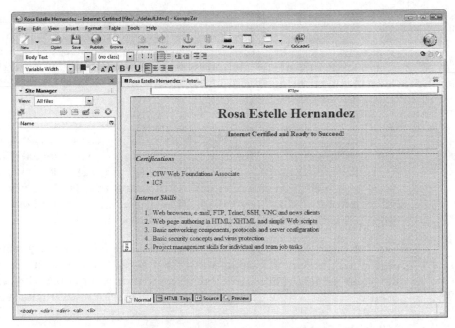

Figure 1-2: KompoZer GUI markup editor

Why learn markup languages?

As already mentioned, most GUI HTML editor applications have not kept pace with the evolution of HTML, and do not provide options for more recent markup standards. However, many of these GUI programs allow you to modify your HTML code manually from the GUI. If you know HTML, you can maximize the benefit of these programs by manually adding code that the GUI editor does not. Further, if you are considering learning any scripting or programming languages, such as JavaScript, you *must* learn how to write code manually.

Learning to write your own markup code in a text editor will enable you to create highly attractive, functional HTML documents, regardless of any other available software. Another reason to use a text editor is so you can learn the fundamentals of markup languages, then update a page to the latest standard or recommendation. You will learn about markup language standards later in this course.

History of Markup Languages

In this section, you will learn about the types of markup languages available to you for creating online documents.

Standard Generalized Markup Language (SGML)

**Standard
Generalized Markup
Language (SGML)**
A metalanguage
used to create
other languages,
including HTML and
XHTML.

metalanguage
A language used for
defining other
languages.

Standard Generalized Markup Language (SGML) is a **metalanguage**, which means that it is used to create other languages, including HTML and XHTML. SGML was originally created by IBM and was standardized in 1986 by the International Organization for Standardization (ISO). SGML is a powerful markup language that describes documents by organizing concepts separately from their visual presentation. However, it is also very complex and difficult to learn.

SGML's purpose was to describe only the information within a document, not the formatting of it. With SGML, you can describe how data elements in the document relate to each other. SGML was not designed to format the data's appearance on the page.

Document Type Definition (DTD)
A set of rules contained in a simple text file that defines the structure, syntax and vocabulary as it relates to tags and attributes for a corresponding document.

SGML essentially requires that you create, or define, your own document language rules. This set of language rules is called the **Document Type Definition (DTD)**. The DTD is generally specified in a separate file, which you reference, or declare, at the beginning of each document that you want to conform to the rules. Once the DTD is established, then all elements in the document must conform to it. You will learn more about DTDs and how to declare them later.

Hypertext Markup Language (HTML)

Tim Berners-Lee of MIT invented Hypertext Markup Language (HTML) with colleagues from CERN (the European Particle Physics Laboratory) as a means of distributing non-linear text, called hypertext, to multiple points across the Internet. Berners-Lee felt that SGML and other languages were needlessly complex and did not suit the need for a cross-platform language that helped format documents.

hyperlinks
Embedded instructions within a text file that link it to another point in the file or to a separate file.

In HTML, one document links to another via pointers called **hyperlinks**. Hyperlinks are embedded instructions within a text file that call another location in the file or a separate file when the link is accessed, usually by a click of a mouse. The global set of linked documents across the existing Internet framework grew into the World Wide Web.

HTML vs. SGML

Like SGML, HTML facilitates data exchange through a common document format across different types of computer systems and networks on the Web. However, HTML does not allow you to define a DTD and has fewer language elements than SGML. As a result, HTML is easier to use and has become the standard method of encoding information for Web documents.

The latest version of HTML, called HTML5, is not based on SGML. This departure has allowed the simplification of HTML structure. For example, the DTD is no longer required.

HTML 3.2 and HTML 4.01 recommendations

OBJECTIVE
2.1.2: HTML and XHTML

HTML 3.2 is an older but functional HTML standard. Some Web pages and HTML editors still use the 3.2 and 4.01 standards.

The HTML 4.01 Recommendation (released in 1999) contained many improvements from HTML 3.2, most notably Cascading Style Sheets (CSS). You can access this standard at *www.w3.org/TR/html4/*. The 4.01 specification included minor modifications to the 4.0 specification.

HTML 4.01 supported multiple spoken languages. For example, HTML 4.01 allowed you to create Web pages that read languages such as Hebrew from right to left. HTML 4.01 also allowed you to create ambitious tables and forms, as well as incorporate scripting languages. You will learn more about scripting solutions, such as JavaScript, later in the course.

 The W3C regulates the development of CSS standards.

HTML 4.01 flavors

As Web pages were developed in HTML 4.01, they had three distinct variants, or "flavors." The HTML 4.01 flavors ensured that you could use the specification and still remain backward-compatible with older Web browsers. Following is a short description of each flavor.

- **HTML 4.01 Transitional** — allowed developers to insert formatting using either CSS or traditional layout instructions (e.g., HTML font, color and phrase elements). This version rendered in browsers that did not support HTML 4.01 features such as CSS. This version also allowed tags that the W3C considered to be less useful, known as "deprecated tags."

- **HTML 4.01 Strict** — required the exclusive use of CSS when defining layout instructions. Deprecated tags were not allowed and generated errors.

- **HTML 4.01 Frameset** — required for pages that used HTML frames, which placed Web pages inside each other to create separate panes in the browser window. Some felt that frames provided additional functionality or enhanced a site's look and feel.

You specify the flavor of HTML by using a document type (<!DOCTYPE>) declaration. You will learn more about the <!DOCTYPE> in this and later lessons.

Many Web pages were written to versions of HTML 4.01. In this course, however, you will create pages using HTML5, which will be discussed shortly. To understand HTML5, you must first be familiar with XML and XHTML.

Extensible Markup Language (XML)

Extensible Markup Language (XML)
A markup language that describes document content instead of adding structure or formatting to document content. A simplified version of SGML.

OBJECTIVE
2.6.1: XML functionality

Extensible Markup Language (XML) is a language used to describe data elements on a Web page. XML enhances the structure and navigation of data. It is not used to format the page's appearance. Businesses use XML because it allows data to be interchanged with all types of applications.

XML is often used with intranets and extranets because these systems tend to focus mostly on sophisticated personal and business transactions. These types of transactions require the elements that XML offers.

XML documents can be formatted into print documents, Web documents, PDF documents, comma-separated values (CSV), Braille, text-to-speech and many other formats. This versatility allows XML to easily format content from a textbook, for example, which can be published to the Web in an e-learning course. Because the documents are well-formed and define only the content, changes can occur on the fly (i.e., dynamically or without interruption), without administrators or programmers manually reformatting the content before transmission.

XML is often misunderstood. Many people think XML is just another set of markup used to format Web pages. This assumption is incorrect. In fact, XML is not used to format Web pages, but to describe the data from which Web pages are created. The W3C governs the development of XML.

Extensible Hypertext Markup Language (XHTML)

Because the requirements for XML and HTML are dramatically different, the developers of HTML decided to create a medium that would merge the two into a markup language called Extensible Hypertext Markup Language (XHTML).

client
An individual computer connected to a network. Also, a system or application (such as a Web browser or user agent) that requests a service from another computer (the server) and is used to access files or documents.

The idea was to make the transition from HTML to XML without making all existing HTML documents unusable in XML **clients**. These requirements meant that XHTML could not completely depart from HTML, nor could it be patterned completely after XML. XHTML documents are not required to render correctly in standard clients, but will have little if any difficulty. For a more detailed discussion about compatibility issues, visit the W3C site at the following URI:

www.w3.org/TR/2002/REC-xhtml1-20020801/#guidelines

 When you use XML, the term Uniform Resource Identifier (URI) is preferred over the standard HTML term Uniform Resource Locator (URL).

Two versions of XHTML were created by the W3C: XHTML version 1.0 and XHTML version 1.1. Version 1.0 became a W3C recommendation in 2000. Version 1.1 earned its original recommendation in 2001. A third version, XHTML 2.0, was abandoned by the W3C in 2009 in favor of a new XHTML5 version, which is still under development. It is important that you are familiar with XHTML because you will encounter Web pages designed using it. Table 1-1 shows the various XHTML specifications.

Table 1-1: W3C XHTML specifications

XHTML Version	W3C Status	Notes
XHTML 1.0	Recommended in 2000	Still used in some production environments
XHTML 1.1	Recommended in 2001	Still used in some production environments; provided "modularization"
XHTML 2.0	Abandoned in 2009; it did not provide backward compatibility	The W3C decided to pursue an XHTML version based on HTML5 instead
XHTML5	Working draft	Under development as part of the HTML5 specification

As you have learned, HTML describes only a document's visual layout, and XML allows you to describe the function and context of the information contained in a document. XHTML allows HTML to become XML-compliant. Thus XHTML extends HTML by allowing the convergence of HTML documents with XML structure, creating forward-compatibility for documents. For more information about how XHTML, XML and HTML work together, visit *www.w3.org/MarkUp*. You can read the W3C's XHTML 1.0 specification at *www.w3.org/TR/xhtml1*.

HTML5

HTML5 is the latest version of HTML under development by the W3C. This course will focus on this specification. At the time of this writing, HTML5 was a W3C working draft. The W3C has created an HTML5 logo to market the technology, shown in Figure 1-3.

Figure 1-3: HTML5 logo

HTML5 provides modern requirements for the Internet with fewer plug-ins, such as the ability to standardize how video and audio are presented on a Web page. To that end, HTML5:

- Introduces the <video> element, which is designed to eliminate the need to install third-party plug-ins (such as those for Adobe Flash or Microsoft Silverlight).

- Adds the <audio> element, which allows pages to seamlessly add audio files for events such as podcasts.

offline storage
The ability for Web browsers and online services to download and access content and services without being connected to the Internet.

- Establishes ways to enable drag-and-drop capability for Web pages without using third-party add-ons.

- Gives developers more native tools such as download progress indicators, image captioning options and form validation tools to use on a page.

- Provides developers with a native option for **offline storage**, and enables applications to run as expected even without network connectivity.

geolocation
An HTML5 Application Programming Interface that allows developers to retrieve the geographical location information for a client-side device.

- Allows developers to retrieve the geographical location information for a client-side device, called **geolocation**. Examples include using the Global Positioning System (GPS) of a mobile device to determine the device's location, which allows Web services to be provided based on the client's location.

You will learn more about HTML5 throughout this course. To view the HTML5 specifications, go to: *http://dev.w3.org/html5/spec/Overview.html*

Choosing and applying a language standard consistently

Whether you develop your own Web pages using HTML5, HTML 4.01, XHTML 1.1 Transitional, or any other flavor of these markup languages, it is important that you adopt a single W3C standard and apply it consistently throughout your document, Web pages or site. Otherwise, your pages may have difficulty rendering properly in user agents. This best practice also applies when you are using other types of languages in your online documents and sites, including CSS, scripting languages such as JavaScript, programming languages, and so forth.

Markup code validation

It is possible to validate all markup code automatically. Many validators exist, but the most authoritative is the W3C Markup Validation Service (*http://validator.w3.org*).

Using this service, you can upload local HTML files for validation, or provide the URL of a Web page to validate it. In this course, you will use the W3C validation service to validate your HTML5 code. However, it is important to note that this validator reads the <!DOCTYPE> declaration on an HTML page and validates according to the specified DTD. So, if your document references an older HTML 4.01 Strict DTD, then the validator will validate code according to the HTML 4.01 Strict specifications.

To reiterate, make sure you adopt a single W3C standard and apply it consistently so that when you validate your markup code, the code and your specified DTD will match, and the results of the validation process will be legitimate.

Validating your markup code is worthwhile because validated code is most likely to be interpreted accurately by the majority of user agents. As a result, your pages will render as you expect and will be available to a larger audience.

Following are some tips to consider when validating your markup code:

- Do not be discouraged when you see multiple problems reported for a page. Sometimes one small flaw can cause the remaining code on the page to fail validation, even if the remaining code is actually valid.

- When errors are reported, search through the code carefully to find the true problem. Sometimes when a validation program finds a problem, it does not report the correct cause or it may not report the cause clearly.

- Make sure that you are validating the correct file.

CIW Online Resources – Online Exercise

Visit CIW Online at *http://education.Certification-Partners.com/CIW* to complete an interactive exercise that will reinforce what you have learned about this topic.

Exercise 1-1: Comparing markup languages

Universal markup creation

Good Web page coding generally involves ensuring that the content is rendered appropriately regardless of the browser used to render it. To ensure this type of consistent, or universal, rendering, Web page developers can apply certain practices to their coding that result in universal markup:

OBJECTIVE
2.1.8: Using a single
W3C standard

- Follow W3C standards carefully.

- Choose one standard version of any given language you use, and apply that standard consistently throughout your document, pages or site.

Creating universal markup code is important for several reasons:

- Your pages will be ensured to render in future versions of most browsers.

- Your pages will be more scalable. This means that as you add more sophisticated content, make pages searchable or use the content in ways you have not yet imagined, you can still use markup you created without having to revise the code extensively.

- Your pages will be more accessible to disabled users. You will be able to more easily make your pages compliant so that your site is available to the widest possible audience and does not present a liability to your organization.

In some situations you may find that universal markup seems unnecessary. For example, if you are writing markup code for a page for your company's intranet, and all employees use the same browser, you can feel comfortable using proprietary language extensions and technology. In this case, you can be relatively sure that your HTML5 code will render consistently in that browser every time. But suppose the company's browser choice changes. Most situations call for pages that can be viewed in a variety of browsers, so creating universal markup is always good coding practice.

 Consistent use of an HTML standard — such as HTML5, for example — can improve your page's ability to rank higher in a search engine results page.

In the following lab, you will visit the W3C Web site to learn more about commonly used markup languages. Suppose your project manager has asked you to research current Web standards. She has heard that HTML 4.01 is common but that newer standards exist, and she wants to know the best sources for this type of information. What Web pages would you research or recommend to explain Web standards?

 Lab 1-1: Reviewing W3C standards

OBJECTIVE
2.1.2: HTML and
XHTML

In this lab, you will visit the W3C Web site to learn more about commonly used markup languages.

1. First, you will learn more about the HTML5 specification. Open a browser and visit **www.w3.org/TR/html5/** Scroll through the specification to learn more about HTML's relationship to SGML, as well as HTML elements.

2. Next, learn more about XML by visiting **www.w3.org/XML**.

3. Visit **www.w3.org/TR/xhtml1/** to learn more about XHTML 1.0 and **www.w3.org/TR/xhtml11/** to learn about XHTML 1.1.

4. Now, visit the W3C home page at **www.w3.org**. Review the mission of the W3C, then browse through the site.

5. Visit the W3C Markup Validation Service at **http://validator.w3.org** and learn more about this service.

6. Further familiarize yourself with HTML, XML and XHTML by accessing Google, Bing or another search engine, and entering search strings such as the following: **"HTML versus XHTML"**

7. Consider the sources presented in your search results. Link to some that look reliable, and read the various explanations that you find to better understand the differences between HTML and XHTML.

In this lab, you visited the W3C Web site and other sites to learn more about HTML, XML and XHTML.

The HTML Web Development Trifecta: HTML5, CSS and JavaScript

The future of Web design lies within three technologies: HTML5, Cascading Style Sheets (CSS) and JavaScript. These technologies used together provide Web pages that easily adapt to smartphones, tablets, gaming devices and smart TVs, as well as to traditional PCs.

Apple co-founder Steve Jobs provided a great argument for using these technologies in his famous "Thoughts on Flash" blog. (Adobe Flash is a browser plug-in that provides multimedia such as video, animation, interactive games and audio.)

> "...we strongly believe that all standards pertaining to the web should be open. Rather than use Flash, Apple has adopted HTML5, CSS and JavaScript — all open standards. Apple's mobile devices all ship with high performance, low power implementations of these open standards. HTML5, the new web standard that has been adopted by Apple, Google and many others, lets web developers create advanced graphics, typography, animations and transitions without relying on third party browser plug-ins (like Flash). HTML5 is completely open and controlled by a standards committee, of which Apple is a member."

HTML5, CSS and JavaScript are sometimes called the "HTML5 family. " Table 1-2 explains the functions of each technology.

Table 1-2: HTML5 family

Technology	Description
HTML5	Markup language used for structuring and presenting Web page content
Cascading Style Sheets (CSS)	Style sheet language that provides the formatting and "look" of a Web page or document written in a markup language
JavaScript	Scripting language that provides dynamic, interactive capabilities to Web pages

This course teaches the basics of HTML5 and CSS. Several JavaScript examples will be included to show interactive HTML5 elements, but JavaScript is fairly complex and is covered in a separate CIW course.

CIW Online Resources – Online Exercise

Visit CIW Online at *http://education.Certification-Partners.com/CIW* to complete an interactive exercise that will reinforce what you have learned about this topic.

Exercise 1-2: The HTML Web Development Trifecta

CIW Online Resources – Course Mastery

Visit CIW Online at *http://education.Certification-Partners.com/CIW* to take the Course Mastery review of this lesson or lesson segment.

SDA Lesson 1 - Part A

Web Site Development Principles

You need more than knowledge of markup languages and talent for design to contribute to a successful Web development team. You also need to understand the business concerns and issues associated with Web development, from copyright issues to site development planning. The following sections discuss many responsibilities of a Web project manager. You may have a different role on a Web development team, but understanding project management makes you a stronger and more valuable team member.

OBJECTIVE
2.14.2: Web project management fundamentals

Project management and the Web development project cycle

Creating a Web site requires you to work closely with individuals and teams of individuals. To work smoothly with other teams, you must carefully outline and communicate the project's steps. While you may not manage the project, at the very least you will be part of it. So you must understand the typical Web development project cycle. Consider the following steps:

- Create and document an initial Web site plan.

- Obtain relevant input from stakeholders.

- Communicate the Web site plan.

- Consider technical and non-technical concerns.

- Develop the site.

- Publish the site.

- Manage the site.

Each step is discussed in the following sections.

 Part of the management cycle is optimizing pages so that they rank highly in search engine results pages.

OBJECTIVE
2.7.3: Accessibility standards and compliance

Developing accessible Web pages

You must design your Web pages with accessibility in mind so that your pages are available to all visitors of your site. For example, consider that the baby-boomer generation (anyone born between 1946 and roughly 1964) commands an enormous amount of income. As this generation ages, its members will develop sight, hearing and cognitive challenges. Ignoring these common disabilities in your design means that you will exclude this group of individuals. As a result, you will not have as popular or as lucrative a site as you may like.

Americans with Disabilities Act (ADA)

The Americans with Disabilities Act (ADA) was enacted in 1990 to protect the civil rights of disabled people. This law has many sections, and includes mandates for equal employment opportunities and public accommodations for disabled people. It also includes mandates that electronic information be accessible to disabled people. Significant compliance failures are subject to financial penalties.

According to the U.S. Justice Department, the ADA also applies to cyberspace communications. In an opinion letter dated September 9, 1996 (*www.usdoj.gov/crt/foia/cltr204.txt*), the U.S. Department of Justice stated the following:

"Covered entities under the ADA are required to provide effective communication, regardless of whether they generally communicate through print media, audio media, or computerized media such as the Internet. Covered entities that use the Internet for communications regarding their programs, goods or services must be prepared to offer those communications through accessible means as well."

Because it is an active law, the ADA is relevant to anyone designing pages in the United States, and anyone creating sites that will be visited by users who live in the United States. The standards are officially known as the U.S. Department of Justice ADA Standards for Accessible Design. Any penalties are the result of prosecution brought by the U.S. Justice Department; lawsuits from individuals and class action suits are not possible. The Justice Department tries to determine good-faith efforts before bringing lawsuits, and generally punishes only violators who exhibit long-term, wanton disregard for the standards. To learn facts and myths about ADA, visit *www.usdoj.gov/crt/ada/pubs/mythfct.txt*.

As a Web designer, your job is to create what the Department of Justice calls "reasonable accommodation" in your Web sites for people with various disabilities. You must make reasonable accommodations if you are a covered entity, which according to ADA is any "private employers, state and local governments, employment agencies and labor unions". Critical ADA compliance factors to consider when creating reasonable accommodations in your Web sites include:

- Ensuring that all images have text-based descriptions so that sight-impaired visitors can access sites through screen-reader technology.

- Providing text-based alternatives to all non-text content (e.g., Java applets).

- Providing forms that are easily read by screen-reading technology.

 Tech Tip *Video is not ADA-compliant because sight-impaired visitors cannot see it. Video with audio but no alternative text support is a problem because hearing-impaired visitors cannot hear it.*

For more information about ADA, visit the following sites:

- The ADA Home Page (*www.ada.gov*)

- A paper that summarizes ADA from a legal perspective, "Applying the ADA to the Internet: A Web Accessibility Standard" by Cynthia D. Waddell, J.D. (*http://people.rit.edu/easi/law/weblaw1.htm*)

- Usability.gov, which is a U.S. Department of Health and Human Services site (*www.usability.gov*)

- An accessibility article on the All Things Web site (*www.pantos.org/atw/35588.html*)

- Current Web design articles in About.com's Web Design/HTML section (*http://webdesign.about.com/od/accessibilityvalidators/a/use_acces_valid.htm*)

Additional disabilities acts and initiatives

Following is a partial list of disabilities acts and initiatives for various nations:

- Canada's Common Look and Feel Standards for the Internet page (*www.tbs-sct.gc.ca/clf-nsi/index_e.asp*)

- The Australian Government's Guide to Adopting the W3C Web Content Accessibility Guidelines (WCAG)(*www.finance.gov.au/publications/wcag-2-implementation/docs/wcag-transition-strategy.pdf*

- India's Maharashtra Right to Information Act (*http://righttoinformation.gov.in/*)

- The e-Japan Priority Policy Program (*www.kantei.go.jp/foreign/it/network/priority-all/index.html*)

Additional information about various national laws and standards is available on the W3C at *www.w3.org/WAI/Policy*.

Web Content Accessibility Guidelines (WCAG)

Web pages should be accessible to all people, including those with disabilities. To assist in this mission, the W3C has created the Web Accessibility Initiative (WAI). The WAI has developed the Web Content Accessibility Guidelines (WCAG) to provide a universal set of standards promoting accessibility. According to the WAI, the Web's full potential can only be realized by "promoting a high degree of usability for people with disabilities." The WAI works with worldwide organizations in five main areas: technology, guidelines, tools, education and outreach, and research and development.

 The European Union and Australia have mostly adopted the WCAG standards.

WAI aims to ensure that core technologies used on the Web, such as HTML, Cascading Style Sheets (CSS), Extensible Markup Language (XML) and the Document Object Model (DOM), are equally accessible to all users, including those with physical, visual, hearing and cognitive disabilities. (You will learn more about these technologies later in the course.) For example, a person with a visual disability may be unable to view a multimedia presentation on the Web. One way to solve this problem is to include text equivalents of the presentation in the code. The multimedia player, such as Apple QuickTime or Microsoft Windows Media Player, could then access the text equivalent and present it to the user in Braille or as speech.

The WAI works with numerous W3C Working Groups to ensure that the standards for various W3C technologies include accessibility options. For example, the HTML standard supports improved navigation, extended descriptions of complex graphics, and multimedia captions. It also supports device-independent user interface descriptions that allow users to interact with Web pages using mouse, keyboard or voice input.

You can visit the following Web sites to learn more about Web page accessibility for disabled people:

- Web Accessibility Initiative (WAI) (*www.w3.org/WAI*)

- Web Content Accessibility Guidelines (WCAG) Recommendation (*www.w3.org/TR/WCAG20*)

- The WAI Policies page (*www.w3.org/WAI/Policy*)

- The WAI Evaluation page (*www.w3.org/WAI/eval*)

- Curriculum for Web Content Accessibility Guidelines 1.0 (*www.w3.org/WAI/wcag-curric*)

Following are additional WAI concerns and standards:

user agent
Any application,
such as a Web
browser, mobile
phone, smartphone
or help engine, that
renders HTML for
display to users.

- **User agent accessibility** — A **user agent** is any device used to view a Web page. The most common user agent is a Web browser. Additional user agents include mobile device applications, such as smartphones and tablets. The W3C User Agent Accessibility Guidelines document is available at *www.w3.org/TR/UAAG20*.

- **WCAG checklist** — A checklist for the accessibility guidelines detailed in the WCAG is available at *www.w3.org/TR/WAI-WEBCONTENT/full-checklist.html*.

- **Accessibility for developers** — The W3C also addresses ways to ensure that development tools can be used by disabled people. For more information, read the W3C Authoring Tool Accessibility Guidelines at *www.w3.org/TR/WAI-AUTOOLS*.

Accessibility extensions include the following:

- Adobe Dreamweaver includes alternative text for all images and multimedia elements. Screen readers read aloud this alternative text for disabled users. Learn more at *www.adobe.com/accessibility/products/dreamweaver/overview.html*.

- Adobe Flash Professional includes extensions that have captioning and video accessibility features at *www.adobe.com/accessibility/products/flash/*.

- Microsoft provides extensive information about accessibility features for all of its operating systems and products at *www.microsoft.com/enable/training/default.aspx*.

Although different situations should be considered when designing Web documents, each accessible design choice generally benefits several disability groups, and the Web community as a whole. For more detailed information, you can read the WAI specification at *www.w3.org/TR/WAI-WEBCONTENT/*.

Section 508 of the Rehabilitation Act

On June 21, 2001, the U.S. government implemented Section 508 of the Rehabilitation Act: Electronic and Information Technology Accessibility Standards. Section 508 requires that all electronic and information technology developed, procured, maintained or used by federal agencies be comparably accessible to users with disabilities. Section 508 is based on the Priority 1 and 2 checkpoints of the W3C's WAI Web Content Accessibility Guidelines 1.0. You can learn more about Section 508 by visiting the following URLs:

- Federal Information Technology Accessibility Initiative, Section 508 home page (*www.section508.gov*)

- U.S. Access Board, Section 508 of the Rehabilitation Act (*www.access-board.gov/508.htm*)

The chief purpose of Section 508 is to ensure that disabled individuals have a comparable level of access to information. Each standard aims to ensure that Web page design and other computer-based elements do not limit access to information by disabled users. Section 508 includes the following standards for Web sites:

- All non-text elements must have a text-based equivalent.

- If using multimedia, all equivalent information must be properly synchronized with the multimedia so that disabled persons are not at a disadvantage.

- Information must be equally available in color and without color.

- Documents must be made available without requiring an associated style sheet.

- Text descriptions must be made available for all image maps.

- Client-side image maps should not be used because they cannot be properly presented to visually impaired users.

- If using tables for data, you must identify all row and column headers.

- If a table has two or more rows or columns, you must use row and column headers.

- Sites that use frames must have titles that easily enable alternative browsers to navigate through each frame.

- If necessary, a separate text-only site should be made available to ensure access.

- When scripting technology is used to enable a site feature (e.g., a form), a plaintext alternative must be available that allows an assistant application to read the feature.

You can visit *www.section508.gov/index.cfm?fuseAction=stds* to read the Section 508 standards.

CIW Online Resources – Online Exercise

Visit CIW Online at *http://education.Certification-Partners.com/CIW* to complete an interactive exercise that will reinforce what you have learned about this topic.

Exercise 1-3: Web accessibility measures

In the following lab, you will visit sites that post accessibility standards. Suppose you belong to a Web development team. Your project manager approaches you and asks about common Web accessibility standards. She has a half-hour available for you to show her some resources on the Web. What sites would you visit?

Lab 1-2: Viewing accessibility standards sites

OBJECTIVE
2.7.3: Accessibility standards and compliance

In this lab, you will view sites devoted to Web accessibility standards.

1. Open a Web browser.

2. Visit the following sites:

   - The W3C Web Content Accessibility Guidelines (WCAG) site at **www.w3.org/TR/WCAG20**

   - The Section 508 site at **www.section508.gov**

   - Canada's Common Look and Feel for the Internet 2.0 site at **www.tbs-sct.gc.ca/clf2-nsi2/index-eng.asp**

3. Read some information at each site you visit. How does each site define accessibility? How are the standards similar and different among sites? Can you see the ways in which accessibility standards are applied to these sites?

4. Conduct searches on the Internet for additional accessibility standards relevant to your particular situation. What other standards can you find?

In this lab, you viewed sites devoted to Web accessibility standards.

OBJECTIVE
2.12.1: Validating
Web documents

Verifying Web page accessibility

You can manually verify Web page accessibility, but it is much quicker to use automated accessibility validators. Table 1-3 describes some of the most common tools.

Table 1-3: Accessibility validators

Validator Tool	Description	Web-Based or Stand-Alone Tool?	URL
W3C Page Validator	Powerful HTML and XHTML validator	Web-based and Firefox add-on	*http://validator.w3.org* *https://addons.mozilla. org/en-US/firefox/ addon/page-validator/*
Total Validator	Powerful HTML and XHTML validator	Firefox add-on	*https://addons.mozilla. org/en-US/firefox/ addon/total-validator/*
Cynthia Says	A free site devoted to the W3C Web Content Accessibility Guidelines (WCAG)	Web-based	*www.cynthiasays.com*
Vischeck	A free service that simulates how a site will appear to color-blind users	Web-based	*www.vischeck.com/ vischeck*
MAGpie	A free application that validates Web sites, and creates audio captions and multimedia descriptions	Stand-alone	*http://ncam.wgbh.org/ invent_build/web_ multimedia/tools- guidelines/magpie*

Tech Tip

Partial color blindness is much more widespread than commonly realized. If your target audience is the entire world, read about color blindness to determine which color combinations are most easily read by the largest number of people. For information, color deficiency simulations and links to color-blindness tests, visit www.visibone.com/colorblind.

Additional Web page accessibility validation tools are available at *www.w3.org/WAI/ER/ tools/*. It is important to understand that these automatic validators may not find issues related to the latest accessibility standards. Manual validation is generally the most thorough approach.

General Web page accessibility considerations

You have now learned about many accessibility standards, guidelines and validation tools. The following sections discuss common Web page challenges and resolutions.

Addressing visual challenges

Following are some common challenges and solutions for accommodating Web users with vision impairment:

- **Text readability** — Make sure that fonts used are the correct size.

- **Text support for images** — All images must be described in text using special HTML code.

- **Screen-reader support** — Ensure that all pages and page elements can be rendered by audio screen readers.

Addressing audio challenges

Following are some common challenges and solutions for accommodating Web users with hearing impairment:

- **Alternative audio support** — If you include audio content on a page, make sure that a text-based equivalent is readily available for hearing-impaired users.

- **Alternative speech input** — If your site includes the ability for speech input, make sure that an equivalent keyboard entry mechanism is available.

- **Text support for audio elements** — Make sure that any audio elements are clearly marked with alternative text so that readers can obtain the information.

Addressing cognitive and technical challenges

Following are some common challenges and solutions for accommodating Web users with cognitive impairment or equipment limitations:

- **Page content that flashes, flickers or strobes** — Such content may cause problems for those with neurological disorders.

- **Alternative navigation** — Navigation aids should be provided to help those with lower cognitive skills.

- **Audio support** — Audio transcriptions of text-based content may help users with reading disabilities such as dyslexia.

- **Low-resolution alternatives** — Design Web pages so that they do not require large, expensive screen resolutions, or provide low-resolution alternatives.

In the following lab, you will use a Web page accessibility-testing strategy. Suppose your Web development team has created a site following the WCAG standards. You are assigned to validate the site. One step you would perform in this validation process is ensuring that the site can be easily browsed by a text-based editor.

 Lab 1-3: Using a text-only browser to evaluate accessibility

In this lab, you will conduct a partial validation test to determine the accessibility of a site for users employing voice-recognition software. Sight-impaired Web users often use voice-recognition software to augment or replace their limited ability to view a Web page. Voice-recognition software is capable of reading text, but not images, on a Web page. You can use a text-based browser to determine how well a site uses text to describe its images.

1. Verify that you have created the **C:\CIW\Site_Dev\Lab Files** directory on your computer, and that the **Lab Files** folder contains subfolders and student files for all lessons in this course. If this directory does not exist, log on to CIW Online now, and extract the files for the **Site Development Associate** course.

   Note: Instructions for using the CIW Web Foundations supplemental files are provided in the front matter section of this book.

2. Open **Windows Explorer** and navigate to the directory **C:\CIW\Site_Dev\Lab Files\ Lesson01\Lab_1-3**. Copy the **Lynx** directory to your Desktop.

*Note: If you cannot obtain the Lynx\ directory, use a Web browser to access a Win32 version of Lynx from **www.fdisk.com/doslynx/lynxport.htm**, then follow the remaining steps in this lab.*

3. Once you have copied the Lynx application to your Desktop, open a command prompt and change to the Desktop\Lynx\ directory using the following command:

    cd desktop\lynx

4. Launch the Lynx text-only browser by entering the following command in the command prompt:

    lynx http://www.ada.gov/

5. You will see the ADA Home Page appear in the Lynx browser, similar to Figure 1-4.

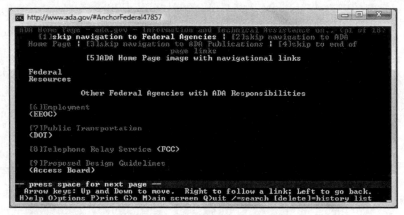

Figure 1-4: Official ADA home page in Lynx Web browser

6. You cannot use your mouse to navigate through Lynx. Following are common Lynx commands you can use to navigate:

    •   **G** — allows you to specify a URL (precede all URLs with *http://* or *https://*)

    •   **H** — summons the Help page, if present

    •   **UP ARROW key** — moves to the top of the page

    •   **DOWN ARROW key** — moves to the bottom of the page, by link

    •   **RIGHT ARROW key** — moves to the next page

    •   **LEFT ARROW key** — moves to the previous page

    •   **Q** — quits Lynx (by first pressing Q, then pressing Y)

7. Review the ADA guidelines discussed previously in this lesson.

8. Navigate through the official ADA home page. How well are the images described when viewing this page in a text-only format? Does this page follow its own guidelines?

9. Visit the following page, and consider how this page follows ADA guidelines:

    http://people.rit.edu/easi/law/weblaw1.htm

10. Visit additional sites, including the following:

- Amazon.com (***www.amazon.com***)

- CNN (***www.cnn.com***)

- BBC (***www.bbc.co.uk***)

11. How well are images described when viewing these pages in text-only format? Do these pages follow other accessibility guidelines?

12. When you are finished viewing these sites, press **Q** then press **Y** to quit Lynx, then type ***Exit*** and press **ENTER** to close the command prompt.

13. As a class, discuss how these sites follow or do not follow ADA guidelines.

In this lab, you considered user disabilities in regard to Web page creation.

In the preceding lab, you used Lynx to test Web-accessibility standards. Lynx is a free, open-source, text-only browser. Lynx supports the HTTP, HTTPS, FTP and NNTP protocols. Users with disabilities, especially visually impaired people, often use text-based browsers to view the Web. In some cases, users may elect to disable graphics to view Web pages more quickly than if the graphics were visible. You can use Lynx to view your Web page to see how understandable your Web page is when the graphics are eliminated.

Many spider programs view your Web page the same way Lynx does. By using Lynx to test your Web pages for accessibility, you may be able to make appropriate changes to allow your site to score higher in Web search engine search results, thereby increasing your exposure.

Creating and documenting an initial Web site plan

OBJECTIVE
2.7.2: Web site diagram

Before you can create any HTML code, you must first create a plan for the site. This plan has several names, including:

- Site diagram.

- Storyboard.

OBJECTIVE
2.13.4: Web site plan documentation

Regardless of the name you use, this plan must include the following:

- A statement discussing the purpose and intended audience for the site. This statement may evolve over time, but it is important to begin with this statement to remind everyone involved why the site is being developed and to steer all efforts in the proper direction.

- A rough outline of the pages needed, including:

  — The default page (e.g., index.html), also called the home page.

  — Sections of the site (e.g., products, sales, international, contacts).

  — An estimate of the technologies required (e.g., databases, CGI, search capability, indexes).

Your Web team cannot create this plan in isolation. You must obtain input from stakeholders.

Wireframing

Wireframing is another helpful tool for Web site planning. Wireframing is the process of developing an outline for a Web presence. Steps in the wireframing process usually include:

- Determining the purpose and objective of the Web site. Is this an e-commerce Web site? An informational Web site? A company intranet?

- Identifying all stakeholders for the site.

- Outlining the basic steps of the development process.

- Identifying steps for managing the project.

- Outlining site navigation.

- Identifying the technologies that are invoked with each user request.

As you can see from this list of tasks, quite a bit of work occurs before pages are created. Sometimes, software can help you with wireframing and project management.

Wireframing software can include:

- Microsoft Sketchflow (*www.microsoft.com/expression/products/sketchflow_overview.aspx*)

- Gliffy (*www.gliffy.com*)

- Web Site Wireframe Tool (*http://wireframe.talltree.us/default.asp*)

- HotGloo (*www.hotgloo.com*)

Additional tools are profiled at Speckyboy Design Magazine (*http://speckyboy.com/2010/01/11/10-completely-free-wireframe-and-mockup-applications*).

Determining the audience and message

Successful Web sites have a strong, central theme aimed at a distinct audience. They have the ability to support this theme by providing clear explanations and related services. You must start with a strong message, then consider how this message will be presented. Even the best looking Web page or site will fail in its purpose if it does not have a clear message.

As you determine your audience, consider eliciting input from various parties, including:

- **Customer representatives** — Organizations often have important customers attend meetings and provide input. Customer representatives can teach you about the various types of messages that appeal most to potential customers. For example, some may want to focus on the value of a particular product, regardless of cost. In other instances, customers may help you focus on a message that shows your products to be inexpensive. Once you have surveyed customers to determine what the market wants, you can begin to craft Web pages that clearly convey your company's message to its intended customers.

- **Suppliers** — If you are planning for large sales as a result of your Web effort, make sure that your product suppliers are ready for this. Otherwise, you could damage the company's reputation by making promises that cannot be kept. Even though a Web authoring team works mostly on creating markup pages, your Web site's ability to communicate with the public means that such business concerns are essential for the overall success of the project.

- **Shareholders** — If your organization is publicly owned, you may need to obtain input from shareholders about the look and feel of the site.

OBJECTIVE
2.7.4: Technical and
audience standards

Validating design issues

The design elements with which you display information on your site can be just as important as the information itself. As previously discussed, the front end you present to users may determine whether users remain at and return to your site. Consider the following design concepts:

- **Message** — Deliver a coherent message for each page. Information that is not relevant or otherwise distracts readers from a well-conceived central idea should be placed on another page or eliminated.

- **Fonts** — If specifying fonts, make sure that you use common ones so that browsers do not have difficulty rendering them. Use proper sizes; small fonts are difficult to read.

- **Images** — Make sure that all images used on a page contribute to either the page's navigability or its message.

- **Color** — Take time to consider color combinations so that your pages are as attractive and readable as possible.

Validation should occur on a regular basis as the site is being developed. Although a final validation is necessary, the final validation should not be the only one. As you validate design issues, consider the following:

OBJECTIVE
2.15.6: Diversity and
corporate culture

- **Organizational design standards** — You have already learned about the importance of branding standards. As you help develop Web pages, make sure that you are following developed rules and advice from your department and others. Such standards help support decisions concerning your organization's branding and marketing standards.

OBJECTIVE
2.19.4: Ethnic and
cultural issues

- **Ethnic diversity** — You may be asked to tailor messages to particular cultures and ethnicities. Project management will ensure that such needs are considered and recommended during planning meetings. It is your responsibility as a designer to create pages that implement all recommendations.

Your development team will also want to consider demographic and cultural issues, including:

- **Language choice** — Some organizations will need to use only one language for their sites, such as English. Others may need to create multiple sites in various languages to accommodate an international audience. Still others may offer an immediate choice of one or two languages because the government of the country in which they reside demands such accommodations, for example.

- **Common color schemes** — Preferences for color combinations differ from one culture to the next. Remain sensitive to and informed about such preferences.

- **Messages that appeal to customers** — You may need to alter your message about a particular product or activity if you present it to another culture. Consider the expectations and preferences of specific cultures so that your message is as clear and appealing as possible.

OBJECTIVE
2.19.3: Corporate
culture

In the following lab, you will review Web sites from major manufacturers to learn how they address different cultures. Suppose your project manager has asked you to research sites that address cultural diversity, including sites that target populations using different languages. Consider the types and sources of examples that you could provide.

Lab 1-4: Researching ways that Web sites address cultural diversity

In this lab, you will review Web sites from major manufacturers to learn how they address different cultures.

1. Open your Web browser. Visit and compare the following sites:

   www.toyota.com

   www.toyota.ca

2. After you have reviewed these sites, answer the following questions:

   - What language choices were offered at the *www.toyota.com* site? Why?

     _____

   - What language choices were offered at the *www.toyota.ca* site? Why?

     _____

     _____

   - What differences in color schemes exist? Why?

     _____

3. Compare the following Web sites from Ford Motor Company:

   www.ford.com

   www.ford.ru

4. After you have reviewed these sites, discuss the following questions as a class:

   - What differences exist in the color schemes, if any? Why?
   - Review the images and technologies used. Which site uses more active content?
   - Does one site offer more car models than the other?
   - What audience does the *www.ford.com* site seem to consider the most?

5. Visit additional sites and compare color schemes, languages and message approaches. Use a search engine to help you find examples of multicultural international approaches. What types of businesses tend to be most accommodating?

In this lab, you reviewed Web sites of major manufacturers to see how they tailor their company messages to various cultures.

Obtaining relevant input from stakeholders

OBJECTIVE
2.7.1: Stakeholder
input

When creating a Web site, stakeholders are relevant organization employees or contributors who can provide or help determine the following information:

- The purpose of the Web site.

- The site's look and feel.

- The services that the audience requires from the site.

- Funds available to develop the site.

- Development timelines. Although your team will largely determine how long it will take to create the site, your team will also have to coordinate with other departments in the organization. For example, the sales and marketing teams are likely to have important input about when the site is published, as well as its look and feel.

OBJECTIVE
2.13.2: Company
site requirements
and collaboration

As you work with your stakeholders, remember the following:

- People who will approve your project often have no technical expertise in your field. Nevertheless, remember that they are essential to the success of your project.

- Be prepared to explain non-technical needs to a technical audience. In other words, make sure that you can present business concerns to IT professionals in ways that will help ensure that your needs are met.

OBJECTIVE
2.13.1: Site
development
teamwork

Your site development team can consist of diverse professionals whose focuses and concerns will differ. However, each will have valuable contributions, and you must be able to communicate effectively with all of them. Following are some examples of team members who might collaborate with you on a Web development project:

- A representative from marketing to help guide branding issues

- An IT worker responsible for configuring servers and network access

- A representative from sales who can provide additional information about specific customer needs

- Members of the Web development team who will use Web technology to create the best site for the organization's needs

Once you have obtained all essential input, you can create your initial storyboard. Figure 1-5 shows a sample storyboard for a relatively simple site.

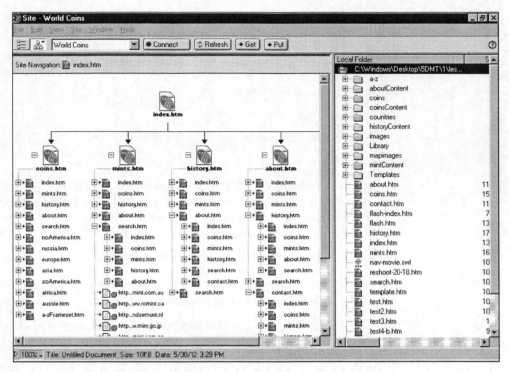

Figure 1-5: Sample storyboard

site map
A brief, hierarchical representation of a Web site that enables visitors to quickly identify areas of the site and navigate to them.

You and your team will develop this initial storyboard into a completed Web site. The storyboard also provides a **site map** to help visitors quickly find resources on your site.

OBJECTIVE
2.13.4: Web site plan documentation

Documenting and communicating the plan

In addition to creating a site storyboard, you must also document decisions made in all meetings. All plans must be distributed and approved. Any decisions involving changes in dates and allocations of funds may require further approval from the organization.

As the plan moves toward finalization, you must communicate it effectively using at least some of the following strategies:

*   Calling relevant parties to ensure that everyone is satisfied

*   Sending e-mail messages

*   Sending postal ("snail mail") messages if necessary

*   Sending fax messages

A telephone call is appropriate at times, but because phone calls are not usually recorded, they cannot be readily recalled and referenced. E-mail and paper-based transmissions can be stored for later retrieval, and used for reference and accountability.

Communicating the Web site plan

As you communicate the Web site plan, you will make oral and written presentations. Following are some typical strategies to consider.

OBJECTIVE
2.13.5: Web site plan communication

Oral presentations and presentation aids

As you give oral presentations about your Web site plan, use presentation aids and tools to help illustrate your plan:

OBJECTIVE
2.15.3: Presentation
software

- **Presentation software** — Slide-based software, such as Microsoft PowerPoint and Google's Presentations application within Google Docs, is common and user-friendly. Presentation software creates a sense of professionalism.

- **Overhead projection** — You may need to create transparencies of statistics and marketing ideas. Be prepared to bring an overhead projector.

OBJECTIVE
2.15.2: Presentation
aids

- **Whiteboards** — You can bring your own whiteboard or use one that is already in the presentation room. A whiteboard helps you to present your ideas as well as write ideas gathered from your audience. You should always take your own set of notes during a team presentation, but you can also use a whiteboard or poster paper to record open discussions (often called brainstorming). Such discussions are very helpful because they show that you are listening to ideas.

- **Easel and poster paper** — If a whiteboard is not available, bring an easel and poster paper so you can take notes for everyone to see. Because an easel and poster paper are portable, you can keep this record of audience feedback.

- **Charts** — Pie charts graphically present information about a topic, showing the relative percentages of all constituent elements. For example, a pie chart can help you show the size of a particular market niche you are targeting. Bar charts are helpful for showing trends or a particular project's progress.

- **Published handouts** — Your audience can use handouts as notes from the meeting. If you want to emphasize a particular portion of a presentation, back it up with a handout.

Presentation tools help you convey information, and also prove that you have properly prepared for a meeting and are not wasting your audience's time.

Leading discussions

Project managers generally lead and moderate meetings related to a Web development project. Consider the following strategies that you can use to effectively take the lead during a meeting:

OBJECTIVE
2.15.7: Meeting
leadership

- **Make introductions** — As you introduce people, explain their roles on the team.

- **Recall past business** — Make sure that each team builds on past decisions and considers past discussions in a meaningful way. At all times, try to make any repeated discussions culminate in a decision that allows the group to show progress on the project.

- **Create a list of action items, including timelines** — A list will help you communicate your team's progress.

- **Monitor time** — Even if important information is imparted in your meetings, if they are too long then important participants may not want to attend again.

- **Ensure proper discussion focus** — Provide an agenda of meeting topics so participants come prepared and expecting to discuss only relevant issues. Consider announcing a time limit for a particular discussion if you fear that it may continue too long.

- **Handle heated discussions** — Changing focus may be especially important if a discussion becomes too heated or if animosity develops among participants.

- **Distribute minutes** — Meeting notes, or minutes, help all parties see progress result from meetings. Minutes also help everyone identify unfinished business, as well as determine any particular topics that were omitted.

OBJECTIVE
2.15.4: Technical
concept
clarification

Considering technical and non-technical concerns

In your meetings, you are likely to find that although everyone may share the same goal, they may not be able to communicate specific needs to each other. A common problem is that some team members do not have much technical knowledge, but nevertheless have ideas that are essential for the success of the site. Often, the non-technical employees in your meetings can ensure funding for your project.

It is the project leader's responsibility to ensure that input and requests from team members with little or no technical knowledge are heard and seriously considered. Similarly, you must ensure that project members with technical experience clearly convey their capabilities, limits and needs to non-technical team members. Otherwise, team members will constantly speak past each other, and confusion will result. Confusion can increase especially if project members work remotely. Ways to ensure clarity both in meetings and in communication include:

- **Regularly asking if anyone has questions** — This strategy helps some team members speak up. However, less outgoing individuals who have questions may still hold back.

- **Asking team members to summarize their understanding of decisions** — Although this strategy puts some people on the spot, this is preferable to having team members remain confused about the project's direction.

- **Asking a third party to deliver a summary of progress** — This third party can attend your meeting and ask questions of team members. By listening to responses, you can gauge overall team participation and understanding.

- **Writing regular updates about the project** — Make sure that in your updates you translate technical requirements into non-technical language, and vice versa.

Developing the site

Once you have obtained enough information and created a definitive plan, you can begin developing the site. As your team develops the site, you will be engaged in various activities, including:

- **Creating markup code** — You will develop pages that fulfill all design standards.

- **Testing functionality** — Make sure that the site performs well technically before it is published to the Web. This involves testing the site in multiple browsers, for example.

- **Approving the site** — All stakeholders will need to approve your team's work. Make sure that all parties have seen the site before publication, and make sure that you have documented this fact.

- **Publishing the site** — The site must be properly placed on a Web server. You may also participate in decisions such as whether you will configure your own Web server or use a Web server configured by another provider.

OBJECTIVE
2.14.3: Pre-launch
functionality testing

2.12.3: Testing pages
in browsers

Testing pages in multiple Web browsers

As you develop Web pages, make sure that you test your Web pages using multiple Web browsers. A different generation of the same browser may interpret HTML somewhat differently. For example, Internet Explorer 9 and higher uses an HTML-rendering engine that has been significantly revised from version 8. Similarly, current versions of Firefox have a significantly revised rendering engine. You should always consider how each vendor and each version implements HTML standards differently.

If you are preparing a site for public use, it is advisable to write your HTML code using the most widely supported standards.

The HTML code used in this course will function in all browsers. However, there will always be subtle differences from browser to browser.

OBJECTIVE
2.7.5: Usability and
browser
compatibility

In some situations, you may feel it is unnecessary to test your pages on a wide variety of browsers. For example, you may not need to perform as many tests for the company intranet if the company has standardized to one browser, such as Windows Internet Explorer. Nevertheless, it is always good practice to ensure that your code is compatible with all browsers so that your browser options are flexible.

Browser types and versions

Table 1-4 discusses browsers to consider for your Web site testing process.

Table 1-4: Commonly used Web browsers

Browser	Description	Download Location
Windows Internet Explorer	A proprietary Microsoft browser installed by default on all Windows operating systems.	*www.microsoft.com*
Mozilla Firefox	An open-source browser. Firefox versions are available for various operating systems, from Windows to Linux.	*www.mozilla.org*
Google Chrome	An open-source browser from Google. Chrome has many new features, such as a clean interface, automatic crash recovery, multi-threading capability, improved sandboxing, isolated tabs and privacy mode.	*www.google.com/chrome*
Opera	An alternative Web browser with extended language support.	*www.opera.com*
Lynx	A command-line text-only Web browser. Often used by those with shell accounts and those who are visually impaired because it can be used with software that renders text into voice. A binary version is included with most versions of UNIX/Linux.	The source code is available at *http://lynx.isc.org*. A Windows binary is available at *www.fdisk.com/doslynx/ lynxport.htm*

Remember that Web browsers are not the only user agents that render HTML pages. Additional user agents include:

- Smartphones.
- Tablets.
- Gaming consoles.
- Other devices that read markup language.

When testing your Web pages for browser compatibility issues, check the following:

- **Rendering of tables** — If you use HTML tables to format content, some browsers may not render the information proportionally, which can distort the way information appears on the page. Some browsers also do not support table options.

- **Strictness levels** — Older browsers may not be able to render the newer versions of HTML or XHTML well.

- **Color support** — If you use background colors or colors within tables, your customers' browsers may not render them exactly as you have intended.

- **Images** — As you already know, some Web browsers do not support images at all. Some browsers do not render background images, whereas others do. Always provide alternative text descriptions for images, and use background images sparingly.

- **Scripting languages** — Make sure that any scripting language you use is supported by the majority of Web browsers.

- **HTML version** — Choose a version of HTML that you know most browsers will support. The HTML5 specification is a solid choice because it is backward-compatible and can render in most browsers.

As a general rule, the closer you adhere to W3C standards, the more consistently your Web pages will render in various browsers. Also, be conservative when using elaborate features that may not render well in certain browsers. Finally, as you develop your Web pages, use features that are supported by the most commonly used browsers.

Managing the site

OBJECTIVE
2.14.4: Existing site management

You are unlikely to develop and post a site that never needs modification. In fact, managing a site usually requires more time and work than initially developing it. As part of a team that manages a site, you must:

- **Create new content** — The perception that a site has failed to remain current can be damaging. Innovation and fresh content are both essential to managing a site that stays popular.

- **Update dead links** — For various reasons, links that once functioned may fail over time. A link can become invalid because a page's location was changed on the hard drive, or because the link pointed to an external Web site that no longer exists or has changed its structure. You can use automated applications to check your site for dead links. However, someone must still manually alter any invalid links to make them valid again.

- **Remove old sites** — Sometimes an entire site becomes invalid. It is your duty to remove such sites from the Internet.

OBJECTIVE
2.14.5: Content maintenance

- **Remove unused pages** — Pages on Web sites sometimes become stale, especially if they are tied to a marketing campaign. If they cannot be updated, they must be removed.

- **Ensure connectivity** — You or a member of the IT department may be assigned to ensure that the site is active and that enough bandwidth is available. You may have to upgrade or downgrade bandwidth, depending upon customer volume. You do not want customers to be frustrated by slow site access, but you also do not want to pay for unused bandwidth.

trouble ticket
A record of a problem related to a service provided by an ISP or cloud service provider. Used to record receipt of a complaint and track resolution of the problem.

- **Report access troubles** — Sometimes you need to contact your ISP and begin a **trouble ticket** to begin resolving a problem. It may also be your responsibility to follow up with problems to ensure they are properly resolved.

- **Process feedback from customers and stakeholders** — Your team will be asked to make changes to the site periodically. Some changes may be subtle; others may require considerable effort on your part to make the site fulfill its potential and truly benefit your organization.

OBJECTIVE
2.13.6: Site
feedback and
improvement

Obtaining feedback

Your Web team must process various types of feedback. Feedback can include:

- **Direct contact with customers** — People who frequent the site may contact you directly through feedback forms to inform you about desired changes.

- **Feedback from upper management** — Executive officers may request changes to the site in order to improve the company's image.

- **Feedback from sales and marketing** — Sales representatives often receive comments from their customers about desired changes. Addressing such reports of customer requests is essential to the site's success.

troll
A Web user who publishes negative comments or submits feedback simply to annoy or anger.

As you receive feedback, you must be able to distinguish between serious feedback and nuisance input. Some individuals scour Internet sites and pretend to provide serious feedback, when in fact they are just trying to cause problems. Such users are often called **trolls**. Trolls can employ various tactics, including sending annoying e-mail messages, submitting Web forms full of negative comments, or writing blogs or articles that disparage your site.

You and your team must also be aware that some people who are sincere about their feedback may have idiosyncratic perspectives. In any case, you should always work to obtain a consensus of opinion that includes reliable sources, then obtain appropriate stakeholder approval before making any changes.

OBJECTIVE
2.15.1:
Management and
customer feedback

Ways to obtain quality feedback

Your team can ensure that you obtain quality feedback by:

- **Providing Web forms on the site that ask for customer input** — Such forms should be available only to serious customers and/or members of the organization. For example, make the form available only to users who have paid for a service or provided verifiable identity. Otherwise, you increase your chances of receiving prank information from trolls.

- **Conducting surveys in person** — You or other team members can contact customers at the direction of your team leader. Such surveys should be directed to your top customers. Make sure that surveys are quick and to the point. You may also want to offer your customers a valuable product, service or discount in exchange for responding to the survey.

- **Conducting surveys via e-mail or text** — If you want to contact more people, an e-mail survey may be appropriate. However, be sure to send surveys only to established customers. Otherwise, your organization may receive a bad reputation as a "spammer."

OBJECTIVE
2.15.5: Feedback
interpretation

As you process and interpret feedback, you should ask the following questions:

- Which suggestions should be taken seriously?

- Does this feedback apply directly to the Web site, or could this problem be solved by requesting that sales and/or marketing personnel work directly with complaining customers?

- What changes will please the majority of customers?

- How much will proposed changes cost? You must consider whether requested changes are economically feasible and worth the extra investment.

- How long will it take to make the proposed changes?

- Who must you contact in order to obtain approval and/or funding for the proposed changes?

Intellectual property

Intellectual property is a unique product or idea created by an individual or organization, and that generally has commercial value. When creating a Web site, you must consider legal issues related to ideas, products and images that are widely available. You cannot "borrow" information from other Web sites. Table 1-5 describes common intellectual property issues and terminology.

Table 1-5: Intellectual property issues and terms

Intellectual Property Term	Description
Trade secret	Intellectual property that must remain private for a company to retain viability. Examples include proprietary code, business plans and sales contacts.
Copyright	The legal ownership of expression by an author. According to most developed countries, copyrighted intellectual property becomes the property of the author for a certain number of years. Copyright protection ensures that the person or group who owns the copyright has the right to publish or otherwise distribute material, and control how it is redistributed. In most countries, a copyright can be sold by its owner.
Trademark	A unique word, phrase or symbol that is claimed or officially registered by an organization with the government. Trademarks can include logos, phrases, company names and so forth. If a logo, word or phrase is trademarked, then only the organization that registered it can use it.
Licensing	The legally authorized use of another person's or entity's copyrighted intellectual property. The terms of the license are generally dictated by the copyright holder. Licenses require contracts and usually an exchange of money, services or both.
Infringement	Any violation of a copyright or trademark. Copyright and trademark infringement are punishable crimes.
Plagiarism	A specific instance of infringement in which an individual or entity claims to have created content (e.g., images, writing or other exact expressions) that was in fact created by other developers. Proven plagiarism can result in severe reprimands, loss of employment, corporate lawsuits and financial penalties.

Copyright scope, reach and time limits

No copyright or trademark is permanent. Legal registrations must be renewed, so if you have trademarked or copyrighted a particular portion of your Web site, then you must manage this intellectual property. Research the laws for your own country to avoid surprises.

The legal issues described here apply to all phases of Web development. Do not ignore these concepts; doing so could lead to your dismissal and to legal action against your company. Precedent court rulings have held violators liable even when they claimed ignorance of the law.

 You may be tempted to use other people's words and ideas when optimizing pages. Avoid that temptation. One way to create original yet relevant content is to work with another individual. Talk out your ideas. You will be surprised at how you can create an optimal page that is both original and relevant.

Ethical issues regarding copyright, trademark and plagiarism

Ethics is the study of making proper choices to ensure that other people's rights are not violated. Consider the following ethical points as you create markup code and design Web pages:

- You cannot copy a site's code or look without the owner's explicit permission. You can create entirely new code that provides a similar look and feel, but consider the perception you present if your site looks just like another.

- Borrowing a lot of code from a site infringes upon the author's copyright.

- The owner of a copyright may allow copyrighted material to be used by others. This permission may be exchanged by contract, for a fee or simply for proper attribution. Most major Web sites post their copyright and licensing contact information.

- All aspects of a Web site are copyrighted. Do not "borrow" images, text, logos, music, scripts, applications or code. Seek proper permission if you find an element on a site that you want to use.

- You cannot provide a link from your Web site to another site without permission because such a link generally implies that the two sites have a business relationship.

- You cannot copy or translate the content of another Web site without explicit permission.

Copyright and trademark laws are country-specific. The World Wide Web allows a person from one country to view information from all over the world. Suppose your employer asks you to research national and international copyright laws. What steps will you take?

Avoiding copyright infringement, trademark infringement and plagiarism

Stealing the intellectual property of others is a serious matter. You must avoid even appearing as if you have stolen information. Ways to avoid problems include:

- **Reviewing all Web site content for originality** — This includes code, images and text. The review must be independent. In other words, choose someone who is not on your team but who will work diligently to highlight any potential infringement issues.

- **Conducting regular content reviews** — A single content review at the end of the project may not solve infringement problems. Regular reviews are likely to encourage development team members to change their practices so that you do not have a large problem to resolve near a deadline.

- **Obtaining express, written consent for any material you use** — Make sure that written consent is properly stored for later retrieval, and that developers do not take advantage of this consent. Even specific design concepts are copyrighted, so if you "borrow" someone else's unique expression for your own site, you may incur legal action. Of course, images and code are all protected by copyright.

- **Creating reasonable deadlines** — Busy developers often take shortcuts to meet deadlines. Work with your project manager to ensure that deadline pressure does not contribute to a team's tendency to copy content.

 Plagiarism is never justified. When in doubt, simply consider another approach to expressing an idea. Never steal ideas or expressions of ideas from others and claim them as your own.

Avoiding copyright and trademark infringement is essential. So is avoiding plagiarism. Suppose your program manager asks you to find authoritative evidence of intellectual property laws. Where could you find this information?

Outsourcing

Increasingly, Web development work (including site design) is being outsourced to workers in remote locations. When outsourcing occurs, a local team of workers often remains to perform some tasks (sometimes permanently, sometimes only for a short time). This local team is usually charged with managing the project. The outsourced team will probably perform the Web page coding and other tasks that the local team cannot complete.

When working with remote teams and even other companies, you must consider the following:

- **Non-Disclosure Agreement (NDA)** — An NDA is a legally binding contract signed by both parties stating that they will not reveal any trade secrets or intellectual property owned by the other.

- **Legal consultation** — When signing NDAs and other documents is necessary, you should first retain legal counsel. Otherwise, you may make commitments that you cannot fulfill. Any contract breach can make your company liable for a lawsuit.

OBJECTIVE
2.20.2: Non-Disclosure Agreement (NDA)

Non-Disclosure Agreement (NDA)

An NDA protects the following intellectual property from unauthorized use by contractors, partners or others who are allowed access to it:

- Ideas and concepts

- Specific plans

- Code

- Written documents

Most NDAs specify penalties if stipulated violations occur. One problem with an NDA is that it takes time to agree about its content. If you involve several individuals on an NDA, then the timeline on a project might increase.

OBJECTIVE
2.20.3: Legal team consultation

Consulting with legal teams

You may have to consult with legal teams in the following situations:

- As you create NDAs

- If you decide to use a marketing campaign, trademark or copyrighted idea similar to another company's

- If you must investigate infringement by other companies against your intellectual property

In the following lab, you will investigate intellectual property concepts and laws. Suppose your project manager assigned you to work closely with a legal team. Before meeting with this team, you want to obtain some preliminary information about intellectual property concepts and laws. The sites you review in this lab provide this type of information.

| **Lab 1-5: Investigating intellectual property concepts and laws**

In this lab, you will learn more about intellectual property concepts and laws.

1. One of the missions of the United Nations Educational, Scientific and Cultural Organization (UNESCO) is to ensure cooperation among nations regarding copyright laws. The UNESCO Universal Copyright Convention enables various countries to cooperate so that copyright is protected across the world. Open your browser, and visit the following site to learn more about the UNESCO Universal Copyright Convention:

   http://portal.unesco.org/en/ev.php-URL_ID=15241&URL_DO=DO_TOPIC&URL_SECTION=201.html

2. The Berne Convention is another international effort to protect copyright. Visit the following page of the World Intellectual Property Organization (WIPO) site to read more about it:

   www.wipo.int/treaties/en/ip/berne/trtdocs_wo001.html

3. Copyright law has many facets and differs among countries. Visit the following site to review copyright laws specific to the United States:

   www.copyright.gov/title17/

4. Visit the following site to learn more about general copyright issues:

   http://whatiscopyright.org

5. Using Google, Bing or another search engine, research the meaning of the word *plagiarism*.

6. As a class, answer the following questions:

   • Which parties are responsible for protecting copyright?

   _____

   • What is plagiarism?

   _____

   _____

   • What can you do as a developer to ensure that you do not engage in activities such as copyright infringement and plagiarism?

   _____

   _____

   _____

In this lab, you investigated aspects of copyright and trademark law. You also researched the meaning of the word plagiarism.

CIW Online Resources – Online Exercise

Visit CIW Online at *http://education.Certification-Partners.com/CIW* to complete an interactive exercise that will reinforce what you have learned about this topic.

Exercise 1-4: Reviewing Web site development principles

Hosting and Web Service Providers

When deciding how your Web site will be hosted on the Internet, you have several options. The first decision is whether your company will host the site in-house or use some form of service provider to do the hosting for you.

Table 1-6 compares benefits and drawbacks of configuring your own hosting solution and using other providers. You will learn more about Internet Service Providers (ISPs) and cloud service providers in the sections that follow.

Table 1-6: Configuring your own server vs. using service providers

Web Service Provision	Benefits	Drawbacks
Configuring your own hosting solution	-You have more control over your services. -You have more choices.	-You must purchase and house all necessary hardware and software. -Configuring your servers will take time and expertise. -You must manage your own server, including security services.
Using an Internet Service Provider (ISP)	-You do not need to purchase hardware or software. -The ISP will configure the server for you.	-You have fewer choices in the configuration. -An ISP provides only basic services (e.g., limited CGI and small databases). -You are dependent upon the ISP's management and security services.
Using a cloud service provider	-You do not need to purchase additional hardware or software. -A cloud service provider will do more than configure your server; it will also provide completed and finished services for your organization. -The cloud service provider will also create custom solutions.	-A cloud service provider often charges a flexible subscription fee that varies upon the resources used (e.g., software licenses and hardware). -As with an ISP, you are dependent upon the cloud service provider's management, security services and uptime reliability.

Web service providers

You do not have to buy, configure and maintain your own Web server to host your site. An Internet Service Provider (ISP) can provide preconfigured servers and as much bandwidth as you are willing to pay for. Quality ISPs generally understand the needs of their customers, and they probably already provide many of the scripts and tools you need.

A cloud service provider may be appropriate if your company requires more complete services than an ISP provides.

Co-location, dedicated hosting and virtual servers

OBJECTIVE
2.18.3: Hosting
options

Table 1-7 summarizes the benefits and drawbacks of hosting solutions provided by service providers.

Table 1-7: Service provider hosting solutions — benefits and drawbacks

Hosting Solution	Description	Benefits	Drawbacks
Co-location	The service provider allocates space for your equipment. You provide the server hardware, and the provider supplies space and necessary bandwidth for your server.	-You have complete control over your equipment. -You do not have to share server resources with any other party. -You have a choice over both hardware and software configuration.	-This option is more costly. -If your equipment experiences problems (either hardware or software), your provider will give fee-based support because the hardware and software are yours. -You may need to fix any problems yourself. -You are responsible for your own security.
Dedicated hosting (or co-hosting)	The service provider gives you access to a dedicated server that it owns.	-You have less up-front cost. -Your site can be launched more quickly because most providers have preconfigured servers. -You do not need to purchase a server and associated software. -You do not need server configuration knowledge. -The service provider configures the system, then allows you to access the system and upload files.	-You are limited to the operating systems and services offered. -You must inquire about the level of customer support. Many providers do not provide extensive customer service, which may lead to long wait times in case of problems. -Some providers allow you total control over your dedicated host. In such cases, you (or a consultant) must secure your systems.
Virtual server	One Web server contains your site and several other sites.	-You have less up-front cost and faster deployment time. -The Web service is generally running already. You simply provide your thoroughly tested code.	-You rely upon the provider's server configuration. -You have no control over the server. You control only your Web files. -If the provider's security is lax, then your virtual server may be easily compromised. -You have less flexibility in Web server functions.

OBJECTIVE
2.18.2: Cloud service
providers

Internet Service Provider (ISP) vs. Cloud Service Providers

Remember that an Internet Service Provider (ISP) provides bandwidth and possibly Web server space.

A cloud service provider is prepared to provide more complete services, including:

Software as a-Service (SaaS)
Software that is hosted centrally on the Internet and accessed by users with a Web browser.

- **Software as a Service (SaaS)**, such as e-mail, accounting, human resources management, customer-service relationship, Web hosting, and nearly any type of software.

- Backup services and nearly unlimited hard drive space on a pay-as-you go subscription.

- Advanced Web and database connectivity, including the creation of custom CGI applications.

- Enterprise resource planning (ERP), which is the ability to automate the planning and operations of your entire organization (e.g., hiring, termination, manufacturing, marketing).

OBJECTIVE
2.18.2: Cloud service
providers

Costs of using a cloud service provider

Costs associated with a cloud service provider include:

- **Database connectivity** — Cost is based on the amount of database support you require.

- **Per-service costs** — Each additional service you use will increase costs.

- **Bandwidth** — In addition to increasing (or decreasing) bandwidth, you can also pay the cloud service provider to closely monitor bandwidth usage.

- **Customer support** — A cloud provider can provide customer service to your company, just like an ISP. Some providers also offer support to your customers, allowing you to avoid the hiring, training and maintenance costs of creating your own team.

- **Security** — Larger cloud service providers have their own security auditing teams.

- **Application development** — A cloud service provider will either have its own application development team or will have relationships with remote development teams that can create custom applications for you.

OBJECTIVE
2.18.2: Cloud service
providers

Negotiating Web services and communicating needs

When working with an ISP or cloud service provider, be prepared to detail your needs. Clearly provide information such as:

- Potential amount of traffic.

- Hard drive space you will need.

- Database and CGI needs.

- Additional services (e.g., custom applications).

As you contact the ISP or cloud service provider sales representatives, obtain prices for each of the services you need. Then, negotiate your prices with service provider representatives by:

- **Indicating your present needs** — Discuss plans in which you pay full price now then negotiate lower prices later, or vice versa.

- **Asking to talk to the sales representative's manager** — The manager has the decision-making power to negotiate lower costs.

- **Asking your manager to discuss prices with the sales representative or with the representative's manager** — Escalating negotiations can enable exceptions and swifter decisions.

You may be able to negotiate lower costs based upon the nature of your organization. If your organization is not-for-profit or associated with education, for example, you may be able to obtain price discounts for services.

OBJECTIVE
2.18.5: Site
information
management

Information you need from your service provider

If you use an ISP or cloud service provider, you will need to obtain the following information from the provider:

- **Account information** — This includes user names and passwords of all accounts associated with your server. The service provider may issue you multiple user names. Write the information carefully and store it in a secure place (e.g., a locked safe).

- **IP addresses and DNS names of the server**.

- **Instructions about file and directory locations**.

- **The service provider's contact information** — Such information includes Help Desk support numbers (and possibly the names of dedicated help desk workers), e-mail and texting numbers.

The Habitat for Humanity Web Site

Habitat for Humanity (also known simply as Habitat) is a not-for-profit, volunteer-driven organization that builds and sells homes for families across the world. The potential homeowner becomes a partner in building the home, and contributes to the actual building process as much as possible. This practice is called "sweat equity." Volunteers also help build the home. For years, Habitat has specialized in helping young people across the world contribute their time to help others obtain decent housing. The Habitat for Humanity site is shown in Figure 1-6.

Figure 1-6: Habitat for Humanity site

Habitat for Humanity has built more than 150,000 homes across the world. Habitat also arranges no-interest mortgages and reasonable payment schedules for the homeowner, in cooperation with businesses and charitable organizations.

Habitat for Humanity has allowed CIW to use an earlier prototype version of its Web site as an example of a commercial-grade site. This permission is in no way an endorsement of CIW or Certification Partners. Habitat's permission to use portions of its site in labs teaching site development skills does not represent any sort of alliance or partnership. Students will build prototype pages using Habitat for Humanity content, which is owned and copyrighted by Habitat for Humanity. The prototype pages that students build do not necessarily represent, duplicate or simulate the current live Habitat for Humanity Web site, which can be visited at www.habitat.org.

Visit the current live version of the Habitat Web site at *www.habitat.org.* As you review the Habitat site, evaluate the site's ability to convey Habitat's message and achieve its goals. As you do so, consider the following questions:

- What strategies does the Habitat site adopt to obtain volunteers for building homes?

- What technologies (e.g., search engines, PDF documents) are used on this site to help achieve its goals?

- What front-end issues should be considered for this site?

- Review the site for offered features. What back-end technologies will be required to fulfill the offered features?

CIW Online Resources – Course Mastery

Visit CIW Online at *http://education.Certification-Partners.com/CIW* to take the Course Mastery review of this lesson or lesson segment.

SDA Lesson 1 - Part B

Case Study

Plan It Out

Seamus was assigned to create a Web site plan for a charity organization. He must ensure that the site includes the following features:

- A message stating the purpose of the charity

- An online form that will receive personal information from potential volunteers and place it into a database

Seamus' first step was to discuss the plan with stakeholders. He did not have a stakeholder group, so he obtained representatives from the following departments:

- Marketing

- IT

- Web development

Eventually, all parties were able to agree on a site plan. After creating the site plan, Seamus' project manager asked him to help present this plan to upper management. Seamus decided to use the following:

- Web page examples provided via an overhead projector

- A handout listing the names of the stakeholders, as well as projected costs and timelines

Upper management was very pleased, although they did have a few specific feedback points that they asked Seamus to consider. The project was approved, and Seamus was able to work closely with the project manager to create the site.

*   *   *

As a class, consider this scenario and answer the following questions:

- What other features might benefit this site?

- What other stakeholders could have been consulted?

- What additional presentation aids could have helped Seamus make a positive impression?

Lesson Summary

Application project

The ability to write markup code manually is important because many GUI editors do not use the latest markup language standards and are not proficient at connecting to databases. HTML is still an evolving language, so you should be ready to modify existing code at any time.

To research the most current Web standards and recommendations, use your browser to access the W3C site (*www.w3.org*). Locate the following information:

- What is the most recent version of HTML?

- What new developments have occurred?

- What additional technologies does the W3C discuss in relation to HTML?

- What is the future of HTML in general? Why was XHTML deemed necessary?

When you are finished with your research, visit the Habitat for Humanity site (*www.habitat.org*). Then answer the following questions:

- What is the message of this site?

- What technical people would you need to help develop this site? For example, consider the site's search engine.

- What input from non-technical people was necessary to develop this site?

Skills review

In this lesson, you learned about the origins of HTML and the purpose for its creation. You learned that the W3C is the standards organization governing the evolution of HTML, XML and XHTML. You also learned that HTML editors may provide a simple interface to help you create HTML pages, but without the core knowledge to write HTML code manually, you are limited in your Web page development. After you learn how to write HTML code, the possibilities are limitless. Finally, you studied principles of Web site accessibility, planning, development, hosting and management.

Now that you have completed this lesson, you should be able to:

✓ 2.1.1: Relate the history of markup languages to current techniques and technologies, including Standard Generalized Markup Language (SGML), previous versions of Hypertext Markup Language (HTML).

✓ 2.1.2: Identify the format and various versions of HTML, including HTML 4.01, Extensible HTML (XHTML), HTML5.

✓ 2.1.8: Explain the importance of consistently developing to a single W3C standard (e.g., HTML5).

✓ 2.6.1: Describe the functionality of XML.

✓ 2.7.1: Obtain input from stakeholders about acceptable technologies and color combinations.

✓ 2.7.2: Create an initial Web site diagram (i.e., a story board or prototype), and translate it into a site map.

✓ 2.7.3: Verify compliance with government and industry accessibility standards, including W3C Web Accessibility Initiative (WAI), U.S. Government Section 508, Americans with Disabilities Act (ADA).

✓ 2.7.4: Validate Web page design according to technical and audience standards adopted by employers.

✓ 2.7.5: Verify Web site usability, viewability and browser compatibility.

✓ 2.12.1: Test and validate Web documents.

✓ 2.12.3: Test Web pages in multiple browsers.

✓ 2.13.1: Work as a team member to develop pages and sites.

✓ 2.13.2: Collaborate with technical (e.g., IT) and non-technical (e.g., marketing) members of the organization to ensure sites meet requirements.

✓ 2.13.3: Determine information and audience requirements for a site, including stakeholders such as customers, employees, shareholders, suppliers.

✓ 2.13.4: Document a Web site plan.

✓ 2.13.5: Communicate the Web site plan effectively, both orally and in writing.

✓ 2.13.6: Obtain and document feedback, then improve the site, including working closely with sales and marketing to evaluate site effectiveness.

✓ 2.14.1: Define legal issues related to a Web site, including trademarking, licensing, copyrighting, licensing copyrighted materials, scope of copyright, reach of copyright, copyrighting process, copyright infringement and consequences.

✓ 2.14.2: Identify fundamentals of project management, including major stages of a Web design/development project cycle.

✓ 2.14.3: Identify processes of pre-launch site/application functionality testing, including checking links, testing with various browsers, testing against corruption of your e-commerce site, load testing, access to the site, testing with various speed connections.

✓ 2.14.4: Manage existing sites (e.g., remove dead links and/or upgrade connectivity when necessary).

✓ 2.14.5: Remove old sites and pages.

✓ 2.15.1: Identify ways to elicit useful feedback from management and customers.

✓ 2.15.2: Use presentation aids and support material, including charts, tables, figures, written content, overhead projection.

✓ 2.15.3: Use presentation software (e.g., slide-based software).

✓ 2.15.4: Clarify technical concepts for a non-technical audience, and use strategies to retain listener interest.

✓ 2.15.5: Interpret verbal, non-verbal and written feedback.

✓ 2.15.6: Address diversity and corporate/organizational culture when communicating your message by customizing meeting and message delivery, and listening for responses.

✓   2.15.7: Identify ways to lead meetings (e.g., make introductions, invite questions, set time frames, set action times, monitor time, ensure proper discussion focus, publish minutes).

✓   2.18.1: Investigate costs associated with placing and developing your own server.

✓   2.18.2: Identify costs associated with using a cloud service provider.

✓   2.18.3: Distinguish among dedicated hosting, co-location and virtual servers.

✓   2.18.4: Activate features provided by managed services (e.g., CGI, forms).

✓   2.18.5: Manage information relevant to a site (e.g., account information, passwords, IP addresses).

✓   2.19.3: Consider corporate/organizational culture when designing page layout.

✓   2.19.4: Demonstrate sensitivity to ethnic and cultural issues in page layout and design.

✓   2.20.1: Obtain proper permissions from developers when repurposing content (e.g., other developers' code, images, concepts).

✓   2.20.2: Create and sign a Non-Disclosure Agreement (NDA) when necessary.

✓   2.20.3: Identify situations in which it is necessary to consult with a legal team.

✓   2.20.4: Identify ethical concerns when developing a Web site.

CIW Practice Exams

Visit CIW Online at *http://education.Certification-Partners.com/CIW* to take the Practice Exams assessment covering the objectives in this lesson.

SDA Objective 2.01 Review	*SDA Objective 2.14 Review*
SDA Objective 2.06 Review	*SDA Objective 2.15 Review*
SDA Objective 2.07 Review	*SDA Objective 2.18 Review*
SDA Objective 2.12 Review	*SDA Objective 2.19 Review*
SDA Objective 2.13 Review	*SDA Objective 2.20 Review*

Note that some objectives may be only partially covered in this lesson.

Lesson 1 Review

1. List three operating systems and three browsers on which HTML will function.

    _____

    _____

2. What is the purpose of a tag in markup languages?

    _____

3. What W3C project promotes Web page access for disabled Web users?

    _____

    _____

    _____

4. Why is it important to relate technical concepts to non-technical people during planning meetings?

    _____

5. When working with a service provider to upload a Web site, what is some of the essential information you will need?

    _____

    _____

    _____

    _____

Lesson 2:
HTML5 Coding

Objectives

By the end of this lesson, you will be able to:

✎ 2.1.3: Use HTML elements and tags to format paragraphs and text.

✎ 2.1.7: Add comments to HTML code and document page/site creation.

✎ 2.1.8: Explain the importance of consistently developing to a single W3C standard.

✎ 2.7.4: Validate Web page design according to technical and audience standards adopted by employers.

✎ 2.9.2: Create a Web page using the HTML5 standard.

✎ 2.12.1: Test and validate Web documents.

Pre-Assessment Questions

1. Which choice represents recommended HTML tag use?

   a. <p>Web page text</p>
   b. <p>Web page text<p>
   c. </p>Web page text</p>
   d. Web page text</p>

2. What HTML element is recommended to create boldface text?

   a. <bold>
   b. <em>
   c. <strong>
   d. <val>

3. How many heading styles (such as H1, H2, etc.) are available when using HTML?

   _____

OBJECTIVE
2.1.8: Using a single
W3C standard

Introduction to Using HTML

In this lesson, you will learn how to use standard HTML elements and tags to create functional documents. These documents are commonly referred to as pages when written for the Web or for any other application. The default or starting page of a Web site is called the home page for that site.

This course demonstrates the HTML5 standard. Remember that when you begin creating a Web page or site, you should first choose the W3C HTML standard that you will use. Then stick to your chosen standard, applying it consistently throughout your document, pages and site. This practice ensures that your elements and markup are universal and your pages will render properly in any user agent that your site visitors use.

CIW Online Resources – Movie Clips

Visit CIW Online at http://education.Certification-Partners.com/CIW to watch a movie clip about this topic.

Lesson 2: HTML5 Coding

Elements and Markup Tags

HTML elements are specific components of an HTML document that can provide content and attributes to a Web page. Each element provides meaning to the page, such as identifying the title of the document or specifying where a video or audio file should be placed. These elements are interpreted by Web browsers and other user agents so that the Web page renders properly.

In a nutshell, HTML documents can be described as a collection of elements. Without elements, a Web page would have no structure or formatting.

The majority of HTML elements include a start tag and end tag, also called markup tags. Markup tags enclose elements in angle brackets, or wickets. Please note that the terms "elements" and "tags" are used interchangeably by many Web developers.

Tags embed the element information in the document so that a user agent will render text or other content as instructed by the associated element. For example, the <strong> element is rendered using a start tag, <strong>, and an end tag, </strong>. The text surrounded by the start and end tag is rendered as bold font when viewed in a browser.

For example, bold text identified in an HTML document is written as:

```
<strong> The text between the start and end tag of the strong element appears in
bold when viewed in a Web browser. </strong>
```

The Web browser renders the HTML document text in bold, but the element and its tags do not appear:

Text between the start and end tag of the strong element appears in bold when viewed in a Web browser.

The combination of elements, markup tags and standard text is loosely referred to as either code or markup. Although markup languages are not programming languages, the elements and tags instruct the browser to perform certain actions, and so the use of the term "code" is appropriate in this context.

Container tags and empty tags

There are two types of HTML tags:

- **Container tags** — tags that come in pairs. Container tags use starting and ending tags. For example, when you want emphasis (italic) text, you will contain the text between starting and ending <em> </em> tags. These tags are also called the opening and closing tags.

- **Empty tags** — tags that stand alone. Empty tags are those that do not directly format a specified block of text, and therefore one tag can execute the instruction. For example, if you want to create a line break, you insert the <br> tag at the point you want the break to occur.

HTML allows you to use some empty tags, but good coding practice requires you to use container tags. HTML encourages you to use only container tags or empty tags that were meant to be stand-alone tags.

Figure 2-1 demonstrates the proper use of a container tag. The <title> tag contains text between an opening and a closing tag. Note that the closing tag includes the slash (/) character.

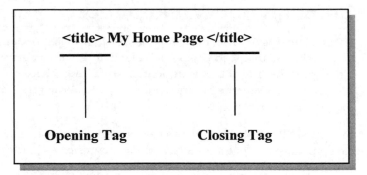

<title> My Home Page </title>

Opening Tag   **Closing Tag**

Figure 2-1: <title> tag pair as container for page title text

Container tags are also known as non-empty tags. You will learn more about creating the appropriate tags throughout the rest of this course.

Empty tags can be written with a slash after the element to become a stand-alone non-empty tag. A good example is the <br> element. It is an empty tag used to create a line break in an HTML document. When coding the <br> tag, it is written as <br/>. Other empty tags are written this way, including the <meta/> and <link/> tags. You will experiment with the <br/>, <meta/>, and <link/> tags later in this lesson.

What constitutes a tag?

A tag can consist of the following three items inside the angle brackets:

- **An element** — provides the main instruction of the tag. An element is required in every tag. Elements include <body>, <p>, <h1>, <title>, <table> and many others.

- **An attribute** — specifies a quality or describes a certain aspect of the element. For example, a hyperlink is added to a Web page by using the <a>, or anchor, element. The *href* attribute is added, which identifies the hyperlink reference. Many elements require specified attributes, but some do not. An attribute is required in a tag only if the element requires it.

- **A value** — gives value to the element and its attribute. For example, <a href="http://www.ciwcertified.com"> has a value that instructs the hyperlink to access the CIW Certified Web site. Like attributes, values are optional in a tag unless required by a specified attribute to the element. Values are used only with attributes; elements do not take values directly. Values should be surrounded by quotation marks; they are not required, but placing values in quotation marks is considered good coding practice.

Be sure to close any quotation marks that you open. If you do not close them, the page content up to the next occurrence of the quotation mark character may disappear.

Some elements, such as <br>, do not use attributes or values. Others, such as the <a> element, are almost always used with attributes and values. It is important that you understand this terminology as you continue throughout the course.

CIW Online Resources – Movie Clips

Visit CIW Online at http://education.Certification-Partners.com/CIW to watch a movie clip about this topic.

Lesson 2: Building a Basic Web Page

OBJECTIVE
2.1.3: HTML text
formatting

Document Structure Tags

HTML5 documents usually contain most of the following document structure components:

- **<!DOCTYPE> declaration** — The <!DOCTYPE declaration is the first tag in an HTML document. It informs the interpreter (usually a Web browser) what version of HTML the Web page is written in. Previous to HTML5, the <!DOCTYPE> declaration was an SGML statement and required a fairly complex declaration. In HTML5, however, the tag is written as only <!DOCTYPE html>. The declaration is not case-sensitive, but it is almost always written in uppercase letters by Web developers (it will be uppercase in this course).

- **<html> tag** — The <html> tag is used as a container for the entire HTML document. It nests all code except for the <!DOCTYPE> declaration.

- **<head> tag** — The head section allows you to insert <meta> tags (which describe the nature of the document), links to style sheets, and the <title> tag.

- **<meta> tags** — The <meta> tag can specify various information about the document, known as metadata. This metadata can include a document description, revision dates, and keywords to help search engines index the page. It also specifies the HTML5 character set used, which is usually UTF-8. The <meta> tag is placed within the <head> container tags.

- **<link> tag**— The <link> tag references a style sheet and is recommended for HTML5. A style sheet usually has a .css file name extension and a file name similar to the page to which it is linked (e.g., syb.css for the HTML page named syb.html). Style sheets are often placed in a subdirectory for the Web page. This subdirectory contains all images and associated files for the page. The <link> tag is placed within the <head> container tags.

- **<title> tag** — This tag identifies the document title. Most browsers will display the title in the browse's title bar. The <title> tag is placed within the <head> container tags.

- **<body> tag** — This tag begins the body of the document and includes all the content of the Web page, such as the text, video, hyperlinks and images. The <body> tag is placed after the <head> tag.

OBJECTIVE
2.7.4: Technical and
audience standards

If your document fails to include these basic structure elements, it may still validate, given the flexible nature of HTML5. However, the document may or may not render in older browsers that do not support HTML5, such as Internet Explorer versions prior to IE9. You will learn more about backward-compatibility issues later in this course.

These basic structural elements are greatly simplified from previous HTML and XHTML versions. The following code displays the basic HTML5 document structure tags:

```
<!DOCTYPE html>
 <html>
 <head>
<meta name="keywords" content="HTML5, basics, elements, tags"/>
 <meta name="author" content="Sampson Avilla"/>
 <meta charset="utf-8"/>
<link rel="stylesheet" type="text/css" href="stylesheet.css"/>
<title>HTML5 Structural Elements</title>
 </head>
 <body>
```

As you learn HTML5, you will start with the structural elements common to most HTML documents. These include:

```
 </body>
 </html>
```

Previous HTML and XHTML documents were different because the <!DOCTYPE> declaration included a Document Type Definition (DTD) file which referenced a specific HTML or XHTML standard. The DTD file is no longer required in HTML5. For example:

```
<!DOCTYPE html PUBLIC "-//W3C//DTD XHTML 1.0 Transitional//EN"
 "http://www.w3.org/TR/xhtml1/DTD/xhtml1-transitional.dtd">
```

Are HTML tags case-sensitive?

HTML tags are not case-sensitive, but older XHTML tags are case-sensitive. Because XML is case-sensitive in that it requires strict conformance to letter case specified in a given DTD, it was decided that all XHTML document elements and attributes should be developed in lowercase letters to ensure consistency, compatibility and conformance.

The benefit to writing code in lowercase is that the code is now compliant with both HTML and XHTML, and will render in all user agents that follow W3C standards. This practice has been widely adopted for all HTML coding.

Document type declaration (<!DOCTYPE>)

document type declaration (<!DOCTYPE>)
A declaration of document or code type embedded within an HTML, XHTML, XML or SGML document; identifies the version and markup language used. Denoted by the <!DOCTYPE> declaration at the beginning of the document.

The **document type declaration**, or <!DOCTYPE> declaration, describes the markup language and version of your code. It is placed at the very top of your document.

Prior to HTML5, the <!DOCTYPE> declaration was technically not XHTML or HTML; it was actually SGML. It included a reference to the Document Type Definition (DTD) for the markup version used. For instance, the XHTML 1.0 Transitional <!DOCTYPE> declaration contained a reference to *www.w3.org/TR/xhtml1/DTD/xhtml1-transitional.dtd*. If you followed the link, you could read the XHTML 1.0 DTD.

 Be careful not to confuse the document type declaration (<!DOCTYPE> declaration) with the Document Type Definition (DTD). The <!DOCTYPE> declaration is a statement that identifies code versions in a document. The DTD is a separate, older document containing a set of rules for structure, syntax and vocabulary, used commonly with XHTML and XML. Previous versions of HTML also included a <!DOCTYPE> declaration that contained a DTD document reference. The DTD applied the rules of the specified language version.

If you do not specify a <!DOCTYPE> declaration, then two problems may arise:

- You may not be able to control how your code renders in the future.

- You will not be able to use a markup validator, because the validator cannot determine the type of markup you are using (e.g., HTML5, XHTML Transitional or HTML 4.01).

Some examples of <!DOCTYPE> declaration statements follow.

HTML 2.0
The following <!DOCTYPE> declaration is used for HTML 2.0 files:

```
<!DOCTYPE HTML PUBLIC "-//W3C//DTD HTML 2.0//EN">
```

HTML 3.2
The following <!DOCTYPE> declaration is used for HTML 3.2 files:

```
<!DOCTYPE HTML PUBLIC "-//W3C//DTD HTML 3.2 Final//EN">
```

HTML 4.01
The following <!DOCTYPE> declarations are used for files written in the specified flavors of HTML 4.01 (the Web addresses are optional):

- **HTML 4.01 Transitional**

```
<!DOCTYPE HTML PUBLIC "-//W3C//DTD HTML 4.01 Transitional//EN"
"http://www.w3.org/TR/html4/loose.dtd">
```

- **HTML 4.01 Strict**

```
<!DOCTYPE HTML PUBLIC "-//W3C//DTD HTML 4.01//EN"
"http://www.w3.org/TR/html4/strict.dtd">
```

- **HTML 4.01 Frameset**

```
<!DOCTYPE HTML PUBLIC "-//W3C//DTD HTML 4.01 Frameset//EN"
"http://www.w3.org/TR/html4/frameset.dtd">
```

XHTML 1.0
XHTML 1.0 approximates the HTML 4.01 <!DOCTYPE> declarations. If you are using the XHTML Transitional flavor and you are not including XML in your document, there will be little difference between an HTML 4.01 and an XHTML 1.0 document. The following

<!DOCTYPE> declarations are used for the specified flavors of XHTML 1.0 (the Web addresses are optional).

- **XHTML Transitional**

  ```
  <!DOCTYPE html PUBLIC "-//W3C//DTD XHTML 1.0 Transitional//EN"
  "http://www.w3.org/TR/xhtml1/DTD/xhtml1-transitional.dtd">
  ```

- **XHTML Strict**

  ```
  <!DOCTYPE html PUBLIC "-//W3C//DTD XHTML 1.0 Strict//EN"
  "http://www.w3.org/TR/xhtml1/DTD/xhtml1-strict.dtd">
  ```

- **XHTML Frameset**

  ```
  <!DOCTYPE html PUBLIC "-//W3C//DTD XHTML 1.0 Frameset//EN"
  "http://www.w3.org/TR/xhtml1/DTD/xhtml1-frameset.dtd">
  ```

HTML5

HTML5 is not based on SGML, so the traditional <!DOCTYPE> declaration is not required and there is no DTD required. However, it is important to include the <!DOCTYPE> declaration to ensure the browser can identify the version of HTML used in the Web page. The following <!DOCTYPE> declaration s used for HTML5 files:

    <!DOCTYPE html>

By using the <!DOCTYPE> declaration, you will improve your page's ability to work with various browsers. The <!DOCTYPE> declaration can help you create a more efficient interface. However, most of its functionality occurs within process.

The <html> tag

The opening <html> and closing </html> tags must encompass all markup for the entire page. The <html> tag can include several attributes, including:

- **manifest** — an attribute used for offline browsing. It lists the address of the HTML document's cache manifest. The manifest attribute requires each page you want cached to include the attribute. This technique is considered more reliable than a traditional browser cache.

- **lang** — configures the page to use a particular language. For instance, a Web document written in English would use <html lang="en"> and a document written in French would use <html lang="fr">. This attribute is helpful for search engines and speech synthesizers. It is a universal attribute that can be used with many different elements besides <html>.

- **xmlns** — If your content needs to conform to XHTML, then specify the XML namespace attribute The default entry is *xmlns="http://www.w3.org/1999/xhtml"*.

The <head> tag

The <head> and </head> tags encompass several page elements, including:

- The <meta> tag.
- The <link> tag that references a CSS file, if present.
- The <title> tag.

The <meta> tag

character set
The group of symbols used to render text on a page.

Unicode
A universal character set designed to support all written languages, as well as scholarly disciplines (e.g., mathematics).

The <meta> tag can specify various information, or metadata, about the document. Attributes of the <meta> tag include the following:

- **charset** — specifies the **character set** used in HTML documents (which is often set by the Web server for HTML documents, rather than by the document itself). It usually specifies the **Unicode** character set, which is standard in today's Web pages:

```
<meta charset="utf-8"/>
```

- **name** — values include "keywords," "description" and "author. " This attribute must be accompanied by the *content* attribute. The "keywords" value of the *name* attribute allows you to specify individual words as the value in the accompanying *content* attribute; these words are used by search engines to match pages to search keywords, and to describe the meaning of the document. The "description" value of the *name* attribute allows you to specify entire sentences as the value in the accompanying *content* attribute; these sentences display in search engines to describe the purpose of the document.

- **content** —When paired with the *name* attribute, the *content* attribute values can supply keywords, author name, page descriptions and so forth, as previously described. Following are some examples.

To provide keywords for search engines, you can use the <meta> tag as follows:

```
<meta name="keywords" content="TCP/IP, networking, Java, CIW, certification"/>
```

If you want to use the <meta> tag to provide a detailed description of your page, use syntax similar to the following:

```
<meta name="description" content="You can enter a useful description of the
page here. You can use sentences, as you would in an e-mail or letter, but
keep it concise."/>
```

To specify the author of the Web page, use the <meta> tag with the "author" value:

```
<meta name="author" content="Rosa Estelle Rodriguez"/>
```

An extended discussion of the <meta> tag is beyond the scope of this course. However, the <meta> tag is a very effective back-end tool for ensuring that your pages work well across networks. The <meta> tag was discussed in this section because it is placed within the document structure tags.

The <link> tag

Style sheet references are specified with the <link> tag in the <head> section, usually before the <title> tag. The <link> tag and CSS are recommended for HTML5. The link must point to a CSS file that is simple ASCII text.

The <title> tag

The <title> tag is the first tag that allows you to specify content that will appear on the page. Any text you enclose with this tag appears in the page title box at the top of a browser. This text also appears in the history list and on the page when printed. Title text becomes the Bookmark name if the page is bookmarked or added to a browser Favorites folder.

The <body> tag

All content viewed by a Web browser or other user agent needs to be placed between the <body> and </body> tags. This content includes text, images, video, tables, lists and hyperlinks. The <body> tag no longer has attributes with HTML5. The previous formatting attributes have been replaced by CSS and the inline CSS style attribute.

CIW Online Resources – Online Exercise

Visit CIW Online at *http://education.Certification-Partners.com/CIW* to complete an interactive exercise that will reinforce what you have learned about this topic.

Exercise 2-1: Document Structure Tags

Web Site File Structure

When creating a Web page, you must consider the site's structure. Your HTML and images will be uploaded to a server eventually, so it is always good practice to organize your files as you create them. Figure 2-2 illustrates a typical Web site file structure.

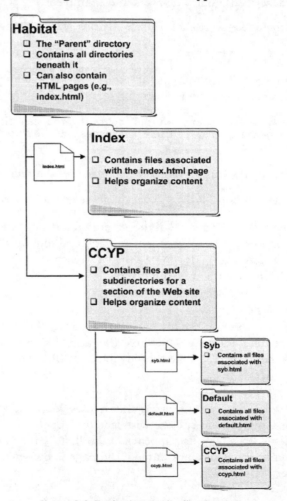

Figure 2-2: Typical Web site file structure

As shown in this figure, the HTML pages are usually placed in a directory, and all images and files used in that page are stored in subfolders with the same name.

In this course, you will work on selected pages from a previously live version of the Habitat for Humanity Web site. All necessary files are provided. Specifically, you will work on a Summer Youth Blitz page, which resides in the Habitat\CCYP\ directory.

CIW Online Resources – Course Mastery

Visit CIW Online at *http://education.Certification-Partners.com/CIW* to take the Course Mastery review of this lesson or lesson segment.

SDA Lesson 2 - Part A

Preparing Your Development Environment

Before you begin creating Web page code, you should:

- **Obtain a text editor** — Most operating systems have their own editors, so you do not need to download and install one. However, you may prefer to obtain a text editor that automatically numbers lines so you can easily reference your code. It is best to use a text editor that automatically saves standard ASCII text. Applications such as Microsoft Word can save to standard ASCII text only if you explicitly command them to do so. Common text editors include Notepad, WordPad, Vi, Pico and Emacs.

- **Install multiple browsers** — You will need to test your code in multiple environments.

- **Set file preferences** — The Windows operating systems do not show file name extensions by default. You will be working with files with various extensions (e.g., .html, .css, .txt), so you will need to be able to see them. You can set preferences in Windows 7 by selecting Start | Control Panel | Appearance and Personalization | Folder Options, then selecting the View tab. Deselect the Hide Extensions For Known File Types check box so that you can view all file name extensions.

OBJECTIVE
2.1.3: HTML text formatting

In the following lab, you will create a simple HTML page. Suppose you have been assigned to create a basic markup page as a placeholder for a page that will describe a summer youth program for Habitat for Humanity volunteers. This simple file should be named syb.html and should validate as HTML5. What steps would you take to create this simple page?

Lab 2-1: Creating a simple HTML5 page

OBJECTIVE
2.9.2: Creating pages with HTML5

In this lab, you will create a basic file directory structure, and you will create an HTML page then validate it as HTML5.

OBJECTIVE
2.12.1: Validating Web documents

1. If necessary, configure your operating system so that you can read the full extensions of all file names. This will allow you to find your HTML files more easily. In Windows 7, select **Start | Control Panel | Appearance and Personalization | Folder Options**, then select the **View** tab. Deselect the **Hide Extensions For Known File Types** check box. Select the **Show Hidden Files, Folders, And Drives** radio button. Click **OK** to close the Folder Options dialog box. Close the Control Panel.

2. Right-click the **Desktop** and select **New | Folder**.

3. Name the new folder *Habitat*.

4. Double-click the **Habitat** folder to open it. Inside, create a subfolder and name it *CCYP*.

5. Double-click the **CCYP** folder to open it.

6. When you are finished, review the directory structure you have created. In Windows Explorer, it should appear off of your Desktop as Habitat\CCYP\.

7. The Habitat\CCYP\ folder will eventually contain the syb.html file, among others. You have now created a standard directory structure for a Web site in which you can organize your images and CSS pages.

8. Right-click inside the **Habitat\CCYP** folder, and select **New | Text Document**. Name the new text document *syb.html*. A warning dialog box will appear stating "If you change a file name extension, the file might become unusable. Are you sure you want to change it?" Click **Yes**. You are changing a text file into an HTML document.

9. Right-click the **syb.html** file and open it in **Notepad**. If Notepad does not appear when you right-click, select **Choose Default Program**. Click the down arrow next to **Other Programs** and double-click **Notepad**. You will see that the syb.html file is currently empty.

10. In the blank syb.html file, enter the following code exactly as written:

```
<!DOCTYPE html>

<html>

<head>
<meta name="keywords" content="CIW, HTML5, Habitat for Humanity"/>
<meta name="description" content="Simple XHTML page for Habitat site"/>
<meta charset="UTF-8"/>
<title>Habitat for Humanity International Summer Youth Blitz Program</title>
</head>

<body style="background-color:white">

Join a Summer Build for Teenagers.
The Summer Youth Blitz is a unique service experience for a diverse group of
youth, ages 16 to 18, from high schools and youth organizations around the
United States. This page will validate as HTML5.

</body>
</html>
```

11. Once you have inserted this code, save your changes. Make sure that your file is named syb.html, not syb.txt or anything else. You may have to close Notepad to rename the file.

12. Now, open **syb.html** in a Web browser by right-clicking the file, selecting **Open With**, and choosing an HTML5-compliant browser. It should resemble Figure 2-3.

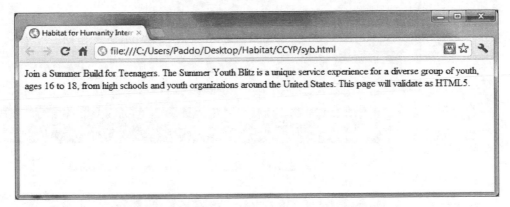

Figure 2-3: File syb.html in Chrome

Note: You can use any Web browser. In fact, you are encouraged to view code in multiple browsers to ensure that you are creating pages that render well in various environments.

13. As you can see, you have created a rudimentary Web page that will validate as HTML5, as long as you have entered the code correctly. To verify this, visit **http://validator.w3.org**. You will see the W3C Markup Validation Service Web page, as shown in Figure 2-4.

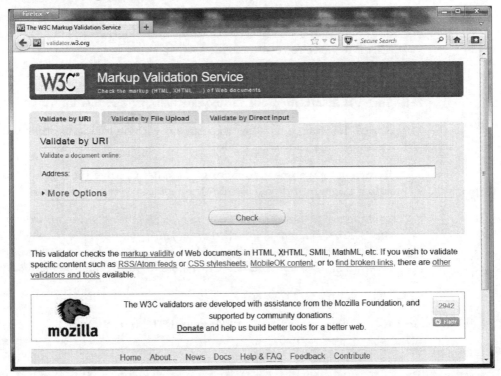

Figure 2-4: W3C Markup Validation Service Web page

14. Click the **Validate By File Upload** link. To the right of the File text box, click the **Browse** button. Navigate to the **syb.html** file you have created and select it by double-clicking.

15. Click the **Check** button.

16. If your code does not validate, make appropriate changes. Warnings are OK and do not mean you made an error. In Figure 2-5, the warning states that the W3C

validator checked the document with an experimental HTML5 conformance checker. The checker may not be up to date with cutting-edge HTML5 code.

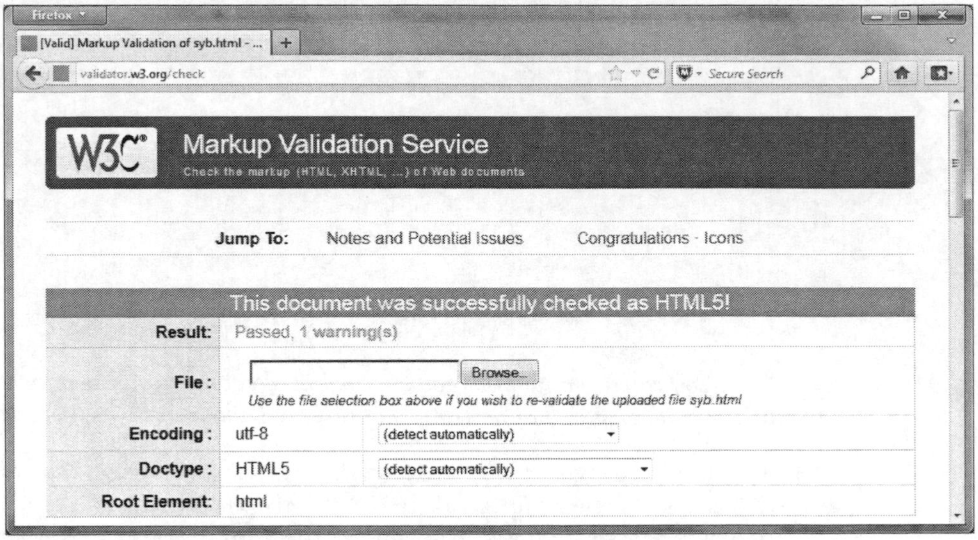

Figure 2-5: Successful HTML5 validation with one warning

17. Once your code validates, change the background color of your page to light blue. To do this, find the <body style="background-color:white">tag, then change the *style* attribute value to read as follows:

    ```
    <body style="background-color:lightblue">
    ```

18. Save **syb.html**, then open it in your Web browser again.

19. Notice the change in color. Experiment with changing to other background colors. Then validate your code again.

20. Return your Web page to its original state. Change the *style* attribute back to the value "background-color:white" then validate your HTML again.

    Tech Note: The background color is typically identified in an external CSS file to which the HTML document is linked. For this lab, you used the inline CSS style attribute, which provides style to an individual file. It overrides any styles identified in the external style sheet. You will learn more about CSS in the next lesson.

21. Close your Web browser.

In this lab, you created and validated an HTML5 document.

Paragraph Formatting and Block-Level Elements

block-level element
A markup element that affects at least an entire paragraph.

text-level element
A markup element that affects single characters or words.

Markup elements that affect an entire paragraph or multiple paragraphs are referred to as **block-level elements**. Elements that can affect something as small as a character or a word are referred to as **text-level elements**. Block-level elements are automatically preceded and followed by paragraph breaks. Text-level elements are not followed by breaks unless the breaks are manually added.

Paragraph breaks and line breaks

OBJECTIVE
2.1.3: HTML text
formatting

The most basic block-level element is the paragraph element. The line break element is technically a text-level element, but it is included here in the context of formatting paragraphs. The <p> tag defines the start of a new paragraph, and a closing </p> tag specifies the end of the paragraph.

The <br> tag inserts a simple line break into the document. Because the <br> tag usually breaks a line of text, it never spans words or multiple lines of text, as does the <p> tag.

The <br> tag does not use a separate closing tag, so it follows a unique tag syntax. A closing slash is appended to every line break tag to make it a stand-alone non-empty tag, as follows:

In the following lab, you will use HTML tags to insert paragraph and line breaks. Suppose the marketing and legal departments have created several paragraphs of text for the syb.html page, and you are assigned to insert this text. You can use the <p> and <br> tags to format information on the page and make it easy to read.

 Lab 2-2: Creating paragraph breaks and line breaks with HTML

In this lab, you will use the <p> and <br> tags to add paragraph breaks and line breaks to a Web page.

1. **Editor:** Open the file **syb.html**, which you edited in the previous lab.

2. **Editor:** Delete all text located between the <body></body> tags except for the "Join a Summer Build for Teenagers" line. Place your cursor on a new line just below "Join a Summer Build for Teenagers."

3. **Editor:** Minimize **syb.html**.

4. Navigate to the **C:\CIW\Site_Dev\Lab Files\Lesson02\Lab_2-2** directory. Copy the file **syb.txt** to your Desktop, then open it in the text editor. Notice that the text is organized into five separate paragraphs.

5. Copy the contents of the syb.txt file and paste it into **syb.html** (between the <body></body> tags except for the "Join a Summer Build for Teenagers" line). Save the **syb.html** file.

6. Load **syb.html** into a browser. You will now see more text on the Web page, but it is not organized into paragraphs when you view it in a browser.

7. Edit the text in syb.html to add paragraphs breaks that will be recognized by a browser. Add the following code shown in bold:

```
Join a Summer Build for Teenagers.
<p>
The Summer Youth Blitz is a unique service experience for a diverse group of
youth, ages 16 to 18, from high schools and youth organizations around the
United States. During this program, 15 to 20 youth participants and adult
leaders "blitz build" an entire Habitat house in two weeks.
</p>
<p>
The house build, an unfamiliar activity for most, provides a common,
nonthreatening ground for building relationships and teams.
</p>
```

```
<p>
In the evenings, the youth participate in activities like team-building games,
leadership development, local cultural events or community dinners.
</p>
<p>
This program is sponsored by national grant donations and coordinated by the
Campus Chapters and Youth Programs department of Habitat for Humanity
International. For the past several years, funding has allowed for three blitz
builds per summer--two in the United States and one outside the country. The
builds take place during the months of June, July and August.
</p>
<p>
If you're interested in participating, and are between the ages of 16 and 18
years old, you must submit an application, which is available during January
and February.
</p>
```

8. Load **syb.html** into your browser. You will see that the text is now separated into paragraphs, as shown in Figure 2-6.

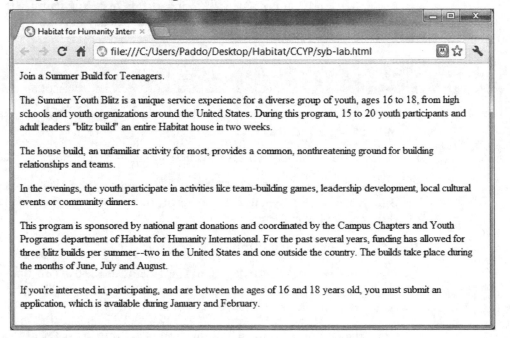

Figure 2-6: File syb.html after adding <p> tags

9. Notice that using the <p> tags has created paragraphs. Now, add some <br/> tags to see the difference between a line break and a paragraph break in HTML. Open the **syb.html** file again and enter the following <br/> tags as indicated in bold:

```
Join a Summer Build for Teenagers.
<p>
The Summer Youth Blitz is a unique service experience for a diverse group of
youth,<br/>ages 16 to 18,
from high schools and youth organizations around the United States.
<br/>During this program, 15 to 20
youth participants and adult leaders <br/>"blitz build" an entire Habitat
house in two weeks.
</p>
<p>
The house build, an unfamiliar activity for most, provides a common,
<br/>nonthreatening ground for building
relationships and teams.
</p>
```

```
<p>
In the evenings, the youth participate in activities like team-building games,
<br/>leadership development,
local cultural events or community dinners.
</p>
<p>
This program is sponsored by national grant donations and coordinated by the
Campus Chapters<br/> and Youth
Programs department of Habitat for Humanity International. For the past
several years, <br/>funding has allowed
for three blitz builds per summer--two in the United States and one outside
<br/>the country. The builds take
place during the months of June, July and August.
</p>
<p>
If you're interested in participating, and are between the ages of 16 and 18
years old, <br/>you must submit
an application, which is available during January and February.
</p>
```

10. Notice that you entered the stand-alone non-empty <br/> tag, rather than encompassing text between <br> and </br>.

11. Reload your file in the browser. You should now see the lines break across the page, as shown in Figure 2-7. Notice that although the lines break, no extra returns are added after the line breaks, as they are with the paragraph breaks.

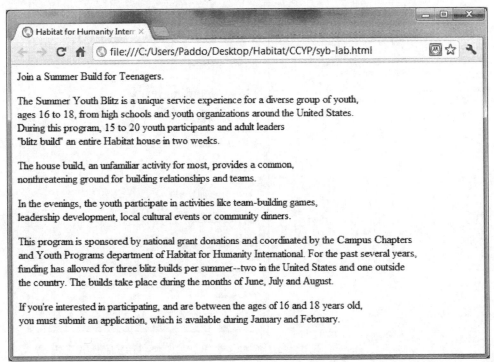

Figure 2-7: File syb.html after adding <br/> tags to create line breaks

12. Close all browser and editor windows.

In this lab, you used the <p> and <br> tags.

The preceding lab demonstrates that the appearance of text in the editor will not necessarily match the appearance of text in the browser. Do not become frustrated when the text in your browser does not appear as you intended. Determine what needs to be done to achieve the desired appearance, and add the appropriate code to your file.

OBJECTIVE
2.9.2: Creating
pages with HTML5

Heading levels

Even the most basic documents will usually include at least one heading, and more likely several. Denoting text as heading elements emphasizes the start of different sections on your page and draws attention to that text. Heading tags have built-in styles associated with them. For example, text formatted as a heading level 1 element is rendered by default in a large, bold, serif font.

HTML uses six heading styles. Heading tags are container tags that encompass the affected text. The <h1> and </h1> tags cause enclosed text to be rendered in the heading level 1 style; the <h4> and </h4> tags cause enclosed text to be rendered in the heading level 4 style, and so forth. The largest heading is level 1. Heading level 4 text is rendered the same size as normal text. Heading levels 5 and 6 are smaller than normal text and should be used sparingly, if at all. Figure 2-8 shows heading appearances relative to normal text.

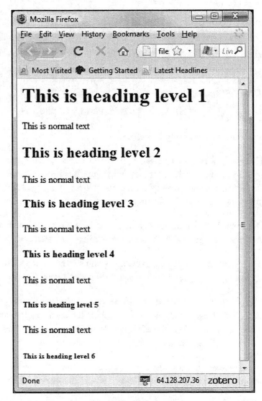

Figure 2-8: Heading-level text and normal text

Because headings are block-level elements, they are automatically preceded and followed by paragraph breaks, regardless of the relative position of the element to other text in the source code. It is important to note that you cannot place any header elements within a set of <p> </p> tags. If you do, your code will not validate as HTML5 and it may not render properly.

Tag nesting in markup

You will often use multiple sets of tags to format some text. Placing a pair of tags within another pair of tags is called tag nesting. You must ensure that your code is properly nested. Proper nesting means that you must open and close a pair of tags within another pair. The following two examples show both proper and improper tag nesting techniques.

> **Proper**: <h1> <em> ... </em> </h1>
>
> **Improper**: <h1> <em> ... </h1> </em>

Notice that in the improper example, the <em> tag (for italic text) is opened within the <h1> tag, but then closed outside the </h1> tag. If you fail to properly nest code, your pages may still render in some user agents, but they will not validate and may fail to render in the future.

Similarly, heading tags (e.g., <h1>, <h2>) should not be used within formatting tags (e.g., <em>, <p>). This tag combination constitutes improper nesting because the elements are incompatible, and will therefore prevent your code from validating.

In the following lab, you will use HTML to create headings. Suppose your project manager has assigned you to add headings to a Web page so that readers immediately understand the page's topics. The headings must help organize the content. The page content includes an introduction, the program's sponsors and an application section.

<table>
<tr>
<td>

OBJECTIVE
2.1.3: HTML text
formatting

</td>
<td>

</td>
<td>

Lab 2-3: Using headings in HTML

</td>
</tr>
</table>

In this lab, you will add heading tags to Web page code to help organize the content.

1. **Editor:** Open **syb.html**.

2. Add and edit the code as shown in bold so that it has <h1> tags but no period at the end:

   `<h1>Join a Summer Build for Teenagers</h1>`

   Note: Make sure that the <h1> line is not placed between a set of <p>...</p> tags.

3. **Editor:** Add a line that says ***Sponsors*** just above the fourth paragraph, and make it an h2 heading. Again, make sure that your heading is not between a set of <p>...</p> tags.

4. **Editor:** Add a line that says ***Apply Now!*** just above the last (fifth) paragraph, and make it an h3 heading. Again, make sure that your heading is not between a set of <p>...</p> tags.

5. **Editor:** Save your changes and load the file into a browser. Your screen should resemble Figure 2-9. When you are finished, validate your code.

Figure 2-9: File syb.html after adding heading, paragraph and line break tags

6. Close all browser and editor windows.

In this lab, you used markup headings.

OBJECTIVE
2.9.2: Creating
pages with HTML5

fixed-width font
A font in which
every character,
including the space
character, has
equal width. In
proportional-width
fonts, letters such as
I and J have less
width than M or B.

Primitive formatting with the <pre> tag

Sometimes, you may want to use text that has already been formatted in a table or with a **fixed-width font**, such as Courier or Lucida Sans Typewriter. With the preformatted text tag (<pre>), all line breaks and spacing will be displayed in the browser exactly as they appear in the original text. The text will display in a fixed-width font, usually Courier.

The <pre> tag allows you to display plaintext files in their original format. It is commonly used to display tabular data. The <pre> tag is a container tag, requiring a closing </pre> tag.

 To learn more about the <pre> tag, visit www.w3schools.com/html5/tag_pre.asp

As you will learn in a later lesson, HTML tables are more attractive and functional for presenting tabular data. However, if you have preformatted data and little time, the <pre> tag is quick and simple to use.

OBJECTIVE
2.9.2: Creating
pages with HTML5

Indenting and centering text

When you want to center a paragraph of text, you must use an inline CSS *style* attribute in the paragraph tag. The syntax is as follows:

```
<p style="text-align:center"> This text is centered. </p>
```

In this example, the <p> tag encompasses the text you want to format. The *style* attribute tells the browser that the paragraph text should be aligned to the specified value, "center".

You can use the *style* attribute for many formatting functions. Most often, you will use it to format content in an individual HTML file when you are not using CSS or when you want to override the external CSS file. For example, you can center text, tables and images. You can also use the *style* attribute to justify items to the right or left on a page. For example, consider the following code:

```
<p style="text-align:right"> This text is aligned to the right. </p>
```

In this example, the text would render on the right side of the page.

The <blockquote> tag centers and indents a block of text. As its name suggests, it is often used to format quotes within a Web page. Do not use <blockquote> tags within <p> tags, and do not use <h1> tags within <blockquote> tags. Doing so will prevent your code from validating.

In the following lab, you will use HTML to center and indent text on a Web page. Suppose your project manager has seen your HTML work thus far and asked you to continue formatting the document. She has suggested indenting and centering some text to enhance the page's appearance. She has also asked you to add some contact information at the bottom of the page.

 Lab 2-4: Indenting and centering text with HTML

OBJECTIVE
2.1.3: HTML text
formatting

In this lab, you will use HTML to indent and center text in the file you created in previous labs.

1. **Editor:** Open **syb.html** and scroll to the bottom of the file.

2. **Editor:** Add the following line just above the </body> tag:

   ```
   <p style="text-align:center"> For more information, contact us at (800) 422-
   4828, ext. 2220. </p>
   ```

3. **Browser:** Load the **syb.html** file. You will see that your new line is centered. Validate your code at ***http://validator.w3.org***.

   Note: Properly nest code, or else it may fail validation, render incorrectly, or both.

4. Use the **<blockquote>** tag to indent all of the text beneath each header, as follows:

   ```
   <h1>Join a Summer Build for Teenagers</h1>
   <blockquote>
   <p>
   The Summer Youth Blitz is a unique service experience for a diverse group of
   youth, <br/>ages 16 to 18,
   from high schools and youth organizations around the United States.
   ```

```
<br/>During this program, 15 to 20
youth participants and adult leaders <br/>"blitz build" an entire Habitat
house in two weeks.
</p>
</blockquote>
```

5. Repeat this formatting for the entire page by enclosing each text paragraph in <blockquote> tags, except the last "For more information" line. Do not format headings as blockquotes. Notice that the tags are properly nested: The <blockquote> tags are not placed inside of the <p> tags, nor are the <h1> tags inside of a <blockquote> tag. When you are finished, resize your browser window so your page resembles Figure 2-10.

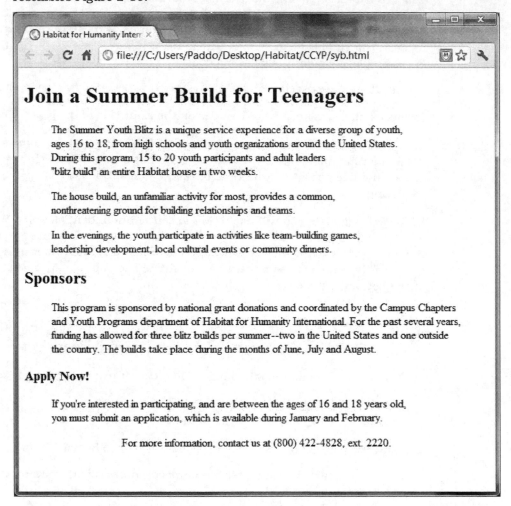

Figure 2-10: File syb.html after indenting with <blockquote> and centering text

6. Close all browser and editor windows.

In this lab, you used HTML to center and indent text in a Web page.

Additional block-level elements

You can incorporate additional block-level elements into your pages. These include forms, horizontal ruling lines, and lists.

By this point, you should understand how to use the most common block-level tags:

- `<p>`

- `<h1>` through `<h6>`

- `<blockquote>`

`<p style="text-align:center">` Other elements are discussed later in this lesson and in the lessons that follow.

 Additional paragraph tags are not added to your code when you use block-level elements. The block-level elements are interpreted by the client browser, which automatically includes the additional spacing.

Text-Level Elements

Text-level elements can affect a section of text as small as a single character or as large as an entire page. In the discussion that follows, you will learn how to use several text-formatting elements to emphasize text and embellish your pages.

Bold and italic text

Simple text-level elements include the following:

- `<strong>` for **bold** text

- `<em>` for *italic* text

Underlined text will not be covered in this course. As a general rule, you should never use underline because this convention designates hyperlinks in Web page text. It will confuse your Web page viewers. If you still want to use underlined text, visit the CSS page at *www.w3schools.com*.

Text-formatting tags are simple to use. Open the tag before the text to be affected, and close the tag where you want that effect to end. Ensure that tags are nested properly: The tag that opens first closes last, and the tag that opens last closes first..

Phrase elements and font style elements

The `<strong>` element and the older `<b>` element both create bold text. However, each element accomplishes this effect differently. The difference is that `<b>` specifically means apply the bold font style, whereas `<strong>` indicates that the text is to be given a strong appearance. In short, `<b>` represents a font appearance instruction, whereas `<strong>` represents the weighting of the phrase relative to surrounding text. The `<b>` element is called a font style element; `<strong>` is called a phrase element. The same is true of the older `<i>` element and the current `<em>` element, respectively, which both create italic or emphasized text.

Outside of ancient rhetoric, there is no such thing as "bold" speech, but the term "strong" can be used both to denote bold text when printed and strongly spoken text when output through an audio device.

For printed output, you can use phrase and font elements interchangeably. However, if you are coding for the future (as you should be), you should consider how the markup might be used in a different context, then apply the most appropriate tag.

As a general rule, use CSS to achieve a richer effect. Phrase elements are used more often for individual pages instead of entire Web sites.

Many text-level phrase elements output the same appearance. For example, the <code>, <kbd> and <samp> tags all make text appear in a fixed-space font. Phrase tags distinguish normal italic text from word definitions or variable program code within the HTML document. Using phrase tags is also beneficial because it is much easier to search for a specific tag within an HTML file instead of searching all italic, fixed-space or bold text.

Table 2-1 lists text-level phrase elements, their usage and their appearances. Font-style elements are slowly disappearing from the Web and are not emphasized in this course.

Table 2-1: Text-level HTML phrase elements

Phrase Element	Usage	Appearance
<em>	For emphasis	*italic text*
<strong>	For stronger, bolder text	**bold text**
<dfn>	For word definitions	*italic* text
<code>	For program code examples	`fixed-space font`
<kbd>	For user keyboard text to be typed	`fixed-space font`
<samp>	For program sample output	`fixed-space font`
<var>	For variable text in program code	*italic text*

In the following lab, you will use text-level phrase elements to format text on a Web page. Suppose your project manager has asked you to add emphasis to certain phrases with formatting such as italic or bold type. You could perform these steps to add the proper elements to your Web page code.

 Lab 2-5: Using text-level phrasing elements in HTML

OBJECTIVE
2.1.3: HTML text formatting

In this lab, you will add text-level phrasing elements to the file you worked with in previous labs.

1. **Editor:** Open syb.html.

2. **Editor:** In the first full paragraph, find the phrase "*Summer Youth Blitz*" and add the <em> tag as shown:

   `<em>Summer Youth Blitz</em>`

3. **Editor:** Save the file.

4. Review your work in a browser, and then validate it.

5. **Editor:** Find the phrase "*and are between the ages of 16 and 18 years old,*" and add the <strong> tags as shown:

   `<strong>and are between the ages of 16 and 18 years old</strong>,`

6. Save your code and load it into a browser. Your page should resemble Figure 2-11.

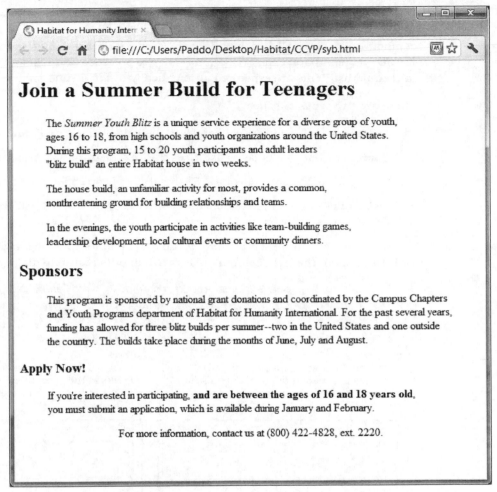

Figure 2-11: File syb.html after adding text-level phrase elements

7. **When time permits:** Experiment with using the <code>, <kbd> and <samp> tags. Be sure to delete these tags when you are finished experimenting.

8. Close all browser and editor windows.

In this lab, you added text-level phrasing elements to a Web page.

Now that you know how to use the text-level phrase elements, you will work with lists.

Lists

A common markup function is to create bulleted and numbered lists. Lists are compound, block-level elements. Encompassed within list definition tags are individual list item tags. A paragraph break automatically precedes and follows the entire list. Individual list items are separated automatically by single line breaks.

There are two types of lists:

- **Ordered list** — a numbered list. Uses the <ol> element and requires a closing tag.

- **Unordered list** — a bulleted list. Uses the <ul> element and also requires a closing tag.

Both list types use identical syntax. Each list item is specified using the list item element:

- **List item** — specifies list items in an ordered or unordered list. Uses the <li> element and requires a closing tag.

Contrast the code in the left column of Table 2-2 and its resulting display in Figure 2-12, with the code in the right column of Table 2-2 and its resulting display in Figure 2-13.

Table 2-2: Ordered and unordered list syntax and display

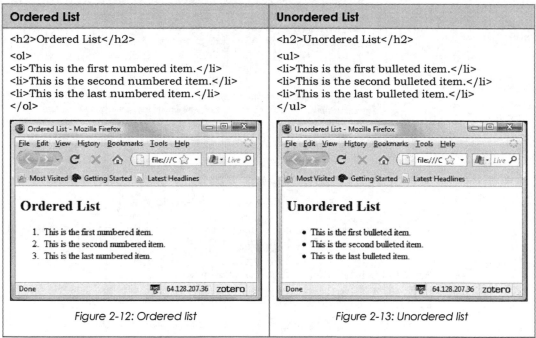

Ordered List	Unordered List
<h2>Ordered List</h2> <ol> <li>This is the first numbered item.</li> <li>This is the second numbered item.</li> <li>This is the last numbered item.</li> </ol>	<h2>Unordered List</h2> <ul> <li>This is the first bulleted item.</li> <li>This is the second bulleted item.</li> <li>This is the last bulleted item.</li> </ul>

Figure 2-12: Ordered list   *Figure 2-13: Unordered list*

In the following lab, you will use HTML to create bulleted and numbered lists. Suppose your supervisor has given you the following text to add to the Web page:

> "During the house build, you will: help lay the foundation, assist in framing the home, and do simple carpentry under supervision."

You can see that a list format would work well for this multi-point information. You can experiment with both an ordered and an unordered list. Which is most appropriate for the information?

Lab 2-6: Creating lists with HTML

OBJECTIVE
2.1.3: HTML text
formatting

In this lab, you will create a bulleted list and a numbered list on a Web page.

1. **Editor:** Open **syb.html**.

2. Create empty space by adding a return immediately beneath the </p> tag located after the text that reads "*for building relationships and teams.*"

3. Add the text shown and format it as an unordered (bulleted) list. Make sure that the list (beginning with the <ul> tag) is not placed within a set of <p> tags:

```
<blockquote>
<p>
The house build, an unfamiliar activity for most, provides a common,
<br/>nonthreatening ground for building relationships and teams.
</p>
<p>During the house build, you will:</p>
<ul>
<li>Help lay the foundation. </li>
<li>Assist in framing the home. </li>
<li>Do simple carpentry, under supervision. </li>
</ul>
</blockquote>
```

4. **Editor:** Save your changes and view the page in a browser. Your page should resemble Figure 2-14.

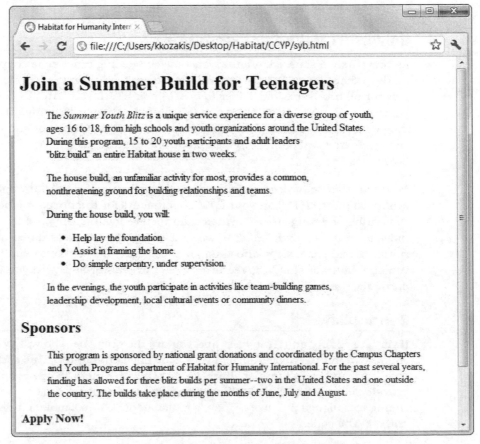

Figure 2-14: File syb.html after adding bulleted list

5. Validate your code at **http://validator.w3.org**.

6. Change your unordered list to an ordered list, then validate your code again. View the page with the ordered list in the browser. Do you think a numbered list format is more appropriate for this information than a bulleted list?

7. Change your code back to an unordered list, then close all editors and browsers.

In this lab, you created ordered and unordered lists.

Good Coding Practice

Now that you have learned the basics of working with HTML5 elements and tags, you should consider not simply which elements to use, but how to best use them in conjunction with your text.

Forward-compatibility

Remember that good coding practice involves writing code for forward-compatibility. That means you should always make your code cleaner to allow an easier transition to updated standards in the future. Such practices include:

- Closing all tags.
- Using lowercase letters within tags.
- Surrounding attribute values with quotation marks.

OBJECTIVE
2.1.8: Using a single W3C standard

Universal markup and consistency

As previously discussed, another facet of good coding practice is creating universal markup that applies W3C standards consistently and thus renders consistently across most or all browsers. Remember to choose one HTML standard for your Web document, pages or site, then apply that standard carefully and consistently throughout. Applying the syntax rules of multiple standards in the same document or site not only prevents your code from validating but also produces unexpected rendering results in your users' browsers.

Note that this point does not contradict the previous point about applying the stricter syntax rules of XHTML in your HTML documents for the purpose of forward-compatibility. Using stricter syntax than required will rarely produce output problems. Inconsistency is mostly an issue with the older HTML standards because their looser rules allowed some sloppier coding practices to render without penalty. Keep in mind that you should understand the requirements of whichever standard you are using, and be particularly aware of syntax and tag usage.

Readability

If you are coding an HTML page and you are the only one who will ever look at the code, you may think the appearance of your code does not matter. This statement is basically true. But suppose you must share your work with others. Some coding techniques provide better readability, and make finding and changing code a simple operation. Other coding techniques produce a busy, confusing format that makes it difficult to decipher and edit the code.

Examine the two boxes of HTML code in Figure 2-15. Both sets of code will render the same in a browser, but clearly one set of markup is easier to read than the other. Suppose you were hiring someone to write HTML code for you. Would you be more inclined to hire the developer of the code on the left, or the developer of the code on the right? The code on the right is much more readable.

```
<html><head><title>Overview
</title></head><body><h1>
Looking Back</h1></body>
</html>
```

```
<html>
<head>
<title>Overview</title>
</head>
<body>
<h1>Looking Back</h1>
</body>
</html>
```

Figure 2-15: Same HTML code with different line breaks

Exceptions

In some cases, you may find it impossible to make the code more readable without affecting the way it renders in the browser. With older XHTML code involving images or the <div> tag, you may find that entering random white space can affect rendering in certain browsers. Always try to make your code readable, but verify that it renders properly.

OBJECTIVE
2.1.7: HTML code
comments

Adding hidden comments

You can hide comments within your HTML source code that will not appear on the page. The syntax for including a comment within your HTML document is as follows:

```
<!-- comment text here -->
```

When to use comments

When creating markup pages, you can use comments to:

- "Comment out" code to see how a page will appear without a particular markup element.

- Inform others about important elements in the code you are creating.

- Remind yourself why you inserted a particular piece of code.

- Insert programming code, such as JavaScript.

CIW Online Resources – Online Exercise

Visit CIW Online at *http://education.Certification-Partners.com/CIW* to complete an interactive exercise that will reinforce what you have learned about this topic.

Exercise 2-2: Using comments

In the following lab, you will insert hidden comments into your HTML code. Suppose your project has incurred a change and you have been asked to temporarily remove the bulleted list. You can use hidden comments to add notes to the file that document this change, and also make it easy to reverse it if necessary.

Lab 2-7: Documenting and commenting HTML code

In this lab, you will document your HTML code and "comment out" certain portions.

1. **Editor:** Open the **syb.html** file.

2. **Editor:** Comment out your bulleted list and the introduction to it using the <!-- and --> tags.

```
</p>

<--
<p>During the house build, you will:</p>
<ul>
<li>Help lay the foundation. </li>
<li>Assist in framing the home.</li>
<li>Do simple carpentry, under supervision. </li>
</ul>
-->

</blockquote>
```

3. Save your changes and view your edited file in a browser. You will no longer see the bulleted list and its introduction.

4. Validate your code to ensure that you have used the comments properly. Sometimes adding comments can cause you to mistakenly omit closing tags and/or interrupt a nesting sequence.

5. Document the reason that you removed the bulleted list by creating another comment immediately after the bulleted list you just commented out:

   `<!-- Bulleted list removed at the request of supervisor, Jane Doe.-->`

6. Near the bottom of the file, just above the </body> tag, document your code so that another developer can identify who wrote it. Insert your name, the date, and a statement that this code validates to HTML5:

   `<!-- Your Name, Today's Date. This code validates to HTML5-->`

7. Validate your code again.

8. Review your code in the text editor. Make sure that it is easy to read in terms of good coding practice.

9. **If time permits:** Create additional comments explaining the code.

10. Close all editors and browsers.

In this lab, you documented and commented out portions of your markup.

CIW Online Resources – Course Mastery

Visit CIW Online at *http://education.Certification-Partners.com/CIW* to take the Course Mastery review of this lesson or lesson segment.

SDA Lesson 2 - Part B

Case Study

HTML Convert

Vlad works as a developer on his company's Web team. He has been assigned to convert the Web site's code from HTML 4.01 to HTML5. He developed a conversion plan that included the following steps:

- Use a valid <!DOCTYPE> declaration for all pages.

- Ideally, use style sheets. Developers do not necessarily need to use CSS, but it is recommended.

- Identify deprecated and forbidden tags already in use. Determine replacement tags and/or other methods of achieving the same effects using proper HTML5 markup.

- Estimate the necessary time and resources to make these changes.

Vlad presented to his project manager an example of a converted page, a new style sheet, and an estimate for the time it would take to complete the conversion process. His project manager was able to obtain funding for the conversion.

*   *   *

As a class, discuss the following questions.

- Suppose Vlad uses a GUI HTML editor. What changes and/or updates must he make?

- What <!DOCTYPE> declaration should Vlad choose if he wants the site to be HTML5-compliant as quickly as possible?

- Considering that Vlad must identify and change deprecated tags, should he add time to the project?

Lesson Summary

Application project

You have already learned many of the basic tags that HTML provides for formatting text and paragraphs. In the lessons that follow, you will learn how to incorporate graphics, create links, use external CSS, work with tables and create HTML forms. Now, consider the following:

- What is the difference between a container element and an empty element? Consider that a container element must contain the text that it formats between opening and closing tags.

- Review all the HTML code you have created. Verify that it adheres to the good coding practices discussed in this lesson. If not, modify your code as necessary and save the files. As your Web site becomes more complicated throughout this course, you will be able to quickly locate code for modification within your files.

Skills review

In this lesson, you learned to use container and stand-alone HTML elements and their tags. You learned the basic structure elements that must be present in any HTML document. You learned how to format both text and paragraphs, and how to create a bulleted list and a numbered list. Finally, you were introduced to the concept of good coding practice, and the importance of correct application and sequence of your code.

Now that you have completed this lesson, you should be able to:

✓ 2.1.3: Use HTML elements and tags to format paragraphs and text.

✓ 2.1.7: Add comments to HTML code and document page/site creation.

✓ 2.1.8: Explain the importance of consistently developing to a single W3C standard (e.g., HTML5).

✓ 2.7.4: Validate Web page design according to technical and audience standards adopted by employers.

✓ 2.9.2: Create a Web page using the HTML5 standard.

✓ 2.12.1: Test and validate Web documents.

CIW Practice Exams

Visit CIW Online at *http://education.Certification-Partners.com/CIW* to take the Practice Exams assessment covering the objectives in this lesson.

SDA Objective 2.01 Review

SDA Objective 2.07 Review

SDA Objective 2.09 Review

SDA Objective 2.12 Review

Note that some objectives may be only partially covered in this lesson.

Lesson 2 Review

1. Markup tags include container, empty and stand-alone non-empty tags. Which tag types are valid in HTML?

   _____

   _____

2. Are HTML tags case-sensitive?

   _____

   _____

3. What three items can be contained inside the angle brackets (wickets) of an HTML tag?

   _____

   _____

4. What is the function of the <!DOCTYPE> declaration?

   _____

   _____

5. Define text-level element.

   _____

   _____

6. What notation can you use to write a note to yourself or others in the HTML code that will not appear in the page when rendered in a browser?

   _____

   _____

7. Should all values be placed in quotation marks for HTML?

   _____

   _____

Lesson 3: Cascading Style Sheets (CSS) and Graphical Elements

Objectives

By the end of this lesson, you will be able to:

- 2.2.1: Incorporate graphical images into HTML pages.

- 2.2.2: Distinguish among and identify the uses and benefits of various graphic file formats, including GIF, GIF89a, JPEG, PNG, TIFF, BMP.

- 2.2.3: Add tiled images and colors to Web page backgrounds.

- 2.2.6: Insert horizontal rules into Web pages.

- 2.3.1: Define the browser-safe color palette.

- 2.3.2: Identify ways that color affects the principles of line, value, shape and form in Web pages.

- 2.3.3: Identify and demonstrate the impact of color combinations to various audiences and cultures.

- 2.3.4: Evaluate Web page design and layout.

- 2.8.1: Explain how to structure Web documents with CSS.

- 2.8.2: Identify ways to apply styles with CSS.

- 2.21.1: Use CSS and HTML5 elements to create document structure.

- 2.21.2: Distinguish between fixed-width and liquid design layouts.

Pre-Assessment Questions

1. Name the three standard image file formats supported across the Web.

   _____

   _____

2. Define hexadecimal color values. Why would you use a hexadecimal value instead of the name of a color?

   _____

   _____

   _____

3. Which property determines the image that will be tiled behind the contents of a page?

   a. The background-image property of external CSS
   b. The background attribute of the <body> tag
   c. The background-image property of the <body> tag
   d. The img property of the <background> tag

Cascading Style Sheets (CSS)

You have already learned that a Cascading Style Sheets (CSS) document is an external text file that determines how to display the look and feel of HTML elements in your Web pages. It contains formatting instructions that can define the font, color and phrase elements used on a particular markup page.

If all pages on your site are linked to the same external style sheet, then one simple change to the style sheet will change all elements across the site. If you then want to change those instructions (for example, the style of <h1> headings), you need not change every page manually. You need only change a line in the style sheet file, then all your <h1> headings will change their appearance to conform to the style sheet. This technology can save a great deal of development and maintenance time, as well as make a more consistent, accessible interface.

CIW Online Resources – Movie Clips

Visit CIW Online at http://education.Certification-Partners.com/CIW to watch a movie clip about this topic.

Lesson 3: Cascading Style Sheets (CSS) and Graphical Elements

The problem with HTML and styles

CSS was created to solve a problem with HTML. The developers of HTML intended the standard to identify only the content and structure of a document, such as <title> and <body>, not the style, look and feel of the content.

When style elements for HTML4 were introduced without style sheets, the HTML standard grew complicated very quickly. Developers had to check each page of a Web site to ensure it had the correct style tags for each element. Imagine the time and difficultly involved with this task.

To save developers from insanity, the W3C quickly went into action and standardized CSS. It greatly simplifies the application of style to Web sites. Today a background image can be added to all Web pages with one change to an external CSS file.

Benefits of using CSS

CSS benefits include:

- **Consistency** — CSS easily gives an entire site a consistent look and feel.

- **Easy change management** — You have the ability to change the look and feel of an entire site by simply changing one part of a single line of code, rather than having to change possibly thousands of lines in hundreds of Web pages.

CSS versions

Currently, three standards exist for style sheets:

- **Cascading Style Sheets (CSS1)** — governs the basic structure of style sheets.

- **Cascading Style Sheets 2 (CSS2)** — adds more capabilities to the CSS1 specification, including the ability to support media types (such as specific printers) and work with tables.

- **Cascading Style Sheets 3 (CSS3)** — provides a modularized standard so that when changes need to be made to a specification, only a particular module within CSS3 will need to be updated, rather than the entire standard. This will allow for a more flexible and timely upgrade of the standard as a whole. New functions are being added to CSS3 to enhance its support of borders, backgrounds, colors, text effects and so forth.

OBJECTIVE
2.8.2: Applying CSS styles

HTML5 adopts CSS as the preferred way to format a page. The standard has evolved over the years and continues to build upon itself. For instance, HTML 4.01 and XHTML 1.0 used CSS1 and CSS2. HTML5 uses CSS1, CSS2 and CSS3. Any given Web page will include CSS rules from all three versions.

Because CSS3 contains the latest instructions, most non-HTML5-compliant browsers cannot interpret it. Most of the basic Web page formatting uses CSS1 and CSS2. When you validate your CSS pages throughout this introductory course, the CSS code will usually validate as CSS2.

Tech Tip *Proper use of style sheets is foundational for creating pages that rank highly in search engines.*

CSS terminology

Before you deploy CSS, you should learn its terminology. The most important terms to understand are selector, property, value, declaration and rule. The following code from a CSS file illustrates the anatomy of these style sheet elements as they are found in linked, or external, style sheets. Inline CSS styles are declared differently, as you learned in the previous lesson.

```
body {background-color:lightblue;}
```

The syntax terms of this CSS code are listed in Table 3-1.

Table 3-1: CSS syntax terms

CSS Syntax	Term
body	Selector
{	Opening curly brace
background-color:	Property
lightblue;	Value
}	Closing curly brace

selector
In a style sheet, any element to which designated styles are applied.

This CSS file entry creates a light blue background color for the Web site. To make such a change, you must identify the element you want to apply the style in. Any element you want to affect is called a **selector**.

After you have chosen a selector, you can customize it by selecting a property and setting a value. By selecting a property, you will change the way the selector renders in the browser. For example, you could alter the selector's color, size, background, font family, font size and so forth. These changes will apply to all subsequent instances of the element you define as a selector.

 In CSS, values do not require quotation marks. Also, CSS syntax should be written in lowercase.

A property must then have a value. For example, if you want to change a selector's size property, you must set a value to specify that size. Or you could decide to change the background color of your pages to teal, and so forth.

In the following example, you will see a CSS declaration, which consists of a property and a value. A declaration must always end with a semicolon.

```
background-color:teal;
```

rule
In a style sheet, a format instruction that consists of a specified selector and the properties and values applied to it.

The name for a selector, property and value all grouped together is a **rule**. The following rule will change the color of the body background to teal, then set the font color to white:

```
body {background-color:teal;color:white;}
```

CSS declarations and rules are reviewed in Table 3-2.

Table 3-2: CSS declarations and terms

CSS Syntax	Term
`background-color:teal;`	Declaration
`body {background-color:teal;color:white;}`	Rule

To define multiple declarations for one selector within a rule, as in the previous example, you must separate each declaration with a semicolon. You must also place a semicolon between the last value of the declaration and the end bracket.

Notice from these examples that the properties and the values must be placed within curly braces. This practice is standard for all style sheet rules, except when declaring inline styles. You will learn more about different ways to define styles shortly.

 CIW Online Resources – Online Exercise

Visit CIW Online at *http://education.Certification-Partners.com/CIW* to complete an interactive exercise that will reinforce what you have learned about this topic.

Exercise 3-1: Introduction to CSS

Proper CSS structure

Following is the accepted structure of rules within a style sheet:

```
body
{
font-family:arial, verdana, helvetica;
color:gray;
font-size:14px;
}

h1
{
font-family:arial, sans-serif;
color:black;
font-size:36px;
}
```

Notice that the opening and closing curly braces and each declaration are placed on separate lines. This spacing is considered good coding practice because it makes the CSS file easier to read.

If you want a particular rule in a style sheet to be ignored, you can "comment out" the entry by placing it in between the /* and */ characters. You can also add comments to explain the rules to others. In the following example, the words "STYLE SHEET FOR SYB.HTML" or "A comment is added here" will not be read:

```
/* STYLE SHEET FOR SYB.HTML */
/* A comment is added here */
```

Inheritance

The concept of inheritance is essential to CSS. In fact, the word "cascading" refers to inheritance. The style you define will flow, or cascade, throughout the documents, unless another style defined inside of a page specifically overrides it. Many styles can be used together to create a completely formatted document. For example, a style sheet rule will override the default <body> font color, which is black. All these characteristics, whether they are defined in a style sheet or exist by default, are inherited throughout the rest of the document.

As you learned in the previous lesson, styles specified using the inline CSS style attribute within an HTML page will override external CSS entries.

Adding CSS to HTML

Now that you understand basic CSS terminology and syntax, you will learn how to implement it in an HTML document. You can apply CSS styles to HTML documents in several ways. You can:

- Declare an inline CSS style attribute.

- Link to an external style sheet.

- Create an internal style sheet.

In the previous lesson, you worked with inline CSS style attributes. In this lesson, you will learn how to link to and modify an external style sheet.

This lesson will not cover importing style sheets. Certain older browsers may crash when rendering pages with an import statement. If you want to use an external style sheet, use a linked style sheet rather than an imported style sheet.

OBJECTIVE
2.8.2: Applying CSS styles

In the following lab, you will use an external style sheet. Suppose your project manager reviews some of your pages and requests that you eliminate the background color from all pages. You could perform this task quickly and simply by editing the style sheet.

Lab 3-1: Using an external style sheet with HTML

In this lab, you will attach an external style sheet to an HTML document, then edit the style sheet's background color declaration.

1. **Windows Explorer:** Navigate to the **Habitat\CCYP** folder on your Desktop and create a subfolder named **syb**. If you have not created a Habitat\CCYP\ directory, please do so now. The new folder (Habitat\CCYP\syb\) will contain the style sheet as well as all images and other files for the syb.html page.

2. **Windows Explorer:** Navigate to **C:\CIW\Site_Dev\Lab Files\Lesson03\Lab_3-1**. Copy the file **syb.css** to the Habitat\CCYP\syb\ folder on your system. If you just created the Habitat\CCYP\ directory, then copy the lab file **syb.html** to the Habitat\CCYP folder.

    Note: Remember that you are going to place all files associated with your syb.html document in a specific subfolder. In this case, files will be in the syb subfolder, including the CSS file.

3. **Editor:** Open the Habitat\CCYP**syb.html** file, and enter the code shown in **bold** to the <head> element. Also delete the inline CSS style attribute and value shown in ~~strikethrough~~ from the <body> element.

    ```
    <!DOCTYPE html>

    <html>

    <head>
    <meta name="keywords" content="CIW, HTML5, Habitat for Humanity"/>
    <meta name="description" content="Simple XHTML page for Habitat site"/>
    <meta charset="UTF-8"/>
    <title>Habitat for Humanity International Summer Youth Blitz Program</title>
    <link rel="stylesheet" type="text/css" href="syb/syb.css"/>
    </head>

    <body style="background-color:white">
    ```

    Note: Make sure you delete the inline CSS style attribute (style="background-color:white") within the <body> tag. Do not delete the actual <body> tag or the closing wicket. The attribute must be deleted because inline CSS overrides external CSS. Also, please note that only the beginning of the HTML document is shown in this lab step to save space.

4. **Editor:** Save your changes.

5. Open **syb.html** in your Web browser. You will not notice any changes because the style entries in the CSS file are currently commented out using the syntax /*   */.

6. Open the file **syb.css** in Notepad. Remove the comments from the line that begins with *body*. Make sure to remove both the beginning /* and ending */ characters of the comment. When you are finished, save your changes. Keep **syb.css** open.

7. Before you close syb.css, review the entry. Note especially the *background-color:tan* entry.

8. After you have removed the comment from the body entry and reviewed all entries, close **syb.css**, making sure that you have saved your changes.

serif
A font style that uses characters with small decorative additions at the outermost points of the characters, called strokes. Includes the Times and Times New Roman fonts.

9. Refresh your browser's display. Notice that the page's background color has changed to tan. Also, notice that the font type (i.e., the font face) has changed. Instead of the standard **serif** font most Web browsers use, you now see the **sans-serif** Arial font.

10. Open **syb.css** again and change the *body* entry so that it reads **background-color:white**, then save and close the file.

11. Refresh your browser's display. What color is the background?

sans-serif
A font style that does not use decorative strokes at the tips of characters. Includes the Arial font family.

12. Visit the W3C CSS Validation Service at **http://jigsaw.w3.org/css-validator** and validate your CSS file.

13. Close any **Notepad** windows.

In this lab, you used an external style sheet.

CIW Online Resources – Movie Clips

Visit CIW Online at http://education.Certification-Partners.com/CIW to watch a movie clip about this topic.

Lesson 3: Creating CSS

Separating Content in HTML

Several simple graphical elements can be added to a Web page to provide structure and visual interest. One such element is the horizontal rule, or <hr> element, which is simple to add. The <hr> element is used to define a thematic break in a Web page, such as a topic change, or to separate content. It creates a horizontal line that separates one part of the Web page from another.

To add a horizontal rule to your page, insert an <hr> tag at the position where you want the line to appear. In HTML, <hr> is an empty tag that should be written as <hr/>. This tag format is called a "stand-alone non-empty tag." This tag is written similarly to the break, or <br/> tag, that you learned about in the previous lesson.

OBJECTIVE
2.2.3: Background images and colors

2.2.6: Horizontal rules

Consider the following code:

```
<h1>Horizontal Rules</h1>
<hr/>
Horizontal rules: Lines used to make visual divisions in your document.
```

This code will render in a browser as shown in Figure 3-1.

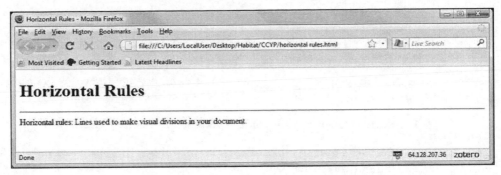

Figure 3-1: Page displaying horizontal rule

By default, these lines include a 3-D shading effect, which can be removed. In addition, the lines can be set to various sizes and widths. Because the line is added by a single tag, <hr>, how is this other information passed to the browser?

HTML5 does not support layout attributes for the <hr> tag. Any styles must be applied using CSS. Common styles added to the <hr> element are alignment, size and width.

Using CSS to stylize horizontal rules

In the previous lesson, you learned about the three components of a tag: an element, attributes and values. You also learned about the inline CSS *style* attribute's properties and values. The *style* attribute is a universal attribute that can be added to any HTML element.

Adding inline CSS style attributes to HTML elements is time-consuming. It is much more practical to style HTML elements using an external CSS file. You are learning inline CSS style attributes to introduce you to CSS. As you progress through the course, you will work with external CSS files more often.

The *style* attribute has a *width* property that can control how far the line extends across the screen. By default, the value of the *width* value is 100 percent. Thus the line in the preceding figure extends from the left margin across to the right margin in the browser window, or the entire width of the window. If you want the line to extend across only 50 percent of the window, you would write the tag as follows:

```
<hr style="width=50%;"/>
```

Note that the property name (in this case, *width*) precedes an equal sign (=). Following the equal sign is the desired value for this property, in this case "50%". The property and value must always be enclosed in quotation marks.

You can use the *height* attribute with the style attribute as well. For example, to create a line 10 pixels high spanning halfway across the page, you could use either of the following syntax options:

```
<hr style="width=50%; height=10px;"/>
<hr style="height=10px; width=50%;"/>
```

The order in which the properties appear is not dictated. However, you cannot reverse the properties and value; the property must always precede the equal sign, and the properties and values must always be enclosed in quotes and separated by semicolons.

In the following lab, you will add horizontal rules to a Web page. Suppose your project manager suggests that the syb.html page could use a visual separation or graphic of some sort between the page content and the contact information at the bottom. You can add a horizontal rule to serve this purpose.

Lab 3-2: Assigning inline CSS attribute values to the <hr> tag in HTML

In this lab, you will learn how to assign and change the values of inline CSS attributes in the <hr> tag.

1. **Editor:** Open the version of **syb.html** you edited in the previous lab.

2. **Editor:** Enter the following code, just above the "*For more information . . .* " line near the bottom of the page:

   `<hr/>`

3. **Editor:** Save your changes.

4. **Browser:** Load **syb.html**. You will see a horizontal line appear in the document.

5. Edit the <hr> tag you have inserted so that the line spans 80 percent of the Web page's width and is 5 pixels in height. The line is centered by default. Enter:

   `<hr style="width:80%; height:5px;"/>`

   When you are finished, a horizontal line will appear, as shown in Figure 3-2.

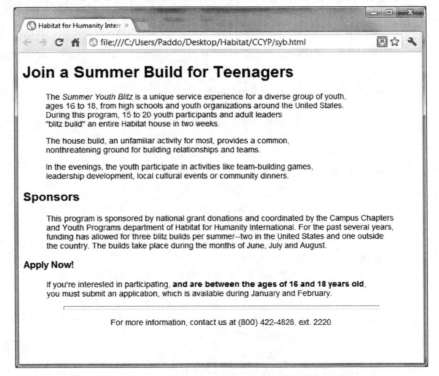

Figure 3-2: Customizing <hr/> element with inline CSS style attributes

6. Visit the W3C Markup Validation Service at ***http://validator.w3.org*** and validate your code.

In this lab, you inserted and customized a horizontal line in your HTML page.

Many Web authors choose to insert images and bars instead of using HTML horizontal lines. You may have a reason to choose the <hr> element in the future because it may designate some contextual meaning or introduce a thematic change in your Web page.

OBJECTIVE
2.2.1: Images

2.2.3: Background
images and colors

Images in Web Pages

You may have heard the saying that a picture is worth a thousand words. Most Web pages incorporate graphical images in their designs. Images add interest to a page, but they provide more than just aesthetics. Images are memorable and can be used to create a mood, emphasize a point or sell a product.

Images can be big or small; they can function as links; they can be used to launch script actions; and they can be used as image maps. Although scripting is not discussed in detail in this course, you will be introduced to clickable image maps in a later lesson. In this lesson, you will focus on using images purely as graphical enhancements.

When chosen carefully, images can greatly enhance your pages. However, too many images can slow page loading, waste costly online time, and even displease users by making the page look too cluttered. Be creative but sparing in your use of images.

The <img> tag displays a graphical image on your page. The key attributes that are required in this tag are *src* (abbreviation for source) and *alt* (alternative text for the image if it cannot be seen). You use the *src* attribute to specify the name and, if necessary, the location of your image file.

The <img> tag is an empty tag but should be treated as a stand-alone non-empty tag:

```
<img src="imagefile.png" alt="Alternative text goes here"/>
```

For the <img> tag to validate as HTML, it must include the *src* and *alt* attributes. You will learn more about the *alt* attribute shortly.

If you upload your Web pages to a Web server and the images do not appear, check the <img src=" "> value of each image. If you created all of your images in a separate directory, make sure you uploaded that directory as well.

CIW Online Resources – Movie Clips

Visit CIW Online at http://education.Certification-Partners.com/CIW to watch a movie clip about this topic.

Lesson 3: Inserting a Graphic into an HTML5 Page

Image file formats

OBJECTIVE
2.2.2: Graphic file
formats

The three universally supported Web image formats are:

- Graphics Interchange Format (GIF).

- Joint Photographic Experts Group (JPEG).

- Portable Network Graphics (PNG).

Windows Internet Explorer and Mozilla Firefox also support the display of Windows Bitmap (BMP) images when used in HTML documents.

JPEG

The Joint Photographic Experts Group (JPEG) format supports literally millions of colors, and is typically used for photographs and complex images. If you want the highest image quality, generally you would use a JPEG file.

This format also supports compression, meaning that you can reduce the image's file size. However, the more an image is compressed, the more its quality is reduced. For this reason, standard JPEG image compression is called "lossy" compression. JPEG compression is copyrighted in many countries. As a result, applications that use JPEG and other copyrighted materials may cost more or have limitations placed on them.

To learn more about the JPEG format, visit The JPEG Committee home page (*www.jpeg.org*) and the Independent JPEG Group home page (*www.ijg.org*).

GIF

Graphics Interchange Format (GIF) files support 256 colors, rather than the millions of colors available to JPEG images. GIFs are best suited for line art, custom drawings and navigational images. GIF has two versions:

- GIF 87a

- GIF 89a

GIF 89a is more popular because it supports the following techniques:

- **Transparency** — the ability to make any part of the image invisible so the page background shows through. The image thus appears to blend into the background.

- **Interlacing** — the ability for an image to render gradually as it downloads.

- **Animation** — a series of images appearing in sequence to create the effect of motion.

GIF and its compression format are also copyrighted in many countries, making it somewhat controversial. You will learn more about animation, transparency and interlacing later in the course.

PNG

Portable Network Graphics (PNG) has emerged as a standard format for images on the Web and is widely implemented. The PNG format was developed using open standards, which means that it does not have the same legal liabilities as other formats (e.g., GIF). However, older browsers do not render the PNG format. PNG images provide the following features:

- **Transparency** — similar to GIF 89a.

- **Interlacing** — similar to GIF 89a.

- **Compression** — lossless, unlike standard JPEG compression. Also, the compression used in the PNG format is not copyrighted, which has helped ensure developer and user agent vendor support.

- **Animation** — less popular than animated GIF, but gaining attention.

You can learn more about the PNG format at LibPNG.org (*www.libpng.org*), the free reference library for PNG images. Table 3-3 provides a summary of the features provided by the three common image formats.

Table 3-3: Features common to major image file formats

Format	Transparency	Interlacing	Compression	Animation
GIF 89a	Yes	Yes	Yes	Yes
JPEG (standard)	No	No	Yes	No
PNG	Yes	Yes	Yes	Yes

 If you spend time browsing images on the Internet, you may be tempted to use graphics created by others in your Web pages. Be aware that any content — text, sound files or images — is the sole property of the original owner. You may be subject to penalties under copyright laws if you use someone else's creation without express, written permission.

Using the *alt* attribute with images

Every image used in HTML5 is required to contain the *alt* attribute with a corresponding value. The *alt* attribute specifies alternative text to appear while the graphic is loading, or in place of the graphic in non-graphical browsers such as Lynx. This alternative text will also display if the image fails to load or if the user has configured his or her browser not to display images.

The syntax for using the *alt* attribute is as follows:

```
<img src="image.png" alt="This text should describe the image."/>
```

The tag is closed using the HTML non-empty tag format. Any other use of the <img> tag will not validate as HTML.

 Tech Tip *Search engines will rank a page higher in a search engine results page if it consistently uses the alt attribute effectively. Remember to include a short but useful description of every image.*

Combining background images and background colors

You can specify both an image and a color for the background in a Web page. In fact, it can be advantageous to specify both, in case a background image becomes unavailable for some reason.

If you use a style sheet and specify both image and color as a background, then the background image will always render first. If the image cannot be found, a background color will then appear. All values specified in style sheets will override anything specified in the HTML itself.

In the following lab, you will incorporate images in a Web page. Suppose the marketing team and another member of your Web development team have collaborated to create an image for your Web site. You have been asked to insert the image into a page you have developed, and you have been given the same image in the three standard file formats. You must choose an image format and insert it in the appropriate location on the page.

Lab 3-3: Incorporating images in an HTML page

In this lab, you will learn how to place and align an image relative to text in a Web page.

1. Navigate to the **C:\CIW\Site_Dev\Lab Files\Lesson03\Lab_3-3** directory, and copy the following files to the **Habitat\CCYP\Syb** directory:

    SYBcollage2.gif
    SYBcollage2.jpg
    SYBcollage2.png

2. Open the **Habitat\CCYP\Syb** directory, and view each image by double-clicking on it. See if you notice any difference among the three image formats.

3. Right-click each image and select **Properties**. What is the file size of each image type (GIF, JPEG and PNG)?

4. As a class, discuss the following points about these image formats:

    *   The larger the image file size, the longer it takes users to download.

    *   Older browsers may not be able to render PNG images.

    *   GIF and PNG images can be interlaced, animated or made transparent. Standard JPEG images do not support these features.

    *   JPEG images offer the highest image quality.

    *   PNG and standard JPEG images can be compressed; however, the higher the compression, the lower the image quality.

5. Now you will insert an image into your Web page. Open **syb.html** in a text editor.

6. Insert the SYBcollage2.png image by entering the code indicated in bold:

    ```
    <blockquote>
    <img src="syb/SYBcollage2.png" alt="Join a summer build!"/>
    </blockquote>
    <h1>Join a Summer Build for Teenagers</h1>
    ```

    Note: The code you typed inserted a file from the Syb\ subfolder. You will learn more about how to specify files in other directories later in this lesson.

7. Load your edited page into a browser. You should see the image shown in Figure 3-3.

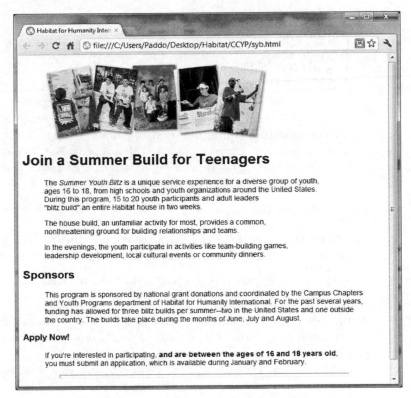

Figure 3-3: File syb.html after adding image

8. Validate your code.

9. Delete the code **alt="Join a summer build!"**. Now revalidate your code. What were the results, and why? How does validated HTML help users with disabilities?

_____

_____

_____

10. Reinsert the code **alt="Join a summer build!"** where it was.

11. Comment out the **<blockquote>** tags that encompass the <img> element and its values using the **<!-- ... -->** comment tags. This will stop the .PNG image file from loading. **Save** your file.

12. Next, you will center the image using CSS. This task requires you to create a class in the CSS file and reference it within the HTML document. The class is simply a set of instructions. Once the class is set up, it will be easy to center your images.

   Note: The image element attributes used to align images are no longer supported in HTML5. CSS classes must be created in order to comply with HTML5.

13. **Editor:** Open the **syb.css** file. To create a class, add the following CSS rule to the bottom of the css file:

```
    img.center
{
display: block;
margin-left: auto;
margin-right: auto;
}
```

You created instructions for a "center" class for the "img" element (img.center) that will be referenced within the HTML document. The image will display as a block element so that it does not merge with any text. The "auto" margin to the left and right creates an equal area on both sides of the image. This technique centers the image, regardless of the size of the browser window.

14. Save the **syb.css** file.

15. **Editor:** Open the **syb.html** file. Create a new line that inserts and centers the JPEG image using the *center* class you created for the <img> element:

```
<img src="syb/SYBcollage2.jpg" alt="Join a summer build!" class="center"/>
```

16. Save the **syb.html** file and open it in a browser. It should resemble Figure 3-4. Resize the browser window. Notice that the image repositions itself to the center of the page regardless of the browser window's size.

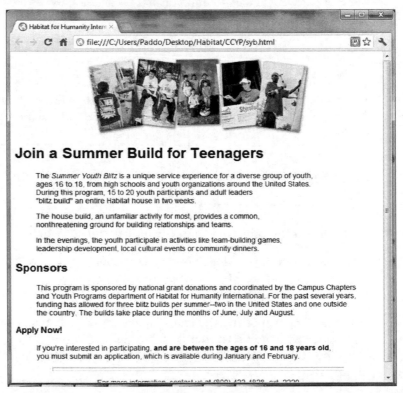

Figure 3-4: Centering image by creating CSS center class

17. When you are finished, comment out the <img> tag you just created for the .JPG image:

```
<!--
<img src="syb/SYBcollage2.jpg" alt="Join a summer build!" class="center"/>
-->
```

18. Remove the comment notations from the <blockquote> tags around the <img> tag for the .PNG image. Your code should now render the .PNG image.

In this lab, you added image files to a Web page. You used the required *alt* attribute, and you experimented with image placement using the <blockquote> element and the CSS *center* class.

OBJECTIVE
2.2.1: Images

2.2.3: Background images and colors

Aligning images relative to text

After you start working with images, you will see that placing an image on your page is only the first step. You must know how to position images relative to text on a page.

External CSS

External CSS classes are useful for floating images to the left or right of text in HTML5. The syntax for the *CSS class* entries are as follows:

```
img.floatleft
{
float: left;
margin: 5px;
}
```

In this example, the image class is defined as *floatleft*. The float property specifies that the image will float to the left of the text. The margin property specifies that the image will include a five pixel margin around it. This will provide a small cushion between the image and the text.

The HTML document needs the following code to access the CSS class:

```
<img src="syb/SYBcollage2.png" class="floatleft" />
```

You can use any name you would like for class: *floatleft* is a good descriptor. If the class was created to float text to the right, it could be named "floatright" with a float value of "right."

Inline CSS style attribute

INSTRUCTOR NOTE:
Aligning images relative to text using CSS can be tedious and can sometimes produce unsatisfactory results. Many developers use HTML tables instead because the image can be placed in one cell and the text in another. Students will learn about HTML tables later in this course.

Although it is not the best method to use if you are developing sites with multiple pages, the inline CSS style attribute can also be used for floating images to the left and right of text:

```
<img src="syb/SYBcollage2.png" style="float:left; margin: 5px;" />
```

Table 3-4 lists the values that you can use to align images to text.

Table 3-4 Using CSS to align images to text

Alignment Option	Description	Code

bottom	The default alignment. The bottom of the image is aligned with the baseline of adjoining text.	The CSS class can be written as:
		
		CSS file:
		`img.bottom {vertical-align:baseline;}`
		
		HTML file:
		`<img src="syb/SYBcollage2.png" class="bottom" />`

middle	A vertical — not horizontal — alignment option. This value aligns the middle of the image to the baseline of adjoining text.	The CSS class can be written as:
		
		CSS file:
		`img.middle {vertical-align:middle; margin:5px;}`
		
		HTML file:
		`<img src="syb/SYBcollage2.png" class="middle" />`

top	Aligns the top of the image with the top of adjoining text.	The CSS class can be written as:
		
		CSS file:
		`img.top {vertical-align:top;}`
		
		HTML file:
		`<img src="syb/SYBcollage2.png" class="top" />`

left	Floats the image to the left of the text paragraph into which the `<img>` tag is inserted. The top of the image will align with the left and top of the adjoining text.	The CSS class can be written as:
		
		CSS file:
		`img.floatleft {float:left; margin:5px;}`
		
		HTML file:
		`<img src="syb/SYBcollage2.png" class="floatleft" />`

right	Floats the image to the right of the text paragraph into which the `<img>` tag is inserted. The top of the image will align with the right and top of the adjoining text.	The CSS class can be written as:
		
		CSS file:
		`img.floatright {float:right; margin:5px;}`
		
		HTML file:
		`<img src="syb/SYBcollage2.png" class="floatright" />`

The <img> element includes two traditional attributes that are helpful:

- *height* — resizes the image's original height dimension in pixels
- *width* — resizes the image's original width dimension in pixels

INSTRUCTOR NOTE:
Point out that when the "left" or "right" value is specified, the image is aligned vertically to the top by default.

In the following lab, you will use CSS with the <img> tag to align images relative to text on your Web page. Suppose your project manager has notified you that several images will be incorporated into a Web page you are developing. You will need to experiment with aligning the images and text. Proper alignment of page components in relation to each other are an important part of Web design that can greatly improve — or degrade — a page's appearance and effectiveness.

 Lab 3-4: Aligning images relative to text with HTML

In this lab, you will practice CSS techniques to align your images relative to nearby text.

1. **Editor:** Open **syb.css** and add the following rule. This rule will float an image to the right of the text:

```
img.floatright
{
float:right;
margin:5px;
}
```

2. Save the file.

3. **Editor:** Open **syb.html**.

4. Find the <img> tag and edit it as follows so that it aligns to the right of the text:

```
<blockquote>
<img src="syb/SYBcollage2.png" alt="Join a summer build!" class="floatright"/>
</blockquote>
```

5. View your page in a browser. It should resemble Figure 3-5.

Figure 3-5: Floating image to right of text

6. Change your code so that the image aligns to the left and the text wraps to its right. Then change it so the text wraps to the top of the image, then again so text wraps to the middle of the image. Be sure to view the page each time in your browser, and note the differences.

7. Now, modify the *margin* value to "40" in the CSS file:

```
img.floatright
{
float:right;
margin:40px;
}
```

8. Save the CSS file and refresh your browser. Notice that the margin around the image increases. Experiment with a larger value, such as **"60"**, **"100"** or **"200"**.

   Note: These values may seem large, and will probably make the image seem out of place. Simply experiment with these values. Remember that a pixel is a very small unit of measurement. The number of pixels per inch is determined by the monitor's screen resolution.

9. When you are finished experimenting, change the *margin* value back to **"5"**.

10. **Editor:** Finish this lab by positioning the image to the right of the text (as you did at the beginning of the lab).

11. Validate your HTML and CSS files using the W3C validation services.

In this lab, you learned to position images in relation to text with HTML and CSS.

Resizing images

At times, you will want to use an image in a size other than its natural size. If you need to resize an image, you must maintain its relative measurements. For example, if you have an image that is 200 pixels wide by 300 pixels tall, you probably would not want to change the size to be 100 pixels wide by 300 pixels tall because this would distort the image, making it appear taller and narrower than it was originally. If you were trying to shrink this image to one-half its size, you would instead change the width to 100 and the height to 150. By shrinking both dimensions by an equal percentage (in this case, by 50 percent), you maintain the original ratio of the image.

The syntax for specifying image height and width information is as follows:

```
<img src="imagename.gif" height="HeightInPixels" width="WidthInPixels"/>
```

If you are not certain of the original dimensions of your image, you can ensure that the size will be changed proportionately by specifying either the height or the width; the other measurement will then be calculated proportionately for you based on the original image size.

CIW Online Resources – Course Mastery

Visit CIW Online at *http://education.Certification-Partners.com/CIW* to take the Course Mastery review of this lesson or lesson segment.

SDA Lesson 3 - Part A

HTML Entities

Occasionally, you will need to include a non-keyboard character in your Web page. These special characters are called HTML entities. For example, mathematics professors who use HTML pages to show math problems may want to use the "less than" (<) and "greater than" signs (>). And most companies use the © and ® symbols to indicate their copyrights and trademarks on their Web sites.

You can include non-keyboard characters in Web pages by using either the ANSI character value or the special HTML code for the character. These special character values can be read by HTML interpreters, which cannot otherwise recognize non-keyboard characters. The HTML code combination, called the escape sequence, consists of the ampersand (&), followed by a code for the specific character you want to generate on the page, followed by a semicolon (;). For example, to generate the "less than" symbol on a Web page, you would use the following special character code as text on your HTML page:

```
&lt;
```

Using the escape sequence is also called "escaping" because it does not allow the browser's HTML interpreter to read the characters as literal text or HTML commands. In the Resources directory of the supplemental files for this course, the file named charcodes.html provides a list of codes for special characters. Table 3-5 defines some of the most commonly used special characters. As you can see, each special character code begins with the ampersand and ends with the semicolon character.

Table 3-5: HTML entity codes

Character	Description	Code
©	Copyright symbol	© or ©
®	Registered trademark symbol	® or ®
é	Acute accent (over letter e)	é To create an acute accent over another character, such as o, enter: ó
<	Less-than symbol	&lt;
>	Greater-than symbol	&gt;
&	Ampersand ("and")	& or &
£	Pound sterling sign	&#163;
ü	Umlaut (over letter u)	ü To create an umlaut over another character, such as i, enter: ï
ñ	Tilde (over letter n)	ñ To create a tilde over another character, such as o, enter: õ
"	Quotation marks	&quot;
@	At symbol	&#64;
Non-breaking space	Inserts an extra space. Often used to create indentations in a paragraph, or create additional spaces between words.	

For a list of additional HTML entities, visit *www.w3schools.com/tags/ref_entities.asp* or *www.w3.org/MarkUp/html-spec/html-spec_13.html*.

Non-breaking spaces

You will often see * * in HTML code, especially in code created by GUI-based Web authoring applications. The HTML special character code for a non-breaking space can be used to insert more than one space in succession when needed. You will find this character to be useful because more than one successive space is ignored in HTML. However, a non-breaking space is never ignored. Use non-breaking spaces sparingly. The following code ensures an indentation before the line "This begins an indented paragraph":

```
<p>
      This begins an indented paragraph.
</p>
```

In the following lab, you will create a symbol on a Web page using an HTML entity. Suppose your project manager mentions that the Web page you will post to the public contains original text and images that could be subject to copyright infringement. You can use special character code to add a copyright statement to your page.

 Lab 3-5: Adding a copyright statement with an HTML entity

In this lab, you will add a copyright statement to your page using the HTML entity code to create the copyright symbol.

1. **Editor:** Open **syb.html**.

2. Insert the following statement at the bottom of the page, just above the </body> tag:

```
<p style="text-align:center">&copy; 2012 Habitat for Humanity
International</p>
```

3. Save your changes, then view your page in a browser. You will see the copyright symbol at the bottom of the page, as shown in Figure 3-6.

Figure 3-6: Adding copyright symbol to Web page

4. Validate your code, and test it in multiple browsers.

In this lab, you added a copyright statement using HTML special character code.

OBJECTIVE
2.2.3: Background
images and colors

hexadecimal
A base-16 number system that allows large numbers to be displayed by fewer characters than if the number were displayed in the regular base-10 system. In hexadecimal, the number 10 is represented as the letter A, 15 is represented as F, and 16 is represented as 10.

Specifying Colors

You have learned that you can specify colors for the page background in HTML and CSS documents. In the previous examples, you used words for values, such as "teal" and "tan". Alternatively, you can also use a **hexadecimal** code to specify color values.

Colors are often specified in terms of their RGB values. RGB stands for Red Green Blue. You may know that if you were mixing paint, the mixture of red, green and blue together creates a rather muddy color. But on a monitor screen, you are mixing light, and the mixture of red, green and blue light produces white, which is the presence of all colors. Black is the absence of all colors. In RGB code, the higher the numeric value representing a color, the lighter that color will be. The lower the value, the darker the color. Figure 3-7 demonstrates the composition of a hexadecimal color code.

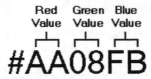

Figure 3-7: Red hex value + green hex value + blue hex value = hexadecimal color code

Colors are specified in RGB values ranging from 0 to 255. The hexadecimal value FF represents 255. Therefore, the hexadecimal value #FFFFFF represents the highest possible value for all three RGB colors, producing white. The hexadecimal value #000000 represents the absence of all colors, or black. The number symbol (#) is not required by current generation browsers, but you should include this symbol for full backward-compatibility. The Resources directory from the supplemental files for this course contains a file named 216color.html that provides the RGB and hexadecimal codes for browser-safe colors, which will be discussed further in the next section. You can also visit the Browser-Safe Web Palette page at *www.lynda.com/resources/webpalette.aspx* (provided by Lynda Weinman) or the Visibone Webmaster's Color Laboratory at *www.visibone.com/colorlab* (provided by Bob Stein).

Browser-safe color palette

OBJECTIVE
2.3.1: Browser-safe
color palette

dithering
The ability for a computer to approximate a color by combining the RGB values.

inline images
Images rendered in a Web page.

When you use a color in a Web page (whether for a background, font or image), you are enabling a combination of RGB values. This limited color palette is necessary because many computer screens have limitations.

You will want your pages to render consistently no matter which browser or operating system is used to view them. In other words, if you define a blue background color, you will want it to appear the same in a Macintosh system using a version of Safari or Firefox as it would in a Windows system using a version of Internet Explorer. You also want your image colors to appear consistently. If your HTML code asks for a color that the browser or operating system cannot support, the computer will compensate through **dithering**. The results of dithering are unpredictable and often unattractive.

When Netscape Corporation marketed the first browser that supported **inline images**, it created a standard of 216 colors that would render consistently, known as the browser-safe color palette. Chrome, Firefox, Internet Explorer and other browsers conform to this list of colors.

Sometimes the browser-safe color palette is called the Web-safe color palette.

As mentioned, the file in your Resources directory named 216color.html contains a list of the 216 colors in the browser-safe palette. To further ensure cross-browser capability, you can specify colors in hexadecimal format, rather than by name.

CIW Online Resources – Online Exercise

Visit CIW Online at *http://education.Certification-Partners.com/CIW* to complete an interactive exercise that will reinforce what you have learned about this topic.

Exercise 3-2: Specifying colors

Page Colors and Backgrounds

OBJECTIVE
2.2.3: Background images and colors

2.3.2: Color vs. line, value, shape and form

You can add color information to the <body> tag in an HTML page to control the colors of the page background, as well as the colors of the text and links on the page. In addition, you can tile an image across the page for a background.

Background color

To specify a color for a page background, you add the *background-color* property to the *body* selector in an external CSS file using the following syntax:

```
body
{
font-family:arial, verdana, helvetica;
color:black;
font-size:14px;
background-color:white;
}
```

If you change the *background-color* value to the hexadecimal value #AA08FB, the background color of the page will become bright purple.

Background image

To specify an image for a page background, add the *background-image* property to the body selector. You must specify the location of the image using the following syntax:

```
body
{
background-image:url('paper.gif');
}
```

Text color

To designate the color of text on a page, use the *color* property in the body selector of the CSS file. View the preceding background color example for the syntax. Various color values, such as hexadecimal values, can be used instead of words.

Hyperlink color

Later in this lesson, you will learn how to create hyperlinks. If you are using hyperlinks, you can control the colors of links depending on whether the link has been visited or not. Hyperlinks use the anchor, or <a> element, in HTML files. CSS allows different link states to be defined in the anchor selector. Table 3-6 describes two of the link states.

Table 3-6: Color attributes available for various hyperlink states of anchor selector

Anchor Link State	Sample Declaration	Description
a:link	{color:#0000FF;} {color:blue;}	Determines the color of unvisited links
a:visited	"{color:#FF0000;} {color:red;}	Determines the color of visited links

In the following lab, you will change Web page colors and backgrounds. Suppose your project manager has asked you to experiment with color combinations for your Web site's pages, text and links. She has also given you an image to use as a page background. Which background will work better for the Web page? And should you specify colors using color names or hexadecimal codes?

 ### Lab 3-6: Changing page colors and backgrounds with HTML

In this lab, you will use hexadecimal code to specify Web page colors. You will also use an image for a page background.

1. **Editor:** Open **syb.css**.

2. **Editor:** Change the following value to the *background-color* property of the body selector:

   `background-color:#CCCCCC;`

3. View the page in a browser. You will see that the background is gray.

4. Edit the CSS body selector to add the text *color* property as shown:

   `color:#0099FF;`

5. Load your page into the browser again. Notice that the text color has changed.

   Note: Remember that it is always considered best practice to use style sheets instead of inline CSS style attributes whenever possible

6. Return the *background-color* and *color* properties in the body selector back to their original values:

   ```
   body
   {
   font-family:arial, verdana, helvetica;
   color:black;
   font-size:14px;
   background-color:white;
   }
   ```

7. Save the **syb.css** file.

8. Go to the **C:\CIW\Site_Dev\Lab Files\Lesson03\Lab_3-6** directory, and copy the file **background.jpg** to the **syb** subfolder you have been using.

9. Now add this image as a background image by adding the *background-image* property to the CSS body selector as follows:

```
body
{
font-family:arial, verdana, helvetica;
color:black;
font-size:14px;
background-color:white;
background-image:url('background.jpg');
}
```

10. Refresh your browser. Your page will now have a purple background, due to the JPEG image you just inserted. The image is tiled by default.

   Note: The background image overrides the background color. Also, the URL reference for the background.jpg image does not require a directory path to the syb folder because the .css file and the background.jpg image are located in the same folder.

11. Remove the purple background image (background.jpg) declaration from the style sheet so that your document's background is white again.

12. When your page renders as expected, save and validate the HTML and CSS files using the W3C validation services.

In this lab, you used hexadecimal color values and inserted a background image using HTML.

Specifying Font Information

CSS allows you to change the size, color and typeface of the text. CSS supports many font-related selectors and properties, including:

- *font-family* — specifies the typeface (i.e., font name) to be used. A *font-family* value must include quotation marks if it has multiple words, such as "Times New Roman." You should also list backup fonts in the *font-family* value, such as Times New Roman, Arial, and Verdana. If the first font is not supported, the next value will attempt to render.

- *font-size* — takes values in pixels, with 16 being the normal size of default text. The *font-size* value is specified with the "px" abbreviation for "pixels." No spaces can exist between the number value and the abbreviation. For example, *font-size=16 px* would not render properly, but *font-size=16px* (with no space) would work correctly. Headings (h1 through h6) should be used whenever possible instead of the *font-size* property.

- *color* — uses the same values that you learned for specifying a page background color.

 If you specify a font that is not available on all systems, some users will not see the font face you chose. Instead, the font will display as a default font face. Be aware of this when planning your page and include backup font-family values.

In the following lab, you will format text on a Web page. Suppose your Web team agrees that you should experiment with one of the site pages to see if a different font style would work well. You can use CSS to try some different font formatting styles.

Lab 3-7: Formatting text with CSS

In this lab, you will learn how to change the font style of text using CSS.

1. **Editor:** Open **syb.css**.

2. Delete the comments from the **h1** heading selector, as shown:

    ```
    /*
    h1
    {
    font-family:arial, sans-serif;
    color:black;
    font-size:32px;
    }
    */
    ```

3. **Browser:** Open the **syb.html** file. Did the h1 style change? It may be difficult to notice.

4. **Editor:** Open the **syb.css** file and add "courier new" with quotation marks as the first font-family value:

    ```
    h1
    {
    font-family:"courier new", arial, sans-serif;
    color:black;
    font-size:32px;
    }
    ```

5. **Browser:** View the **syb.html** file. The h1 font-family change is noticeable with the courier new font.

6. **Editor:** Delete the comments from the h2 heading selector. Change the font-size value to **20** pixels. Add **"courier new"** with quotation marks as the first font-family value, as shown:

    ```
    /*
    h2
    {
    font-family:"courier new", arial, sans-serif;
    color:black;
    font-size:20px;
    }
    */
    ```

7. **Editor:** Delete the comments from the h3 heading selector. Change the color value to **blue**. Add **"courier new"** with quotation marks as the first font-family value, as shown:

    ```
    /*
    h3
    {
    font-family:"courier new", arial, sans-serif;
    color: blue;
    font-size:16px;
    }
    */
    ```

8. When you are finished, your page should resemble Figure 3-8.

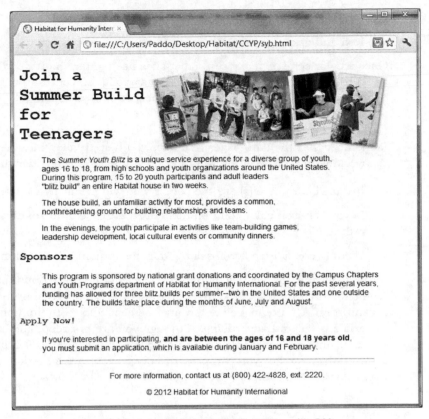

Figure 3-8: Modifying heading styles with CSS

9. When your page renders as expected, validate your code at ***http://validator.w3.org***.

In this lab, you used CSS to format Web page text.

With practice, you can embellish your HTML pages quickly and easily by using CSS to add graphical elements and styles.

Web Design Issues

Thus far, you have created a Web page that validates to HTML5. You have also learned many page elements. Before continuing, it is important to consider some Web design issues, including color combinations and ways to structure documents.

OBJECTIVE
2.2.3: Background
images and colors

2.3.3: Impact of
color choices

Color combinations

Color combinations are important to a Web site's look and feel because they can impose tone and mood. Color choices can convey the personality of a site, and thus its sponsoring organization, as serious, playful, trendy, conservative, creative, studious or authoritative, for example. Certain color combinations can also make a site easier — or more difficult — to read and view. Following are some examples of popular color combinations for Web sites:

- Gray, green and white (e.g., *www.w3schools.com*)

- Blue and white (e.g., current live Habitat for Humanity site, *www.habitat.org*)

- Red and white (e.g., *www.linux.org*)

- Red, white and gray (e.g., *www.cnn.com*)

- Red and gray (e.g., *http://espn.go.com*)

Once a color scheme is chosen, most sites use lighter shades of chosen colors for background. A lighter background acts as a foil (i.e., contrast) to the foreground text and images, making the site appear more polished and professional.

Culture and audience issues

Remember that the Web pages and sites you help develop may be available to anyone in the world with a browser and an Internet connection. Consider the following issues:

- From what culture(s) are the people who will primarily view this site?

- Is your chosen color combination effective in the cultures this site targets or in most cultures?

- What is considered "professional" for the audience that will most likely view this site?

In the following lab, you will consider some color combinations that could be used for a Web site. Suppose the marketing department is in charge of branding for your organization. That team will determine the best color combinations for all company materials, sites and advertising. Although you are not responsible for choosing the color scheme, your project manager has asked you to research and compare some color combinations so that you can present information to the marketing team about the way that colors in the company Web pages will render in browsers.

 Lab 3-8: Comparing Web site color combinations

In this lab, you will compare color schemes used in organization and corporate Web sites.

1. Open your browser and visit **www.w3schools.com**.

2. What color scheme is used for this Web site? Is it easy to read, distracting or unnoticeable? What type of mood or personality does this site's color scheme convey? And what does the look and feel of the home page make you think about its sponsoring organization?

3. Visit the following sites and consider the same questions for each:

   www.habitat.org
   www.microsoft.com
   www.CIWcertified.com

In this lab, you compared common color combinations used in Web sites, and you considered their effects on users.

OBJECTIVE
2.3.4: Page design and layout

Page layout

Web page layout is the placement of all page elements — including text, images, headings, navigation menus and so forth — relative to each other. A good page layout makes the page aesthetically pleasing, and easy to scan, read and navigate. Following are some layout guidelines to consider when designing your Web pages:

- **Be succinct** — Limit words to clear, necessary verbiage, especially on the home page. Most users simply scan pages quickly looking for specific information or links to it. Let users navigate to additional pages if they want more information.

- **Make sure that each page focuses on one topic** — No tangent message, regardless of its importance, should be added to a page. Use links to point users to appropriate related topics on separate pages.

- **Divide the page into three sections** — Use the left side of the page for navigation, the upper section of the page for a topic title (as well as navigation), and the middle section of the page for the information.

- **Include navigation aids** — A common way to enable navigation is to place links at the top and bottom of the page, and within the body of the page, to reduce the need for users to scroll.

- **Place comments in each section of code** — Comments help explain changes you have made to the code or page. You can indicate the nature of the change, including the date you made the change and your name or initials, or you can explain the nature of the markup. For example, the syb.html page has three headings (h1, h2 and h3). You could comment each of these sections of the narrative.

Tech Tip   *Effective page layout is essential for effective search engine optimization.*

OBJECTIVE
2.8.1: Structuring documents with CSS

2.21.1: Document structure with HTML5 and CSS

Document structure and style sheets

When Web pages were first being developed, early designers would use the <table> tag to format pages. Tables were necessary to divide the pages into sections because the Cascading Style Sheets (CSS) standard had not yet been developed. By using tables, designers could ensure that all page elements aligned and rendered consistently.

Today, the use of the <table> tag to format pages is considered improper practice by the W3C. Pages formatted with the <table> tag will not pass W3C validation tests, no matter what standard you use.

Following the use of tables, developers began to add structure to an entire page by using the <div> tag. It provided a way of dividing a page using an *id* attribute. Once a name was specified for a document section using the *id* attribute, developers could define this section's place in the document (as well as its contents) in a linked style sheet. That strategy gave developers granular control over the document, and ensured that the style sheet — rather than the HTML tags — governed the document's structure.

HTML5 with CSS has introduced a more effective and simple way to structure Web pages. Instead of using the <div> tag as a "jack of all trades" element with its array of attributes, the developers of HTML5 created specific elements to define the document structure. These elements include <header>, <footer>, <nav>, <article>, and <aside>. A basic Web page structure is shown in Figure 3-9.

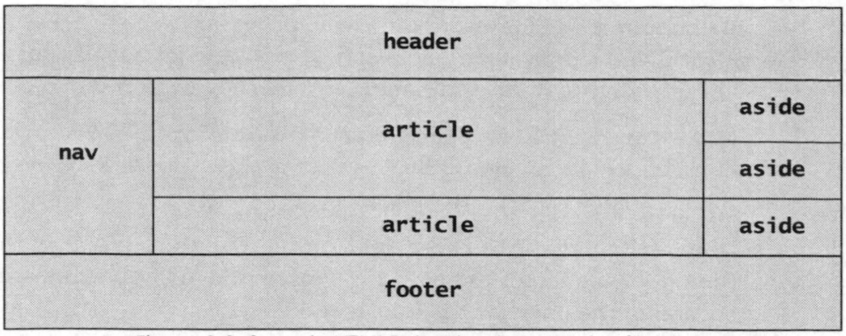

| header |
nav	article	aside
		aside
	article	aside
footer

Figure 3-9: Sample HTML5 structural elements of Web page

As shown in the figure, a developer can structure the Web page with elements that are easily interpreted and native to any HTML5-compliant browser, regardless of whether the browser is on a mobile device, laptop or tablet. The structure elements can be defined as:

- **<header>** — Top of the Web page, similar to the header in a word-processing document.

- **<nav>** — Defines navigation links, such as hypertext menus to access various pages of the Web site.

- **<article>** — Web site content, such as company services, articles, blogs, images and videos.

- **<aside>** — Content that is "aside" from the article content, such as advertisements or news feeds.

- **<footer>** — Bottom of the Web page, similar to the footer in a word-processing document.

The header might contain the company logo; the footer could include copyright and contact info; the nav section may contain navigational links to other resources on the site; the articles could be blogs, tweets, video, social networking posts, news articles, or any other content; and the aside could be advertisements, highlighted resource links, and even more content.

The following HTML sample demonstrates a way to define part of a document's overall structure and add images using the <nav> tag:

```
<!-- NAVIGATIONAL SIDEBAR -->
<nav>
<img height="129" src="syb/SYBSumReptCV.jpg" width="100" alt="Link to a PDF
file. Go to www.adobe.com to download Adobe Reader"/>
<br/>
<br/>SYB
<br/>Summary Report
</nav>
```

This HTML code can now be controlled through an external style sheet. The following style sheet entry defines formatting for the section of code created by the <nav> tag in the preceding HTML sample:

```
nav
{
float:left;
width:165px;
background:#fc3 url(navbg_04.gif) repeat-y top right;
height:662px;
}
```

In this CSS code, the navigational sidebar is made to appear (i.e., float) on the left side of the document. A background image (navbg_04.gif) is specified and will appear at the top right of the sidebar. The *repeat-y* entry ensures that the image is tiled vertically in the background. The sidebar will always appear 165 pixels wide and 662 pixels high. You could repeat these structural properties and values for each structural element of the HTML document, then use CSS to control the rendering of each section in the document.

If necessary, you can adjust the formatting any time by modifying the CSS entries. For example, suppose you were to add more text to a page, which makes the page longer. If you were using a sidebar image, this image may then be too short, making the page look awkward. To solve this problem, you could increase the sidebar image's height to accommodate the change by adjusting the *height* property's pixel value in the style sheet. You can also use CSS to move images to specific locations on your pages.

Alternatively, the following example shows an inline CSS style attribute declared inside an HTML <p> tag:

```
<p style="text-align:center; margin-right:12px;"/>
```

This tag uses the inline CSS style attribute to align text to the center of a right margin that begins 12 pixels into the document. This style will apply only to this <p> tag, and not to any others.

For more information about using proper CSS layout, visit the following sites:

- W3C — Home Page of Cascading Style Sheets (*www.w3.org/Style/CSS/Overview.en.html*)

- w3schools.com — CSS tutorials and reference (*www.w3schools.com/css/css_intro.asp*)

You will learn more about applying styles with CSS throughout this course.

Fixed-width vs. liquid design layouts

OBJECTIVE
2.21.2: Fixed-width
vs. liquid design

Web designers have no control over their site visitors' browser window sizes, the Web browsers used or the fonts installed on visitors' computers. Yet despite this, many designers try to control the way that Web page elements will render on the screen.

There are two page-layout methods that designers use to control the placement of Web page elements when rendered in the browser:

- **Fixed-width layout** — also known as absolute positioning. Achieved by assigning specific pixel widths to elements using the HTML5 structural elements or the <div> tag. This layout ensures that the text, images and layout will not vary from browser to browser. The problem with using a fixed-width layout is that the elements may not render as expected when users change the size of their browser windows.

- **Liquid layout** — also known as relative positioning. Achieved by assigning percentage values to elements. With this layout, the size of an element is flexible and will change dynamically depending on the size of the browser window. For example, you can specify in the CSS width property that Element A will occupy 35 percent of the screen and Element B will occupy the remaining 65 percent. If the user resizes the browser window, the elements will resize correspondingly.

There is great debate concerning the use of fixed-width versus liquid design layouts in Web pages. General industry consensus indicates that implementing a liquid design layout using CSS is the preferred method of designing Web pages.

Relative path names

Most Web developers use subfolders to organize images, style sheets and Web pages. Currently, your HTML pages are configured to refer to all images and style sheets in the same directory (e.g., a folder on your Desktop). As the site grows, your HTML pages will refer to subdirectories. A reference to a file within a directory or subdirectory is called a relative path.

A relative path statement allows you to specify subdirectories (i.e., subfolders), as well as directories above the one where your page currently resides. A relative path assumes that the directory in which the HTML file resides is the current (i.e., "home") directory. All other directories exist either beneath the current directory (i.e., subdirectories) or above the current directory (i.e., parent directories) in a hierarchical structure.

For example, if you place the SYBcollage2.png file into the Syb\ directory, and your Web page's <img> tag needs to reference this image file, then you must change your *src* attribute value to include the new subdirectory location, as follows:

```
<img src="Syb/SYBcollage2.png" alt="PNG image"/>
```

If you omit the subdirectory reference to Syb/ before the image file name, then your HTML page will look for the SYBcollage2.png image file in its existing directory, and not in a subdirectory named Syb. Thus the page will render without the image file, and a small box with an X will appear in its place.

White space, the <img> tag and HTML

With HTML, if you add a space or use the ENTER key to create a return within the <img> tag, the additional space will not be rendered in a browser. In XHTML, however, sometimes adding spaces or hard returns within or even between <img> tags will cause white space to appear on the page. Therefore, be careful when working with <img> tags in XHTML so that you do not add unintentional white space.

HTML5 and Older Browsers

Support for Internet Explorer 8, 7 and 6

HTML5 is not supported by Internet Explorer 8 or earlier. This is a challenge because Windows XP and Vista cannot run IE9, which is the only Internet Explorer version that supports HTML5. The simple solution is to install the latest version of the Chrome or Firefox browsers on Windows XP and Vista systems.

But what about your site visitors? You cannot force them to install Chrome or Firefox. They may be using IE8, 7 or 6. The only way to support these older IE browsers is to add JavaScript code to your HTML documents and a new rule to CSS.

Because older IE browsers will not recognize the new HTML5 elements, such as <header>, <footer>, <article>, etc. JavaScript must be used to create these elements in your Web page so older IE browsers will recognize them.

Note: JavaScript coding is beyond the scope of this course. This code is provided to demonstrate how JavaScript is used to support older browsers.

HTML5 document additions

At a minimum, the basic HTML5 structural elements should be created by adding JavaScript in the <head> element:

```
<script>
document.createElement("article");
document.createElement("footer");
document.createElement("header");
document.createElement("nav");
</script>
```

CSS document additions

The new HTML5 structural elements must also become block-level elements in CSS for consistent styling. A block-level element is a large block of content, such as a paragraph or a structural element that starts a new line of text or a new section.

```
header, nav, article, footer
{
display:block;
}
```

Adding all HTML5 elements

Each new HTML5 element must be added. This can be a long and laborious task, so the best solution is to implement a mini-script developed by Remy Sharp, available at *http://remysharp.com/2009/01/07/html5-enabling-script.*

Instructions for enabling the script are included at the Web site. Remy Sharp's code has been utilized by Google, MIT and nearly all Web developers across the globe. It is the *de facto* standard for supporting HTML5 for older IE browsers.

In the following lab, you will see how the HTML structural elements and CSS can be used to create document sections. Suppose members of your Web team have added images and page structure to an HTML page. The new document structure includes four sections:

- **A navigation bar in the header of the page** — with links to the rest of the site. This section will contain several images.

- **A navigation bar on the left side of the page** — with links that explain additional Habitat youth programs. This section will contain a background image, an image that will eventually link to a PDF file, and several button-style images, the first of which will eventually link to another page.

- **A body content section** — with the narrative (which you have already marked up) about the Summer Youth Blitz program.

- **A footer section** — with text-based navigation to help ensure accessibility.

The page and a style sheet have been developed already. You have been assigned to review the page and add comments to make sure that the document is properly structured. You have also been asked to verify that the document refers to the correct style sheet.

Lab 3-9: Using HTML5 and CSS to structure a page

In this lab, you will review the structure of a Web page. Specifically, you will see the way that HTML5 and CSS can be used to create document sections.

1. **Editor:** Close **syb.html**.

2. **Windows Explorer:** Create a subdirectory off of **Habitat\CCYP\Syb** named *Old*.

3. **Windows Explorer:** Move the contents of the Habitat\CCYP\Syb\ folder to the **Habitat\CCYP\Syb\Old** folder.

   Note: These actions will not delete or move your existing syb.html page, because it is not in the Habitat\CCYP\Syb\ folder.

4. Move the existing **syb.html** file into the **Habitat\CCYP\Syb\Old** folder.

5. **Windows Explorer:** Go to the **C:\CIW\Site_Dev\Lab Files\Lesson03\Lab_3-9** directory, and copy the contents of the Syb\ folder into the **Habitat\CCYP\Syb** folder.

   Note: Copy the contents of the Syb\ folder, but not the folder itself.

6. Go to the **C:\CIW\Site_Dev\Lab Files\Lesson03\Lab_3-9** folder, and copy the **syb.txt** file from this folder to your **Habitat\CCYP** directory.

7. Open **syb.txt**. Verify that the style sheet links to the **\Syb\syb.css** file.

8. In **syb.txt**, scroll down to the following code:

   ```
   <header>
   ```

9. Add the following comment immediately above the code block:

   ```
   <!-- HEADER -->
   ```

10. You have identified the top section of the page. Now, find the following text:

    ```
    <nav>
    ```

11. Immediately above this text, enter the following comment:

```
<!-- NAV -->
```

12. You have just marked the navigation section of this page. Next, find the following text:

```
<article>
```

13. Immediately above the text you just found, enter the following comment:

```
<!-- ARTICLE -->
```

14. Find the following text:

```
<footer>
```

15. Immediately above the text you just found, enter the following comment:

```
<!-- FOOTER -->
```

16. You have now commented each of the sections of your page. Review each section carefully. Notice that HTML5 structural elements are used to create each section.

17. Save syb.txt as **syb.html** in the Habitat\CCYP directory, and view it in a browser. Your page should resemble Figure 3-10.

Figure 3-10: syb.html Web page using HTML5 structural elements and CSS

18. **Editor:** Open **syb.html** in your editor. Find the section marked with the comment <!-- HEADER-->. Notice the <header> tag immediately beneath the comment. Each HTML5 structural element has a counterpart in the Syb\syb.css file because each tag, in conjunction with your linked style sheet, helps define the structure of this HTML page.

19. **Editor:** Open the **Syb\syb.css** file. Compare the structural tags with the corresponding entries in the style sheet. For example, notice that the *nav* entry in syb.css inserts an image named navbg_04.gif into the file. No reference to this image exists in syb.html. Therefore, you can use style sheets to add images.

20. Review the other sections of your page, and compare them to the style sheet.

21. Cut one of the HTML5 structural tags, then load the page in a browser to see the impact. Return to the editor, and Undo your changes to restore the document.

    Note: You can restore the document by using the Undo feature in WordPad or Notepad. If necessary, you can also copy the complete file from the Finished folder for this lab.

22. From **syb.html**, comment the reference to the style sheet, then reload the page in the browser. Notice that the document's structure is no longer intact because the style sheet, in conjunction with the HTML5 structural tags, now defines the structure of this HTML page. Remove the comment notation.

23. Validate your code. Correct all problems so that the code validates as CSS and HTML5.

24. If you like, remove the background image (background.jpg) from the page. What background color would you recommend for this page? Add it now.

In this lab, you added structure to your page using images and CSS.

CIW Online Resources – Course Mastery

Visit CIW Online at *http://education.Certification-Partners.com/CIW* to take the Course Mastery review of this lesson or lesson segment.

SDA Lesson 3 - Part B

Case Study

A Sharper Image

Iain works on the Web development team for a prominent community college system in the Southwest part of the United States. He was assigned to create several new Web pages, most of which would include detailed images. These images would aid navigation and provide vital registration instructions for the college students.

Iain was experienced with HTML and did not feel it was important to spend time validating all code because he was very busy. After creating and posting the new pages, however, Iain began receiving complaints from students who used text-based browsers. These students complained that they could not see (or hear) the registration instructions.

To solve this problem, Iain added the *alt* attribute to each <img> tag to describe each image with text. Although it would have taken him more time to include the *alt* attribute in his initial page development, Iain found that the *alt* attribute resolved the complaints.

* 　　　 * 　　　 *

As a class, discuss the following issues that might arise when incorporating images in Web pages:

- Most people use browsers that support images. Why is it important to support all browser types in this situation?

- How could validation have saved Iain development time? What other advantages would have come from initial validation?

Lesson Summary

Application project

When you incorporate an image into your Web page, you should consider the image's usefulness to the rest of the page. Images are generally effective only if they complement the text or overall message of the page.

Many Web sites offer copyright-free graphic files for site designers to use. These sites provide coordinated graphics such as buttons, bullets, rules and backgrounds that can help create a theme for your site. Use a search engine to locate free Web graphics, or visit the Yahoo! Directory at *http://dir.yahoo.com/*, and navigate to Arts & Humanities | Design Arts | Graphic Design | Web Page Design And Layout | Graphics. Add a new, free, non-copyrighted image to your Web page. After you finish, revert your file to its original state for the remaining lessons.

Skills review

In this lesson, you were introduced to CSS and graphical Web page elements such as horizontal rules, images and colors. You learned how to position graphics relative to text on a page, and how to resize images for display using CSS. In addition, you applied CSS to font families, font size and font colors. You also learned about special characters, and about using HTML5 structural elements to add structure to a Web document.

Now that you have completed this lesson, you should be able to:

✓ 2.2.1: Incorporate graphical images into HTML pages.

✓ 2.2.2: Distinguish among and identify the uses and benefits of various graphic file formats, including GIF, GIF89a, JPEG, PNG, TIFF, BMP.

✓ 2.2.3: Add tiled images and colors to Web page backgrounds.

✓ 2.2.6: Insert horizontal rules into Web pages.

✓ 2.3.1: Define the browser-safe color palette.

✓ 2.3.2: Identify ways that color affects the principles of line, value, shape and form in Web pages.

✓ 2.3.3: Identify and demonstrate the impact of color combinations to various audiences and cultures.

✓ 2.3.4: Evaluate Web page design and layout.

✓ 2.8.1: Explain how to structure Web documents with CSS.

✓ 2.8.2: Identify ways to apply styles with CSS.

✓ 2.21.1: Use CSS and HTML5 elements to create document structure.

✓ 2.21.2: Distinguish between fixed-width and liquid design layouts.

CIW Practice Exams

Visit CIW Online at *http://education.Certification-Partners.com/CIW* to take the Practice Exams assessment covering the objectives in this lesson.

SDA Objective 2.02 Review

SDA Objective 2.03 Review

SDA Objective 2.08 Review

SDA Objective 2.21 Review

Note that some objectives may be only partially covered in this lesson.

Lesson 3 Review

1. What attribute allows inline CSS to be applied within HTML document tags?

   _____

2. What is the term for the grouping of a CSS selector, property and value?

   _____

3. Name the alignment options available for aligning images relative to text.

   _____

4. What is the function of the *alt* attribute?

   _____

   _____

5. What standard of 216 colors was introduced to render Web page colors consistently across different browsers?

   _____

   _____

Lesson 4: Hyperlinks

Objectives

By the end of this lesson, you will be able to:

✧ 2.1.4: Create HTML hyperlinks for text, images, local files and remote sites (internal and external links).

✧ 2.14.4: Manage existing sites (e.g., remove dead links and/or upgrade connectivity when necessary).

✧ 2.16.6: Identify the importance of online indexing and cataloging.

Pre-Assessment Questions

1. Which term describes the underlined, colored text on a Web page that a user can click to access another Web page?

   a. Fully qualified URL
   b. Anchor
   c. Hyperlink
   d. Partial URL

2. When are partial URLs used with hyperlinks?

   a. When using an external image as a link
   b. When linking to another location on the same site
   c. When linking to an external Web site
   d. When accessing a system file on the Web server

3. What is the term recommended by the W3C for a link to a resource? What is the other common term for such a link?

   _____

   _____

Introduction to Hyperlinks

The characteristic that makes the World Wide Web a "web" is the linking capability that connects Web pages to other files across the Internet. Hyperlinks are in fact more fundamental than the ability to include multimedia objects in your HTML documents. Even users with non-graphical browsers, such as Lynx, can select hyperlinks in Web pages to navigate and explore the Web. The critical element is the ability to move from page to page by clicking linked text or images.

A hypertext link is a word or phrase in an HTML document that is specially tagged as a link using the anchor element, <a>. By default, hyperlinks appear blue and underlined in the browser. You can use CSS to make hyperlinks appear in any color you like. An image or icon can also be enclosed in anchor tags and used as a link to another file. In both cases, clicking the link will take the user to the link's specified destination.

You can create links to external files as well as to points within the current file. On a long page, you can use links to jump between sections of the page; such a link is called an internal link.

CIW Online Resources – Movie Clips

Visit CIW Online at http://education.Certification-Partners.com/CIW to watch a movie clip about this topic.

Lesson 4: Hyperlinks

OBJECTIVE
2.1.4: HTML
hyperlinks

The Anchor Element

Links are created with the anchor element, <a>. Anchor elements are container tags that encompass the text or image (or both) to be used as the link. The *href* attribute is used to specify the link's hypertext reference, or the target of the link. You can specify a fully qualified URL or a relative URL reference for any file, page or site.

The W3C considers URLs part of a Uniform Resource Identifier (URI). Sometimes URLs are called URIs when referring to Web addresses. Both are correct, but Web addresses are specifically locators, as opposed to the broader "identifier" term. The terms are used interchangeably. This course will use "URL" throughout.

The syntax for using the anchor element to create a link is as follows:

```
<a href="URL"> linked text or image (or both) </a>
```

Table 4-1 lists examples of values for the URL when referencing external links.

Table 4-1: URL options for external links

Type of Reference	Description	Examples
Fully qualified URL (also called absolute URL)	A URL (i.e., URI) that contains a full path to a resource, including the protocol indicator. Also known as a hard link.	http://www.someserver.com/somepage.html or ftp://ftp.someserver.com/pub/somefile.ext or c:\intetpub\wwwroot\ccyp\syb\syb.html
Partial URL (also called relative URL)	A URL that assumes the current document's path. All references are made from the document's current directory.	syb.html or ../css/stylesheet.css or pub/images/mybullet.gif

As you read absolute and relative URLs, you must understand how browsers interpret them. Table 4-2 summarizes common URL paths. As you read this table, assume that all references are to the same page, index.html.

Table 4-2: URL paths

URL	Description
/mysite/index.html	The initial forward slash (/) instructs the browser to look for a directory named mysite that is off of the root directory. If you were to insert this reference into a page on your Windows system, your browser would interpret the first forward slash as C:\, and would look for the mysite/ directory, which would contain the index.html file. If this page were on a Web server, the link would refer to the Web server's root directory (e.g., /var/www/mysite/ in Linux/UNIX or C:\inetpub\wwwroot\ in Windows).
mysite/index.html	The absence of any initial characters instructs the browser to look for the mysite subdirectory. This subdirectory begins off of the same level as the current page. The index.html page resides inside of the mysite subdirectory.
../mysite/index.html	The initial two periods and forward slash (../) instruct the browser to look for a directory named mysite that begins one level higher than the page you are currently viewing.

Tech Tip

Windows and UNIX/Linux systems use different naming conventions for their paths. Windows path names use back slashes, whereas UNIX/Linux paths use forward slashes. Also, Windows paths can use drive names (e.g., C:\), whereas Unix/Linux paths do not.

Specifying protocols

Hyperlinks do not have to point only to HTTP addresses. You can create hyperlinks for various protocols. Table 4-3 describes several protocols you can specify in a hyperlink URL.

Table 4-3: Protocols in hyperlink URL references

Protocol	Hyperlink HTML Example
HTTP	Visit the <a href="http://www.CIWcertified.com">CIW<a/> site.
HTTPS (Secure HTTP)	Visit our <a href="https://www.CIWcertified.com">secure CIW<a/> site.
FTP	Download the file from our <a href="ftp://ftp.server.com">FTP server.</a>
E-mail	You can send e-mail to us at <a href="mailto:info@ciwcertified.com">info@ciwcertified.com</a>.

Problems when creating hyperlinks

Many Web developers commit the same common errors when writing HTML code to create hyperlinks on their Web pages. As you use the <a> element, make sure that you:

- **Use a closing anchor tag** — You must place the </a> tag after the page text to be affected.

- **Place quotation marks around the value** — The value of the *href* attribute is the target of your link; for example:
  "http://www.habitat.org"

- **Include the closing bracket at the end of the opening <a> tag** — The following example is a common oversight:
  <a href="http://www.habitat.org" Habitat </a>
  The tag should read as follows:
  <a href="http://www.habitat.org"> Habitat </a>

Table 4-4 lists some problems you might experience when creating links in HTML, with troubleshooting techniques that you can use to solve these problems.

Table 4-4: Troubleshooting HTML hyperlink problems

Problem	Solution
Text and images disappear	The <a> tag is not properly closed with </a>, or you have not placed quotation marks around a value. Review your tags carefully.
All successive Web page text is a hyperlink	The <a> tag is not properly closed with </a> in the correct location. Review your tags carefully.
Garbled code appears on screen	One or more <a> tags may be missing an opening or closing angle bracket (i.e., wicket). Review each <a> tag carefully.
Code will not validate due to a problem <a> tag	A closing tag may be missing or mistyped (such as <a/> instead of </a>). Review your tags carefully.

Creating Local Hyperlinks

OBJECTIVE
2.1.4: HTML
hyperlinks

A local hyperlink is a link you create from one file on your local system to another file on your local system. You create these types of links when you are developing your own pages and linking them to form a site. Your files can be uploaded to a Web server in the same directory structure you save on your system, so your file references can remain unchanged as long as your directory structure persists. Creating local hyperlinks involves determining the location of the file to which you want to link, relative to the location of the file from which you are linking.

In the following lab, you will create local hypertext links in a document. Suppose you have been assigned to link your Web page to other pages on the site. You need to determine page text that will clearly identify hyperlinks so your users know where each link will take them. You also need to provide a link to a report in PDF format. You must supply page text for each hyperlink, as well as the HTML code that will create the hyperlink function that links the pages of your site to each other.

Lab 4-1: Creating local text hyperlinks in HTML

OBJECTIVE
2.1.4: HTML
hyperlinks

In this lab, you will create local hyperlinks from the syb.html page to other pages that are stored on your hard drive.

In the first five steps, you will populate and verify the Habitat folders on your Desktop. In the rest of the lab, you will create links from syb.html to files in these directories.

1. Navigate to the **C:\CIW\Site_Dev\Lab Files\Lesson04\Lab_4-1** folder. Copy the **index.html** file and the **index** directory to the **Habitat** folder on your system. This page and its associated directory re-create a prototype version of the Habitat for Humanity home page.

2. From the **Lab Files\Lesson04\Lab_4-1** folder, copy the **default.html** file and the **default** directory to the **Habitat\CCYP** subfolder. (Notice that you are copying to a different location than in Step 1.) This file and directory re-create a prototype Campus Chapters And Youth Programs page.

3. From the **Lab Files\Lesson04\Lab_4-1** folder, copy the **ccypintl.html** file and the **ccypintl** directory to the **Habitat\CCYP** subfolder (the same location as in Step 2). This file and directory re-create a prototype International Programs page.

4. From the **Lab Files\Lesson04\Lab_4-1** folder, copy the file **application.html** and the **application** directory to the **Habitat\CCYP** subfolder (the same location as in Steps 2 and 3). This file and directory re-create a prototype Summer Youth Blitz Application Form page.

5. Verify that your Desktop directories are now populated as follows:

   • **Habitat** should contain **index.html** and the **index** directory.

   • **Habitat\CCYP** should contain **application.html**, **ccypintl.html**, **default.html** and all associated directories for these files. It should also contain **syb.html** and the **Syb** directory from the previous lesson. If not, copy the syb.html and the Syb\ directory from the Lab_4-1 folder.

   Note: The directories you copied and verified in Steps 1 through 5 contain Web pages to which you will link in this lab. You will create links to these directories in the following steps.

6. Open **syb.html** in a text editor. Scroll to the bottom of the page, to the footer section.

7. At the bottom of the page, find the text that reads *International Programs*. Surround this text with the opening and closing anchor tags to create a hyperlink to the ccypintl.html page:

   ```
   <a href="ccypintl.html">International Programs</a>
   ```

Note: You do not need to specify a subfolder for this relative URL because ccypintl.html is in the same folder as syb.html.

8. Save the page, then open it in a browser. Scroll to the bottom of the page. The phrase International Programs should now be a hyperlink, indicated as blue underlined text, as shown in Figure 4-1.

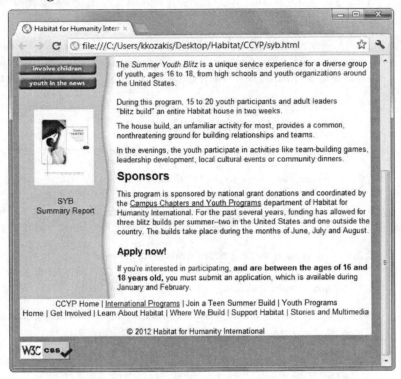

Figure 4-1: Page syb.html with hyperlink in footer section

9. Click your new link to verify that it is valid. The International Programs page should appear in your browser.

10. Validate your code at ***http://validator.w3.org***.

11. Open **syb.html** in the text editor and again scroll to the bottom. Find the text that reads *CCYP Home*. Surround this text with the opening and closing anchor tags to create a hyperlink to the **default.html** page that resides in the same folder (i.e., on the same level) as syb.html:

```
<a href="default.html">CCYP Home</a>
```

Note: Understand that this code refers to a page on the same level (in the same directory) as the page you are currently editing.

12. Save the file. Test your code in a browser. You should see that the text CCYP Home at the bottom of the page is now a hyperlink.

13. Click the link to verify that it points to the correct page. You should see the Campus Chapters And Youth Programs home page appear in the browser.

14. Open **syb.html** again in the text editor and again scroll to the footer. Find the text that reads *Home*. Create a link for this text pointing visitors to the **index.html** page that resides in the **Habitat** directory (one directory up from syb.html):

```
<a href="../index.html">Home</a>
```

Note: This code ".." refers to a page one directory up from the current directory. Remember that in Step 1, you copied this file and a directory to the Habitat\ folder, not to the Habitat\CCYP\ folder.

15. Save the file. Test your code in a browser, then validate it at **http://validator.w3.org**. Resolve any code problems before continuing the lab.

16. In **syb.html**, find the text that reads ...*You Must Submit An Application* (in the Apply Now! section). Create a hyperlink from the word ***Application*** to the file **application.html**, which resides in the same directory as syb.html.

17. Find the phrase *Join a Teen Summer Build*, and create a hyperlink from this phrase to the current page (syb.html). Save the file.

18. Check your work by viewing it in a browser then validating it. Resolve any problems.

19. Next, you will link to a PDF document. Verify that Adobe Reader is installed on your system by selecting **Start | All Programs** and looking for the Adobe Reader icon. If your system does not have Adobe Reader, go to ***www.adobe.com*** to download and install it. Adobe Reader is free software that allows you to view PDF files.

20. Verify that the file **AME_AnnualReport.pdf** is in the Habitat\CCYP\Syb\ subfolder. If it is not present, copy the PDF file from **C:\CIW\Site_Dev\Lab Files\Lesson04\Lab_4-1\Syb** to the **Habitat\CCYP\Syb** subfolder.

21. In **syb.html**, find the text that reads *SYB
Summary Report*. It is located at the end of the <nav> section. Create a link from this text to the PDF file.

22. Save the file, then refresh **syb.html** in the browser. Verify your relative link to the PDF. When you click the **SYB Summary Report** link, Adobe Reader should automatically launch and download the report file.

23. Browse all your local links to verify that they work.

24. You can change the default appearance of a hyperlink using CSS. In your editor, open the file **Habitat\CCYP\Syb\syb.css** (which is the style sheet for syb.html) and find the following entry:

```
/*
a
{
color: #093
}
*/
```

25. Notice that this CSS entry for hyperlinks is commented out. The entry instructs all hyperlinks to be displayed in green, rather than the default blue. Delete the comment notation **/* */**, then save and close the **syb.css** file.

26. Reload the **syb.html** page in the browser, and notice that the hyperlinks are now green instead of blue. All links on this page will now appear green, even if visitors click them.

27. Now, change all of your headings (e.g., <h2> and <h3>) to appear purple. Do this by opening the **Habitat\CCYP\Syb\syb.css** style sheet file and adding the following line to the end of the h2 and h3 styles:

```
color: purple;
```

Note: Be sure to include the semicolon (;) after the style to separate it from any other styles you add.

28. Save your changes to **syb.css** and to **syb.html**. Verify and validate your work. Resolve any problems. When you are finished, your page should resemble Figure 4-2.

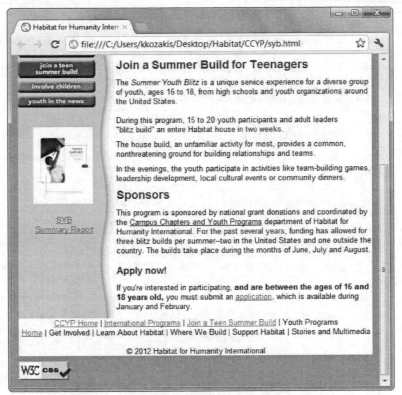

Figure 4-2: Page syb.html after adding local hyperlinks

In this lab, you created hyperlinks in a Web document.

Creating External Hyperlinks

An external hyperlink is a link you create from a file on your system to a separate file on the Internet. You add these types of links to your own pages to reference other Web sites' pages. Creating external hyperlinks involves determining the full URL, including the protocol indicator, for the Web page to which you want to link. Remember that you should not provide a link from your site to another site without first obtaining permission from that site's owner, because such a link may imply a business relationship or endorsement.

In the following lab, you will create external hyperlinks. Suppose your project manager has assigned you to work on the Summer Youth Blitz page for a sister site to Habitat. You need to link this page to the live *www.habitat.org* site. However, some of the links should remain local.

Lab 4-2: Creating external hyperlinks in HTML

In this lab, you will use the anchor element to link text from one file to another file on an external Web site.

OBJECTIVE
2.1.4: HTML
hyperlinks

1. Open **syb.html** in a text editor. Scroll to the bottom of the page, to the footer section.

2. Your project manager has provided you with the information in the following table. Using this information, add the appropriate links from specified page text in the footer section of syb.html to the specified external pages on your system.

Page Text to Tag as Hyperlink	URL Value to Reference
Youth Programs	*http://www.habitat.org/youthprograms/*
Get Involved	*http://www.habitat.org/getinv/*
Learn About Habitat	*http://www.habitat.org/how/*
Where We Build	*http://www.habitat.org/intl/*
Support Habitat	*http://www.habitat.org/support/default.aspx*
Stories and Multimedia	*http://www.habitat.org/stories_multimedia/*

3. When you are finished adding all HTML anchor tags to the file, save **syb.html**. Then load the page in a browser. It should resemble Figure 4-3.

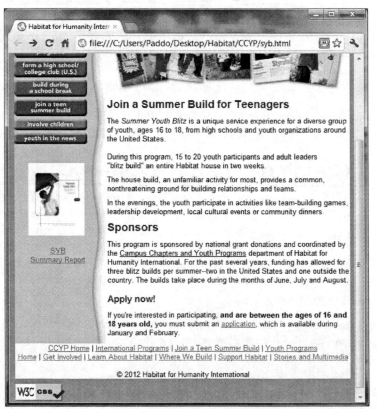

Figure 4-3: Page syb.html after adding remote hyperlinks

4. Validate your code at ***http://validator.w3.org***. Resolve any problems, then save and close **syb.html**.

5. Consider the names of the hyperlink text that you inserted. How might you change the names so that they are more descriptive? Search engines will rank a page higher if they see that hyperlinks have been given descriptive names.

In this lab, you created absolute links to an external site.

Using Images as Hyperlinks

You are not limited to using text to provide a link to another file. You can create a hyperlink from a graphical image by surrounding the image tag with opening and closing anchor tags.

In the following lab, you will create hyperlinks from image files. Suppose your project manager has suggested that the images on your Web page serve no purpose other than to be aesthetically appealing. Although this role is acceptable for images, you consider a way to add functionality to the images on your Web page.

 Lab 4-3: Using images as hyperlinks with HTML

OBJECTIVE
2.1.4: HTML
hyperlinks

In this lab, you will create hyperlinks from several images on a Web page.

1. Open **syb.html** in a text editor.

2. Find the <img> tag for the **sybheaders_03.jpg** image. You can use the search feature in your text editor (e.g., select **Edit | Find** in Notepad).

3. Create a hyperlink from this image as follows:

```
<a href="http://www.habitat.org/how/factsheet.aspx"><img height="22"
src="syb/sybheaders_03.jpg" width="72" id="FAQs" alt="Click here to get facts
about Habitat."/></a>
```

Warning: Do not introduce any additional spaces or returns in this particular code. Otherwise, your page may not render as expected because the HTML code sometimes reflects spaces you introduce. Enter this code exactly as it appears with no returns.

4. Your project manager has provided you with the information in the following table. Using this information, create links to the indicated images.

Image File to Tag as Hyperlink	Image Label	URL Value to Reference
sybheaders_03.jpg	FAQs	*http://www.habitat.org/how/factsheet.aspx*
sybheaders_04.jpg	History	*http://www.habitat.org/how/historytext.aspx*
sybheaders_05.jpg	Newsroom	*http://www.habitat.org/newsroom/default.aspx*
sybheaders_06.jpg	Gift cards	*http://www.habitat.org/support/giftfromtheheart.aspx*
sybheaders_07.jpg	Photos	*http://www.habitat.org/photogallery/album.aspx*

Image File to Tag as Hyperlink	Image Label	URL Value to Reference
sybheaders_08.jpg	Apply!	*http://www.habitat.org/youthprograms/ages_14_25/asbw_default.aspx*
Intlbutton1.gif *(This image is in a new location in the HTML file)*	International programs	*http://www.habitat.org/youthprograms/ages_14_25/international/international_default.aspx*

5. When you are finished adding all HTML anchor tags to the file, save **syb.html**. Then load the page in a browser. Verify that the page renders as expected, and click your new links to test them.

6. Validate your code at ***http://validator.w3.org***. Resolve any problems, then save and close **syb.html**.

In this lab, you created hyperlinks from images to related Web site pages.

So far, you have created external links using full and partial URLs. In the next section, you will learn how to create an internal link to a different area within the same page.

OBJECTIVE
2.1.4: HTML
hyperlinks

Creating Internal Links

On a long Web page, you may want to include links that target other areas within the same page so that users can easily find the information that interests them. An internal hyperlink provides this link from one point to another in a Web page.

Internal links require internal bookmarks, called anchors, to identify the point that the link will reference within the page. Creating an internal link requires two steps. You must first use the anchor element, <a>, with the *id* attribute to define an area as a target (the bookmark or anchor). Then, in another portion of the page, you create the link that points to the bookmark using the anchor element with the hypertext reference (*href*) attribute as you have already learned. The syntax for creating an internal link is as follows:

```
<a id="targetArea1">
target anchor text or image (or both)
</a>

… other page content here …

<a href="#targetArea1"> text/images linking to targetArea1 </a>
```

The *id* attribute of the <a> element identifies an internal bookmark or anchor in the page. Note that for the *href* value, the # symbol is used. This symbol, called a hash, tells the browser to look for an anchor by this name within the current document. Without this hash, the browser will look for an external file by that name.

In this example, the <a id> tag appears above the <a href> tag in the code. These tags can appear in either order in a document — it simply depends on whether the target <a id> appears above or below the link to it <a href> on the rendered page.

CIW Online Resources – Online Exercise

Visit CIW Online at *http://education.Certification-Partners.com/CIW* to complete an interactive exercise that will reinforce what you have learned about this topic.

Exercise 4-1: Creating internal hyperlinks

OBJECTIVE
2.16.6: Online indexing and catalogs

Creating a glossary

A glossary provides a helpful navigation feature, especially if your site introduces concepts and terms to an audience that is unfamiliar with your practices. A glossary is one way to help index and catalog your site.

In the following lab, you will learn how internal hyperlinks are created. Suppose your project manager has asked you to help index and catalog the Web site. You know that a glossary is a useful way to do this. You can create a glossary using internal hyperlinks to index your site and provide helpful information to your site's visitors.

Lab 4-4: Using internal hyperlinks

In this lab, you will examine and use an HTML document that includes internal hyperlinks.

1. **Windows Explorer:** Copy the **internal.txt** file and the **internal** folder from the **C:\CIW\Site_Dev\Lab Files\Lesson04\Lab_4-4** folder to the Habitat folder on your Desktop.

    Note: Be sure to copy both the file and folder.

2. **Editor:** Open **internal.txt**.

3. **Editor:** Save this file as **internal.html**. Make sure that both internal.html and the internal\ directory are in the Habitat folder on your Desktop. The code in internal.html refers to files in the internal\ directory using relative paths.

4. Examine the following code with your instructor:

```
<!DOCTYPE html>
<html>
<head>
<meta name="Keywords" content="CIW, Web Foundations Associate, Example"/>
<meta name="Description" content="For the CIW Web Foundations Associate
courses"/>
<meta charset="utf-8"/>
<link rel="stylesheet"  type="text/css" href="internal/internal.css"/>
<title>Habitat for Humanity International Glossary </title>
</head>
<body>

<h1><a id="TermTop">
Glossary of Terms
</a></h1>

<h3>
<a href="#First">A-D</a> |
<a href="#Second">E-H</a>|
<a href="#Third">I-K</a>|
<a href="#Fourth">L-O</a>|
```

```
<a href="#Fifth">P-T</a>|
<a href="#Sixth">U-Z</a>|
</h3>
<blockquote><p>Click the link for the group of letters representing the start
of the term you want to see defined.</p></blockquote>

<h3><a id="First">A-D</a></h3>

<strong>Term:</strong> Definition of term.<br/>
<strong>Term:</strong> Definition of term.<br/>
<strong>Term:</strong> Definition of term.<br/>
<strong>Term:</strong> Definition of term.<br/>

<br/>
<blockquote><a href="#TermTop"><img src="internal/returnup.gif" alt="Return to
the top"></a> Click on the image to the left, or <a href="#TermTop">here</a>,
to return to the top.</blockquote>

<h3><a id="Second">E-H</a></h3>

<strong>Term:</strong> Definition of term.<br/>
<strong>Term:</strong> Definition of term.<br/>
<strong>Term:</strong> Definition of term.<br/>
<strong>Term:</strong> Definition of term.<br/>

<br/>
<blockquote><a href="#TermTop"><img src="internal/returnup.gif" alt="Return to
the top"></a> Click on the image to the left, or <a href="#TermTop">here</a>,
to return to the top.</blockquote>

<h3><a id="Third">I-K</a></h3>

<strong>Term:</strong> Definition of term.<br/>
<strong>Term:</strong> Definition of term.<br/>
<strong>Term:</strong> Definition of term.<br/>
<strong>Term:</strong> Definition of term.<br/>

<br/>
<blockquote><a href="#TermTop"><img src="internal/returnup.gif" alt="Return to
the top"></a> Click on the image to the left, or <a href="#TermTop">here</a>,
to return to the top.</blockquote>

<h3><a id="Fourth">L-O</a></h3>

<strong>Term:</strong> Definition of term.<br/>
<strong>Term:</strong> Definition of term.<br/>
<strong>Term:</strong> Definition of term.<br/>
<strong>Term:</strong> Definition of term.<br/>

<br/>
<blockquote><a href="#TermTop"><img src="internal/returnup.gif" alt="Return to
the top"></a> Click on the image to the left, or <a href="#TermTop">here</a>,
to return to the top.</blockquote>

<h3><a id="Fifth">P-T</a></h3>

<strong>Term:</strong> Definition of term.<br/>
<strong>Term:</strong> Definition of term.<br/>
<strong>Term:</strong> Definition of term.<br/>
<strong>Term:</strong> Definition of term.<br/>

<br/>
<blockquote><a href="#TermTop"><img src="internal/returnup.gif" alt="Return to
the top"></a> Click on the image to the left, or <a href="#TermTop">here</a>,
to return to the top.</blockquote>

<h3><a id="Sixth">U-Z</a></h3>

<strong>Term:</strong> Definition of term.<br/>
```

```
<strong>Term:</strong> Definition of term.<br/>
<strong>Term:</strong> Definition of term.<br/>
<strong>Term:</strong> Definition of term.<br/>

<br/>
<blockquote><a href="#TermTop"><img src="internal/returnup.gif" alt="Return to
the top"></a> Click on the image to the left, or <a href="#TermTop">here</a>,
to return to the top.</blockquote>

<hr/>

<p>
    <a href="http://validator.w3.org/check/referer"><img
        src="internal/valid-css.gif"
        alt="Valid HTML5 and CSS!" height="31" width="88" /></a>
</p>

</body>
</html>
```

5. **Browser:** Load the file **internal.html**. Your page should resemble Figure 4-4.

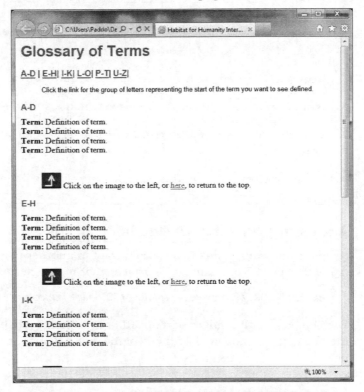

Figure 4-4: Demonstration glossary file for internal links

6. **Browser:** Click **U-Z**, the last link at the top of the page. You should see the section heading that matches the link you clicked. This section is near the end of the document, as shown in Figure 4-5.

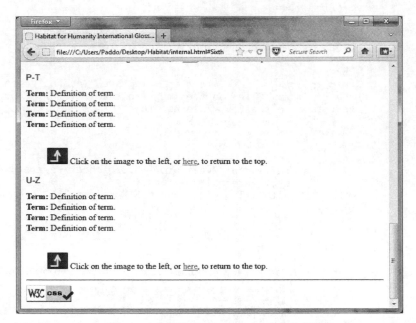

Figure 4-5: After accessing internal link

7. **Browser:** Click any of the arrow images to return to the top of the page.

8. Practice navigating through this page to make sure that all links work correctly.

9. Validate the code at ***http://validator.w3.org***. When you are finished, close your browser.

In this lab, you examined and used a glossary that demonstrates internal hyperlinks.

Accessing an external file's internal link

Suppose you want to link to a specific point in another page without first accessing the top of that page. To link to an internal anchor in another file, use the following syntax:

```
<a href="URL/filename.ext#AnchorID">link text or image</a>
```

You can start with a full or partial URL, but you must specify the file name, followed by the hash symbol, followed by the *id* of the internal anchor to which you want to direct the link.

OBJECTIVE
2.14.4: Existing site
management

link rot
The phenomenon in
which hyperlinks on
a Web site gradually
become invalid as
referenced Web
page content, links
and page locations
change.

Managing Hyperlinks

Periodically, you will need to check both the external and internal hyperlinks on your Web pages to verify that they still work. Links can become invalid for a variety of reasons, most commonly because a referenced page is moved or deleted, or because page content is changed and anchors are renamed or lost. This phenomenon is known as **link rot**.

In addition to annoying users, a bad hyperlink will cause a page to be ranked lower by a search engine such as Google, Yahoo! or Bing. To avoid this problem, you can use automated link-checking software to validate the hyperlinks on your pages. This type of software has the ability to report the state of all site links. Following are some common link-checking software tools:

- **W3C Link Checker** (*http://validator.w3.org/checklink*)

- **Sourceforge Link Checker** (*http://linkchecker.sourceforge.net/*)

- **Link Alarm** (*www.linkalarm.com/*)

Consider that automatic link-checking software can identify invalid links for you, but you still must manually update your HTML code to delete or modify any invalid links. Even if you use automatic link-checking software, it is advisable to check your hyperlinks manually as well. Although a link may still be valid, the content of either the target page or the page with the link can change in ways such that a link is no longer relevant or appropriate.

 Dead hyperlinks are a major factor in having an otherwise good page get ranked lowly by a search engine.

CIW Online Resources – Course Mastery

Visit CIW Online at *http://education.Certification-Partners.com/CIW* to take the Course Mastery review of this lesson or lesson segment.

SDA Lesson 4

Case Study

The Missing Link

Omar works on a Web development team that just posted a site. This site contains both internal and external hyperlinks. Only three days after the site was posted to the production server, Omar found that four external hyperlinks were already invalid. To solve this problem, he checked each link manually and edited the HTML code to validate each one.

After this experience, Omar wanted to manage the hyperlinks more closely and be notified of any problem links immediately. He obtained automatic link-checking software, which checks all site links periodically then sends an e-mail message reporting the status of every link. After installing this software, Omar was confident that his site's links would always remain valid.

*   *   *

As a class, consider this scenario and discuss the following points:

- After Omar installs automatic link-checking software, will his site links always remain valid? Why or why not?

- Why would it be important to occasionally check your hyperlinks manually?

- Why would it be important to use both external and internal links on your Web site?

Lesson Summary

Application project

This lesson taught you about internal, external and local hyperlinks in Web documents. Take some time to learn more about the attributes available to the <a> element. Visit the following sites to read about hyperlink options:

- W3C (*www.w3.org*)

- W3Schools (*www.w3schools.com*)

As you visit these sites, research the capabilities and limitations of HTML5 in relation to the <a> element. What styles can CSS provide the <a> element?

Skills review

In this lesson, you learned to create hyperlinks from text and images to other Web files and sites. You learned that you could use full or partial URLs in your links, and you learned to link to an internal anchor point within the current document or even in another document.

Now that you have completed this lesson, you should be able to:

✓ 2.1.4: Create HTML hyperlinks for text, images, local files and remote sites (internal and external links).

✓ 2.14.4: Manage existing sites (e.g., remove dead links and/or upgrade connectivity when necessary).

✓ 2.16.6: Identify the importance of online indexing and cataloging.

CIW Practice Exams

Visit CIW Online at *http://education.Certification-Partners.com/CIW* to take the Practice Exams assessment covering the objectives in this lesson.

SDA Objective 2.01 Review

SDA Objective 2.14 Review

SDA Objective 2.16 Review

Note that some objectives may be only partially covered in this lesson.

Lesson 4 Review

1. Name the two types of URL you can reference when creating hyperlinks to an external site or to another page on the same site.

   _____

2. Within an anchor element (<a>), the *href* attribute performs what function?

   _____

   _____

3. You are creating an image hyperlink. What HTML code links the image *zoomap.jpg* to the *map.htm* Web page?

   _____

4. You want to create a hyperlink that provides the end user with a pre-addressed blank e-mail message when he or she clicks the link. You want to pre-address the e-mail messages to *info@habitat.org*. The hyperlink text should read "*Please send e-mail to info@habitat.org.*" What HTML code would create this hyperlink?

   _____

5. Describe the syntax used to link to an internal anchor in another file without first accessing the top of that page.

   _____

   _____

   _____

Lesson 5:
HTML Tables

Objectives

By the end of this lesson, you will be able to:

✐   2.1.5: Design and format HTML tables to present information in an organized way.

Pre-Assessment Questions

1. Which table element encloses table cell contents?

    a. <tr>
    b. <th>
    c. <td>
    d. <table>

2. Which table element allows you to add a descriptive title that appears above the table by default?

    a. <border>
    b. <caption>
    c. <title>
    d. <table>

3. What CSS property manipulates the amount of space between cell borders in a table?

    _____

OBJECTIVE
2.1.5: HTML tables

Introduction to HTML Tables

When you want to display data that is best suited to a tabular format, you can use the set of table tags provided in HTML. Tables can provide useful and attractive grids for Web page content. As you learned earlier in this course, you can also use the <pre> tag to structure tabular data. However, the <pre> tag does not allow you to format data exactly as you want it. The <table> tag gives you many formatting options.

Figure 5-1 describes the individual elements that compose a table. Each of these elements will be explored in this lesson.

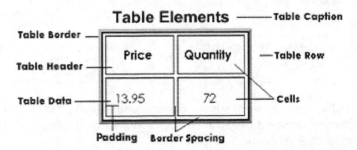

Figure 5-1: Table elements and CSS properties for HTML pages

The code for the table in the preceding figure could be written as follows:

```
<table border="1">
<caption>Table Elements</caption>
<tr>
<th>Price</th>
<th>Quantity</th>
</tr>
<tr>
<td>13.95</td>
<td class="center">72</td>
</tr>
</table>
```

The table style could be defined in CSS as the following:

```
table, td, th
{
border:1px solid gray;
}
td, th
{
padding:15px;
}
td.center
{
text-align:center;
}
```

Table element attributes are not supported in HTML. CSS must be used. The only <table> element attribute still used is *border*, which simply states if the table has a border or not. The border attribute has a value of "0" for no border, and "1" for a border. The style of the border is defined in CSS.

Table 5-1 describes the table element tags that correspond to each element in the preceding figure.

Table 5-1: Table element tags

Element	Tag	Required?	Description
Table	<table>...</table>	Required	Creates a table. Contains all other table elements.
Table caption	<caption>...</caption>	Optional	Adds a caption or title, which appears above the table by default.
Table row	<tr>...</tr>	Required	Contains all data for a table row.
Table header	<th>...</th>	Optional	Typically designates cells in the top row or left column. By default, text in a header cell will appear bold and centered.
Table data	<td>...</td>	Required (unless <th> is being used)	Designates table cell contents. By default, the data is left-justified.

Tables can be very complex or very simple, as is the one you will create in the next lab. Straightforward tables are easy to create if you understand where to place each element and CSS property.

CIW Online Resources – Movie Clips

Visit CIW Online at http://education.Certification-Partners.com/CIW to watch a movie clip about this topic.

Lesson 5: HTML Tables

CIW Online Resources – Online Exercise

Visit CIW Online at *http://education.Certification-Partners.com/CIW* to complete an interactive exercise that will reinforce what you have learned about this topic.

Exercise 5-1: Defining table structure

CSS Properties for All Table Elements

The CSS properties for tables can be used for any element used in the table. For example, the <table> element defines the overall table structure, but the CSS properties used to provide its style are also used for the <th>, <tr> and <td> elements.

Recall that the *border* attribute determines whether a border will appear around the table. By default, borders do not appear. If the value is "1", a border appears. If the value is "0" or the attribute does not exist, a border does not appear.

Table 5-2 describes CSS properties used to create tables.

Do not confuse the border property with the border attribute. In CSS, the border property determines the style of the border, but only after it is activated in the HTML document with the <table border="1"> tag.

Table 5-2: CSS properties used for <table> element

Property	Description	Values
border	Determines the style of the border.	- border width (e.g., *1px*) - border line style (e.g., *solid*) - border color (e.g., *gray*)
border-collapse	Collapses the borders of adjacent cells into a single border instead of separating them.	- *collapse*
border-spacing	Determines the amount of space between the borders of adjacent cells.	- Number of pixels
padding	Determines the amount of space between cell data and the cell border.	- Number of pixels
width	Determines how far the table or cell will extend horizontally across the page.	- Number of pixels - Percentage of the browser window — number followed by percent symbol (%)
background-color	Determines the background color for table elements.	- Color name (e.g., *green*) - Hexadecimal code (e.g., *#00FF00*)
text-align	Aligns text horizontally.	*-left* *-center* *-right* *-justify*
vertical-align	Aligns content vertically.	- *top* - *bottom* - *middle*

CIW Online Resources – Online Exercise

Visit CIW Online at *http://education.Certification-Partners.com/CIW* to complete an interactive exercise that will reinforce what you have learned about this topic.

Exercise 5-2: CSS properties for all table elements

In the following lab, you will create tables using HTML5 and CSS. Suppose you notice that the content on the syb_day.html page would work well in a tabular format, which improves readability and adds visual interest. You can organize the existing content into an HTML table by adding the appropriate element structure. Then you can supply a couple sentences to introduce the table, as well as a table caption with the title for the table: "A Day in the Life of a Habitat Worker."

Lab 5-1: Creating HTML tables to organize content

In this lab, you will convert existing content into tabular format by creating an HTML5 table.

1. From **C:\CIW\Site_Dev\Lab Files\Lesson05\Lab_5-1**, copy the file **syb_day.html** and the **syb_day** folder to the **Habitat\CCYP** directory. The syb_day.html file should reside on the same level as syb.html, default.html and other Web page files.

2. Load the file **syb_day.html** into your browser. It should resemble Figure 5-2. Notice that the content is not presented in tabular format.

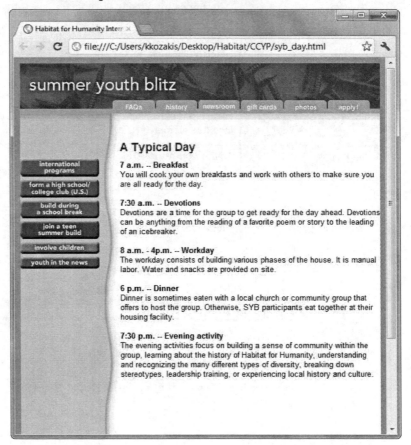

Figure 5-2: Page syb_day.html presented without table

3. Open **syb_day.html** in a text editor.

4. Search for the following line of code:

   `<h2>A Typical Day</h2>`

5. Use the **Edit | Cut** command (or **CTRL+X**) to cut all content that refers to the "*typical day*," including all text and markup tags. Start by cutting the **<p>** tag located below the line specified in the previous step, continue through the text that ends with "*experiencing local history and culture*," and also include the **
** tags and the **</p>** tag just above the closing </article> tag. (Do not cut the </article> tag.)

6. Open a second instance of Notepad, and paste the text you just cut into a new file.

7. Save this new file as **old.txt**. In later steps in this lab, you will copy the content (but not the markup) from this text file into the new table you create in syb_day.html. For the purpose of learning tables, it is best to begin by creating the table elements first, then adding content to the table later.

8. Minimize **old.txt**.

9. Maximize **syb_day.html**. Add opening and closing tags to create a table where the text once existed:

    ```
    <table>
    </table>
    ```

10. In **syb_day.html**, create some white space by entering several returns between the opening and closing <table> tags you just entered.

11. By default, tables do not render with a visible border. Give the table a border by adding the **border="1"** attribute and value to the opening **<table>** tag. You now will be able to see your work better.

12. Create a table caption that reads **A Day in the Life of a Habitat Worker**.

13. Consider the content on the original page. As you format the content into a table, you will need to label each column heading with the type of information that column will contain. What categories of information does the existing content provide? Answer the following question in the space provided: How many columns will your table need, and what will each column be titled?

    _____

14. You are now ready to create a header row for the table. Between the opening and closing <table> tags, insert a **<tr>** tag. Remember to close the table row with a **</tr>** tag, and use good coding practice by placing each new element on its own line.

15. Now, insert the necessary number of **<th>** tags between the <tr> </tr> tags to create the table header cells. When you are done, you should have three <th> tags, all properly closed with </th>.

16. The table header row will require the most tag information. When you are finished, your code should appear as follows:

    ```
    <table border="1">
    <caption>
    A Day in the Life of a Habitat Worker
    </caption>
    <tr>
    <th>Time</th>
    <th>Activity</th>
    <th>Description</th>
    </tr>
    </table>
    ```

17. Add the next row to your table. Use the **<tr> </tr>** tags again, but instead of using three sets of <th> tags within the row, use three sets of **<td>** tags to create the cells because this row is not a table header.

18. Within the <td> tags, enter the following content from old.txt:

> ***7 a.m.***
> ***Breakfast***
> ***You will cook your own breakfasts and work with others to make sure you are***
> ***all ready for the day.***

19. The next task involves centering text in table data. Because not all table data will be centered, a class must be created in CSS. The class will then be specified in the HTML document. To create the class, open **syb_day/syb_day.css**.

20. In the **syb_day.css** file, add the following rule:

```
td.center
{
text-align:center;
}
```

21. Add the ***center*** class to center the content that appears in the first two cells you specify with <td> tags. When you are finished, your code should appear as follows:

```
<tr>
<td class="center">7 a.m.</td>
<td class="center">Breakfast</td>
<td>You will cook your own breakfasts and work with others to make sure you
are all ready for the day.</td>
</tr>
```

22. Insert the following text, with <p> </p> tags, just above the table and just below the phrase *A Typical Day*:

```
<p>Why is our program so popular? Because it gives you the opportunity to help
others. Below are some examples of activities.</p>
```

23. Save the file, then view your page in a browser. You should see a table caption introducing a table with three columns, a header row and one row of information, as shown in Figure 5-3.

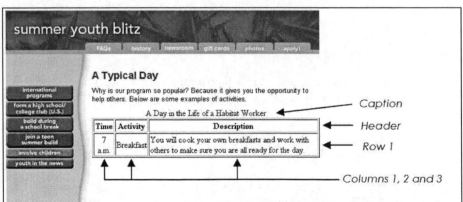

Figure 5-3: Page syb_day.html with content in tabular format

24. If your table does not render correctly, review your code and make any necessary changes. When the page renders correctly in the browser, validate your code at **http://validator.w3.org**. The file is short at this point so errors will be easier to locate and correct.

25. Add four more rows to your table, so that you have five rows containing the content you cut from the page. (This content is now in the old.txt file you created, so copy it

from there.) Center the content that appears in the first two cells you specify with
<td> tags in each row.

26. Notice that the <tr> tags add rows, but that the <td> tags add cells to contain
content. The content in each cell is categorized by the column headers, which are
defined by the <th> tags.

27. To ensure the table font matches the document font, add the following code to the
syb_day.css file. Tables often look better when the table text is slightly smaller than
the surrounding text, so the font size will be adjusted from 80% to 70%. The width of
the table will be set to 90% of the section width so that a margin appears:

```
table
{
font-family: Arial, Helvetica, Geneva, Swiss, sans-serif;
font-size: 70%;
width:90%;
}
```

28. To center the table in the Web page section, a *class* must be created in **syb_day.css**,
similar to centering an image. The *margin-left* and *margin-right* properties are set to
auto. This automatically creates equal spacing on both sides of the object, whether it
is a table or an image.

```
table.center
{
margin-left: auto;
margin-right: auto;
}
```

29. Add the center *class* to the **syb_day.html** file by adding the following code in bold:

```
<table class="center" border="1">
```

30. To improve readability, add five pixels of padding to all table data. This will create
white space around the data. Enter the following code in **syb_day.css**:

```
td
{
padding:5px;
}
```

31. The last adjustment will be the width of the "Time" column. The table would look
better if the text "a.m." and "p.m." were on the same line as the time (e.g., 7 a.m.).
The width can be adjusted by adding a *class* that specifies the header's width in
pixels. Add the following code to **syb_day.css**:

```
th.width
{
width:50px;
}
```

32. Add the *class* to the **syb_day.html** file:

```
<th class="width">Time</th>
```

33. When you are finished, save **syb_day.html** and **syb_day.css** and load them into a
browser. If your table docs not render as expected, review your code. Edit the code as
necessary until it renders as shown in Figure 5-4.

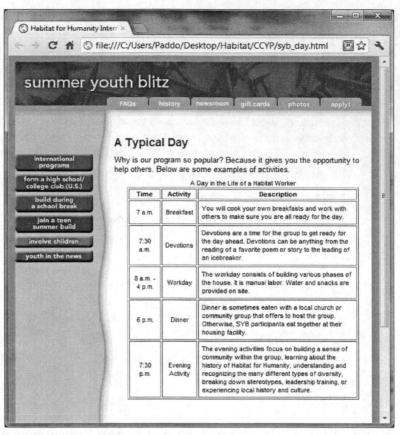

Figure 5-4: Page syb_day.html with table

34. Validate your code and resolve any issues. You will edit this table further in a later lab.

In this lab, you converted existing content into tabular format by creating an HTML table.

OBJECTIVE
2.1.5: HTML tables

Table and Data Alignment Options

Frequently you will want to align cell content in a manner that differs from the default alignment. Following are the defaults for table data:

- Content in table header cells is aligned both horizontally and vertically to the center of the cell.

- Content in table data cells is aligned horizontally to the left and vertically to the center.

Table data alignment can drastically affect the look of a table. For instance, if each row uses a different horizontal alignment, the table may not appeal to viewers. For the best visual result, align content consistently within columns.

So far, you have examined only tables with single lines of cell content. Now consider the example in Figure 5-5.

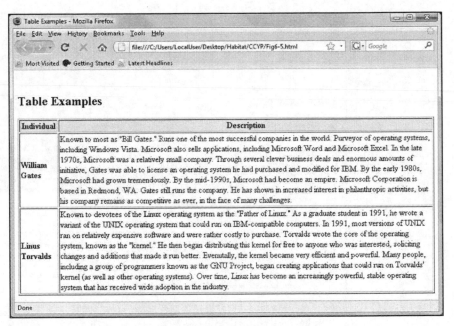

Figure 5-5: Alignment of cell content

You can change the alignment for an individual cell or for an entire row. The CSS property you use to specify horizontal alignment is *text-align*. For vertical alignment, use the *vertical-align* property.

Either of the following code samples in Figure 5-6 could be used to produce the alignment shown in Figure 5-7.

HTML document code:

```
<tr>
<td>
William Gates
</td>
```

Corresponding CSS document code:

```
tr
{
vertical-align:top;
}
```

HTML document code:

```
<tr>
<td class="valign">
William Gates
</td>
```

Corresponding CSS document code:

```
td.valign
{
vertical-align:top;
}
```

Figure 5-6: Two ways to change vertical alignment

The code example on the left in the preceding figure sets the alignment of the entire row to "top", meaning that all cell content in that row will start at the top of the cell. The code example on the right creates a *class* named *valign* that specifies a vertical alignment only for the cell containing "William Gates". This *class* can be used in any <td> tag.

The cell to the right of "William Gates" is already aligned to the top because it is completely full, so the appearance generated by either choice will match that shown in Figure 5-7. (The second row was left unchanged for contrast.)

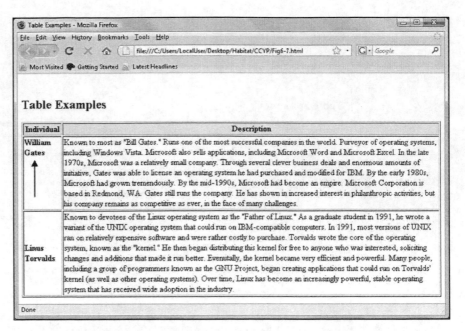

Figure 5-7: After specifying vertical alignment affecting cell or row containing "William Gates"

You can also align the contents of any table cell horizontally to the left, right or center.

OBJECTIVE
2.1.5: HTML tables

Height and Width of Table Elements

You can change the height or width of the table and individual cells by specifying pixel or percentage values. Examine Figure 5-8.

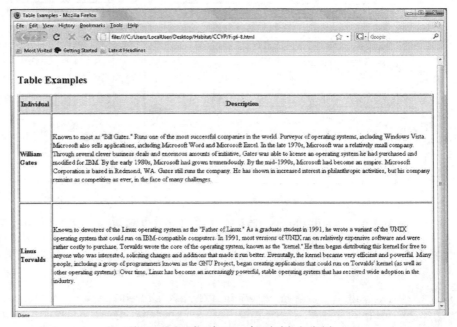

Figure 5-8: After increasing table height

In the preceding figure, the table rows increased in size because the *height* property of the CSS *table* rule was set to 500 pixels. You could also specify a percentage of the browser window. Note that the additional height was equally distributed among the various rows.

In Figure 5-9, the *height* property has been deleted from the CSS *table* rule, and is set only for the cell containing the word *Description*. The cell height has been set to 75 pixels. If you mistakenly set multiple values in multiple cells, the highest value will take precedence; the order of entries does not matter.

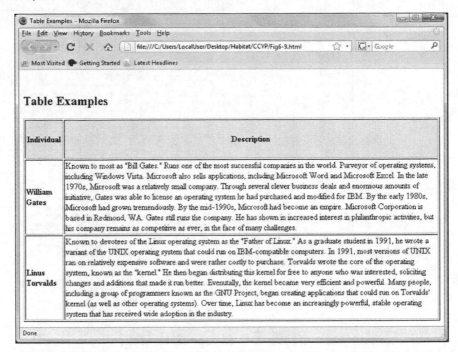

Figure 5-9: After specifying and adding CSS class td.height {height: 75px;} *in table cell*

In Figure 5-10, all *height* properties have been deleted, except that the width of the first column (with the title *Individual*) has been set to 50 percent of the browser window.

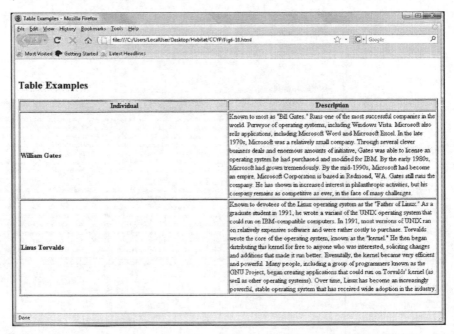

Figure 5-10: After specifying and adding CSS class th.width {width:50%;} *to first <th> tag*

In Figure 5-11, the table width has been changed to 70 percent of the screen and the table has been centered.

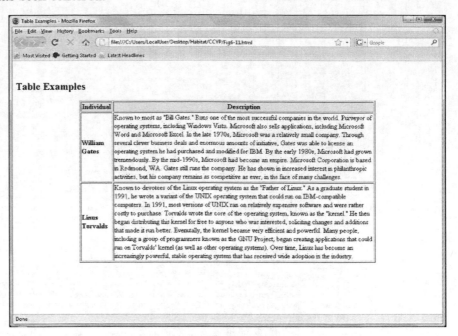

Figure 5-11: After centering table

OBJECTIVE
2.1.5: HTML tables

Column and Row Spanning

Sometimes you will want a column to span across two or more cells. In other cases, you may need a cell to span more than one row. Figure 5-12 demonstrates a cell that horizontally spans two columns.

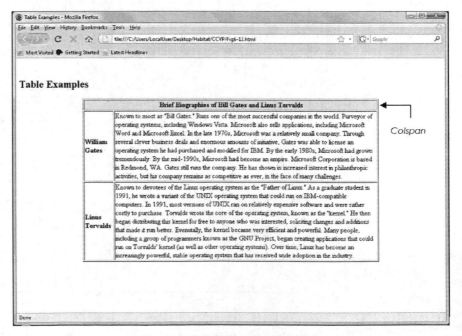

Figure 5-12: Using colspan attribute

The following code created the spanned column in the preceding figure:

```
<tr>
<th colspan="2">
Brief Biographies of Bill Gates and Linus Torvalds
</th>
</tr>
```

Notice that one of the <th> headings has also been removed. This change is logical because now one <th> tag is occupying both spaces. Figure 5-13 shows a cell (i.e., column) that vertically spans two rows.

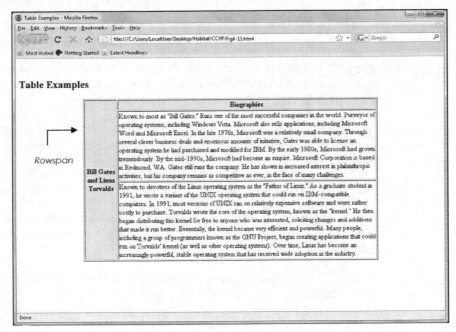

Figure 5-13: Using rowspan attribute

The following code created the spanned row in the preceding figure:

```
<tr>
<th rowspan="3">
Bill Gates and Linus Torvalds
</th>
<th>
Biographies
</th>
</tr>
```

Note that the *colspan* and *rowspan* attributes can also be used with the <td> tag.

In the following lab, you will customize an HTML table. Suppose you want to add some formatting to your Web page table and the content organized within it. You can use CSS font style, color, alignment and spacing options to modify the table's appearance. Your formatting choices will improve the table's readability, as well as make it more visually exciting.

Lab 5-2: Customizing HTML tables with CSS formatting

OBJECTIVE
2.1.5: HTML tables

In this lab, you will modify table data with formatting options to make it more aesthetically pleasing.

1. Open **syb_day.html** and **syb_day/syb_day.css** in an editor. If necessary, you can also copy them from your student Lab 5-2 folder and paste them in your Habitat/CCYP folder, similar to step 1 of the previous lab.

2. Find the table caption, which reads *A Day in the Life of a Habitat Worker*. Notice that it is in a standard font. Add the **<strong>** tag to make this caption bold.

3. Use CSS to change the first **<tr>** element so the background color of the table headers is light blue *("#6699FF")*. Load the page in a browser to see how it renders, then validate your code at ***http://validator.w3.org***.

4. Find the first **<th>** heading tag. Change the **width** property used in its CSS *class* to a value of **"93"**. Load the page in a browser to see how it renders, then validate your code.

5. Change the **padding** attribute in the CSS table data (*td*) rule to a value of **"3"**.

6. Experiment with other modifications and formatting additions to the table. For instance, add background colors to table cells and rows, change the font colors, or collapse the border so only one line appears around each cell.

7. In the HTML document, insert a blank line between the end of the table and the footer section by adding a **
** tag immediately after the closing table tag </table>. Load the page in a browser to see how it renders, then validate your code.

8. You have now placed all of the page's content into a table. However, the changes you made may have caused the yellow navigation (*nav*) sidebar graphic (navbg_04.gif) to be too short or too long for the page. Open the style sheet and find the **nav** and **article** entries.

9. Adjust the **height:** value of the *nav* and *article* entries so that the yellow sidebar graphic is the same length as the table. The height values should be the same to ensure the footer is evenly spaced beneath them. Experiment with the setting until the *nav* and *article* sections look even when rendered in the browser.

10. When you are finished, your page may resemble Figure 5-14, depending on how you experimented and customized your table.

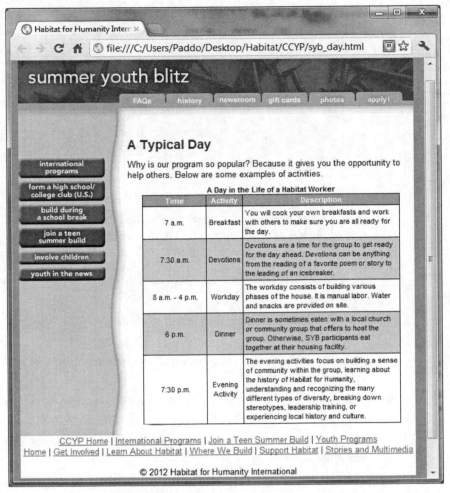

Figure 5-14: Page syb_day.html with customized formatting

11. **If time permits:** Remove the border around the table and refresh your browser. Use the **border="1"** attribute and value in the **<table>** tag to reapply the border.

In this lab, you customized the appearance of a table and its content.

HTML Tables vs. CSS Page Structure

HTML tables have often been used to create content structure for entire Web pages. In HTML5, however, you should not use tables to structure a page. Instead, the W3C recommends that you use the new HTML5 document structure tags.

As you learned earlier in this course, HTML5 with CSS has introduced a more effective and simple way to structure Web pages. Instead of using the <div> tag as a "jack of all trades" element with its array of attributes, the developers of HTML5 created specific elements to define the document structure. These elements include <header>, <footer>, <nav>, <article> and <aside>. Review the simple Web page structure shown in Figure 5-15.

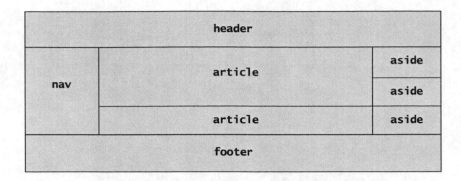

Figure 5-15: Sample HTML5 structural elements of Web page

As shown in the figure, a developer can structure the Web page with elements that are easily interpreted and native to any HTML5-compliant browser, regardless of whether the browser is on a mobile device, laptop or tablet. The structure elements can be defined as:

- **<header>** — Top of the Web page, similar to the header in a word-processing document.

- **<nav>** — Defines navigation links, such as hypertext menus to access various pages of the Web site.

- **<article>** — Web site content, such as company services, articles, blogs, images and videos.

- **<aside>** — Content that is "aside" from the article content, such as advertisements or news feeds.

- **<footer>** — Bottom of the Web page, similar to the footer in a word-processing document.

The header might contain the company logo; the footer could include copyright and contact info; the nav section may contain navigational links to other resources on the site; the articles could be blogs, tweets, video, social networking posts, news articles, or any other content; and the aside could be advertisements, highlighted resource links, and even more content.

Tech Tip

A search engine will automatically rank a page lower if the page uses tables for structure. Use the HTML5 structure elements and CSS instead. Also, if you overuse a table on a page, you may also experience problems. Use tables tastefully and sparingly.

CIW Online Resources – Course Mastery

Visit CIW Online at *http://education.Certification-Partners.com/CIW* to take the Course Mastery review of this lesson or lesson segment.

SDA Lesson 5

Case Study

To Use Tables or Not To Use Tables

An-Mei supervised a Web development team responsible for converting the company Web site's HTML 4.0 code into HTML5. She began the project by reviewing the existing Web pages and code with her team.

An-Mei and her team found that most of the existing pages had used HTML tables to structure all content, rather than only the content that lent itself to a tabular format.

An-Mei chose to limit the use of tables whenever possible, reserving them for content that required a structured layout, such as numbers, dates and other items often viewed within spreadsheets or complex lists.

An-Mei directed the team to remove all HTML tables used for page structuring, and to replace the structure using the HTML5 structure elements instead. Although this change required a significant investment of time, the team found that the time was well spent. Without the table structuring, all pages could be quickly updated, and future modifications to the site content were easier. Upper management was pleased that Web site updates were implemented more readily than in the past.

*　　　*　　　*

As a class, discuss the ways that HTML tables can improve a Web page.

* What types of content benefit from a tabular structure? What types of content do not?

* Are there any advantages in using an invisible HTML table to structure an entire Web page? Why did Web developers use them for so many years? What disadvantages does the table structure pose?

* Is such a situation likely to occur in the workplace when you are dealing with a business or organization Web site? Why or why not?

Lesson Summary

Application project

Tables are useful for presenting information that naturally lends itself to tabular format. HTML allows you to do this. In the past, tables have been used to add structure to a Web page. However, the W3C recommends against this practice for HTML5, so you should use the HTML5 structure elements instead.

Visit *www.w3schools.com* and *www.w3.org*, and review the <table> element. Then browse some sites, visiting some that include tables. See how other Web developers use tables to organize content. Do you think tables provide an effective presentation? What types of content are best suited for tabular presentation?

Skills review

In this lesson, you learned to create and manipulate HTML tables. You used the basic structure tags to generate a table, rows and individual cells. You also aligned cell content, learned how to span cell content across rows and columns, and added background colors to both tables and cells. Finally, you learned that manipulating a border can dramatically affect the appearance of your table.

Now that you have completed this lesson, you should be able to:

✓ 2.1.5: Design and format HTML tables to present information in an organized way.

CIW Practice Exams

Visit CIW Online at *http://education.Certification-Partners.com/CIW* to take the Practice Exams assessment covering the objectives in this lesson.

SDA Objective 2.01 Review

Note that some objectives may be only partially covered in this lesson.

Lesson 5 Review

1. The size of an HTML table can be modified by specifying measurements in either of which two units of measure?

    _____

2. What element can be used instead of the <table> element to create a simple table by preserving spacing and line breaks in preformatted text?

    _____

3. What components of table appearance can be formatted using the CSS *text-align* property or by creating a CSS *class* that specifies either a *right, left* or *center* justification value?

    _____

    _____

4. What is the default alignment of the content in table data cells?

    _____

5. What attributes are used to span a single cell across multiple rows or columns, respectively?

    _____

Lesson 6:
Web Forms

Objectives

By the end of this lesson, you will be able to:

- 2.4.1: Construct and test HTML forms.

- 2.4.2: Identify ways that CGI scripts can parse and transmit information from a form, including e-mail, FTP, HTTP, HTTPS.

- 2.4.3: Diagram a fundamental CGI session.

- 2.18.4: Activate features provided by managed services (e.g., CGI, forms).

Pre-Assessment Questions

1. Which form field offers a round option field in a group of two or more mutually exclusive options?

   a. Submit button
   b. Check box
   c. Scrolling select list
   d. Radio button

2. Which type of button clears all form data and sets all form fields back to the default values?

   a. Default button
   b. Radio button
   c. Reset button
   d. Submit button

3. What tag is used in a select list to identify the text that will appear as list choices?

   _____

Introduction to Web Forms

Web sites use forms to obtain input from users. You can create several types of fields in one form to collect various types of user input. Such input can include the user's name, address and credit card number, for example. The information a user enters into the form is then submitted to a server where it is stored and/or processed.

After a user has entered information into a Web form, he or she clicks the form's Submit button. Submitting the form uploads or e-mails the user's information to the receiving server. Many Web forms also provide a Reset button that clears entered data instead of submitting it, and resets the form fields to the default values.

Forms are of little use without an application on a Web server to process the submitted information. CGI scripts perform this information processing. The following sections discuss the ways that CGI scripts receive and process Web form information. The rest of the lesson will teach you how to develop Web forms using HTML.

CIW Online Resources – Movie Clips

Visit CIW Online at http://education.Certification-Partners.com/CIW to watch a movie clip about this topic.

Lesson 6: Web Forms

Web Forms and CGI

To be truly functional, a form requires the use of a **Common Gateway Interface (CGI)** program to process the script. CGI is the *de facto* standard, but other technologies can be used to process forms, such as Active Server Pages (ASP) and JavaServer Pages (JSP). CGI programs use **server-side script**. By contrast, **client-side script** is executed on the client computer or browser.

A CGI script residing on a server performs two important functions:

- It receives data from a Web browser.

- Then it processes and formats the data.

Without some sort of CGI script running on the server, the server cannot receive Web form data. Most CGI scripts do more than just receive data; they also remove extraneous information (such as delimiters) and format the data. Many scripts, servers and utilities are available for UNIX, Macintosh and Windows platforms to simplify this process. Such scripting utilities are available commercially, or as freeware or shareware.

Diagramming a CGI session

The following elements are necessary for a CGI session:

- Web browser

- CGI script (a file that contains a programming language such as Perl or PHP)

- Web form

- Web server, with a CGI interpreter

Common Gateway Interface (CGI)
A program that processes data submitted by the user. Allows a Web server to pass control to a software application, based on user request. The application receives and organizes data, then returns it in a consistent format.

server-side script
Code that resides on a server to help process Web form input. Server-side CGI scripts are commonly written in Perl.

client-side script
Code embedded into an HTML page and downloaded by a user; resides on the client and helps process Web form input. Common client-side scripting languages include JavaScript and VBScript.

OBJECTIVE
2.4.3 Diagramming CGI sessions

A CGI script remains on a Web server. The Web forms you will learn to create in this lesson allow users to upload information to your Web server, where information can be processed and acted upon. Actions taken by the Web server and CGI interpreter can include:

- Storing information in a database (for example, bank account updates).

- Searching a database for a product (for example, a book or movie at Amazon.com).

- Sending processed information back to the end user (for example, a new bank account balance or a confirmation that a book was shipped).

Figure 6-1 illustrates the Web form data processing performed via CGI.

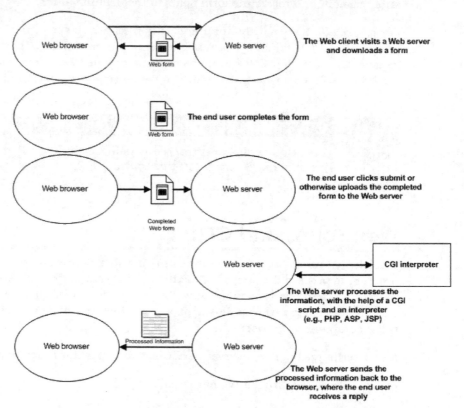

Figure 6-1: CGI session

OBJECTIVE
2.4.2: CGI scripts

Parsing data: Form handling, name=value pairs and CGI

You now understand that a CGI script residing on a server receives data from a Web browser, then processes the data into human-readable format (or any other format you require). Before a CGI script receives any data, however, a user must enter the data into a Web form and submit it. Figure 6-2 shows a simple Web form.

OBJECTIVE
2.18.4: Managed services

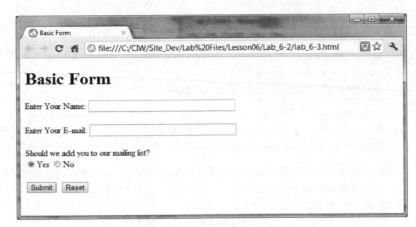

Figure 6-2: Simple HTML form

In this figure, a form allows the user to provide his name and e-mail address, then indicate whether he wants to be placed on the company's mailing list. When the user clicks the Submit Query button, the browser sends the information entered in this form to the Web server as a raw text string.

The basic element of a raw text string is a name=value pair. The *name* attribute of the <form> element organizes information input by the user into name=value pairs. For example, the Web form in the preceding figure organizes user input according to the following code. Pay special attention to the code shown in bold:

```
Enter Your Name: <input type="text" name="Name" size="40"/>

Enter Your E-mail: <input type="text" name="Email" size="40"/>

Should we add you to our mailing list? <br/>
<input type="radio" name="AddToList" value="yes"/> Yes
<input type="radio" name="AddToList" value="no"/> No
```

When the browser sends this data, it will use the *name* attribute values "Name", "Email" and "AddToList" as the basis for creating the raw text string. You can specify any words as *name* values. In this example, the server receives a raw text string that resembles the following:

```
Name=Dimitri+Pappas&Email=student50@class.com&AddToList=yes
```

This raw text string consists of name=value pairs, delimited by ampersands (&). In a name=value pair, entered spaces are replaced with plus signs (+). If a form field is left empty, only the first part of the name=value pair will be returned. For example, if this user left the mailing list option blank, the corresponding name=value pair would return "Email=" without any information after the equal symbol.

After the server receives this information, a CGI script can parse and format the raw text string into a human-readable format similar to the following:

Name:	Dimitri Pappas
E-Mail:	student50@class.com
Mailing List:	Yes

The Web form you will create in this lesson will use Name and Email, as well as other name values that correspond to their functions. Now that you understand how a basic script processes Web form data, consider a commonly used CGI script: FormMail.

Applied example: FormMail

One example of a CGI script is the venerable FormMail script, written by Matt Wright. This script has existed in various versions since 1997. It is written in Practical Extraction and Report Language (Perl) and has the file name FormMail.pl.

FormMail is designed to receive information from a Web form via the Perl interpreter. The script then sends the form information to you via e-mail. You simply check your e-mail to receive results from the script. You can learn more about FormMail at Matt's Script Archive (*www.scriptarchive.com/formmail.html*).

FormMail is popular for many reasons, including the following:

- It is available free of charge from Matt's Script Archive (MSA).

- It is written in Perl, which allows developers to use a free CGI interpreter available in many places, including *www.cpan.org*. Most modern operating systems allow the Perl interpreter to be installed, making Perl one of the more ubiquitous languages. The combination of a free, powerful Perl interpreter and a free, well-written FormMail script is widely appealing.

- FormMail is easy to customize. Wright specifically designed FormMail for ease of use: The developer simply modifies a few portions of the script and it is ready to perform whatever tasks a particular Web form requires.

After you download FormMail, you perform the following simple steps:

- Install Perl on your Web server. Many Web servers already have Perl installed.

- Define the FormMail variables so that the script is capable of receiving information and sending it to you.

- Give executable permissions to the FormMail.pl script on your Web server.

- Refer to the FormMail.pl script in your Web form.

- Wait for users to visit your site, and then check your e-mail for results.

Many organizations and businesses use the FormMail script for various beneficial purposes. Some companies have made money through Web-based sales. Other sites have used the script to help charities and other worthy causes.

Security concerns

Spam has become a concern for most Web users. Some unscrupulous individuals have taken advantage of the FormMail script because older versions could be fooled into sending e-mail to anyone. Some systems administrators still use older versions of the program. Other administrators improperly configure newer script versions, resulting in more spam on the Internet. You should use the latest version of FormMail, which has features that allow its use without inviting abuse from spammers.

A site called the FormMail Hall of Shame contains a list of servers that still allow spam to be sent. You can visit this site at www.softwolves.pp.se/internet/formmail_hall_of_shame/.

Other versions of FormMail

You are not limited to using the original Perl FormMail script. Alternative versions of FormMail are available for PHP (*www.dtheatre.com/scripts/formmail.php*) and ASP (*www.brainjar.com/asp/formmail*), for example.

In the following lab, you will work with the FormMail script. Suppose the Web development director asks what you think about adding a Web form to the company site, and whether you could enable such a form to process data. You profile some of the FormMail script's features and download the script. Then you discuss the potential capabilities with the director. If she decides that a form should be added to the Web site, you can program the FormMail script you downloaded to process information obtained from the Web form.

  Lab 6-1: Studying the FormMail script

OBJECTIVE
2.4.2: CGI scripts

In this lab, you will review the FormMail script and its features.

1. Open a browser and visit ***www.scriptarchive.com/formmail.html***, which is the FormMail home page. Review the description of FormMail, including the Readme file and the FAQ page.

2. Navigate to the **C:\CIW\Site_Dev\Lab Files\Lesson06\Lab_6-1** directory, and copy the **formmail.zip** file to your Desktop.

    *Note: If necessary, go to **www.scriptarchive.com/formmail.html** to visit the FormMail home page and obtain the FormMail script.*

3. Unzip the FormMail file, and extract the **Readme** and **FormMail.pl** files.

4. Open the **Readme** file in WordPad or Notepad.

5. Review the *Necessary Variables* section. This section describes the variables that you must change if you use this script with a Web server.

6. Close the **Readme** file.

7. Open the **FormMail.pl** file in WordPad or Notepad.

8. Review the script and identify the following elements of the script:

    *   **$mailprog** — specifies your e-mail server program. This program could be for Windows or another operating system. Linux/UNIX servers often use Sendmail (*www.sendmail.com/sm/open_source/*) or Postfix (*www.postfix.org*).

    *   **@referers** — helps control who can use the FormMail script.

    *   **@valid_ENV** — allows you to specify the environment variables that will be sent with the script. Remember that FormMail is designed to send to you, via e-mail, the form information submitted by your site visitors. You can use the @valid_ENV section to get information about the host that used your script, such as the user agent (e.g., a Web browser) used to generate the request or the IP address of the user's system. The @valid_ENV element is added as a security measure so that you can learn about the submissions you receive. However, be aware that a malicious user can spoof this information.

- **@recipients** — includes the recipient field (required) and additional optional fields that allow you to control the way that information submitted by users is processed.

9. When you are finished reviewing the FormMail script, discuss the following questions as a class:

- Why is the FormMail script popular?

- How could you use this script in your own situation?

In this lab, you reviewed the FormMail script.

Now that you understand the basic processes and conventions of a Web form, you can begin studying and coding individual form fields.

HTML5 and Forms

The basic form elements and attributes for form creation in HTML5 are little changed from HTML 4.01. The main differences are:

1. Cascading Style Sheets (CSS) are used for all form styles.

2. Advanced features are now available, such as new <form> elements and attributes, and <input> types for better control of validation and input control.

At the time of this writing, many of the new elements and attributes are not supported by most browsers, even the ones that support HTML5. As HTML5 continues to evolve, these new elements and attributes will be adopted.

To learn more about the new HTML5 form elements and attributes, visit the W3Schools HTML5 Forms section at www.w3schools.com/html5/ and click the links in the HTML5 Forms navigation bar.

OBJECTIVE
2.4.1: Creating HTML forms

Basic Tags for Creating Web Forms

You can create a user-input Web form on a Web page by placing HTML code to create various form fields in between a set of HTML <form> tags. Such forms are essential for receiving input from users and for e-commerce.

All elements of the form must be contained in the <form> element section in order for the form to function and process properly. There are many types of fields that you can place in a form, depending on the type of info you want to elicit from users. This section describes the basic HTML tags used to create a Web form. In the sections that follow, you will add a field type to your Web form with each successive lab.

The <form> tag

The HTML <form> tag creates a user-input Web form by encompassing all the content and fields of the form on the page. The <form> tag is a container tag, so it requires both opening and closing tags. In some browsers, if you fail to supply the closing </form> tag, the form will not render. Internet Explorer displays form fields even if no <form> tag is present. However, users would be unable to submit any information because the <form> tag is required to instruct the browser where to send data.

Following is sample syntax for a <form> tag:

```
<form
    method="post"
    action="http://www.anyserver.com/cgi-bin/scriptfile">
            <input .../>
            <select> ... </select>
</form>
```

For now, ignore the <input> and <select> elements.

The <form> element has two main attributes associated with it:

- *method* — specifies which method the browser will use to send form data to a Web server

- *action* — specifies the name and location of the CGI script used to process the form

These attributes are required in the <form> tag in order to process data that users submit in the form.

The method attribute

The *method* attribute specifies the method by which the browser will send form data to a Web server. The *method* attribute takes two values:

- "get" — Form data is appended to the URL of the Web page for use in a query string. This method sends information in cleartext and is thus less secure.

- "post" — Form data is posted to the URL specified by the *action* attribute. Post is the preferred method for sending form data. It can send more characters, although sometimes post requires more processing by the CGI script.

The action attribute

The *action* attribute specifies the name and location of the CGI script used to process the form. The contents of the form will be processed by the script and acted upon according to the instructions in the script.

CIW Online Resources – Online Exercise

Visit CIW Online at *http://education.Certification-Partners.com/CIW* to complete an interactive exercise that will reinforce what you have learned about this topic.

Exercise 6-1: The <form> tag

The <input>, <select> and <textarea> tags

You can use the <input>, <select> and <textarea> tags to create form fields by placing them between the <form> </form> tags.

The <input> tag and the type attribute

The <input> tag is not a container tag; it stands alone. You use <input> to create text boxes, check boxes, radio buttons, and the Submit and Reset buttons.

The <input> element takes the *type* attribute. The value you use with the *type* attribute designates the form field type as a text box, a radio button, a Submit or Reset button, a password field or a check box. For example, to create a radio button with the <input> element, you would use the following syntax:

```
<input type="radio" name="AddToList"/>
```

You can change the value of *type* to create other buttons or fields. You can also add other attributes to customize the field's behavior. To create a password field, for example, you would use the following code:

```
Enter Your Password: <input type="password" name="Password" size="14"/>
```

You will learn more about the *name* and *value* attributes shortly.

The <select> tag

The <select> tag is a container tag used to create single-option and multiple-option select lists. Following is an example of <select>:

```
How often do you want to be updated about Habitat for Humanity?<br/>
<select name="Frequency">
<option>Once a week</option>
<option>Once or twice a month</option>
<option>Once a month</option>
<option value="NotAtAll" >Never</option>
</select>
```

When using the <select> tag, you may want to allow users to select more than one option from the list. If so, you must use the *multiple* attribute with "multiple" as the value. For example, consider the following HTML code:

```
<p>Which countries have you worked in?</p>
<select name="Countries" multiple="multiple" size="4">
<option>Australia</option>
<option>New Zealand</option>
<option>England</option>
<option>France</option>
<option>India</option>
<option>China</option>
</select>
```

This code allows users to select multiple countries, rather than just one.

The <textarea> tag

The <textarea> container tag creates scrolling text area spaces. Users can enter multiple lines of text into a text area; it is larger and allows more input than a text box. Because it is a container tag, you can enter default text between the opening and closing tags, and it will appear in the text area until the user types their input into the field.

CIW Online Resources – Course Mastery

Visit CIW Online at *http://education.Certification-Partners.com/CIW* to take the Course Mastery review of this lesson or lesson segment.

SDA Lesson 6 - Part A

Web Form Fields

Table 6-1 describes each type of form field discussed in this lesson.

Table 6-1: Web form fields

Form Field	Description	Example
Text box	A text field into which a user can enter characters.	Name: [ ]
Radio button	Round option buttons in a group of two or more mutually exclusive options.	**Do you know carpentry?** ◉ Yes ○ No
Check box	Square boxes in a group of two or more non-exclusive options.	**Skills (check all that apply):** ☑ Carpentry ☑ Cement working ☐ Medical care
Single-option select list	A drop-down list of two or more options from which a single selection can be made.	**How often do you want to be updated about Habitat for Humanity?** Once a week ▼ — Once a week / Once or twice a month / Once a month / Never
Multiple-option select list	An exposed list of two or more options, optionally scrollable, from which the user can make multiple selections.	**Please indicate your interests (select all that apply):** Swimming / Diving / Kayaking / Literature
Text area	A scrolling text field into which the user can enter multiple lines of text.	**Comments:** I am looking forward to helping!
Password field	A text box that visually masks the entered characters as asterisks.	**Enter your password:** [********]
File upload	A button and field that allow users to navigate to and select a local file for uploading or other purposes (for example, to validate HTML files).	Choose your file here: [C:\my_application.pdf] [Browse...]

Table 6-1: Web form fields (cont'd)

Form Field	Description	Example
Submit button	A button that, when clicked, causes the form's action statement to process. Labeled "Submit" or "Submit Query" by default, but can display any label.	Submit
Reset button	A button that, when clicked, clears all form data and sets all form fields back to the default values for those fields. Labeled "Reset" by default, but can display any label.	Reset

The value names for each type of form field will be discussed shortly. Figure 6-3 depicts several form fields on a Web page form.

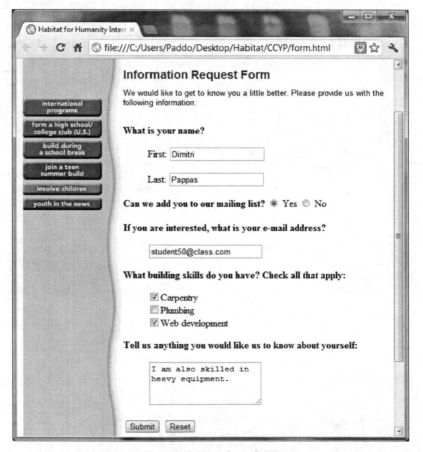

Figure 6-3: Web form fields

Many Web forms use form fields much more sparingly, as shown in Figure 6-4.

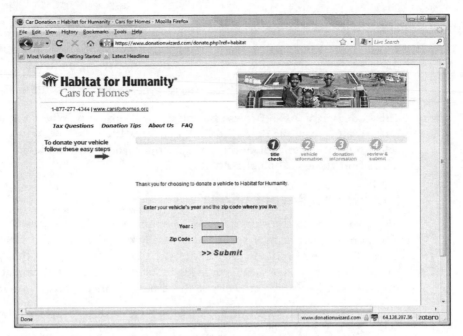

Figure 6-4: Sparing use of Web form fields

In the preceding figure, notice that a small form is embedded within other Web page content. This brief form allows Habitat for Humanity to determine if a Certificate of Title is required to transfer your vehicle donation.

Forms and the *name* attribute

All form field elements share an attribute: *name*. The *name* attribute identifies information you receive from a user and associates it with a value you specify. The *name* attribute helps you organize user input. For example, you could use a series of check boxes to learn about a user's preferences for gardening, sailing and biking, and you could name the group of boxes "Interests." Thus when you receive information from the Web form, the names in your results clearly indicate the user's choices. That is, if the user checks the "sailing" check box, you will receive the following information: *Interests=sailing*.

Text boxes

A text box is used to collect a single line of data from the user, such as name, e-mail or address information. The text box is the most common form field.

The syntax for creating a text box is as follows:

```
<input type="text" name="FieldName"/>
```

If you want the text box to appear with some default text inside, use the additional *value* attribute as shown:

```
<input type="text" name="FieldName" value="DefaultText"/>
```

Additionally, you can use a *size* attribute to specify the width of the text box in characters. The *size* attribute has no effect on the amount of text the user can enter; it restricts only the visual appearance of the field. Contrast this with the *maxlength* attribute. The value of *maxlength* restricts user entries to the specified number of characters; it has no effect on the display width of the field.

File upload

You can allow your site's users to upload files to your site using a Web form. Simply use the "file" value of the *type* attribute to the <input> tag as follows:

```
Provide your resume here: <input type="file" name="UploadedFile"/>
```

This code will create a Browse button on the Web form. When a user clicks the Browse button, a Choose File dialog box will appear, which the user can use to navigate to and select a local file for uploading. An accompanying text box displays the path and file name that the user has chosen.

Submit and Reset buttons

When you specify the <input> tag's *type* attribute value as "reset" or "submit", you create a button that performs a specific action. Clicking the Submit button sends the data from all fields in the form to be processed by the *action* specified in the <form> tag. Clicking the Reset button clears all form fields instead of submitting the data, and resets fields to their default settings. You will use these buttons in the forms you create in this lesson.

The labs in this course provide an overview of the usage and syntax of individual form fields. The action attribute used in the <form> tag will point to an HTML test engine that provides a form response to your browser. Many test engines are available on the Internet that can be helpful for testing form code.

In the following series of labs, you will create a Web form with a variety of form field types. Suppose the Web development director was encouraged by the information you provided her about using the FormMail script for Web form processing. She has decided that a form could be a useful addition to the Web site, and she assigns you to design a model for the Web form. The director will use your model in discussions with upper management, marketing and sales associates to gather input about the types of information that should be collected from your Web site visitors. So you consider the various form fields that you can demonstrate in your model, and the types of user information that each field is most effective for collecting.

Lab 6-2: Creating a simple Web form in HTML

OBJECTIVE
2.4.1: Creating HTML forms

In this lab, you will create a basic Web form using the HTML <form> and <input> tags. The *action* attribute in the <form> tag will point to a public test engine that you can use to check your form output. You would never use this URL in an actual production setting; use it only to verify that your form is functioning as expected.

OBJECTIVE
2.18.4: Managed services

1. **Editor:** From **C:\CIW\Site_Dev\Lab Files\Lesson06\Lab_6-2**, open the file **lab_6-2.txt**.

2. **Editor:** Enter the source code indicated in bold:

```
<!DOCTYPE html>
<html>

<head>
<meta name="Keywords" content="CIW, Web Foundations Associate, Example"/>
<meta name="Description" content="For the CIW Web Foundations Associate
courses"/>
<meta charset="utf-8"/>
<!-- <link rel="stylesheet" type="text/css" href="myform.css"/> -->
<title>Basic Form</title>
</head>
```

```
<body>
<h1>Basic Form</h1>

<form
    method="post"
    action="http://ss1.ciwcertified.com/cgi-bin/process.pl">

Enter Your Name: <input type="text" name="Name" size="40"/>
<br/>
<br/>
Enter Your E-mail: <input type="text" name="Email" size="40"/>
<br/>
<br/>
<br/>
<input type="submit"/>
<input type="reset"/>

</form>

</body>
</html>
```

3. **Editor:** Save the file as **lab_6-2.html**.

4. **Browser:** Open the file **lab_6-2.html**. Your display should resemble Figure 6-5.

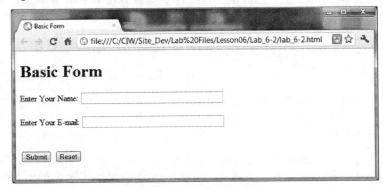

Figure 6-5: Simple Web form

5. **Browser:** Enter a name and an e-mail address into the text boxes, and then click the **Submit** button. You should see in the status bar that a server connection is being made. After a few seconds (or minutes if your connection is slow), you should see the results of your input echoed back to you on a separate page, as shown in Figure 6-6.

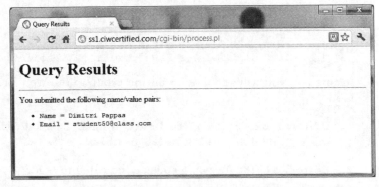

Figure 6-6: Results of submitting data to form's test engine script

6. **Browser:** Click the **Back** button in the browser to return to your Web form page.

7. **Browser:** Click the **Reset** button to clear all form data.

8. Validate your code at *http://validator.w3.org*.

In this lab, you created a simple form, and you saw a CGI script return name=value pairs from the submitted form.

Now that you are familiar with the <input> tag, you will use it to create radio buttons and check boxes in the sections that follow.

Radio buttons

Radio buttons are never used as stand-alone items. They are reserved for two or more mutually exclusive options. To ensure exclusivity, a group of radio buttons must share the same *name* attribute, although they will each use an individual value. The following example code shows two buttons representing mutually exclusive answers to the same question.

```
Do you know carpentry? <br/>
<input type="radio" checked="checked" name="KnowCarp" value="yes"/> Yes
<input type="radio" name="KnowCarp" value="no"/> No
```

The browser will render this code as shown in Figure 6-7.

Do you know carpentry?
⦿ Yes ○ No

Figure 6-7: Radio button group

Notice that in the preceding figure, the Yes option is preselected as a default. This preselection is made possible by the *checked*="checked" attribute and value, shown in the code.

In the following lab, you will add some radio buttons to the Web form. Suppose you want the model form, which you are creating for the Web development director, to demonstrate some mutually exclusive user-input options. Radio buttons provide this capability, and they are a form field type familiar to most Web users. You also consider whether to preselect one of the radio buttons as a default. A default selection can save users time or demonstrate use of the button. However, some users may neglect to change the default selection, even if the preselected choice is not their preference. Can you use this fact to your advantage?

Lab 6-3: Adding a radio button group to an HTML Web form

OBJECTIVE
2.4.1: Creating HTML forms

In this lab, you will add a radio button group to the Web form you created in the previous lab.

1. **Editor:** From **C:\CIW\Site_Dev\Lab Files\Lesson06\Lab_6-2**, open the file **lab_6-2.html** and save it as **lab_6-3.html**.

2. **Editor:** Add the following code as indicated in bold:

```
<!DOCTYPE html>
<html >

<head>
```

```
<meta name="Keywords" content="CIW, Web Foundations Associate, Example"/>
<meta name="Description" content="For the CIW Web Foundations Associate
courses"/>
<meta charset="utf-8"/>
<!-- <link rel="stylesheet" type="text/css" href="myform.css"/> -->
<title>Basic Form</title>
</head>
<body>
<h1>Basic Form</h1>

<form
    method="post"
    action="http://ss1.ciwcertified.com/cgi-bin/process.pl">

Enter Your Name: <input type="text" name="Name" size="40"/>
<br/>
<br/>
Enter Your E-Mail: <input type="text" name="Email" size="40"/>
<br/>
<br/>

Should we add you to our mailing list?<br/>
<input type="radio" name="AddToList" value="yes" checked="checked"/>Yes
<input type="radio" name="AddToList" value="no"/>No
<br/>
<br/>

<input type="submit"/>
<input type="reset"/>

</form>

</body>
</html>
```

3. **Editor:** Save the **lab_6-3.html** file.

4. **Browser:** Load your file. The radio buttons should appear as they do in Figure 6-8.

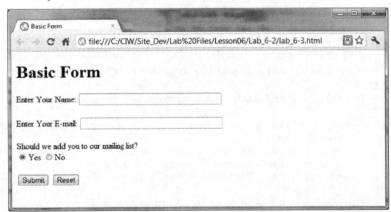

Figure 6-8: Web form after adding radio button group

5. **Browser:** Test the radio buttons by clicking the **No** button, then clicking the **Yes** button. If you can select both buttons simultaneously, you made an error in the *name* attribute for these buttons. To work properly, these buttons must use the same name for their group.

6. **Browser:** If your buttons are working, enter information into the rest of the form, then submit the form. You should see either "yes" or "no" returned for the value of the AddToList field, as shown in Figure 6-9.

Figure 6-9: Form results with radio button group

7. **Browser:** Click the Back button to return to your form page.

8. Validate your code.

In this lab, you added radio buttons to a Web form.

Check boxes

Check boxes are used for a group of non-exclusive choices. You have two options when naming check boxes, and the option you choose depends on how you plan to use the collected data. Consider the following scenario. You want a list of the user's favorite hobbies. You plan to store the user's selections in a database. Are you going to store the user's entire response, which might include multiple hobbies, in a single field? Or do you want each hobby stored in a separate field in the database? Your choice will affect how you name the fields. In the next lab, you will see the results from both options.

The syntax for creating a check box is as follows:

```
<input type="checkbox" name="groupName"/>
```

As with radio buttons, you can preselect check boxes by adding the attribute *checked*="checked" into the tag. Unlike radio buttons, however, you can preselect as many check boxes as you like because check boxes are non-exclusive.

The following code will create a check box section on a form:

```
What skills do have that can help us at Habitat for Humanity? (check all that
apply):<br/>
<input type="checkbox" name="Carpentry"/> Carpentry<br/>
<input type="checkbox" name="Plumbing"/> Plumbing<br/>
<input type="checkbox" name="Financing"/> Financing<br/>
```

This code would render as shown in Figure 6-10.

What skills do you have that can help us at Habitat for Humanity? (check all that apply):
☐ Carpentry
☐ Plumbing
☐ Financing

Figure 6-10: Check box group

In this check box example, the tags could also be written as follows:

```
<input type="checkbox" name="Skills"/> Carpentry<br/>
<input type="checkbox" name="Skills"/> Plumbing<br/>
<input type="checkbox" name="Skills"/> Financing<br/>
```

With this syntax, each choice is treated as part of a single database field named Skills. Either method is acceptable, but one will be more appropriate depending on how you plan to use the data.

In the following lab, you will add some check boxes to the Web form. Suppose you want your model form to demonstrate some non-exclusive user-input options. Check boxes provide this capability, and they are a form field type familiar to most Web users. You consider that your organization could benefit from learning about some of the skills that candidates possess. A group of check boxes is an effective form field for obtaining this type of information.

	Lab 6-4: Adding check boxes to an HTML Web form

OBJECTIVE
2.4.1: Creating HTML forms

In this lab, you will add several check boxes to the Web form you have been building in the previous labs.

1. **Editor:** From **C:\CIW\Site_Dev\Lab Files\Lesson06\Lab_6-2**, open the file **lab_6-3.html** and save it as **lab_6-4.html**.

2. **Editor:** Add the following code as indicated in bold:

```
<!DOCTYPE html>
<html>

<head>
<meta name="Keywords" content="CIW, Web Foundations Associate, Example"/>
<meta name="Description" content="For the CIW Web Foundations Associate courses"/>
<meta charset="utf-8"/>
<!-- <link rel="stylesheet" type="text/css" href="myform.css"/> -->
<title>Basic Form</title>
</head>

<body>
<h1>Basic Form</h1>

<form
    method="post"
    action="http://ss1.ciwcertified.com/cgi-bin/process.pl">

Enter Your Name: <input type="text" name="Name" size="40"/>
<br/>
<br/>
Enter Your E-mail: <input type="text" name="Email" size="40"/>
<br/>
<br/>

Should we add you to our mailing list?<br/>
<input type="radio" name="AddToList" value="yes" checked="checked"/>Yes
<input type="radio" name="AddToList" value="no"/>No
<br/>
<br/>
```

```
What skills do you have that can help us at Habitat for Humanity? (check all
that apply):<br/>
<input type="checkbox" name="Carpentry"/> Carpentry<br/>
<input type="checkbox" name="Plumbing"/> Plumbing<br/>
<input type="checkbox" name="Financing"/> Financing<br/>
<br/>
<br/>

<input type="submit"/>
<input type="reset"/>

</form>

</body>
</html>
```

3. **Editor:** Save the **lab_6-4.html** file.

4. **Browser:** Load your file. The check boxes should appear as they do in Figure 6-11.

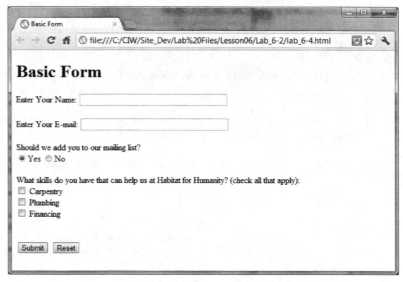

Figure 6-11: Web form after adding check boxes

5. **Browser:** Enter information into the form. Select at least one of the check box options. Then submit the form. Your results should resemble Figure 6-12.

Figure 6-12: Form results with check boxes as separate data fields

6. **Editor:** Open **lab_6-4.html**, and change the check box tags as indicated in bold:

```
What skills do you have that can help us at Habitat for Humanity? (check all
that apply):<br/>
<input type="checkbox" name="Skills"/> Carpentry<br/>
<input type="checkbox" name="Skills"/> Plumbing<br/>
<input type="checkbox" name="Skills"/> Financing<br/>
```

7. **Editor:** Save the **lab_6-4.html** file.

8. **Browser:** Click the **Back** button to return to your form page.

9. **Browser:** Submit the same data again. This time you should see slightly different results, as shown in Figure 6-13.

Figure 6-13: Form results with check boxes as group data field

10. Consider these results carefully. By naming all the check boxes the same, you made them function as a group. If you want to know whether candidates have at least one of the skills listed but you do not need to know which specific skills they checked, then organizing information in this way may help you create a large group to contact. You can use either method to configure your check boxes based on which best suits your needs.

11. Change the check box tags' *name* attribute values back to ***Carpentry***, ***Plumbing*** and ***Financing***, respectively.

12. Validate your code.

In this lab, you added check boxes to a Web form.

Select lists

Select lists are drop-down lists of predetermined options. Depending on the settings, these lists can allow single or multiple selections.

Single-option select list

The syntax for creating a drop-down single-option select list is as follows:

```
<select name="listName">
<option>Option 1 </option>
<option>Option 2 </option>
...
<option>Option n </option>
</select>
```

The value that is passed when the form is submitted is the text to the right of the <option> tag. However, if you want to pass a value different from the text that appears in the list, you can add the *value=""* attribute into any or all of the <option> tags. In the next lab, one option will be set to pass a value different from the one the user will see.

In the following lab, you will add a single-option select list to the Web form. Suppose you want your model form to demonstrate a drop-down list of choices from which users can choose one. A select list provides this capability, and it is a form field type familiar to most Web users. You consider that the marketing team will want to contact candidates via e-mail regularly, so a select list might provide an effective way to learn how often the candidates want to be contacted. How else might this type of list help the marketing team perform tasks?

 Lab 6-5: Adding a single-option drop-down list to an HTML Web form

OBJECTIVE
2.4.1: Creating HTML forms

In this lab, you will add a drop-down select list to the Web form you have been building.

1. **Editor:** From **C:\CIW\Site_Dev\Lab Files\Lesson06\Lab_6-2**, open the file **lab_6-4.html** and save it as **lab_6-5.html**.

2. **Editor:** Add the following code as indicated in bold:

    ```
    <input type="checkbox" name="Financing"/> Financing<br/>
    <br/>
    <br/>

    How often would you like to receive an e-mail from Habitat for Humanity? <br/>
    <select name="EmailFreq">
    <option>Once a week</option>
    <option>Once or twice a month </option>
    <option>Once a month </option>
    <option value="Remove">Never </option>
    </select>
    <br/>
    <br/>

    <input type="submit"/>
    <input type="reset"/>

    </form>
    ```

3. **Editor:** Save the **lab_6-5.html** file.

4. **Browser:** Load the file. The select list should appear as it does in Figure 6-14.

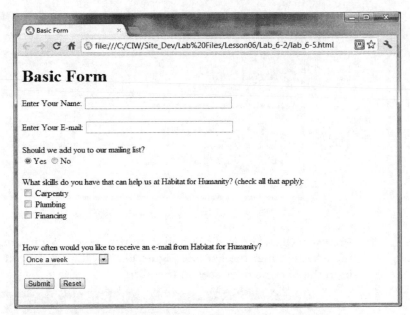

Figure 6-14: Web form after adding select list

5. Click and hold the arrow at the right side of the select-list box to open the drop-down list of items. Select the second list option as shown in Figure 6-15.

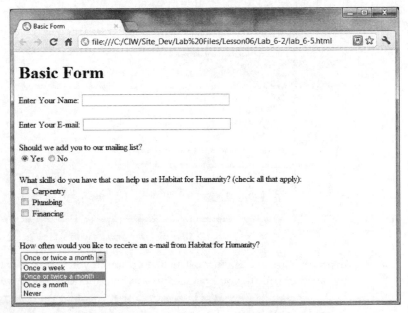

Figure 6-15: Selecting from select list in Web form

6. **Browser:** Fill out the rest of the form and submit it. You should see results similar to Figure 6-16.

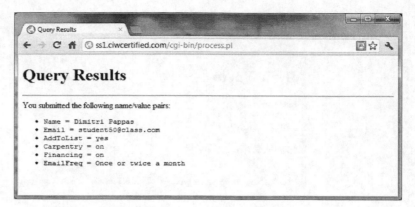

Figure 6-16: Form results with select list

7. **Browser:** Click the **Back** button to return to your Web form page. This time, choose the last option in the list (see Figure 6-17). This option will return a value different from the one the user sees in the form.

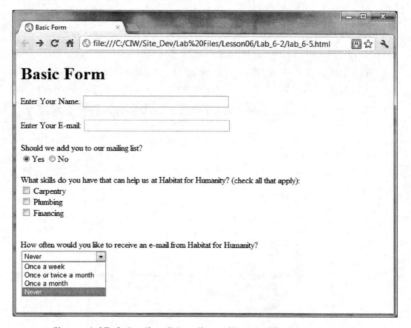

Figure 6-17: Selecting list option with specified result value

8. **Browser:** Submit the form. The last option in your results list should reflect the value of the *value* attribute you specified in the last <option> tag in your code. See Figure 6-18.

Figure 6-18: Form results with select list return value specified

9. Consider these results carefully. Notice that the value returned for EmailFreq is now "Remove" instead of "Never" as it appears in the user's selections. The code you entered for the *value* attribute of this <option> tag created a customized result value. This value would be useful with a CGI script that could automatically remove candidates from a mailing list if they choose the "Never" selection, yet store their e-mail information in a database for later use.

10. Validate your code.

In this lab, you created a single-option drop-down list in a Web form.

Multiple-option select list

Within the <select> tag, you can include the *multiple* attribute as follows:

```
<select name="work" multiple="multiple" size="4">
```

The presence of this attribute automatically changes the select list to allow users to select more than one option. Because multiple selections are possible, these lists are usually presented with several, if not all, options already exposed.

The *size* attribute of the <select> tag controls the number of items that will appear in a scrolling list box. If no size is specified, the number of items that will appear by default depends on the browser.

In the following lab, you will add a multiple-option select list to the Web form. Suppose you want your model form to demonstrate a drop-down list of choices from which users can choose one or more. A select list provides this capability, and it is a form field type familiar to most Web users. You consider that Habitat for Humanity has determined several countries that require workers, so a select list might provide an effective way to learn where candidates would like to work. To facilitate scheduling, you should know all the locations that interest the candidate, instead of limiting his or her choices to just one.

 Lab 6-6: Adding a multiple-option select list to an HTML Web form

OBJECTIVE
2.4.1: Creating HTML forms

In this lab, you will add a multiple-option select list to the Web form you have been building.

1. **Editor:** From **C:\CIW\Site_Dev\Lab Files\Lesson06\Lab_6-2**, open the file **lab_6-5.html** and save it as **lab_6-6.html**.

2. **Editor:** Add the following code as indicated in bold:

```
<option value="Remove">Never </option>
</select>
<br/>
<br/>

Where would you like to work? (choose all that apply):
<br/>
<select name="work" multiple="multiple" size="4">
<option>Australia</option>
<option>Japan</option>
<option>India</option>
<option>England</option>
<option>United States</option>
</select>
```

```
<br/>
<br/>
<input type="submit"/>
<input type="reset"/>
```

3. **Editor:** Save the **lab_6-6.html** file.

4. **Browser:** Load your file. The scrolling select list box should appear as it does in Figure 6-19.

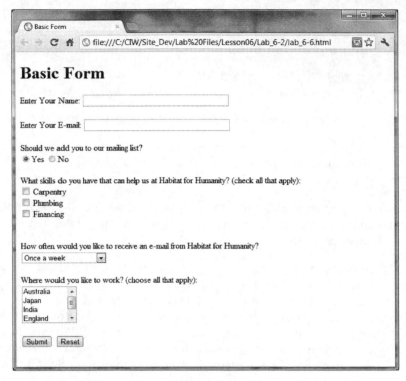

Figure 6-19: Web form after adding multiple-option select list

5. **Browser:** Complete all fields in the form. For the multiple-option select list, hold down the **CTRL** key while clicking to select more than one option (on Windows platforms). Then submit the form. The results should include all of your selections, as shown in Figure 6-20.

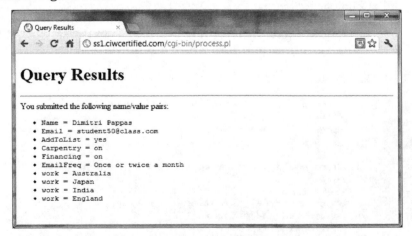

Figure 6-20: Form results with multiple-option selection

6. Use the browser **Back** button to return to your Web form page. Try choosing different selections and submitting the form again to verify that your form works correctly.

7. Validate your code.

In this lab, you added a multiple-option select list to a Web form.

Scrolling text area box

You can use a text area box to gather more than one line of text from a user. The <textarea> tag provides a scrolling text box into which a user can enter a few sentences, an address, a letter to the editor or other text.

The <textarea> tag is a container tag, and the only content this tag can contain is text. Text between <textarea> tags will appear as default text within the box.

The <textarea> element has several key attributes, which you should understand and use. Table 6-2 describes these attributes and accepted values.

Table 6-2: Attributes of <textarea> tag

Attribute	Description	Value
cols	Specifies the width in characters of the scrolling text box.	Integer value (e.g., "25", "40")
rows	Specifies the number of rows of text to display in the box.	Integer value (e.g., "2", "5")
wrap	Specifies whether user-entered text can wrap to new lines in the text box. If "soft" is specified, text continues on one line, so the user must scroll horizontally to read his or her entry. If "hard" is specified, text will wrap to a new line as it approaches the box border. This line wrapping is in appearance only: The text string submitted to the script will take the form of one long line of text. *Note: The wrap attribute was deprecated in HTML 4.01 but was revived in HTML5 with "soft" and "hard" values, instead of the previous "none" and "virtual" values, respectively.*	"soft" or "hard"

In the following lab, you will add a scrolling text area box to the Web form. Suppose you want your model form to demonstrate a text box into which users can enter more than just one short line of text. A scrolling text area box provides this capability, and it is a form field type familiar to most Web users. You consider that the teams analyzing user input from your Web site's form may want to elicit general comments or questions from users. A scrolling text area box is an effective tool for inviting information and feedback that site visitors want your organization to know.

Lab 6-7: Adding a scrolling text area box to an HTML Web form

OBJECTIVE
2.4.1: Creating HTML
forms

In this lab, you will add a scrolling text area box to the Web form you have been building.

1. **Editor:** From **C:\CIW\Site_Dev\Lab Files\Lesson06\Lab_6-2**, open the file **lab_6-6.html** and save it as **lab_6-7.html**.

2. **Editor:** Add the following code to the end of your form as indicated in bold:

   ```
   <option>United States</option>
   </select>
   <br/>
   <br/>

   Comments:<br/>
   <textarea name="comments" cols="30" rows="3">
   </textarea>
   <br/>
   <br/>

   <input type="submit"/>
   <input type="reset"/>
   ```

3. **Editor:** Save the **lab_6-7.html** file.

4. **Browser:** Load the file. The scrolling text area box should appear as it does in Figure 6-21.

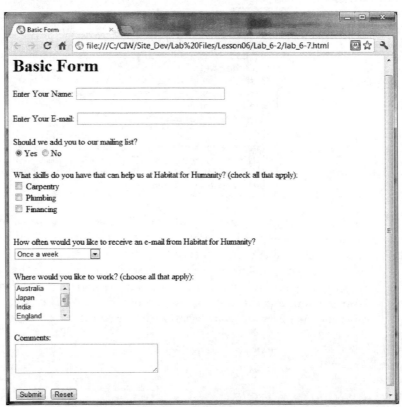

Figure 6-21: Web form after adding scrolling text area box

5. Type text into the scrolling text area box and submit the form. The text you typed should appear at the end of your results listing from the test engine.

6. Validate your code.

7. **When time permits:** Edit the file **lab_6-7.html** so that default text appears in the Comments field. Do this by entering text between the <textarea> </textarea> tags.

In this lab, added a scrolling text area box to the Web form.

You have now worked with several HTML form fields. When you have some time after class, you can practice your Web form-building skills. Suppose you submitted your model Web form to the Web development director as requested. The director is pleased, and so are upper management and the sales and marketing team members who reviewed it. The Web development director has gathered input from these parties, and now has directions for you to create a live Web form for the site. She has asked you to create a form that will:

- Collect a first and last name from each candidate.

- Obtain e-mail address information.

- Obtain information about the candidate's skills.

- Allow candidates to include any additional information about themselves.

This Web form page must also incorporate the look and feel, and other standard elements, of the overall site.

Web forms and CAPTCHAs

To reduce spam submissions sent to your form, consider the use of a CAPTCHA (Completely Automated Public Turing Test to Tell Computers and Humans Apart). A CAPTCHA is a challenge-response mechanism designed to discern between a human and a "bot" in order to detect the automated systems used by spammers for registering e-mail accounts.

A CAPTCHA is an automatically generated image presented to a user who has just submitted information or made a request of a Web server. CAPTCHAs require the user to view the distorted text image, and then enter the text shown in the graphic into a form field before he or she is allowed to proceed with a transaction. The distorted image is easily recognizable by humans, but is a difficult challenge for a machine. When the user provides the correct response to a CAPTCHA, then his or her input is accepted for processing.

Many CAPTCHA services exist, including:

- Captchas.net (*http://captchas.net*)

- Captcha.cc (*www.captcha.cc*)

- Secureimage CAPTCHA (*www.phpcaptcha.org*)

Search engine optimization (SEO) and Web forms

When creating Web forms, you should take search engine optimization (SEO) into consideration. SEO involves learning how a particular search engine (such as Google, Yahoo! or Bing) ranks a Web site. You can use this knowledge to customize a site's Web pages — including the forms used — so that the site is ranked as highly as possible in a search engine's results.

When conducting SEO, consider the following strategies related to forms:

- Create as simple a form as possible. Each additional field you use may reduce your score.

- Some search engines may score pages lower if a CAPTCHA is used. The problem with a CAPTCHA, or any other element that requires human input, is that a bot that encounters it will not take time to read and process all of the page. This can cause the page to be scored lower.

- Give form fields informative, descriptive labels.

- Provide a clear call to action. Do not assume that a Submit button will inform users (or search engine bots) about what they should do.

- Provide alternative text navigation.

CIW Online Resources – Online Exercise

Visit CIW Online at *http://education.Certification-Partners.com/CIW* to complete an interactive exercise that will reinforce what you have learned about this topic.

Exercise 6-2: Web Form Fields

CIW Online Resources – Course Mastery

Visit CIW Online at *http://education.Certification-Partners.com/CIW* to take the Course Mastery review of this lesson or lesson segment.

SDA Lesson 6 - Part B

Case Study

In Good Form

Lola works on the Web development team for her college. She has been assigned to create a Web form that will help the Language Department faculty plan a student trip to Europe in the summer. The faculty advisors want to use the Web page to register interested students, collect itinerary suggestions, and gather information that will help them plan the travel accommodations. Lola's form needs to collect the following information from each interested student:

- Gender

- Languages studied

- Preferred countries to visit

- Hotel room preferences

- Student limitations related to physical abilities, diet, allergies, religious practices, etc.

Lola decides to use the following form elements:

- Radio buttons to indicate gender

- Check boxes to indicate languages studied

- A scrolling text area box to indicate preferred countries

- A drop-down select list to indicate hotel room preferences

- A text box to indicate student limitations

Lola posts the Web form on the Language Department page of the college Web site. She then asks the department faculty members to review the form and let her know if they need any other information from students.

*   *   *

As a class, answer the following questions:

- Did Lola use the correct form fields for the information requested? Why or why not?

- What other form fields could be used for the information requested on this form?

- What other types of information might the faculty members ask Lola to collect for this project? Which form fields would work best for each new type of information? Why?

Lesson Summary

Application project

Web forms are useless unless you can process them. Traditionally, the most popular way to process a form is through the use of a Perl-based CGI script. However, many alternatives to Perl-based CGI have emerged. Alternatives include Active Server Pages (ASP), JavaServer Pages (JSP) and PHP Hypertext Processor (PHP).

Visit several Web sites that use forms. View the Web form source code. Can you determine where the form is processed by viewing the <form> element, and the *method* and *action* attributes?

Skills review

In this lesson, you learned to use each of the major form field elements, and you created a functional Web form. You also saw the different form results that can be returned by setting the form action to point to a public test engine. You can test your knowledge after class by creating a form within a table in a new page.

Now that you have completed this lesson, you should be able to:

✓ 2.4.1: Construct and test HTML forms.

✓ 2.4.2: Identify ways that CGI scripts can parse and transmit information from a form, including e-mail, FTP, HTTP, HTTPS.

✓ 2.4.3: Diagram a fundamental CGI session.

✓ 2.18.4: Activate features provided by managed services (e.g., CGI, forms).

CIW Practice Exams

Visit CIW Online at *http://education.Certification-Partners.com/CIW* to take the Practice Exams assessment covering the objectives in this lesson.

SDA Objective 2.04 Review

Note that some objectives may be only partially covered in this lesson.

Lesson 6 Review

1. You need to create a Web form that asks visitors to enter a password before they can access the next page. What input type would you use?

   _____

   _____

2. Which Web form tag is used to create text boxes, check boxes, radio buttons, and the Submit and Reset buttons, but not select lists?

   _____

3. Which form field allows users to enter text such as a first or last name?

   _____

4. Write the HTML tag to create a scrolling text area box that will report input results by the name of "Feedback." The box should be 30 characters wide and five rows tall.

   _____

5. In HTML, do form tags need to be closed? Why or why not?

   _____

   _____

   _____

Lesson 7:
Video, Audio and Image Techniques

Objectives

By the end of this lesson, you will be able to:

✍ 2.2.2: Distinguish among and identify the uses and benefits of various graphic file formats, including GIF, GIF89a, JPEG, PNG, TIFF, BMP.

✍ 2.2.4: Create and link client-side image maps.

✍ 2.2.5: Perform advanced image formatting techniques.

✍ 2.2.7: Distinguish between raster and vector graphics.

✍ 2.2.8: Scan and edit hard copy sources and images.

✍ 2.2.9: Identify steps for creating images, including resolution, format and layers.

✍ 2.2.10: Identify benefits and drawbacks of using stock photography.

✍ 2.2.11: Create a photo and portfolio management strategy, including online and offline storage, software and services.

✍ 2.10.3: Evaluate the benefits and drawbacks of proprietary technologies such as Adobe Flash and Microsoft Silverlight.

✍ 2.10.5: Create a basic video file using video capture and editing software.

✍ 2.10.6: Insert a video file into a Web page using the HTML5 <video> element and attributes.

✍ 2.10.7: Insert an audio file into a Web page using the HTML5 <audio> element and attributes.

Pre-Assessment Questions

1. What <video> attribute is used to display an image until the play button is selected or the video loads?

    a. image-load
    b. source
    c. poster
    d. src

2. Which <audio> attribute specifies that an audio file will continue to play over and over?

    a. repeat
    b. loop
    c. autoplay
    d. audio/ogg

3. Which syntax is used for defining a circle-shaped hot spot area in an image map?

    a. coords="x1,y1,x2,y2"
    b. coords="radius,y1,x1"
    c. coords="x1,y1,x2,y2,xn,yn"
    d. coords="x1,y1,radius"

Introduction to Web Video, Audio and Image Techniques

A primary ingredient of any successful Web page is well-placed video, audio and images. You have already learned about the video, audio and image file formats used on the Web. In this lesson, you will learn more about techniques used in Web pages, including:

- The <video> element.

- Video format conversion.

- The <audio> element.

- Image maps.

- Image transparency.

- Interlacing.

- Animation.

You will also learn about several methods you can use to create and edit video and images.

CIW Online Resources – Movie Clips

Visit CIW Online at http://education.Certification-Partners.com/CIW to watch a movie clip about this topic.

Lesson 7: Video, Audio and Image Techniques

OBJECTIVE
2.10.6: Inserting video with <video>

The <video> Element

HTML5 has introduced the <video> element to allow developers a standard method to embed video into their Web sites. Prior to the <video> element, browser plug-ins (such as Adobe Flash, Microsoft Silverlight or Apple QuickTime) were required to view video. These plug-ins are not supported by all browsers or devices, so a standardized way to include video was needed.

Embedding video in an HTML5 document is straightforward. See the following code:

```
<video width="360" height="270" controls="controls" poster="image.png">
<source src="video.mp4" type="video/mp4" />
<source src="video.webm" type="video/webm" />
<source src="video.ogg" type="video/ogg" />
Your browser does not support the HTML5 video element.
  </video>
```

Table 7-1 lists the elements and attributes used in the example code.

Table 7-1: Video elements and attributes

Element or attribute	Description
<video> element	Defines a video to embed in the Web page.
width and height attributes	Specifies the width and height (in pixels) of the video window. If not specified, the video size will be determined by the source video file when it loads, which could change the Web page layout considerably.
controls attribute	Adds video controls such as the play, pause, rewind and volume controls. These video controls are native to HTML5.
poster attribute	Identifies an image to be displayed until the play button is clicked or while the video is downloading. If the poster attribute is not specified, the first frame of the video is displayed instead.
<source> element	Defines the media resource. Multiple sources can be listed, such as different types of video formats, to support a variety of devices and browsers.
src attribute	Identifies the location and file name of the media resource.
type attribute	Identifies the format, or MIME type, of the video. The <video> element supports three formats: MP4, WebM and Ogg.
Text	Text enclosed by the <video> element will appear if the browser or device cannot support any of the video formats available.

The MP4 video format (MPEG 4 files) is widely used. YouTube recently reformatted most videos away from Flash, which required a plug-in, to MP4. MP4 often uses the H.264 video codec, which is native to most browsers that support HTML5. This codec uses far less processor and battery power because it does not require a plug-in.

The WebM and Ogg video formats are also used. The WebM video format often uses the VP8 codec. VP8 is an open video compression format owned by Google. Ogg uses the Theora format for HTML5 video, which is a free video compression format that can be distributed without licensing fees.

To ensure all browsers and devices can access your video, you should format your video to these three formats and identify them in the <source> element. If that is not possible, then choose one, such as the MP4 format, as the default format.

In the following lab, you will create a video. Suppose your supervisor has decided that a page on the company Web site should be more accessible to visual and auditory learners. She asks you to post a video on the page that shows you talking about the contents of the Web page. You will need to create a video of yourself reading some of the Web page's content.

OBJECTIVE
2.10.5: Creating
videos

Lab 7-1: Creating a video

In this lab, you will create a video of yourself talking about the Habitat for Humanity Summer Youth Blitz.

Note: This lab assumes your computer has a built-in Webcam and microphone. If it does not, modify the lab to select your external devices.

1. Create a **new folder** named **Lab_7-1** on your Desktop.

2. Open Windows Live Movie Maker by selecting **Start | All Programs | Windows Live Movie Maker**.

3. **Movie Maker:** Click the **Webcam video** button on the toolbar.

4. **Webcam video:** If prompted, select your video and microphone devices. The Webcam tab will open.

5. **Webcam tab:** Center yourself in the Webcam screen. Remember to convey a professional appearance. Click the **Record** button and read aloud the following text while you record yourself:

   The Summer Youth Blitz is a unique service experience for a diverse group of youth, ages 16 to 18, from high schools and youth organizations around the United States.

   During this program, 15 to 20 youth participants and adult leaders "blitz build" an entire Habitat house in two weeks. Apply now!

6. Click the **Stop** button. Save the video as **webcam.wmv** in your Desktop folder **Lab_7-1**.

   Tech Note: Movie Maker only saves files and exports them as .wmv files (Windows Media Video), which is a Microsoft proprietary video format. In the next lab, you will convert the .wmv file to an HTML5-supported .mp4 file.

7. **Movie Maker:** Review your video and re-record it if necessary. Only keep one "take" of your video. Delete all the others.

8. Trim the beginning and end of the video by selecting the **Edit** tab and clicking the **Trim tool** button. Determine the **Set start point** and the **Set end point** to remove any unwanted footage at the beginning and ending of your video. Click **Save trim**.

9. **Optional:** Add a fade-in and fade-out effect to the video by selecting the **Visual Effects** tab. Click the **down arrow** to the right of the effects. Select **Multiple Effects**. In the Add or Remove Effects window, select **Fade in from black** and **Fade out to black** and **Add** them, as shown in Figure 7-1. Click **Apply**.

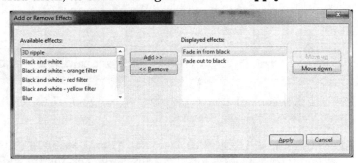

Figure 7-1: Adding fade-in and fade-out effects in Movie Maker

10. **Optional:** Add the text **"The Summer Youth Blitz"** to the beginning of the video and **"Apply Now"** to the end. Do not spend more than 10 minutes creating the video — it does not need to be perfect. Figure 7-2 shows a sample video.

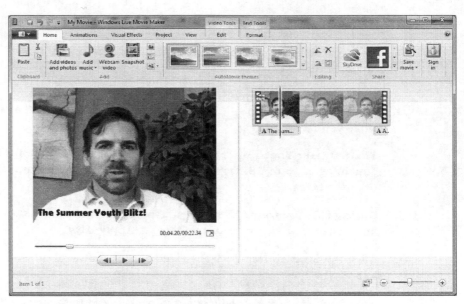

Figure 7-2: Sample video in Movie Maker

11. **Movie Maker:** Save your project as **My Movie.wlmp** to the **Lab_7-1** folder on your Desktop. Keep the program open.

12. Select the **Home** tab and click the **Save movie** button. Save the video as **syb.wmv** to the **Lab_7-1** folder on your Desktop.

13. Exit Movie Maker.

In this lab, you created a video for the Summer Youth Blitz Web page.

In the following lab, you will convert this video to the MP4 video format. Suppose your supervisor has asked you to make the video accessible to those with an HTML5-compliant browser that supports the MP4 format.

Lab 7-2: Converting video to support HTML5 formats

OBJECTIVE
2.10.6: Inserting
video with <video>

OBJECTIVE
2.10.5: Creating
videos

In this lab, you will convert a .wmv video to an HTML5-supported MP4 video format using Free Video Converter Factory.

1. From the **C:\CIW\Site_Dev\Lab Files\Lesson07** directory, copy the **Lab_7-2** folder to your Desktop. This directory contains the video converter application.

2. Open the **Lab_7-2** folder and double-click the **video-converter.zip** file. Extract the video-converter.exe file to the same folder.

   Tech Note: If necessary, visit www.videoconverterfactory.com/free-video-converter/and download the program. Other free video converters are available from HAMSTER soft (http://videoconverter.hamstersoft.com/) and freemake.com (www.freemake.com/free_video_converter/).

3. Double-click the **video-converter.exe** file. This program is called Free Video Converter Factory and has been recommended by Microsoft for converting .wmv to .mp4.

4. **Setup:** The Video Converter Factory welcome screen appears. Click **Next**. Accept the license agreement and click **Next**.

5. In the Select Destination Location window, accept the default settings by clicking **Next**. In the Choose Start Menu Folder window, accept the default settings by clicking **Next**.

6. In the Select Additional Tasks window, make sure the **Create a desktop icon** check box is selected and click **Next**. Verify the settings in the Ready To Install window and click **Install**.

7. When setup is completed, a Completing The Video Converter Factory window will appear. The **Launch Video Converter Factory** check box is selected by default. Click **Finish** and the program will launch.

8. Before you continue, delete the **video-converter.exe** and **video-converter.zip** files from the Lab_7-2 folder. These files are no longer needed.

9. **Video Converter Factory:** Click the **Add** button to select a video file to import. You can also select the **File** menu and choose **Add Files**. Locate and select the **syb.wmv** file you created in the previous lab and click **Open**.

10. In the **Profile** drop-down menu, select **Common Video** and select **MP4 AVC(*.mp4) H.264 Video configure**. The H.264 encoder is required for HTML5 video.

11. Click the **folder** icon next to the **Output** field. Locate and select the **Lab_7-2** folder on your Desktop and click **OK**. Your screen should resemble Figure 7-3.

Figure 7-3: Video conversion from .wmv to .mp4

12. Click the **Start** button. After the conversion is complete, click **Finish**.

13. Exit Video Converter Factory.

14. **Windows Explorer:** Open the **Lab_7-2** folder on your Desktop and double-click the **syb_(new).mp4** file. It should play successfully using the computer's default video player.

15. Rename the file from syb_(new).mp4 to **syb.mp4**.

16. Close Windows Explorer.

In this lab, you converted a video file from .wmv to .mp4 format. The MP4 video format is supported by the HTML5 <video> element, but only with the H.264 codec. Now the video will play in an HTML5-compliant browser without a plug-in.

In the following lab, you will embed your video into the Summer Youth Blitz Web page. Suppose your supervisor has approved the video you created, and now you are ready to insert it on the page.

Lab 7-3: Adding video to an HTML5 Web page

OBJECTIVE
2.10.6: Inserting
video with <video>

In this lab, you will use the HTML5 <video> element to embed a video into a Web page.

1. From the **C:\CIW\Site_Dev\Lab Files\Lesson07** directory, copy the **Lab_7-3** folder to your Desktop. This directory contains the Summer Youth Blitz Web page.

2. Open the **Lab_7-3** folder and open the **lab_7-3.html** file in a text editor.

3. Add the <video> element with a height of 210 pixels. Place it immediately before the "Apply Now" <h3> text in the article section. The width will be determined by its ratio to the height pixel value (standard 4:3 ratio).

4. Add the default video controls (play, pause, volume, etc.) by including *controls="controls"* to the <video> element.

5. Before you add the <source> element, copy the **syb.mp4** video from **Lab_7-2** into the **Lab_7-3\syb** folder.

Note: If you did not create a syb.mp4 video in Lab 7-2, then copy the syb.mp4 file from the C:\CIW\Site_Dev\Lab Files\Lesson07\Finished\Lab_7-2 folder.

6. Nest the <source> element within the <video> element to identify the syb.mp4 video. Add the *src* and *type* attributes with the appropriate values.

7. Add text for browsers that do not support the <video> element. (If the browser does not support the video format or MIME type, an error message will appear and/or the video will not load.)

8. Your code may resemble the following:

HTML code:

```
<video height="210" class="center" controls="controls">
<source src="syb/syb.mp4" type="video/mp4" />
Your browser does not support the HTML5 video element.
 </video>
```

CSS code:

```
video.center
{
display: block;
margin-left: auto;
margin-right: auto;
}
```

9. Save your files and validate both at the W3C validator sites.

10. **Browser:** Open **lab_7-3.html** in Chrome or IE9. Your screen should appear similar to Figure 7-4.

Figure 7-4: Video embedded using HTML5 <video> element

11. **Browser:** Open **lab_7-3.html** in Firefox. Your screen should appear similar to Figure 7-5.

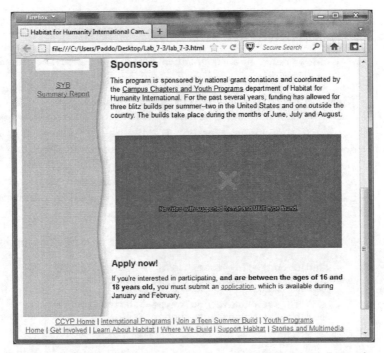

Figure 7-5: Firefox error: "No video with supported format and MIME type found."

Firefox does not support the MP4 video format. How can this issue be overcome with the <source> element? How can it be solved with video formatting? As mentioned earlier in the lesson, multiple video formats can be identified using the <source> element. All three HTML5 video formats can be created and listed (.*mp4*, .*ogg* and .*webm*).

12. **If time permits:** Add the <video> element's *poster* attribute. To do this task, open your Movie Maker project. Scroll through your video, stop on a good frame of yourself, and click **Snapshot**. Save it to the **Lab_7-3\syb** folder as *poster.png*. Use the *poster* attribute to identify the picture. Your snapshot will appear in the video window until the play button is selected.

13. Close your files and browsers.

In this lab, you used the HTML5 <video> element to embed a video into the Summer Youth Blitz Web page.

As you have learned, HTML5-compliant browsers do not necessarily support all the HTML5 video formats. This presents more work for Web developers, who must decide if they want to support all HTML5 video formats or if they want to require users to switch browsers. Table 7-2 lists the HTML5 video formats and shows which HTML5-compliant browsers support each of the formats. (Information is current at the time of this writing.)

Table 7-2: HTML5-compliant browser support for HTML5 video formats and codecs

Video Format/Codec	Supported by Browser?		
	Chrome	IE9 and Safari	Firefox and Opera
MP4/H.264	Yes	Yes	No**
Ogg/Theora	Yes	No*	Yes
WebM/VP8	Yes	No*	Yes
*Manual installation available			
**Windows-only manual installation available for Firefox; no manual installation exists for Opera.			

The <audio> Element

Similar to the <video> element, HTML5 has introduced the <audio> element that allows developers a standard method to embed audio into Web pages. Prior to the <audio> element, browser plug-ins or separate applications (such as Windows Media Center, Apple iTunes, Apple QuickTime, Adobe Flash and Microsoft Silverlight) were required to listen to audio. These plug-ins are not supported by all browsers or devices, so a standardized way to include audio was needed.

Embedding audio in an HTML5 document requires the following code:

```
<audio controls="controls">
<source src="audio.mp3" type="audio/mpeg" />
<source src="audio.wav" type="audio/wav" />
<source src="audio.ogg" type="audio/ogg" />
Your browser does not support the HTML5 audio element.
</audio>
```

As with the <video> element, the *controls* attribute identifies the default audio controls: play, pause, volume, etc. Any text enclosed within the <audio> element will appear to browsers that do not support it.

Multiple sources can be identified with the <source> element to ensure various audio formats are supported. HTML5 supports three audio formats: .mp3, .wav and .ogg.

Not all HTML-compliant browsers support all of these audio formats. Table 7-3 lists the HTML5 audio formats and shows which HTML-compliant browsers support each format. (Information is current at the time of this writing.)

Table 7-3: HTML5-compliant browser support for HTML5 audio formats

Audio Format/Codec	Supported by Browser?			
	Chrome	IE9	Safari	Firefox and Opera
MP3	Yes	Yes	Yes	No
Ogg	Yes	No	No	Yes
Wav	Yes	No	Yes	Yes

In addition to the *controls* attribute, several other attributes are common to both the <video> element and the <audio> element. Two widely used attributes are listed in Table 7-4.

Table 7-4: Additional <audio> and <video> attributes

<audio> and <video> Attribute	Description
loop="loop"	Specifies that the audio or video file will play over and over again without stopping.
autoplay="autoplay"	Specifies that the video will play immediately upon loading.

In the following lab, you will add voice-over audio and audio controls to a Web page. Suppose your supervisor has assigned you a new project. A company Web page needs voice-over audio for auditory learners who visit the page. Voice-over audio is necessary because anyone who visits the page could click the play button to hear parts of the Web page read aloud, not just users who require screen-reader software.

 Lab 7-4: Adding audio to an HTML5 Web page

OBJECTIVE
2.10.7: Inserting
audio with <audio>

In this lab, you will use the HTML5 <audio> element to embed audio into a Web page.

1. From the **C:\CIW\Site_Dev\Lab Files\Lesson07** directory, copy the **Lab_7-4** folder to your Desktop. This directory contains the Summer Youth Blitz Web page completed in Lab 7-3.

    Note: You can also use your final Lab 7-3 files. However, you must copy the voiceover.mp3 file from the C:\CIW\Site_Dev\Lab Files\Lesson07\Lab_7-4\syb\ folder into your existing Lab_7-3\syb folder. You can rename your Desktop Lab_7-3 folder and lab_7-3.html file to Lab_7-4 and lab_7-4.html, respectively, to better follow the lab steps.

2. Open the **Lab_7-4** folder, and then open the **lab_7-4.html** file in a text editor.

3. Add the <audio> element at the bottom of the <article> section.

4. Add the default audio controls (play, pause, volume, etc.) by including *controls="controls"* to the <audio> element. Add a CSS class to center the controls on the Web page.

5. Nest the <source> element within the <audio> element to identify the voiceover.mp3 audio located in your Lab_7-4\syb Desktop folder. Add the *src* and *type* attributes with the appropriate values.

6. Add text for browsers that do not support the <audio> element. (If the browser does not support the audio format, an error message will appear and/or the video will not load.)

7. Add text before the <audio> element to provide instructions for Web page visitors, such as "For audio of this Web page, use the audio controls below."

8. Your code may resemble the following:

HTML code:

```
<p>
For audio of this Web page, use the audio controls below.
</p>

<audio controls="controls" class="center">
<source src="syb/voiceover.mp3" type="audio/mpeg" />
Your browser does not support the HTML5 audio element.
 </audio>
```

CSS code:

```
audio.center
{
display: block;
margin-left: auto;
margin-right: auto;
}
```

9. Save your files and validate both at the W3C validator sites.

10. **Browser:** Open **lab_7-4.html** in Chrome. Your screen should appear similar to Figure 7-6.

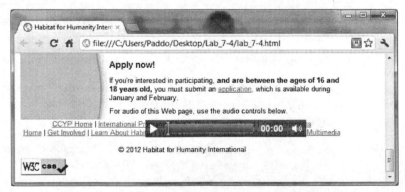

Figure 7-6: Audio embedded using HTML5 <video> element but overlapping text

11. **Editor:** Notice that the audio controls overlap the text on the page. Fix this issue by extending the height of the <nav> and <article> sections in CSS to 915 pixels. This will provide more space on the Web page for the audio controls.

12. **Browser:** Open **lab_7-4.html** in Chrome. Your screen should appear similar to Figure 7-7. The overlapping issue should be fixed.

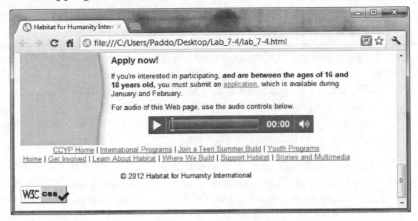

Figure 7-7: Audio embedded using HTML5 <video> element without overlapping text

Firefox does not support the MP3 format. Similar to video, multiple audio formats can be identified using the <source> element. All three HTML5 audio formats can be created and listed (.mp3, .ogg and .wav).

13. Close your files and browsers.

In this lab, you embedded an audio file into a Web page. The MP3 audio format is supported by the HTML5 <audio> element. Your MP3 audio now will play in most HTML5-compliant browsers without a plug-in.

CIW Online Resources – Online Exercise

Visit CIW Online at *http://education.Certification-Partners.com/CIW* to complete an interactive exercise that will reinforce what you have learned about this topic.

Exercise 7-1: HTML5-compliant browser support for video and audio formats

Graphic Types

OBJECTIVE
2.2.2: Graphic file formats

2.2.7: Raster vs. vector graphics

Before learning about image techniques, you should understand the differences between the two types of graphical images used in Web pages:

- **Vector** — graphics that use mathematical coordinates with lines, curves and shapes to create images and specify colors. Vector graphics can be created using various tools, including Adobe Illustrator and Adobe Freehand (*www.adobe.com*). Vector graphics are generally small in file size. Their presentation size can be enlarged or shrunk (i.e., scaled) without losing image quality.

- **Bitmap** — graphics that use small dots (usually thousands) to create images and specify colors. Each dot is mapped to bits stored in a computer's memory. Bitmaps are also called raster graphics, and they include the JPEG, GIF and PNG formats. Digitized photographs are the most common type of bitmap seen on the Web. Bitmap images can be created using tools such as Paint Shop Pro (*www.corel.com*) and The GIMP (*www.gimp.org*). Making bitmap images more detailed can create large file sizes (e.g., 20 MB). Removing pixels and compressing files will decrease file size, but will also reduce image quality.

OBJECTIVE
2.2.4: Client-side
image maps

image map
A Web page image with clickable regions that are defined as "hot spot" hyperlinks to other pages or page sections.

Image Maps

An **image map** is an image that contains clickable regions, sometimes called hot spots. Each hot spot acts as a hyperlink. You define each hot spot with a set of coordinates (indicating its position on the image) and a URL reference. Image map files originally had to be placed on the server and processed there, but now the map information can be processed on the server side or the client side. Client-side image maps use map code embedded within the HTML page.

The most difficult aspect of creating an image map is determining the coordinates of the map areas you want to use as links. After you complete this task, you simply specify the URL that corresponds to each hot spot. Many image-creation applications provide the coordinates of any position in an image as you move your cursor across it. If you do not know the coordinates for different regions of your image but you know the image's pixel height and width, you can perform mathematical calculations to determine which coordinates define which regions.

Examine the graphic shown in Figure 7-8.

Figure 7-8: Image to be used as map

Suppose you want to use this image as a set of hyperlinks that send users to other pages on your Web site. You can create an image map. Because this image consists of six visually separate sections, you could define each of the six sections as a hot spot for a link. Each hot spot can link to a different page.

For example, you could create a hot spot on the section that shows a hand. Because this area is a rectangular shape, you would define that portion of the image using four coordinates, which represent the x and y coordinates for the upper-left and lower-right corners. Coordinates depend upon the pixel size of the image. If you enlarged this image, you would have to change the coordinates. You will learn to determine the coordinates of a hot spot area shortly.

Once you define a hot spot's coordinates, you can point the hot spot to reference a URL so that when a user clicks that area of the image, the file designated by the URL is loaded. The defined hot spot area is not visible on a Web page, although when a user passes his or her cursor over a hot spot, the cursor will change into the pointing-hand icon that indicates a hyperlink.

Web design applications that provide WYSIWYG (What You See Is What You Get) capabilities often provide tools that simplify the image mapping creation process. Adobe Dreamweaver and Microsoft Expression Web both provide this service.

CIW Online Resources – Movie Clips

Visit CIW Online at http://education.Certification-Partners.com/CIW to watch a movie clip about this topic.

Lesson 7: Creating a Basic Image Map

Defining a client-side image map

You can create either client-side or server-side image maps. Client-side image maps are more common. Server-side image maps require a CGI script, so they are not commonly used. The main advantage of a client-side map is that you can place all the code relating to the image map directly into your HTML file. The syntax for defining a client-side map for an image is as follows:

```
<map name="mapname">
    <area shape="shape" coords="coordinates" href="url" alt="description"/>
    <area shape="shape" coords="coordinates" href="url" alt="description"/>
    <area shape="shape" coords="coordinates" href="url" alt="description"/>
</map>
<img src="imagemap.gif" usemap="#mapname"/>
```

Table 7-5 specifies how each element and attribute in this example is used in an image map.

Table 7-5: Image map elements and attributes

Element / Attribute	Description
<img> tag	Specifies an image file in a Web page, as learned in a previous lesson. The *src* attribute specifies the image file name.
<img> tag's *usemap* attribute	Indicates that the image placed in the Web page will use an image map. Note the relationship between the <img> tag's *usemap* attribute value and the <map> tag's *name* attribute value.
<map> tag	A container tag; requires a closing </map> tag. The <map> tag encloses <area> tags. You can define your image map with the <map> tag either before or after the related <img> tag; either sequence is acceptable.
<map> tag's *name* attribute	Provides a reference name for the image map.
<area> tags	Stand-alone tags that define the hot spot regions of the image map. You can define as many or as few hot spot regions as you like within an image map.
<area> tag's *shape* attribute	Accepted values are: - "rect" for a rectangular area (i.e., hot spot). - "circle" for a circular area. - "poly" for any other shape. - "default" to use the entire area
<area> tag's *coords* attribute	The number and meaning of coordinates you specify with the *coords* attribute value will vary based on the *shape* attribute value: - For rectangle areas: $x1,y1,x2,y2$ - For circle areas: $x1,y1,radius$ - For polygon areas: $x1,y1,x2,y2,...xn,yn$ (up to 100 pairs of coordinates)

Table 7-5: Image map elements and attributes (cont'd)

Element / Attribute	Description
\<area\> tag's *href* attribute	Value is a URL specifying the linked page that will load when the user clicks the defined hot spot area of the image map.
\<area\> tag's *alt* attribute	Alternative text must be provided using the *alt* attribute whenever the *href* attribute is used.
Hash symbol (#) in the *usemap* attribute's "mapname" value	Indicates that the "#*mapname*" value represents an image map defined within the same HTML file. If no hash symbol is present here, then the browser will look outside the HTML page for the referenced *mapname* file.

Defining a rectangle hot spot

Any two points can define a rectangle. Each point is represented by a horizontal (*x*) coordinate and a vertical (*y*) coordinate. Rectangles are defined by four coordinates representing the upper-left and bottom-right corners of the rectangle, as shown in Figure 7-9.

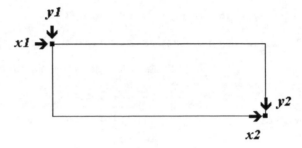

Figure 7-9: Rectangle area defined by four coordinates

You can define a rectangular area using the following syntax:

```
<area shape="rect" coords="x1,y1,x2,y2" href="url" alt="description"/>
```

The *x1* indicates the leftmost point of the area to be defined. The *y1* indicates the topmost point of the area to be defined. The *x2* indicates the furthest point to the right in the area to be defined, and *y2* indicates the lowest point. These four coordinates will necessarily define a rectangle.

Consider the example image shown earlier in this section (see Figure 7-10).

Figure 7-10: Image map example

As mentioned before, coordinates depend upon the pixel size of the image. This image is 130 pixels wide and 97 pixels high. Suppose you want to define a rectangular hot spot over the hand section of this image. The coordinates that define the hand area are 1,52,33,96. If you enlarged this image, you would have to change the coordinates.

In this image, the coordinate 1 represents the distance in pixels from the left edge of the image to the left edge of the hot spot. The coordinate 1 thus represents the left edge of the image. This number is the left *x* coordinate for a rectangle. The coordinate 52 represents the distance in pixels from the top of the image to the top of the same hot spot; this is the upper y coordinate. The two coordinates together, 1 and 52, designate the upper-left corner of the rectangle hot spot. The coordinates 33 and 96 respectively represent the bottom-right x and y coordinates of a rectangle encompassing the hot spot. Each coordinate is measured from the top or left edge of the image.

The HTML area definition for this image hot spot would be written as follows:

```
<area shape="rect" coords="1,52,33,96" href="hand.htm" alt="hand"/>
```

Figure 7-11 shows another image that can function as an image map with rectangular hot spots.

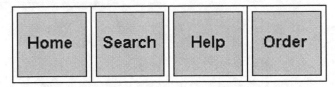

Figure 7-11: Rectangular image with rectangular areas

This image file is 312 pixels wide and 75 pixels high. Each square is 78 pixels wide. Using basic math, you should be able to determine the top-left and bottom-right x and y coordinates for each square area within this graphic. The code for an image map of this graphic could resemble the following:

```
<img src="buttons.gif" usemap="#ButtonMap"/>

<map name="ButtonMap">
    <area shape="rect" coords="0,0,78,75" href="home.htm" alt="home"/>
    <area shape="rect" coords="78,0,156,75" href="search.htm" alt="search"/>
    <area shape="rect" coords="156,0,234,75" href="help.htm" alt="help"/>
    <area shape="rect" coords="234,0,312,75" href="order.htm" alt="order"/>
</map>
```

Defining a circle hot spot

Circles are defined by two coordinates and a radius. The pair of coordinates specifies the circle's center, and the third number specifies the desired radius, or half-width, of the circle.

The syntax for defining a circle area is as follows:

```
<area shape="circle" coords="x1,y1,radius" href="url" alt="description"/>
```

Figure 7-12 shows how the coordinates and radius are determined.

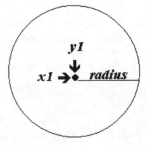

Figure 7-12: Circle area defined by two coordinates and radius

Defining a polygon hot spot

When you need to define an area that is neither a circle nor a rectangle, you can use the *shape*="poly" attribute and value, then specify coordinates for each point that defines the polygon.

Examine Figure 7-13. Note that the coordinates define the points of the polygon in sequence. For example, you could not switch the *x4* and *y4* coordinates with the *x2* and *y2* coordinates without altering the shape of the image.

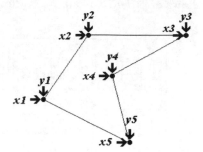

Figure 7-13: Polygon area defined by three or more pairs of coordinates

You can use up to 100 pairs of coordinates to define a polygon. The syntax for defining a polygon area is as follows:

```
<area shape="poly" coords="x1,y1,x2,y2,...xn,yn" href="url"/>
```

In the following lab, you will define hot spot regions in an image. Suppose your project manager has asked you to add a new image to your Web page, and to create several hyperlinks from this image to other Web pages on the site. You review the image, and consider the areas and shapes that would work best as hyperlinks. You also consider that users may or may not use precise aim when they click an area of the image expecting to activate a certain link. You determine the coordinates for hot spot areas on the image, and write the HTML code to create the image map on your page.

Lab 7-5: Defining a client-side image map

In this lab, you will add an image to the Web form page and define an image map for it.

1. From the **C:\CIW\Site_Dev\Lab Files\Lesson07** directory, copy the **Lab_7-5** folder to your Desktop. This directory contains the file lab_7-5.html and others.

2. Open the **Lab_7-5** folder and double-click the **lab_7-5.html** file. You will see a Habitat for Humanity page titled *Information Request Form* appear in your browser.

3. Open **lab_7-5.html** in a text editor.

4. Search for the following text string, which resides in the <nav> sidebar area of the page:

```
<!-- BEGIN IMAGE MAP CODE -->
```

5. Just below the comment you located, insert the following code and text to introduce the image:

```
<p>
<strong>Click anywhere on the image below
<br/> to learn more about
<a href="http://www.habitat.org/intl"> where we build</a>.
</strong>
</p>
```

6. Below the code you just added, write the proper code to insert the **global_village_130_97.jpg** image file using the **<img>** tag. This image resides in the **form** folder and is 130 pixels wide and 97 pixels high. Knowing the width and height of an image is essential when calculating image map coordinates.

7. Add the *width* and *height* attributes to your <img> tag to make sure that the image is the proper size.

8. Use the *alt* attribute to provide some appropriate alternative text for the image. Remember that the *alt* attribute is required with images in order for your code to validate as HTML5.

9. Use CSS to specify that no border appears around the image. Open **form.css** in the **form** folder and enter:

```
img
{
border:0px;
}
```

10. The image should now be inserted in your page without a border. You are ready to begin creating the image map. Add the *usemap* attribute to the <img> tag to refer this image to the map instructions. Use *"#global"* as the attribute value.

Note: Be sure to close your <img> tag properly.

11. Save the file **lab_7-5.html**.

12. Insert a **<map>** tag. Add the *name* attribute with **"global"** as the value.

Note: Be sure to close your <map> tag properly.

13. Using **<area>** tags, insert the image map coordinates for this rectangular image. The following table lists the coordinates that you have already determined for each hot spot in this image, as well as the associated hyperlink reference for each image map area.

Note: Review the lesson if you do not remember the proper syntax for the <area> tag. A finished version of lab_7-5.html is provided in the C:\CIW\Site_Dev\Lab Files\Lesson07\Finished\Lab_7-5\ folder.

Hot Spot Coordinates	Hyperlink Reference URL
0,0,32,51	http://www.habitat.org/intl
33,1,86,50	http://www.habitat.org/wb
86,1,129,50	http://www.habitat.org/prison
1,52,33,96	http://www.habitat.org/lac
34,52,86,96	http://www.habitat.org/disaster
87,52,129,96	http://www.habitat.org/gv

14. As you create the six **\<area\>** tags, be sure that you close each tag properly, and that you use the *alt* attribute for each \<area\> so that users who are using text-only browsers or settings can navigate the image map.

15. Load the page into the browser; it should resemble Figure 7-14. Each square in the new image should link to a unique URL.

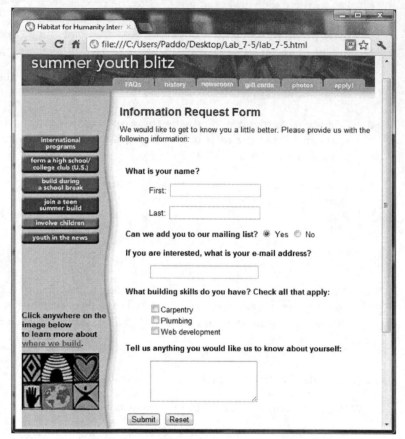

Figure 7-14: Page with image map

16. Verify that the image map functions as expected by testing each link. If the image map does not function correctly, review your code and make any necessary changes. When the image map renders and functions as expected, save the file and validate your code at ***http://validator.w3.org***.

17. As a class, discuss the strengths and drawbacks of image maps, including:

- Their effect on users with disabilities.

- Their effect on users with text-only browsers or settings.

- Their relative worth as navigational aids.

- Their ability to improve navigation.

In this lab, you created an image map and discussed its relative benefits to a Web page.

CIW Online Resources – Online Exercise

Visit CIW Online at *http://education.Certification-Partners.com/CIW* to complete an interactive exercise that will reinforce what you have learned about this topic.

Exercise 7-2: Defining a client-side image map

CIW Online Resources – Course Mastery

Visit CIW Online at *http://education.Certification-Partners.com/CIW* to take the Course Mastery review of this lesson or lesson segment.

SDA Lesson 7 - Part A

Image Transparency

OBJECTIVE
2.2.5: Advanced image formatting

An image that supports transparency provides the visual effect of blending in to the background of your Web page. In function, the page background simply shows through the transparent part of the image file. Most developers use image transparency to remove the blank image background so it appears to float on the page. However, you can make any element of an image transparent, not just its background.

The only Web-ready image file formats that support transparency are GIF 89a and PNG. The GIF 87a and JPEG formats do not support transparency. In Figure 7-15, you see a non-transparent PNG image rendered along the top of the page in the browser. Notice that you can see the image's white background, and that it obscures the page's background.

Figure 7-15: Standard PNG image on Web page without transparency

Although you may want an image to retain its natural background, some designs look better when the images blend with the page background. Figure 7-16 shows the same image from the previous figure now with a transparent background, allowing the page background to show through.

Figure 7-16: Same image with transparent background on Web page

Notice in this figure that you can no longer see the image's original white background; the image background is now transparent. Even if you change the Web page's background or background color, that background will appear through this image's background, making the image appear to float on the page background. Most developers refer to this type of image file as a transparent GIF, but remember that you can achieve this effect with the PNG format as well.

In the following lab, you will work with transparent GIF and PNG image files on a Web page. Suppose your project manager is pleased with the design of a Web page, but not with the graphic at the top. He and others have noted that the white background around the image is distracting, and he wants the image to blend in with other page elements. You send the original image file to a graphic artist on your development team, and she has returned PNG and GIF 89a versions of the image. You can now test both image file formats in the Web page and choose which one to use.

Lab 7-6: Inserting transparent GIF and PNG images in a Web page

OBJECTIVE
2.2.5: Advanced
image formatting

In this lab, you will insert transparent GIF 89a and transparent PNG image files into a Web page.

1. From the **C:\CIW\Site_Dev\Lab Files\Lesson07** directory, copy the **Lab_7-6** folder to your Desktop. This directory contains a copy of the Summer Youth Blitz page. It also contains a subfolder named Transparent\, which contains two transparent images (transSYBcollage2.gif and transSYBcollage2.png).

2. From your Desktop, open **Lab_7-6** and double-click the **index.html** file.

3. You will see a version of the Summer Youth Blitz page open in your browser, this time with two images: a purple background image, and a foreground image showing youths at work on a Habitat project. Notice that the foreground image, SYBcollage2.jpg, has a white background that partially obscures the background image.

4. Open **index.html** in a text editor. Edit the **<img>** tag in this file to replace SYBcollage2.jpg with the file **transSYBcollage2.gif**, which is a transparent GIF 89a

file. Save the **index.html** file, ensuring that the correct path is specified (the transSYBcollage2.gif file resides in the transparent\ subfolder).

5. Refresh **index.html** in your browser. You will now see the transparent image transSYBcollage2.gif in your page, if you referenced it properly in your code. This new image does not have a white background, but a transparent background that allows you to see the purple background image. Notice that the transparent image improves the look of this page.

6. Open **index.html** in a text editor, and edit the **<img>** tag so that it refers to your transparent PNG image, **transSYBcollage2.png**. Save the file **index.html** and refresh it in the browser. Notice that the PNG file also renders with a transparent background. Do you notice any differences between the two transparent image files? Which file type would you prefer to use on your Web page, and why?

In this lab, you inserted a transparent GIF image file and a transparent PNG image file into a Web page.

Image Interlacing

OBJECTIVE
2.2.5: Advanced image formatting

Interlacing is a technique that allows an image to progressively display in a browser as it downloads. The image will appear in stages over the period of downloading time. This action makes your pages more accessible to users with slower Internet connections.

Standard image formats are read from top to bottom. The top of a non-interlaced image will appear after the browser has read 50 percent of the image. The bottom half will render some time later, as shown in Figure 7-17.

Figure 7-17: Non-interlaced image rendering in browser

As you can see, a non-interlaced image can remain invisible or incomplete for some time to a user who is downloading the image across a slow connection.

By contrast, an interlaced image appears to fade in as it renders in the browser because it is interpreted differently. An interlaced image is repeatedly scanned from left to right. The first pass will render roughly 13 percent of the entire image. The second pass delivers 25 percent, and then continues in 25-percent increments until the image renders completely. During this process, the full image will at first appear fuzzy, but will continuously sharpen.

The only Web-ready image file formats that support interlacing are GIF and PNG. Both GIF formats, 87a and 89a, support interlacing. You can create an interlaced image by configuring an image file in a graphics-editing application and saving it as a compatible file type.

CIW Online Resources – Online Exercise

Visit CIW Online at *http://education.Certification-Partners.com/CIW* to complete an interactive exercise that will reinforce what you have learned about this topic.

Exercise 7-3: Reviewing interlaced and non-interlaced images

Animation

OBJECTIVE
2.2.2: Graphic file formats

2.2.5: Advanced image formatting

Creating an animated image involves combining several images in a sequence that is rendered in rapid succession to simulate motion. Some image formats support animation, others do not. You can also use languages and scripts to create animation. The following sections discuss common ways to create animation using Web-based technology.

Animated GIF and PNG

The only Web-ready image file formats that support animation are GIF 89a and PNG. Programs such as the Alchemy Mindworks GIF Construction Set (shown in Figure 7-18) allow you to incorporate several images into one file.

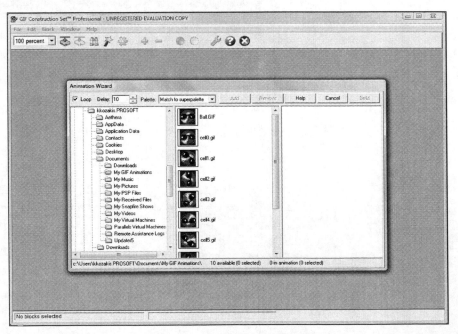

Figure 7-18: GIF Construction Set

Most animation programs allow you to control the way that images render in the browser (e.g., set the interval of appearance between images) and to create many other effects. You can obtain a copy of GIF Construction Set from Alchemy Mindworks (*www.mindworkshop.com/alchemy/gifcon.html*) or from TUCOWS downloads (*www.tucows.com/downloads*).

You can obtain other image animation shareware programs from TUCOWS or from CNET Download.com (*http://download.cnet.com*).

Flash animation

Instead of using sequences of PNG or GIF images, you can create animation using complex scripts, called macros. Adobe (*www.adobe.com*) has incorporated macros to create advanced animation capabilities using its proprietary Flash technology. Flash macros manipulate vector-based graphics to create animated sequences. Many images that appear to be animated PNGs or GIFs may actually be Flash presentations, and vice versa. Flash animations generally provide more sophisticated animation.

Flash-based animated movies are extremely popular but remain a proprietary technology. Flash movies are created using the Adobe Flash CS4 application. Animation creation applications are quite expensive. However, the Flash player, which allows you to view Flash animations, is a free browser plug-in supported by many user agents in various operating systems.

 Tech Tip *If you are interested in learning more about using Flash animation, it is recommended that you pursue the CIW Web Design Specialist course.*

Microsoft Silverlight

You can also create animation using another proprietary technology, Microsoft Silverlight (*www.microsoft.com/silverlight/*). Silverlight is Microsoft's response to Adobe Flash. It is compatible with multiple Web browsers (e.g., Windows Internet Explorer, Mozilla Firefox, Apple Safari) used on Microsoft Windows and Mac OS X operating systems.

Silverlight consists of the Silverlight application for creating Silverlight animations, and the Silverlight plug-in for viewing animations on the Web. The Silverlight plug-in needs to be launched from an HTML page via JavaScript. It is largely designed for online video playback and intense graphical interactivity.

Java applets

Java applets can also provide animated sequences in a Web page. For the animation to render, the user agent must have a Java interpreter installed. Java animations may not render as quickly as Flash or Silverlight movies, due to the nature of the Java interpreter used. Although the Java development environment and all Java players are freely available, Java remains a proprietary technology owned by Sun.

Scalable Vector Graphics (SVG)

You learned about vector graphics earlier in this lesson. Scalable Vector Graphics (SVG) is a W3C-recommended language developed by various vendors, including Adobe, Microsoft and Sun. SVG uses XML to describe graphics and graphical applications.

SVG allows you to create cross-platform animated movies. Not all SVG images are animated, but this application is common because SVG offers comprehensive animation support.

Unlike Java, Flash and Silverlight, SVG is an open standard. However, it provides similar features in addition to animation, including:

- **Compression** — The compression algorithms available in SVG allow you to create high-quality images and movies that are smaller in file size than other formats. SVG images have more efficient compression than JPG or GIF images.

- **Searchable text** — Text within SVG images can be indexed and searched.

- **Zooming** — You can zoom in on portions of an image without losing image quality.

SVG supports other technologies, including JPEG, GIF and Java. As with Flash, Silverlight and Java, a browser must be updated with a plug-in to render SVG data, but all major vendors incorporate support for SVG. To learn more about SVG, visit *www.w3.org/Graphics/SVG*.

Identifying animation techniques

There are at least two ways to learn more about an image or macro. Right-click the object and try to save it; you can then identify its properties. You can also view the source code of a Web page to see how the image or Flash/SVG/Java file was inserted into the page.

OBJECTIVE
2.10.3: Proprietary
technologies

Mobile Device Issues with Animation and Plug-Ins

As you create animated images, remember the following issues:

- **Animation techniques are often proprietary**, so your site visitors may need to download a plug-in. As a result, some users may choose not to visit your site. To solve this problem, you can create another version of your site to accommodate visitors without plug-ins. Remember that some users, such as those viewing your site on a smartphone or tablet, may be unable to access content you create using proprietary technologies. Creating an alternative site requires more time and resources on your part, but it ensures that your site is available to all users.

- **Plug-ins drain system resources.** Plugs-ins are required to view certain content because the content (such as animation or movies) will not play on Web browsers without them. As a result, plug-ins use additional CPU and battery power. This consideration is especially important for users on mobile devices, which depend upon battery power. Battery life can decrease as much as 40 percent on a mobile device when running a plug-in. HTML5 solves this issue by providing native support for animation, movies and other multimedia without the use of plug-ins. CSS and JavaScript are used instead.

 To learn more about plug-in resource usage and other effects on mobile devices, read the "Thoughts on Flash" article from Apple co-founder Steve Jobs at www.apple.com/hotnews/thoughts-on-flash/.

- **Animation may seem useful and interesting, but it is frequently overused.** Animation is often used to provide entertainment rather than information. Consider the purpose of animated images on your site. If they are used to provide information, be sure to include alternative text for users who are interested only in your site's informational content.

- **Animated images can limit accessibility.** Only the oldest browsers have a problem rendering animated images. However, older browsers also cannot render any PNG images. And although relatively few people use very old browser software, consider that people who use mobile phone technology to access Web sites may have problems using animated images.

 When it comes to search engine optimization, using animation too heavily can cause pages to be scored lower in search engine results.

Creating and Managing Images

Images are essential in Web site design. Users have come to expect a visually pleasing experience that can only be achieved with the use of images. As you have seen, images can also be used for navigation in the form of image maps and graphical buttons that link to other pages or resources. On a corporate site, the organization's logo and trademarks are crucial for name recognition and branding.

There are several options you can use to obtain and manage images for use on your Web pages. You can:

- Create original images using image-creation software.
- Scan hard-copy images.
- Use stock photographs.
- Obtain photos from photo-sharing Web sites.
- Use photo management software to organize, edit and share your images.

OBJECTIVE
2.2.8: Scanning and
editing images

2.2.9: Creating
images

Creating and scanning images

Image-creation software applications can often handle a variety of formats, such as GIF, JPEG and PNG. You can use these applications to:

- Create your own graphical images.
- Edit pictures.
- Modify digital photos.
- Create animations.
- Draw or paint images.

Popular image-creation applications include:

- Adobe Fireworks (*www.adobe.com*)
- Adobe Photoshop (*www.adobe.com*)
- Adobe Illustrator (*www.adobe.com*)
- The GIMP (*www.gimp.org*)
- Picasa (*http://picasa.google.com/*)
- Inkscape (*www.inkscape.org*)

Image layers

When you design an image, each individual component of the image can be created on its own layer, thus allowing that component to be manipulated independently of the entire image. A series of layers will compose an entire image, and an image can have as many layers as necessary.

However, although layers are supported in the PNG file format, they are not supported by GIF or JPG formats. This means that when the image is finalized, it must be flattened into a single layer to be exported to those formats, and then the layers can no longer be manipulated. If you maintain a copy of the original layered version of the image, you can make changes easily, and other versions of the image can be exported when necessary.

Scanning images

You can also use a scanner to scan images from a print source. The print source can be a photo, paper document, book, magazine, map or three-dimensional object (as long as it does not have a lot of depth; for example, a coin could be scanned). Unlike a photocopy machine that creates a paper hardcopy of the scanned item, a scanner creates a digital image in memory that you can save and then edit with an image-creation or photo management software application.

All digital images have certain attributes that can drastically affect quality and file size. A few of these attributes are discussed in the following sections.

Pixels

The term "pixel" is short for "picture element." The pixel is the smallest unit displayed by a computer monitor. Pixels in a grid form the building blocks for images that a computer can display.

Color depth

Pixels provide some amount of color information. This information, measured in bits, determines how many colors each pixel can display. For example, pixels with 4 bits of grayscale information can display up to 16 shades of gray. Eight bits of color information per pixel produces up to 256 bits of color information, and so forth. Higher bit values (also called bit depths) result in more intense or realistic colors. As the color depth increases, however, so does the file size.

Image resolution

A user's monitor resolution determines how large onscreen images will be displayed. Screen resolution depends on the number of pixels present in a monitor's height and width. Higher screen resolutions display more pixels per inch (ppi). For example, a 17-inch monitor set to a resolution of 1024x768 will not display as many pixels per inch (ppi) as a 17-inch monitor set to 1280x960.

For printing, greater detail is achieved with higher-resolution images, and this detail is measured in dots per inch (dpi). When scanning images from a print source or importing pictures from a digital camera for use on the Web, it is generally accepted that you should set the resolution to 72 dpi in order to display the image on screen at approximately the same size as the original image.

For Web images, the dimensions of the image in pixels — rather than the dpi or ppi — are most important. When designing a Web site, you will typically resize images to the dimensions you want to use on your Web page.

The relationship between actual size and pixel size can be a bit confusing at first. To understand it, consider an image that is 128 pixels wide by 128 pixels tall. If this image is displayed on a 17-inch monitor set to 1024x768 resolution, the image will occupy one-eighth of the width and one-sixth of the height available on the monitor screen. If the monitor is set to a resolution of 1280x960, then the image will take up less space on the screen. The monitor has not increased in size, and the image is still 128 pixels by 128 pixels. What has changed is that the monitor is displaying more pixels per inch (ppi). Because monitors can be set at different resolutions, there is no way to specify that an image should be 1 inch long, for example, on a Web page. Instead, you specify image size in pixels, such as 150 pixels or 300 pixels.

Using stock photographs

OBJECTIVE
2.2.10: Stock
photography

Stock photography is any group of images for which you can purchase the rights to use in printed material or on a Web site. Photographers file their images with an agency that negotiates licensing fees on the photographer's behalf. Stock photo images are then licensed from the agency.

Many modern stock photography distributors offer still photos, video and illustrations. Millions of photos are available for licensing, and all images on stock photography Web sites include embedded metadata that makes the images easily searchable by keywords.

Licensing stock photos

To use stock images, you must purchase a license. The license is a one-time fee that allows you to use the image(s) multiple times for multiple purposes. Generally, there is no time limit on when the purchaser must use the image, but there is usually a restriction on how many times the image can be reproduced (the specified number of times is often referred to as a print run). For example, a license might allow the purchaser to print 500,000 copies of a brochure using the image.

Two types of licensing are available:

- **Royalty-free license** — allows the buyer to use an image without having to pay a royalty each time the image is used. Royalty-free does not imply that the image is free to use without purchasing a license or that the image is in the public domain. The buyer also does not have the right to resell or transfer the image. The fee for the image is usually based on the size of the digital file. For example, a 600KB image might cost US$50 while a 10MB version of the same image might cost US$200.

- **Rights-managed license** — allows the buyer to "rent" an image through negotiation of a specific price for a specific use. Some rights-managed licenses stipulate exclusivity (i.e., the buyer may restrict similar use of the image by others for the duration of the license). Rights-managed licenses are usually more expensive than royalty-free licenses, but allow for much larger print runs. For example, a magazine with a large print run would use a rights-managed license instead of a royalty-free license. Generally, the fee charged is based on the scope of the project. For example, you might pay US$200 to use an image in a small brochure, or many thousands of dollars to use an image in a national advertising campaign.

Advantages and disadvantages of using stock photos

When developing a Web site, there are both advantages and disadvantages to using stock photography.

Advantages include saving time and money. Image databases are quick and easy to search, licenses can be purchased online, and images can be downloaded for use immediately. In most cases, licensing fees cost much less (especially royalty-free licenses) than hiring a photographer and models, and setting up a photo shoot.

Even if you were to use internal resources for conducting a photo shoot (thereby saving the cost of the licensing fee) you must consider the time factor. Using stock photos increases project speed. Another advantage to using stock photography is that you know exactly what the finished image looks like, while an assignment photo shoot may deliver photos that require editing.

Disadvantages to using stock photography can be the cost associated with the licensing fees and a reduction in creative control. You can select only from the images that are available and you may not be able to find exactly what you want.

Online stock photography resources

There are numerous stock photography Web sites with large databases of searchable photos and videos. These include:

*   Jupiter Images (*www.jupiterimages.com*)

*   Getty Images (*www.gettyimages.com*)

*   Shutterstock Images (*www.shutterstock.com*)

In addition to licensing single images, many sites offer access to collections of images on a monthly or yearly subscription basis.

Microstock photography: iStockphoto

iStockphoto (*www.istockphoto.com*) is an online microstock photography provider. Microstock photography is an offshoot of stock photography. Microstock providers deal almost exclusively over the Internet, accept photographs from amateur photographers as well as professionals, and sell their images at a very low cost (generally from US$0.20 to $10).

Image prices are based on credits. An image may cost between 1 and 20 credits, depending on size, and credits may range from US$0.95 to $1.40 each.

Contributing photographers categorize their images with keywords and upload them to the site's inspection queue, where they are reviewed for quality. Photographers receive a commission of between 20 and 40 percent of every sale. iStockphoto also sells vector graphics and raster illustrations.

Critics of iStockphoto contend that the company is devaluing the stock photography market by selling images so far below accepted price standards. The commission rate is also below the industry norm (50 percent) and based on much lower purchase fees.

Free images

Some Web sites offer digital photos for personal and commercial use free of charge, with certain restrictions. These restrictions can include various stipulations, for example:

*   The domain name of the Web site must not be removed from the photo.

*   The photos may not be resold.

*   The photographer who took the photos retains the original copyright.

A few sites that offer images free of charge include:

- FreeStockPhotos.com (*www.freestockphotos.com*).

- FreeImages.co.uk (*www.freeimages.co.uk*).

- Freepixels (*www.freepixels.com*).

Photo sharing

OBJECTIVE
2.2.11: Photo and portfolio management strategy

Another possible source for free images is photo-sharing Web sites, although photographs on these Web sites are copyrighted to the photographer and you must contact the photographer or owner of the photo to obtain permission to use the images.

Photo-sharing Web sites allow you upload, organize, view, share and download photos and other image files. Some sites are free, whereas others offer subscription-based services. Free sites generally rely on advertising or the selling of prints for revenue. These sites feature ads. Some sites offer subscriptions for their premium services, and a scaled-down version with fewer features as their free package.

Some photo-sharing sites require you to download an application in order to upload and manage photos. Some also support only specific platforms or browsers.

The best photo-sharing sites:

- Allow you to create private and public photo albums

- Include password-protected access

- Prevent unauthorized downloading of photos (e.g., through right-clicking and selecting a Save option)

- Provide online tools for editing photos (e.g., cropping, red-eye removal, etc.)

- Offer the ability to buy and sell prints and other gifts

- Allow you to search for photos by keyword "tags" or date.

Several sites also accept pictures taken with camera phones, and some allow you to upload and share video as well.

History of photo sharing

The first photo-sharing sites appeared in the late 1990s offering photo finishing (e.g., touch-ups, red-eye removal, etc.) and online print ordering.

As digital cameras and camera phones became more widely used, more and more users signed up for photo-sharing services. Today, many photo-sharing sites include social networking and business elements, such as the ability to create and join communities, create private and public photo albums, and sell your personal photographs online.

Modern photo-sharing services strive to make organizing, storing and sharing digital photos convenient, safe and easy. These sites offer various ways to share pictures, including the print purchasing and creation of unique gifts (such as luggage tags, postcards, mugs, mouse pads, calendars, etc.) featuring selected photos.

Some sites are also geared to professional and semi-professional photography enthusiasts who can sell their work, or who want a forum where they can display their photos and receive feedback from other photographers around the world.

Selecting photo-sharing services

When selecting sites and services, consumers should consider criteria such as:

- Relative ease of use.

- Tools for managing photo albums and videos.

- Tools for photo editing.

- Monthly or annual fees.

- Storage space and daily upload limits.

- Presences or absence of ads and spam.

- Ability to buy and sell prints.

- Password-protected access.

Several photo-sharing sites advertise themselves as "family-friendly," prohibiting photos or other media portraying adult content.

Popular photo-sharing sites include:

- Badongo (*www.badongo.com*).

- DotPhoto (*www.dotphoto.com*).

- Webshots (*www.webshots.com*).

- Fotki (*www.fotki.com/us/en*).

- Flickr (*www.flickr.com*).

- SmugMug (*www.smugmug.com*).

- Picasa (*http://picasa.google.com*).

- Snapfish (*www.snapfish.com*).

- Shutterfly (*www.shutterfly.com*).

OBJECTIVE
2.2.11: Photo and portfolio management strategy

Photo management

You can use photo-management software to organize your portfolio. Photo-management software applications often have photo-sharing capabilities, but are designed primarily to enable you to organize, as well as edit, your photos. You can use photo-management software to:

- Scan your hard drive for pictures and create a single, digital library for them.

- Upload photos directly from your camera, scanner or memory card. You can also download photos to your camera.

- Browse, edit and share your photos from the library you create.

- Sort your photos into virtual albums.

- Add tags to photos.

- Conduct searches for photos based on specific criteria.

- Build slide shows with your photos.

- Burn pictures to CDs and DVDs.

Examples of photo management software include:

- Adobe Photoshop Lightroom (*www.adobe.com*).

- Adobe Photoshop Elements (*www.adobe.com*).

- Apple Aperture (*www.apple.com*).

- Apple iPhoto (*www.apple.com*).

- Preclick Gold (*www.preclick.com*).

- ACDSee Pro (*www.acdsee.com*).

- Corel Photo Album (*www.corel.com*).

- FotoTime FotoAlbum (*www.fototime.com*).

- Roxio PhotoShow (*www.photoshow.com*).

CIW Online Resources – Online Exercise

Visit CIW Online at *http://education.Certification-Partners.com/CIW* to complete an interactive exercise that will reinforce what you have learned about this topic.

Exercise 7-4: Creating and managing images

Search engine optimization and images

Consider the following issues in relation to search engine optimization (SEO) and images:

- The file name for an image should be as descriptive as possible. For example, consider an image of a product you want to sell on your SCUBA equipment Web site. Instead of using a name such as *product.gif* for a SCUBA regulator image file, name the image file scubapro_mk-17_regulator.gif. However, do not get carried away and create extremely long file names.

- Use the *alt* attribute in every <img> tag to provide an apt description of the image. Doing so not only improves accessibility, it also compels search engine bots to score the page better.

- Consider using keywords for image file names.

To ensure the most success, take the time to learn exactly what a search engine looks for.

CIW Online Resources – Course Mastery

Visit CIW Online at *http://education.Certification-Partners.com/CIW* to take the Course Mastery review of this lesson or lesson segment.

SDA Lesson 7 - Part B

Case Study

A Web Site's Image

Vivi works on the Web development team for a world-renowned museum in Los Angeles. She supervises the creation of image files that are posted on the site.

Vivi regularly receives new image files from the marketing department to promote exhibits, lectures and other events at the museum. She also keeps a vast catalog of image files representing the museum's offerings, grounds and most famous works. Sometimes she moves popular images to different pages of the site, where they must share space (and memory) with other related image files. She also incorporates some animated images that demonstrate preservation processes, illustrate historical timelines and recapture event highlights.

The museum Web site receives a great deal of traffic from users around the world, with the images being a popular feature of the site. Vivi has developed the following parameters for images that will be posted to the Web site:

- Images must be the best quality possible to display works of fine art.

- Images must be easily downloadable, even by clients with dial-up access (e.g., 56 Kbps or even slower).

- Images must be in formats compatible with even the oldest browsers.

Vivi receives images in various electronic and paper-based formats. She converts all image files to JPEG and GIF formats before posting them on the Web site. She also regularly reviews the visitor feedback comments submitted to the site to monitor any accessibility problems with the images.

                    *   *   *

As a class, discuss this scenario and answer the following questions:

- Why does Vivi use JPEG and GIF images on the site, but not PNG images?

- Is it wise for Vivi to include animated GIF images on the site? Why or why not? Are animated images useful on this Web site? What alternatives could she use for animated content?

- What accessibility challenges are inherent to Vivi's project? Are there any techniques Vivi could use to make image content on her Web site more accessible to users with limited or no image viewing capability?

- How else could Vivi use images effectively on this site?

Lesson Summary

Application project

This lesson discussed using video, audio, image maps, transparent images, interlaced images and animated images as Web page content. Take some time to learn more about each of these techniques. Use Google, Yahoo!, Bing and other search engines to conduct searches for information about each of these techniques.

Also visit Google at *www.google.com* and select the Images and Video links. Google's Image Search and Video Search allows you to search images and videos on the Web using keywords like you would for a Web page search. Experiment by entering keywords in Google Image Search and Video Search, and review the files that are returned in the search results. How does Google know which images and videos match your search criteria? Are all of the image and video files returned in the search results relevant to the keywords you entered? Why or why not?

Remember to consider copyright restrictions when viewing image and animation on the Web, and posting these enhancements to your own Web pages. The images you see on the Web are the copyrighted property of the image file owner. Do not copy an image file you find on the Web and post it on your own site, or you may be subject to copyright infringement penalties. Some images are available for reuse on a copyright-free or permission-only basis. Conduct a search for Web sites providing image files that you are allowed to use for free. Can you find any useful image or animation files?

Skills review

In this lesson, you learned about the HTML5 <video> and <audio> elements. You converted proprietary video formats to HTML5-supported formats. You imbedded both video and audio files into Web pages using the required attributes and elements. You also learned several image techniques to use on your Web pages. You created a client-side image map by determining coordinates, defining image map hot spots and linking image hot spots to other pages. You also learned about image transparency, interlacing and animation. Finally, you learned how to obtain and manage images by creating original images using image-creation software, scanning hard-copy images, using stock photographs, obtaining photos from photo-sharing Web sites, and using photo-management software to organize, edit and share your images.

Now that you have completed this lesson, you should be able to:

✓ 2.2.2: Distinguish among and identify the uses and benefits of various graphic file formats, including GIF, GIF89a, JPEG, PNG, TIFF, BMP.

✓ 2.2.4: Create and link client-side image maps.

✓ 2.2.5: Perform advanced image formatting techniques.

✓ 2.2.7: Distinguish between raster and vector graphics.

✓ 2.2.8: Scan and edit hard copy sources and images.

✓ 2.2.9: Identify steps for creating images, including resolution, format and layers.

✓ 2.2.10: Identify benefits and drawbacks of using stock photography.

✓ 2.2.11: Create a photo and portfolio management strategy, including online and offline storage, software and services.

✓ 2.10.3: Evaluate the benefits and drawbacks of proprietary technologies such as Adobe Flash and Microsoft Silverlight.

✓ 2.10.5: Create a basic video file using video capture and editing software.

✓ 2.10.6: Insert a video file into a Web page using the HTML5 <video> element and attributes.

✓ 2.10.7: Insert an audio file into a Web page using the HTML5 <audio> element and attributes.

CIW Practice Exams

Visit CIW Online at *http://education.Certification-Partners.com/CIW* to take the Practice Exams assessment covering the objectives in this lesson.

SDA Objective 2.02 Review

SDA Objective 2.10 Review

Note that some objectives may be only partially covered in this lesson.

Lesson 7 Review

1. What is one concern regarding plug-ins and mobile devices?

    _____

    _____

2. What are the three video formats supported by the HTML5 <video> element?

    _____

3. What is the easiest way for Web developers to support multiple video formats for different HTML5-compliant browsers?

    _____

4. How can Web developers configure a video to play immediately when it loads?

    _____

    _____

5. What is an image map "hot spot"?

    _____

6. Name the two coordinates used to define a point on any image shape.

    _____

7. Name two Web-ready image file formats that support transparency.

    _____

8. A non-interlaced image will begin to render after the browser has read what percentage of the image file?

    _____

9. Image layers are supported in which file format?

    _____

10. Why should you specify the size of your Web images in pixels?

    _____

    _____

    _____

Lesson 8:
Extending HTML

Objectives

By the end of this lesson, you will be able to:

- 2.1.6: Define the Document Object Model (DOM) and its relationship to Dynamic HTML (DHTML).

- 2.1.9: Add third-party applications to your Web page (e.g., Google gadgets for the Web).

- 2.10.8: Describe various HTML5 Application Programming Interfaces (APIs), including canvas, geolocation, offline Web application, drag-and-drop.

- 2.10.9: Demonstrate basic HTML5 API functionality using JavaScript and HTML5 elements.

- 2.17.1: Compare popular client-side and server-side programming languages, including JavaScript, Java, PHP, Python, .Net, C, C++, Visual Basic, C#.

- 2.17.2: Define Common Gateway Interface (CGI) methods, including .Net, Django, Python, JavaServer Pages (JSP), Server-Side JavaScript (SSJS), Active Server Pages (ASP), PHP Hypertext Preprocessor (PHP), Ajax.

- 2.17.5: Identify the value of n-tier applications and associated techniques in processing online transactions.

- 2.19.1: Identify ways to use additional technologies to provide custom features to an end user (e.g., using JavaScript to detect Web browser type, using cookies).

Pre-Assessment Questions

1. How does an application created in PHP differ from an application created in JavaScript?

    a. The PHP application requires an interpreter.
    b. The PHP application requires an interpreter on a server.
    c. The PHP application requires an interpreter on a UNIX Web server.
    d. The PHP application requires an open-source interpreter.

2. Which HTML5 Application Programming Interface (API) allows a Web program to run locally on a client system?

    a. Offline Web application
    b. Drag-and-drop
    c. Canvas
    d. Geolocation

3. What interpreted, cross-platform, object-based scripting language can add interactivity to a Web page?

_____

Extending HTML

You are not limited to HTML when developing Web pages. In this lesson, you will learn about client-side and server-side Web technologies for extending the capabilities of your Web pages. Technologies discussed in this lesson include:

- Client-side and server-side scripting.

- Document Object Model (DOM) and Dynamic HTML (DHTML).

- HTML5 Application Programming Interfaces (APIs).

- Web application frameworks.

- Databases.

This lesson will also discuss other advanced Web technologies made possible through the combination of HTML5, JavaScript and Cascading Style Sheets (CSS).

CIW Online Resources – Movie Clips

Visit CIW Online at http://education.Certification-Partners.com/CIW to watch a movie clip about this topic.

Lesson 8: Extending HTML

Server-Side and Client-Side Languages

Before you learn about specific server-side and client-side languages, it is helpful to understand some basic programming terms. Table 8-1 describes some essential concepts in programming.

Table 8-1: Basic programming concepts

Concept	Description
Variable	A place in memory used to store information for later use. Variables are used in simple applications and are essential in complex ones. Variables are usually created by using the equal sign (=). For example, to create a variable named James, you would use the following command: James=James. Variables are often referred to as values preceded with a dollar sign ($). For example, the variable named James would be referred to as $James. In many languages, variables are case-specific (e.g., the variable $James is different from the variable $james).
Array	A collection of variables stored in a series. Arrays are used to hold multiple values; a variable can hold only one value.
Function	A line of code that allows you to refer to an entire series of steps or commands. Functions are used to organize code into discrete sections.
Interpreter	Software used to read and process code in standard text files. Interpreters either reside on the server or are downloaded to a client. PHP, Perl and ASP are all languages that use an interpreter. Some CGI applications must explicitly specify the location of the interpreter. For example, Perl requires the first line to include a correct reference, or the script will fail.
Compiler	An application used to process code in standard text files into executable applications. For example, to compile a C application named james.c, you would use the gcc application: gcc james.c -o james.exe.

Table 8-1: Basic programming concepts (cont'd)

Concept	Description
Include	A set of files called a library that you can refer to in your code. Programmers often include libraries in their code to avoid having to re-create code that has already been written.
Print	A command that prints application output to a destination, often a computer screen. For example, you can create an application that prints information to a window on the screen so you can monitor the application's progress. Print is generally part of a programming language's Input/Output library, which is responsible for allowing users to input information (e.g., through a keyboard) or output information (e.g., to a monitor).
Echo	A command that repeats the input you type back to a terminal or an application window. Echo can also be used in an application to repeat input so that it can be processed or forwarded.
Statement	Logical constructs that allow you to control the way that information flows in the application.

Programming statements

Even relatively simple scripts must control the way that information flows within them. Sometimes, an application must determine the action it will take if a certain condition occurs or while a certain condition exists. Table 8-2 describes several programming statements that allow applications to process information.

Table 8-2: Programming statements

Statement	Description
If/then	Executes a process only if a particular condition is true. For example, an application may contain a statement that checks whether the \tmp\ folder is present. If it is, then the application will run. Classic *if/then* statements allow only one condition to occur. Known as a conditional statement.
If/then/else	Similar to an *if/then* statement, but executes a group of additional commands if the given condition is false. For example, an *if/then/else* statement can direct the following logic: If the \tmp\ folder is not available, then check to see if the \temp\ directory is available, or else create a directory named \tmp\. Known as a conditional statement.
Do while	Runs ("do") a specified subprocess while a specified condition is true. For example, an application may continue to present an alternative window while the mouse is being right-clicked. Often used as a part of an *if/then* or *if/then/else* statement, the *do while* statement ensures that an action occurs the entire time a condition is true. Sometimes known as a *repeat until* statement.
Do until	Similar to a *do while* statement, but runs the specified subprocess until a specified number of events have occurred. For example, a calculation process may add the number 1 to the result of the previous statement until the sum reaches 100, then exit.
Break	When placed inside of a statement, allows an application to break out of an infinite loop in case of a problem.

The following sections discuss server-side and client-side Web technologies commonly used to extend Web pages. Each of the languages discussed allows you to implement some or all of the programming statements and concepts described in the preceding tables.

Server-Side Languages

OBJECTIVE
2.17.1: Programming
languages

A server-side language has the following attributes:

- Code is executed by the Web server, not by the Web browser.

- Code is generally placed into files called applications. These applications are assigned execute permissions by the Web server. In some cases, code is embedded into HTML pages.

- Code executes because an interpreter has been installed and activated on the Web server.

Server-side scripts are used for various purposes, including:

- Browser detection.

- Database connectivity.

- Cookie creation and identification.

- Logon scripts.

- Hit counters.

- File uploading and downloading.

Common server-side languages include PHP, Perl, Active Server Pages (ASP), Visual Basic, C, C++, C# and Java. The following sections will discuss each of these languages.

OBJECTIVE
2.17.2: CGI methods

PHP Hypertext Preprocessor (PHP)

PHP is an interpreted server-side scripting language for creating dynamic Web pages. It is embedded in HTML pages but is usually executed on a Web server. The following code example is a very simple PHP CGI application that creates the message "Hello, World" in HTML, then returns a report identifying the browser used to access the Web page. This script can be placed in a Web server's CGI bin directory:

```
<?php
$ua = $_SERVER['HTTP_USER_AGENT'];
{print"
<html>
<head>
<title>PHP Example</title>
</head>
<body>
<h1>Hello, World!</h1>
Your user agent is:<strong>{$ua}.</strong>
</body>
</html>
";}
?>
```

In this code, the syntax *<?php* begins the statement that allows code execution. Figure 8-1 shows the results of this code when viewed in a Web browser (in this case, Mozilla Firefox running on a Red Hat Linux system using the X Window interface).

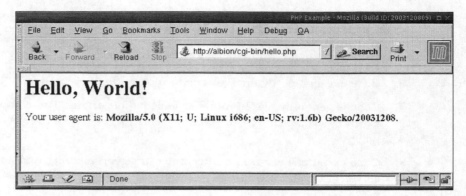

Figure 8-1: Viewing results of "Hello World" PHP script

As you can see, the PHP server-side code has detected and reported the user agent used to access it. However, you can do more with this information than simply return it to the user. You could use this information to customize a user's experience depending upon the browser used. For example, this script could direct Internet Explorer users to one version of the site, and Mozilla Firefox users to another.

Practical Extraction and Report Language (Perl)

Perl is a cross-platform programming language that enables users to write custom CGI programs and system management programs. Perl is a language commonly used for various purposes, including Web server processes. The following example code shows a simple Perl program that performs the same function as the PHP script profiled previously:

```perl
#!/usr/bin/perl
use CGI qw/:all/;
$cgi_object = CGI::new();

print "Content-type: text/html\n\n";
print "<html>\n<head>\n<title>\nPerl CGI
Example\n</title>\n<body>\n<h1>Hello,
World!</h1>\nYour user agent is: <b>\n";
print $cgi_object->user_agent();
print "</b>.</html>\n";
```

In this code, notice the first line that begins with the #! characters. This first line is known as the "shebang." The shebang is used in Perl applications to point to the location of the Perl interpreter. Many problems with Perl scripts originate with an improperly created shebang line.

This code provides only a very simple example of Perl's capabilities.

OBJECTIVE
2.17.2: CGI methods

Active Server Pages (ASP) using VBScript

Active Server Pages (ASP) is Microsoft's original server-side scripting solution. It has largely been supplanted by .NET. You can create ASP applications using VBScript, which is quite similar to JavaScript, except that VBScript is a proprietary Microsoft language. PHP is an alternative to ASP.

The following example VBScript ASP code enables browser detection:

```asp
<%@ LANGUAGE=vbscript %>
<html>
<head>
```

```
<title>ASP CGI Example</title>
</head>
<body>
<h1>Hello, World!</h1>
<%
path = Request.ServerVariables("PATH_INFO")
pagename = Request.ServerVariables("HTTP_HOST")
method = Request.ServerVariables("REQUEST_METHOD")
browser = Request.ServerVariables("HTTP_USER_AGENT")
user = Request.ServerVariables("REMOTE_ADDR")
```

C

C is a powerful compiled programming language that has served as the foundation for other languages, including C++ and Java. Although C was first developed in the late 1960s, it remains popular today. It is mostly used to develop stand-alone applications, rather than Web applications. For example, most daemons (i.e., services) are written in C.

C is a procedural language, meaning that it relies upon subprograms to accomplish a task in an application. Subprograms are contained within an application and are called by various terms depending upon the language used. In C, subprograms are called functions.

C uses standard libraries that you can include in the program. These libraries are common to any C implementation and are designed to save you coding time. Without these libraries, you would be forced into writing hundreds of lines of code each time you created an application. Many different library files exist. C has been organized as a language so that these libraries are standardized and available to everyone.

The following code demonstrates an extremely simple C program:

```
#include <stdio.h>
int main()
{
    printf("Hello, World!\n");
    return 0;
}
```

Notice that this code uses a library inclusion, called *stdio.h*. This inclusion is the standard I/O library, responsible for printing the phrase "Hello, World!" to your screen. The standard I/O library is also responsible for allowing users to input information into applications you write. However, the example code does not contain any logic that allows you to enter information into this program. All C programs must have a main function, which in C begins with the code *int main()*.

C++

object-oriented
A style of programming that links data to the processes that manipulate it.

C++ is another compiled programming language. It is not a proprietary language; compilers are available from a variety of sources, including Microsoft (*www.microsoft.com*) and GNU (*www.gnu.org*). Based on C, C++ is not procedural in nature. Rather, it is an **object-oriented** language. An object-oriented language may include procedural elements, but instead of using subprograms to accomplish a task, a language such as C++ will create an object that can then be manipulated throughout the program. The primary benefit of object-oriented languages is that they allow developers to create efficient, powerful code. Table 8-3 describes common object-oriented language terms used by C++, as well as Java, Visual Basic and C#.

Table 8-3: Object-oriented language terms

Term	Description
Object	A discrete portion of an application. Once an object is instantiated (i.e., created), it can then be used. All objects have specific states and behaviors that can be manipulated. An object is also known as an instance, because an object can be duplicated and then manipulated within a program.
Abstraction	The determination of all elements that make a particular object unique, separate and distinct from another instance of an object.
Class	A group of similar objects.
Polymorphism	The ability of the programming language to make an object behave differently or to take on different characteristics, depending upon its place in an application.
Inheritance	The ability for one class to share characteristics with another class. Characteristics can include an object's state, structure or behavior.

All C++ programs must be compiled to a specific computer type (e.g., IBM-compatible machines that run Windows). Once a C++ program is compiled to a specific type of host, it cannot be run on another (e.g., a Macintosh system) unless an **emulator** is used.

Java

Java is also an object-oriented programming language. Java is a compiled language, like C and C++. Unlike C++, however, Java is designed to allow its applications to run on any operating system that has the Java interpreter installed. As a result, Java has two benefits:

- **Java is object-oriented** — It allows the creation of powerful applications.

- **Java is platform-independent** — You do not compile a Java application to a specific computer type (e.g., IBM, Macintosh or Sun Sparc). Rather, you compile a Java application to a specific Java interpreter. The Java interpreter can be installed on any system, and the Java application can be used on any system running the interpreter.

Uncompiled text files that contain Java code often have the .java file name extension. When a file is compiled into a Java application, the file usually has the .jar extension.

This portion of the course focuses on using Java on the server side. Java is also used to create applets, which are executed by a client's browser and are thus a client-side technology.

JavaServer Pages (JSP) and Java servlets

Java can be used to create a JavaServer Pages (JSP) API. JSP is a technology that uses Java commands embedded into HTML code.

Java can be used to create Java servlets. A Java servlet is an application that must be installed directly onto the remote server; code from a Java servlet is not downloaded to the browser. When using Java servlets, you must perform the following steps:

- Compile the servlet.

- Place the servlet on a server that is capable of handling it.

One of the most popular Web servers that supports JSP and servlets is Apache Tomcat (*http://tomcat.apache.org/*).

The Microsoft implementation of Java is known as J++.

Visual Basic

Visual Basic (VB) is a compiled programming language developed by Microsoft Corporation. It is used for stand-alone applications and server-side Web applications. It is not often used as a client-side application in Web browsers, as is JavaScript or VBScript.

Earlier versions of Visual Basic were more procedural in nature than they were object-oriented. Visual Basic now has more object-oriented capabilities. It is often used in the Microsoft .NET CGI solution. Visual Basic is considered to be easier to use than languages such as C++ and Java, but as a result, this simplicity sometimes does not allow Visual Basic to perform all the tasks that C++ and Java can perform. For more information about Visual Basic, visit the Microsoft Visual Basic Developer Center at *http://msdn.microsoft.com/en-us/vstudio/hh388568*.

C#

C# (pronounced "C sharp") is a compiled object-oriented programming language, and is the proprietary Microsoft competitor to Java. C# was designed to be easier to use (like Visual Basic) but still powerful. C# is also sometimes known as Visual C#, the Microsoft product name. Because C# is a Microsoft-specific language, it has features that make it much easier to develop applications and interfaces for the Windows operating systems. For more information about C#, visit the Microsoft Visual C# Developer Center at *http://msdn.microsoft.com/en-us/vstudio/hh388566*.

CIW Online Resources – Online Exercise

Visit CIW Online at *http://education.Certification-Partners.com/CIW* to complete an interactive exercise that will reinforce what you have learned about this topic.

Exercise 8-1: Reviewing main server-side scripting languages

Server-side includes (SSIs)

A server-side include (SSI) is an instruction within an HTML page that directs the Web server to perform an action. SSI is considered to be an alternative to CGI because it does not use languages such as JavaScript, Visual Basic or Java. Rather, SSI instructions are written in SGML. The instruction is used to dynamically add content to a page just before it is downloaded to a user. SSI can be used to:

- Place the results of a database query into a page.

- Execute other programs.

- Indicate the last time that the displayed document was modified.

- Insert text at the bottom of a page (i.e., a footer). The footer can contain any text you want, from the current date to a customized message.

- Add the current date as a timestamp to a page.

SSI file name extensions

A Web server that supports SSI reads each HTML page for SSI instructions, and then processes the instructions for each user request. Standard practice is for HTML files that use SSI to use the .shtml or .shtm file name extension, rather than simply .html or .htm. The Web server knows to look for files with these extensions.

SSI support in Web servers

Most Web servers include SSI capability. However, the SSI feature may be disabled. For example, if you are using Apache Server, you must edit the *httpd.conf* file to enter the instructions necessary for Apache Server to process the server-side includes found in HTML pages. With Microsoft Internet Information Services (IIS), you must select features in the GUI to enable SSI.

Even though your Web server may be configured to support SSI, it may not be configured to look for the standard .shtml or .shtm file name extensions. In such cases, you can take either of two approaches:

- Find the supported extension type for SSI.

- Define a MIME type for the .shtml or .shtm extensions for the Web server.

Either solution will allow the Web server to process SSI instructions.

Client-Side Languages

OBJECTIVE
2.17.1: Programming
languages

Client-side languages run on the user's computer after the page is downloaded. Therefore, some of the processing burden can be passed from the server to the client machine. Allowing the client to do the work frees the server to perform other, more important functions and services. The following sections discuss JavaScript and VBScript, the two most popular client-side languages.

Issues with client-side languages

Using server-side technologies is sometimes preferable because there are risks inherent in allowing the client to determine the way your Web pages render. Consider the following problems:

- Some clients do not support JavaScript or any other scripting language.

- Users can deactivate script execution in browsers that normally support it. Many companies direct their employees to disable scripting in their browsers due to security concerns. If your page relies upon client-side scripting for browser recognition and/or database connectivity, then your pages may not render as expected to some portion of your audience.

JavaScript

JavaScript is an object-based scripting language that allows developers to add interactivity to their Web pages. JavaScript can be used on the client side or on the server side. When used on the client side, JavaScript code must reside inside HTML documents in order to run. JavaScript can add the following functionality to a Web page or site:

- Pop-up windows, such as alert, dialog and prompt boxes

- Automatic date and time changes

- Images and text that change upon mouse rollover

- Cookie creation and identification

Unlike traditional programming languages, such as C, a scripting language is used within a program to extend its capabilities. If you have ever written a macro in Microsoft Excel or used WordBasic to perform some task in a Microsoft Word document, you have already used a scripting language.

JavaScript syntax closely resembles that of C. The code is placed within your Web document so that when your browser retrieves a page that incorporates JavaScript, it runs the programs and performs the appropriate operations.

JavaScript is object-based, not object-oriented

object-based
Similar to object-oriented programming languages, but does not allow for inheritance from one class to another.

JavaScript is not considered an object-oriented language because it does not support inheritance. JavaScript is an **object-based** language that has a collection of built-in objects, including:

- **Document** — allows you to obtain values from and write values to a document.

- **Navigator** — allows you to determine the type of browser accessing a Web page.

- **Array** — allows you to create a series of variables to later manipulate.

Several additional objects exist. JavaScript allows you to apply methods to all objects. For example, the *document.write* command in JavaScript allows you to write a specified value to a document. To learn more about JavaScript, enroll in the *CIW JavaScript Fundamentals* course.

JavaScript advantages

JavaScript offers programmers several advantages, including a short development cycle, ease of learning, and platform-independence. These advantages make JavaScript a natural choice to easily and quickly extend HTML pages on the Web. Table 8-4 describes these JavaScript benefits.

Table 8-4: JavaScript advantages

Advantage	Description
Quick development	Because JavaScript does not require time-consuming compilation, scripts can be developed in a relatively short period of time. Most of the interface features, such as forms, frames and other GUI elements, are handled by the browser and HTML code, further shortening the development time. JavaScript programmers do not have to create or handle these elements of their applications.
Easy to learn	Although JavaScript shares many characteristics with the Java programming language, the JavaScript syntax and rules are simpler. If you know any other programming languages, it will be easy for you to learn JavaScript.
Platform-independence	Like HTML, JavaScript is not specific to any operating system. The same JavaScript program can be used on any browser on any system, provided that the browser supports JavaScript.

Embedding JavaScript into HTML

JavaScript must reside within an HTML document. It is embedded into HTML code using the <script> tag. Note that JavaScript placement is not restricted to the <body> element. The following example demonstrates the basic structure of an HTML file with JavaScript.

```
<!DOCTYPE html>
<html>
<head>
<meta name="Keywords" content="CIW, Web Foundations Associate, Example"/>
<meta name="Description" content="For the CIW Web Foundations Associate
courses"/>
<meta charset="utf-8"/>
<title>JavaScript</title>
```

```
<script>
JavaScript code goes here
</script>

</head>
<body>

<script>
JavaScript can go here too
</script>

</body>
</html>
```

In JavaScript, the Web author can communicate with the user through the *alert()* and *prompt()* functions. These functions are both properties of the *window* document. The Web author can also use the *document.write()* function to output text to the client window in sequence with an HTML. The *alert()* function displays an alert dialog box. The *prompt()* function requests user input in a text area within a dialog box. The *prompt()* function initiates a conversation, or dialog. The result returned by the *prompt()* can be used as an argument to another method, such as the *document.write()*.

OBJECTIVE
2.19.1: Custom site
feature
technologies

JavaScript and browser detection

JavaScript can also be used to detect browser type and version. Consider the following code:

```
<!DOCTYPE html>
<html>
<head>
<meta name="Keywords" content="CIW, Web Foundations Associate, Example"/>
<meta name="Description" content="For the CIW Web Foundations Associate
courses"/>
<meta charset="utf-8"/>
<title>Browser Detection Using JavaScript</title>
</head>
<body>
<h1> Hello, World!</h1>
<script type="text/javascript" >

document.write("Your user agent is: "+ navigator.userAgent)
document.write(".")
</script>
</body>
</html>
```

In this example, the JavaScript code uses the *write* method of the *document* object and the *userAgent* method of the *navigator* object to write the user agent information to the page. No CGI script is necessary for this code to render; you need only the JavaScript interpreter, which is included in almost all modern browsers by default.

User agents such as Lynx often do not support JavaScript or other forms of client-side scripting.

Practical uses for scripts of this type include:

- Presenting different versions of a site to different browsers.

- Informing users in a corporate intranet to upgrade their browsers to a supported version.

- Ensuring accessibility to disabled users.

Version 2.0

In the following lab, you will use JavaScript code to perform browser detection. Suppose your project manager still wants your Web pages to be able to automatically detect a user's browser type and version. However, she was not satisfied with the PHP solution you demonstrated for her previously. She asks you to demonstrate a similar solution that can be enabled on the client side.

 Lab 8-1: Using JavaScript to detect browser type

In this lab, you will use JavaScript in a Web page to detect the type and version of browsers being used to access the page.

1. From the **C:\CIW\Site_Dev\Lab Files\Lesson08\Lab_8-1** directory, copy the **hello.html** file to your Desktop.

2. **Browser:** Open the **hello.html** file. Your screen should list the browser type and version. The example in Figure 8-2 shows that the browser is Mozilla Firefox 11.0 on Windows NT 6.1 (Windows 7).

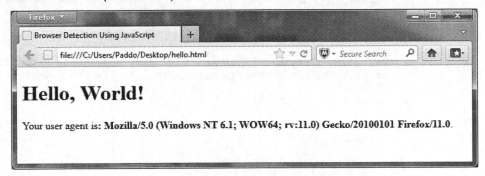

Figure 8-2: Using JavaScript for browser detection

3. Close your browser.

4. As a class, discuss the following questions:

   • What are the benefits of using this client-side script instead of a server-side script?

   • What are the drawbacks of using this client-side script instead of a server-side script?

   • What practical uses are there for this script?

5. **When time permits:** The instructor can upload this page to a Web server, then you can access this page across a network.

In this lab, you used JavaScript to detect browser type and version.

OBJECTIVE
2.19.1: Custom site feature technologies

JavaScript and cookies

You can also use JavaScript to deposit cookies on the system hard drives of users who visit your site. Using simple JavaScript code, you can use cookies to:

• Store passwords.

• Store user preferences.

- Choose which Web pages will be displayed based on the browser version used.

JavaScript can also be used for copyright protection. A simple script can help prevent your Web site from being included in another site without proper recognition.

In the following lab, you will incorporate some simple JavaScript code into a Web page. Suppose your project manager wants a feature on the Web page that asks the user to enter his or her name, then incorporates the user input into a greeting. You can add some JavaScript code to your HTML to create this feature.

 Lab 8-2: Using simple JavaScript to create an interactive Web page

In this lab, you will incorporate a simple JavaScript function into a Web page.

1. From **C:\CIW\Site_Dev\Lab Files\Lesson08\Lab_8-2** directory, copy the file **lab_8-2.html** to your Desktop.

2. **Editor:** Open **lab_8-2.html**, and add the JavaScript code as indicated in bold:

```
<!DOCTYPE html>
<html>
<head>
<meta name="Keywords" content="CIW, Web Foundations Associate, Example"/>
<meta name="Description" content="For the CIW Web Foundations Associate
courses"/>
<meta charset="utf-8"/>

<title>Simple JavaScript</title>
</head>
<body>
<h1> Simple JavaScript </h1>
<script type="text/javascript" >

 alert("You are entering the world of JavaScript");
    document.write("Hello, ");
    document.write(prompt("What is your name?", ""));
    document.write("<br/>Welcome to JavaScript!");
</script>
</body>
</html>
```

3. **Editor:** Save the **lab_8-2.html** file.

4. **Browser:** Open **lab_8-2.html**. Your screen should resemble Figure 8-3.

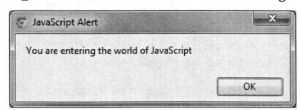

Figure 8-3: JavaScript alert box

5. **Browser:** Click **OK**. A dialog box will appear asking for your name. Enter your name in the text field, then click **OK**. Your screen should resemble Figure 8-4, with your name in the greeting.

Figure 8-4: JavaScript-generated Web page

6. Close your browser.

7. **When time permits:** Add this JavaScript code to one of the Habitat for Humanity pages from the course labs. View your page and test the script in at least one browser. After you verify that the script works, validate your code at **http://validator.w3.org**. Then answer the following question: What will happen when people with voice-recognition software and text-based browsers such as Lynx visit this page?

_____

_____

In this lab, you learned more about the capabilities of client-side JavaScript.

VBScript

You already learned a little about VBScript in the discussion about Active Server Pages (ASP). VBScript is the Microsoft implementation of JavaScript. Like JavaScript, VBScript can be used on the client side or on the server side, and provides access to built-in documents and methods.

VBScript is proprietary, so the VBScript interpreter is installed only in Windows Internet Explorer. If you use VBScript on the client side, then in most cases Internet Explorer will be the only Web browser that will recognize the code you use. However, if you use VBScript on the server side, then any browser can use your pages.

VBScript syntax is quite similar to JavaScript and offers capabilities similar to JavaScript as well. To learn more about VBScript, visit *www.microsoft.com*.

CIW Online Resources – Online Exercise

Visit CIW Online at *http://education.Certification-Partners.com/CIW* to complete an interactive exercise that will reinforce what you have learned about this topic.

Exercise 8-2: Reviewing main client-side scripting languages

Dynamic HTML (DHTML)

Dynamic HTML (DHTML)
An umbrella term that describes the combination of HTML, script, styles and the Document Object Model (DOM) to provides Web page interactivity.

Dynamic HTML (DHTML) is an umbrella term to describe HTML's ability to work with other technologies to provide animation, interactivity and dynamic updating in Web pages. With DHTML, you can create a Web page that reacts to user actions without contacting the server or downloading complex, bandwidth-consuming applications. Because it eases the burden on the server, DHTML is an effective front-end and back-end solution.

You can use DHTML to control the way in which an image will perform. For example, you can animate an image only when a mouse passes over it. Or the page can automatically scroll text headlines. Additional DHTML uses include the following:

- **Automatic adjustment of font sizes and colors** — You can use a DHTML **event handler** to animate text when a user passes a mouse over certain parts of the page.

event handler
A line of code that allows a language to respond to a specific event or user input.

- **Absolute positioning** — You can create text that moves to certain positions in reaction to user input.

- **New document content** — Content can be exchanged dynamically, without having to refresh the browser window.

- **Granular control over animation, audio and video** — Rather than writing page code to constantly present a video clip, you can write code to begin a sequence at a certain time or after a certain event.

HTML5 APIs are the best examples of DHTML because they utilize multiple technologies to extend the functionality of HTML:

OBJECTIVE
2.1.6: DOM and DHTML

- HTML5

- Cascading Style Sheets (CSS)

- JavaScript to access the Document Object Model (DOM)

You have already learned about HTML, CSS, and JavaScript. In the next section, you will learn about the DOM.

Document Object Model (DOM)

OBJECTIVE
2.1.6: DOM and DHTML

The Document Object Model (DOM) is a standard developed by the W3C. It describes the elements, or objects, within a document rendered by a Web browser. It is a vendor-neutral, cross-platform **Application Programming Interface (API)** that specifies how objects in a document can be referred to and manipulated through scripting languages.

Application Programming Interface (API)
A set of universal commands, calls and functions that allows developers to communicate with an application or operating system.

The DOM is meant to be a vendor-neutral, cross-platform standard. With the DOM, you can open a new browser instance and control its functions. For example, you can determine the size of the new browser instance, the toolbars that will be open, and so forth. You can also create pop-up dialog boxes, change the font and colors used in the current document, and alter the address bar or almost any other component of the browser.

Currently, the DOM is not as universal as expected. Most browser vendors either add their own features or do not implement all of the DOM as proposed by the W3C. You can learn more about the W3C DOM by visiting *www.w3.org/DOM/*.

Accessing a browser's DOM

To work with the DOM for any browser, you need to use a scripting language, such as JavaScript or VBScript. JavaScript is more difficult to learn, but more universal. At present, VBScript works only with Windows Internet Explorer.

 Do not confuse the DOM with the Component Object Model (COM). The DOM describes documents within a browser. The COM is a Microsoft specification for creating applications. The Distributed Component Object Model (DCOM) describes the ability to create applications that work well over network connections.

DOM compliance

At one time, browser and technology vendors created separate models. However, the W3C has created a standard DOM, and all future models are based on it. Browser compliance with the W3C DOM is important for the following reasons:

- Compliant browsers have all of the functionality currently needed in your workplace.

- Compliant browsers are able to offer all accessibility features advocated by the W3C.

- Compliant browsers will be able to access popular features in the future.

Choosing a DOM-compliant browser

When choosing a browser, it is often best to use one that follows the DOM most closely. Choosing a DOM-compliant browser helps ensure that all code (e.g., HTML and JavaScript) used by your team will be supported.

In some cases, however, a browser that is less compliant may be the best choice, because the browser may provide other features that make it the best tool for your organization. Factors that might affect browser choice include:

- **Stability and security** — Some of the more popular browsers have experienced serious security issues. Sometimes these problems occur because the code used in the browser is proprietary and therefore "closed"; it cannot be readily reviewed for problems.

- **Authentication features** — Some browsers, such as Windows Internet Explorer, support proprietary authentication features found in IIS. Traditionally, other browsers have not supported these features. Recently, Mozilla Firefox has supported some of Microsoft's proprietary authentication features.

- **Availability** — Most browsers are available free of charge, but some companies do not want to bother with downloading and installing a new browser when an operating system already provides one.

Undefined object error and the DOM

You may receive an undefined object error if you visit a Web page and your browser does not support a specific DOM. In other cases, you may simply view an unformatted document in plaintext. Not all versions of a browser support the same DOM. Therefore, not all objects can be defined.

If a particular DOM is not supported, another browser will usually render the Web page successfully. This relationship is common with Windows Internet Explorer and Mozilla Firefox.

HTML, the DOM and browser compatibility

Most HTML elements and attributes are backward-compatible. However, some of the more ambitious improvements, including frames and the ability to respond to users, do not work well (or at all) with earlier browser versions. Additionally, modern browser versions interpret many HTML commands quite differently, which means that your pages will render differently from browser to browser. Some DHTML solutions will work well in one browser but disable another. JavaScript appears slightly differently, depending on the browser.

CIW Online Resources – Online Exercise

Visit CIW Online at *http://education.Certification-Partners.com/CIW* to complete an interactive exercise that will reinforce what you have learned about this topic

Exercise 8-3: Dynamic HTML (DHTML) and the Document Object Model (DOM)

OBJECTIVE
2.10.8: HTML5 APIs

HTML5 APIs

The future of Web development will probably focus on HTML5 APIs. They provide an open environment for developing Web applications that does not rely on proprietary browser plug-ins. The HTML5 APIs are an excellent example of DHTML.

HTML5 APIs consist of HTML5, CSS and JavaScript. JavaScript is used to access the DOM. As you learned earlier in this course, these technologies used together provide Web pages that can easily adapt to smartphones, tablets, gaming devices and smart TVs, as well as to traditional PCs.

HTML5 APIs are used to create apps for mobile devices, not just Web pages. For example, the mobile apps for Pandora and LinkedIn use HTML5 APIs. Many expect mass adoption of HTML5 APIs in the next few years as mobile devices continue to proliferate.

Some functions of the HTML5 APIs include:

- Media (audio and video).

- Document editing.

- Cross-document messaging.

- MIME type and protocol handler registration.

- Web storage.

For a complete list of HTML5 APIs from one of the W3C members, visit http://platform.html5.org/. You should bookmark this Web page.

You will learn about four popular APIs in this lesson: canvas, offline Web applications, geolocation, and drag-and-drop. You have already learned the basics of the media APIs for audio and video using the <audio> and <video> elements.

CIW Online Resources – Movie Clips

Visit CIW Online at http://education.Certification-Partners.com/CIW to watch a movie clip about this topic.

Lesson 8: HTML5 API

Canvas

canvas
An HTML5 Application Programming Interface (API) used for rendering visual images on the fly by providing scripts with a bitmap canvas.

OBJECTIVE
2.10.8: HTML5 APIs

on the fly
Dynamically created Web page content, as opposed to pre-defined, static content.

Canvas is an HTML API that provides a place on a Web page (a "canvas") where developers can display graphics, animation, video and games "**on the fly**" without the need for a plug-in. Canvas is described by the W3C as an HTML5 element that "provides scripts with a resolution-dependent bitmap canvas, which can be used for rendering graphs, game graphics, or other visual images on the fly." By itself, canvas is a simple pixel-based drawing API that produces a bitmap image.

You can draw objects on a canvas using JavaScript. You can use the canvas to display simple drawings, animations, graphics or graphs; and you can also use it for more advanced tasks that include interactivity, such as video games, simulations, video editing or image configurations.

Previously, users had to install plug-ins such as Adobe Flash Player or Microsoft Silverlight to view these types of files. Moving forward, any user who has an HTML5-compliant browser will be able to have multimedia experiences without a plug-in. Think of the Flash games and videos that have been used on the Web over the years. Now these games and videos can be played through the canvas API.

The canvas API uses fewer resources than a plug-in does (such as battery power and CPU usage). This is especially important with regard to mobile devices, such as smartphones and tablets, that rely upon battery power.

The canvas API by itself is quite boring. It basically requires an advanced Web application developer to fill it in with multimedia content he or she has created. For this course, you will create a simple canvas area on a Web page and add a rectangle to it. This course does not cover Web application development, so the lab is for introduction purposes only.

How it works

The canvas element is defined in HTML with the <canvas></canvas> tag. The canvas element has only two attributes: height and width. These attributes can be omitted; however, the default height of 300 pixels and width of 150 pixels will be applied.

Initially, the canvas element is transparent. Adding some basic styles such as a border, margin, background, etc., will help make it visible in the browser. Styles that are applied will have no effect on the drawing capabilities.

Older browsers do not fully support canvas; therefore, alternative content should be used. The older browsers will ignore the <canvas></canvas> tags and will render the content that is between them. See the following example:

```
<canvas id="myCanvas" width="200" height="100" style="border:1px solid
#000000;">
    Your browser does not support the canvas element.
</canvas>
```

Looking at the preceding code, an older browser will display the text "Your browser does not support the canvas element." All compatible browsers will display the canvas element styled with a solid 1-pixel black border.

The *id* attribute is not specific to <canvas>, however, you should specify a unique *id* to identify it later.

The canvas element uses a DOM method called *getContext*. The *getContext* method needs only one parameter: the type of context. There are two types of context — 2D and 3D. The *getContext* method is a built-in HTML5 object. It has many methods such as circles, rectangles, paths and many more.

Canvas only supports one primitive shape, the rectangle. All other shapes are created by using a collection of functions and combining one or more paths. To draw a rectangle, you must specify the x and y coordinates as well as the width and height of the object you want to draw. Rectangle properties are shown in Table 8-5.

Table 8-5: Canvas rectangle properties

Rectangle Property	Description
fillRect(x,y,width,height)	Draws a filled rectangle.
strokeRect(x,y,width,height)	Draws a rectangular outline.
clearRect(x,y,width,height)	Clears the specified area and makes it fully transparent.

In the following lab, you will explore the canvas API. Suppose your supervisor has informed you that the company Web site will need to move away from the use of plug-ins to display content. You need to start learning about the canvas API to see what it can do.

 Lab 8-3: Experimenting with the HTML5 canvas API

OBJECTIVE
2.10.9: HTML5 APIs
and JavaScript

In this lab, you will view the canvas element with its corresponding JavaScript. The JavaScript code in this lab is beyond the scope of this course. It is provided to show the potential of the canvas API.

1. **Windows Explorer:** Copy the **C:\CIW\Site_Dev\Lab Files\Lesson08\Lab_8-3** folder of your student files to your Desktop.

2. **Editor:** Open the file **canvas-1.html** from the **Lab_8-3\ Desktop** folder. Study the code, which is as follows:

```
<!DOCTYPE html>
<html>
<head>
<meta name="Keywords" content="CIW, Web Foundations Associate, Example"/>
<meta name="Description" content="For the CIW Web Foundations Associate
courses"/>
<meta charset="utf-8"/>
<title>HTML5 Canvas API Example</title>

<style type="text/css">
canvas
{
border: 1px solid #000000;
}
</style>
</head>
```

```
<body>

<canvas id="myCanvas" width="300" height="300">
Your browser does not support the canvas element.
</canvas>

</body>
</html>
```

Within the `<canvas> </canvas>` element, notice that the *id* attribute is called *myCanvas*. The height and width attributes, along with inline styles, are also used. This ensures that the canvas will be visible in the browser.

3. **Browser:** Open the file **canvas-1.html** in your browser (from the same **Lab_8-3** folder on your Desktop). It should resemble Figure 8-5.

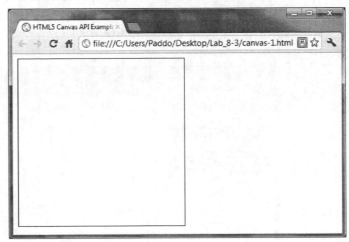

Figure 8-5: Canvas displayed in browser

4. **Browser:** Close the file.

5. **Editor:** Open the file **canvas-2.html** from the **Lab_8-3** folder on your Desktop. Study the code, which is as follows:

```
<!DOCTYPE html>
<html>
<head>
<meta name="Keywords" content="CIW, Web Foundations Associate, Example"/>
<meta name="Description" content="For the CIW Web Foundations Associate
courses"/>
<meta charset="utf-8"/>
<title>HTML5 Canvas API Example</title>

<style type="text/css">
canvas
{
border: 1px solid #000000;
}
</style>
</head>

<body>

<canvas id="myCanvas" width="200" height="100">
Your browser does not support the canvas element.
</canvas>
```

```
<script type="text/javascript">

var c=document.getElementById("myCanvas");
var ctx=c.getContext("2d");
ctx.fillStyle="#FF0000";
ctx.fillRect(0,0,150,75);

</script>

</body>
</html>
```

In the first line after the <script> tag, JavaScript uses the *getElementById* and the *id* attribute that you declared to find your canvas. The next line creates the context object and uses the *getContext* DOM method. The next line creates the rectangle and fills it with color. In the last line, the coordinates are specified and the width and height are defined.

6. **Browser:** Open the file **canvas-2.html** in your browser. It should resemble Figure 8-6.

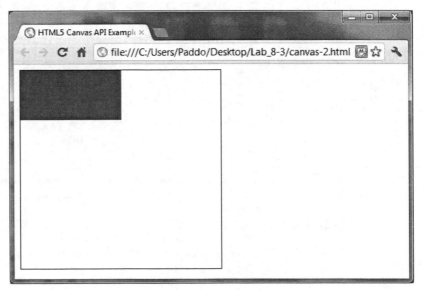

Figure 8-6: Rectangle drawn in canvas

7. **Editor:** Edit the code in **canvas-2.html** to adjust the position, width, height, fill and stroke color. Save your file and view it in a browser when finished.

In this lab, you demonstrated how the canvas element displays in a browser and how to draw a basic rectangle within the canvas.

OBJECTIVE
2.10.8: HTML5 APIs

Offline Web Application

offline Web application
Permits the user to continue working with Web sites and Web documents even when a network connection is unavailable.

Offline Web applications allow users to interact with Web sites while they are offline. This will allow a user to continue to interact with a Web site when a network connection is unavailable. Web pages will store data locally within the user's browser, utilizing the **application cache**, allowing them to continue accessing the site.

This feature is especially helpful when users leave their Internet Service Provider's coverage range. With mobile devices, users may lose connections when traveling through

application cache
A directory on a computer where applications, such as Internet apps, can be stored and run without access to the original application.

manifest
A list of the files that are needed for the Web application to work offline.

valleys, tunnels or other areas without coverage. The offline Web application API allows them to continue working with the application without interruption during coverage loss.

Utilizing a **manifest**, which tells the browser which files to store locally, is what allows the user to continue working without the connection. When the user goes back online, the application cache will automatically update when revisiting the Web site. The application cache will reload that file in the event any of the existing data has changed in the cached files.

In addition to using a Web application when the computer is offline, the application allows quicker loading of the application next time it is used. The application loads quicker because it can be run locally, from the user's computer, instead of having to be downloaded from a server. This process also reduces the load placed upon the server because the server does not have to provide an application each time it is used. The browser only downloads changes or updates from the server.

How it works

To set up a site and its applications to work offline, follow these steps. First, you will need to create a mandatory *cache.manifest* file. The manifest lists the files needed for the Web application to work offline. For example, if a Web site is cached, you would list the main .html file, the .css file, and any images or JavaScript files used.

The file name requires a file name extension of .manifest. The file name itself is usually the application name, such as *mortagagecalculator.manifest* or *date.manifest*.

The manifest file always includes the text "CACHE MANIFEST" in the first line. The contents of the file follow the following format:

```
CACHE MANIFEST
#The CACHE MANIFEST line is required. This line is a comment.
#Blank lines and comments are ignored

CACHE:
index.html
styles.css
actions.js
banner.jpg

FALLBACK:
images/banner.fallback.jpg
/offline.html
*
```

The CACHE MANIFEST line is required to identify the purpose of the code. The next two lines are comments, which are helpful for developers to write notes to themselves and others reading the code.

Next, three section headers that can be used are CACHE, FALLBACK and NETWORK. The CACHE section lists the application files that will be used offline (e.g., cached). The FALLBACK section defines what the user will see in the event a resource does not load. This can be a simple Web page that states "We're sorry, but the Web site or application you requested is unavailable."

The NETWORK section defines an online whitelist. A whitelist includes the files that are never stored. Such files possibly need a server to process and you would not need them locally.

Next, the HTML files that will be cached need to point to the cache manifest file. Include a *manifest* attribute in the <html> tag that identifies the manifest file you are linking to.

```
<html manifest="date.manifest">
```

In the following lab, you will create an offline Web application using the HTML5 offline Web application API. The cached application is a simple JavaScript program that displays the date and time in the browser, even when the browser is offline.

 | **Lab 8-4: Creating an offline Web application**

OBJECTIVE
2.10.9: HTML5 APIs
and JavaScript

In this lab, you will demonstrate how the offline Web application HTML5 API functions. The JavaScript code in this lab is beyond the scope of this course. It is provided to show the potential of the offline Web application API.

1. **Windows Explorer:** Copy the **C:\CIW\Site_Dev\Lab Files\Lesson08\Lab_8-4** folder from your student files to your Desktop.

2. **Editor:** Open the file **date.html** in the **Desktop Lab_8-4** folder. Study the code, which is as follows:

```
<!DOCTYPE HTML>
<html manifest="date.manifest">
<head>
<meta name="Keywords" content="CIW, Web Foundations Associate, Example"/>
<meta name="Description" content="For the CIW Web Foundations Associate
courses"/>
<meta charset="utf-8"/>
<title>HTML5 Offline Web Application API Example</title>

<script src="date.js"></script>
<link rel="stylesheet" href="date.css">
</head>
<body>
<p>The time is: <output id="date"></output></p>
</body>
</html>
```

Notice that in the HTML element, the manifest element is pointing to the manifest file.

3. **Chrome:** Open the file **date.html** in the Chrome browser.

   Note: Depending on the browser that you are using and the security settings, you may be prompted to allow storage for offline use, as shown in Figure 8-7. For this lab, allow local storage.

Figure 8-7: Offline storage prompt as displayed in Firefox

Your screen should resemble Figure 8-8.

Figure 8-8: Offline Web application displayed in Chrome browser

4. The date application will now function regardless of whether the user has an Internet connection. Close the files and exit the browser and editor.

5. **Firefox or IE9:** Open the file **date.html**. The browser may block the script and not respond. Determine if this error is a result of browser incompatibility or if the browser security settings are responsible for the error.

In this lab, you created an offline Web application using the HTML5 offline Web application API.

It is important to note that browsers will continue to display the cached version of an application, regardless of whether it has been updated or changed on the server. To overcome this issue, you must change the manifest file whenever you make changes to the Web application on the server. This will cause the browser to reload the new version of the application. Also, some browsers have limitations on the cache size per site, so do not exceed 5 MB for the downloaded application if possible.

OBJECTIVE
2.10.8: HTML5 APIs

geolocation
The ability to determine a user's location. Web sites can use this information to enhance the user experience and provide location-based services.

Geolocation

The HTML5 geolocation API is used to locate a user's geographical position. The W3C defines **geolocation** as "an API that defines an advanced interface for location information associated only with the device hosting the application, such as latitude and longitude."

Geolocation determines how to display a user's location based on how the user visits a Web site. A number of technologies can be used, such as the user's IP address, wireless network, or GPS hardware utilized on his or her device.

Because this can compromise a user's privacy, the user is usually required to approve the action, depending on the user's security settings. A prompt will display in the browser asking for permission, as shown in Figure 8-9.

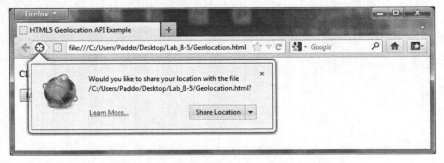

Figure 8-9: Prompt asking for location tracking permission

How it works

Geolocation can determine a user's current position, monitor the user's location, and update any changes to that location. Geolocation uses three methods for getting the location information from the user: *getCurrentPosition*, *watchPosition* and *clearPosition*.

Using JavaScript, the geolocation method starts with the *getCurrentPosition()* method to obtain the user's location. The latitude and longitude of the user are the returned values. The geolocation methods are shown in Table 8-6.

Table 8-6: Geolocation methods

Method	Description
getCurrentPosition()	Retrieves the current geographic location of the user.
watchPosition()	Retrieves periodic updates about the current geographic location of the user.
clearWatch()	Cancels an ongoing watchPosition() call.

Geolocation displays the user's information in a localized map such as the one shown in Figure 8-10.

Figure 8-10: Location of Certification Partners, LLC, using geolocation API on mobile device or PC

In the following lab, you will experiment with the geolocation API. Suppose your supervisor has requested a Web site modification to include the location of site visitors. For marketing purposes, she wants to know each visitor's location so she can determine the nearest retail store that sells your company's products. The following lab will demonstrate how the geolocation API works in a Web page to identify a user's location.

Lab 8-5: Experimenting with the geolocation API

OBJECTIVE
2.10.9: HTML5 APIs
and JavaScript

In this lab, you will demonstrate the functionality of the HTML5 geolocation API. The JavaScript code in this lab is beyond the scope of this course. It is provided to show the potential of the geolocation API.

1. **Windows Explorer:** Copy the **C:\CIW\Site_Dev\Lab Files\Lesson08\Lab_8-5** folder from your student files to your Desktop.

2. **Editor:** Open the file **Geolocation.html** from your **Desktop Lab_8-5** folder. Study the code, which is as follows (the geolocation API code is shown in bold):

```
<!DOCTYPE html>
<html>
<head>
<meta name="Keywords" content="CIW, Web Foundations Associate, Example"/>
<meta name="Description" content="For the CIW Web Foundations Associate
courses"/>
<meta charset="utf-8"/>
<title>HTML5 Geolocation API Example</title>
</head>

<body>
<p id="MyLocation">Click the button to get your position:</p>
<button onclick="getLocation()">My Location</button>
<div id="map"></div>
<script>
var x=document.getElementById("MyLocation");
function getLocation()
  {
  if (navigator.geolocation)
    {
    navigator.geolocation.getCurrentPosition(showPosition,showError);
    }
  else{x.innerHTML="Geolocation is not supported by this browser.";}
  }

function showPosition(position)
  {
  var latlon=position.coords.latitude+","+position.coords.longitude;

  var img_url="http://maps.googleapis.com/maps/api/staticmap?center="
  +latlon+"&zoom=14&size=400x300&sensor=false";
  document.getElementById("map").innerHTML="<img src='"+img_url+"' />";
  }

function showError(error)
  {
  switch(error.code)
    {
    case error.PERMISSION_DENIED:
      x.innerHTML="User denied the request for Geolocation."
      break;
    case error.POSITION_UNAVAILABLE:
      x.innerHTML="Location information is unavailable."
      break;
    case error.TIMEOUT:
      x.innerHTML="The request to get user location timed out."
      break;
    case error.UNKNOWN_ERROR:
      x.innerHTML="An unknown error occurred."
      break;
    }
  }
```

```
</script>
</body>
</html>
```

In the preceding code, the function getLocation() is looking to see if geolocation is supported by the browser. If it is supported, the getCurrentPosition() method is then run, and if it is not supported, an error message will be displayed to the user. If the getCurrentPosition() method is successful, it will then return the coordinates to the function, and the showPosition() function will display the latitude and longitude.

If any errors are found, the showError() function will display any errors that are encountered when the getCurrentPosition() function was run.

3. **Firefox:** Open the file **Geolocation.html** in Firefox. Click the **My Location** button. Your screen should resemble Figure 8-11.

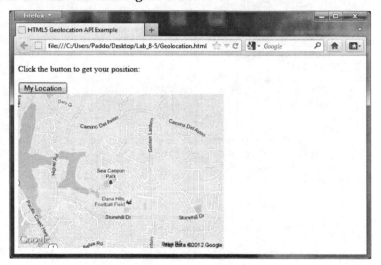

Figure 8-11: Geolocation displayed in Firefox

Note: At the time of this writing, not all browsers supported geolocation. Experiment with different browsers and observe the results.

4. **Chrome:** Open the file **Geolocation.html** in Chrome. Click the **My Location** button. The browser may block the geolocation API from loading. An error message may appear, as shown in Figure 8-12. Determine if this error is a result of browser incompatibility or if Chrome's security settings are responsible for the error.

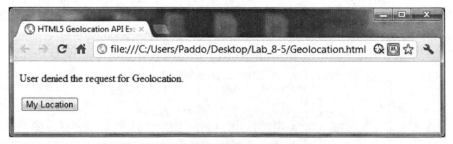

Figure 8-12: Chrome denying geolocation request

In this lab, you demonstrated how the geolocation element displays in a browser using your current location on a map.

OBJECTIVE
2.10.8: HTML5 APIs

drag-and-drop
Functionality that allows a user to grab an object and move it to a different location on a computer screen.

drop zone
An area of a Web page that has been defined as a place where dragged items can be placed.

Drag-and–Drop Functionality

Drag-and-drop functionality on a Web page allows a user to move an item from one place on the page to another by dragging it across the screen and dropping it in a different location. The user can also drag an item off the Web page and drop it into an external application such as a word processor, a photo editor or another browser.

When drag-and–drop functionality is enabled on a Web page, all links, text and image elements are draggable. With the use of a **drop zone** — a place where items can be dropped — many elements can be manipulated.

There are two kinds of drag-and-drop functionality: dragging files from the user's computer onto a Web page; and dragging items to a different location within the same page.

Adding drag-and-drop functionality to your Web pages requires several steps. First, you must specify the HTML element you would like to be draggable. Next, you must add an event listener for the *dragstart* event on any of the HTML draggable elements. Last, you must add an event listener for the *dragover* and *drop* events on any elements that will accept a dragged item.

How it works

First, you have to define an element as being able to be dragged. To do this you must set the draggable attribute to "true".

```
<img id="drag1" src="logo\CIWLogo.png" draggable="true"
ondragstart="drag(event)" width="336" height="69" />
```

You must use the *DataTransfer* object to define the draggable element's data type and value. Assigning an *id* to the item to be dragged will allow that *id* to be saved in the *DataTransfer* object to be used again after the element is dropped.

Next, you must define a drop zone. This is done by creating two events: *dragover* and *drop*. The *dragover* event is called when you drag something over it, and the *drop* event is called when something is dropped.

In the following lab, you will add drag-and-drop functionality to a Web page. Suppose your supervisor asks you to develop a training site for the company's sales team. The company has divisions throughout the globe that manufacture various products. The site must include drag-and-drop functionality so the team members can drag pictures of company products to the correct division of the company that creates each product. You need to start learning about the drag-and-drop API to see what it can do.

 Lab 8-6: Adding drag-and–drop functionality to a Web page

OBJECTIVE
2.10.9: HTML5 APIs
and JavaScript

In this lab, you will demonstrate the functionality of the drag-and-drop HTML5 API. The JavaScript code in this lab is beyond the scope of this course. It is provided to show the potential of the drag-and-drop API.

1. **Windows Explorer:** Copy the **C:\CIW\Site_Dev\Lab Files\Lesson08\Lab_8-6** folder from your student files to your Desktop.

2. **Editor:** Open the file **Drag_and_Drop.html** from the **Desktop Lab_8-6** folder. Study the code, which is as follows (the drag-and-drop API code is shown in bold):

```
<!DOCTYPE HTML>
<html>
<head>
<meta name="Keywords" content="CIW, Web Foundations Associate, Example"/>
<meta name="Description" content="For the CIW Web Foundations Associate
courses"/>
<meta charset="utf-8"/>
<title>HTML5 Drag and Drop API Example</title>

<style type="text/css">
  #div1 {width:350px;height:70px;padding:10px;border:1px solid #aaaaaa;}
</style>
<script type="text/javascript">
 function allowDrop(ev)
  {
   ev.preventDefault();
  }

 function drag(ev)
  {
   ev.dataTransfer.setData("Text",ev.target.id);
  }

 function drop(ev)
  {
   var data=ev.dataTransfer.getData("Text");
   ev.target.appendChild(document.getElementById(data));
   ev.preventDefault();
  }
</script>
</head>
<body>

 <h1>Certified Internet Web Professional</h1>
 <p>Drag the CIW image into the rectangle:</p>

 <div id="div1" ondrop="drop(event)" ondragover="allowDrop(event)"></div>
 <br />
<img id="drag1" src=" logo\CIWLogo.png" alt="CIW logo" draggable="true"
ondragstart="drag(event)" width="336" height="69" />

</body>
</html>
```

In the preceding code, the draggable item — the CIW logo — is set to "true." The *ondragstart* attribute named *drag(event)* function specifies the data that will be dragged (the logo).

The *ondragover* event specifies where the logo can be dropped. By default, data elements cannot be dropped in other elements — they will open as a link when dropped. The *ev.preventDefault()* method is called to prevent that action.

When the logo is dropped, the drop event occurs.

3. **Chrome:** Open the file **Drag_and_Drop.html** in the browser. It should resemble Figure 8-13.

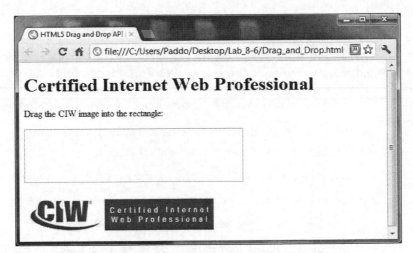

Figure 8-13: CIW logo before it is dragged to new location

4. **Chrome:** Click the CIW logo, drag it into the box and drop it. Your screen should resemble Figure 8-14.

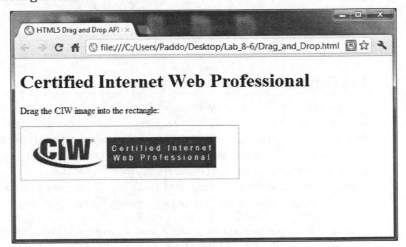

Figure 8-14: CIW logo after it is dropped in new location

5. **Firefox or IE9:** Open the file **Drag_and_Drop.html** in one of these browsers. Does it work in these browsers? Why or why not? Determine whether any errors or lack of response is due to browser incompatibility, or if the browser security settings are responsible for the errors.

In this lab, you demonstrated how the drag-and-drop API works by dragging the CIW logo into a box on a Web page.

CIW Online Resources – Online Exercise

Visit CIW Online at *http://education.Certification-Partners.com/CIW* to complete an interactive exercise that will reinforce what you have learned about this topic.

Exercise 8-4: HTML5 APIs

Web Application Frameworks

A **Web application framework** is a software framework that enables developers to create and manage dynamic Web sites, Web applications and Web services. Software frameworks generally provide common programming code for generic functions that can be selectively overridden by the developer for specific functionality.

Web application frameworks provide software libraries that contain reusable code that developers can use to:

- Help manage the creation and maintenance of online databases.
- Provide Web page security.
- Manage data on the servers that host the Web pages.
- Provide templates that make it possible to change the background of Web pages while keeping the graphics, text and other elements of the page intact.

Two Web application frameworks that are quickly gaining favor with Web site developers are:

- Django.
- Ruby on Rails.

Building Web pages with Django

Django is an open-source Web application framework that is designed to support the development of dynamic Web sites. Django is written in Python, which is an open-source, object-oriented programming language. Python is a highly readable language that emphasizes an uncluttered visual layout by using white space as block delimiters and applying minimalistic syntax and semantics. If you are running a Linux or Mac OS X system, Python is probably already installed. If you are running a Windows system, you will need to install Python (*www.python.org*) before you can install and launch Django.

Django allows developers to easily create complex, database-driven Web sites. Django emphasizes Rapid Application Development (RAD) and the Don't Repeat Yourself (DRY) principle, in which the duplication of elements is kept to an absolute minimum. With the DRY principle, modifying any single element of a system will not change logically unrelated elements, and logically related elements will change correspondingly to ensure uniformity and predictability.

To learn more about Django, visit *www.djangoproject.com*.

Building Web pages with Ruby On Rails

Ruby On Rails is another open-source Web application framework that also emphasizes Rapid Application Development (RAD) and the Don't Repeat Yourself (DRY) principle for rapid Web site development. Ruby On Rails (or "Rails," for short) works with a wide range of Web servers (e.g., Apache, lighttpd), databases (e.g., MySQL, Oracle, SQL Server, DB2) and operating systems (Windows, Linux, Mac OS X). Like Django, Rails emphasizes simplicity and ease-of-use so that developers can create complex Web sites quickly.

To learn more about Ruby On Rails, visit *http://rubyonrails.org/*.

Connecting to a Database

You learned about databases and CGI earlier in this course. However, you should understand that for a database to work, you must:

- **Provide a way for the Web server and database to recognize each other** — For example, Microsoft systems use ODBC.

- **Provide permissions to the database so that it can be read and/or written to** — Most databases allow users to write to them.

CGI and permissions

OBJECTIVE
2.17.2: CGI methods

2.18.4: Managed
services

CGI scripts often fail to execute properly not because they are coded incorrectly, but because the Web server does not have execute permissions. Failure for CGI scripts to execute is caused by the following:

- The Web server does not have the permissions to execute files and scripts.

- The file or script used has incorrect permissions, which prohibits the server from executing the file.

In many ways, these two problems are the same issue. To solve such problems, first make sure that the Web server you are using has all of the necessary permissions. Then, modify the permissions assigned to the file so that it has only enough permissions to function. This allows the Web server to execute the file securely. Allowing a file too many permissions can cause serious security problems.

ISPs and CGI

If you are working with an Internet Service Provider (ISP), you generally need to request the CGI services. Following are the actions you will need to request that the ISP perform:

- **Enable execute permissions on your scripts** — The ISP can assign these permissions after they receive your files.

- **Create a directory that contains available CGI scripts** — This directory is generally called the CGI bin, and is often named *cgi* or *cgi-bin*. The ISP should create this directory with your site files.

- **Provide user names and passwords with enough permissions for the system** — The ISP will usually assign the appropriate permissions. The administrative password for UNIX systems is *root*. The administrative password for Windows systems is *administrator*. However, understand that it is possible for an ISP to create new accounts that may have sufficient permissions to accomplish a task normally reserved for the *root* or *administrator* account.

N-tier applications

OBJECTIVE
2.17.5: N-tier
applications

When discussing databases, three elements are generally involved:

- **Data** — the database file or multiple database files.

- **Business logic** — the SQL coding necessary to create relationships with the data stored in the database.

- **Presentation** — the way that data and business logic are presented on the user screen. Presentation includes Web forms created with HTML, and application-specific interfaces such as Microsoft Access or a Web browser.

In a single-tier database, the data, business logic and presentation are all provided by one application (e.g., Microsoft Access). In a two-tier application, the client is responsible for the business logic and data presentation, and the database is stored on a separate server. In an n-tier solution, all three database elements are separated, as shown in Figure 8-15.

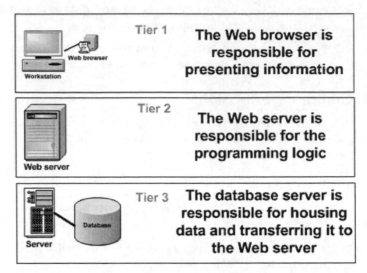

Figure 8-15: N-tier application

This lesson has discussed basic CGI and database concepts, which are often n-tier solutions. Table 8-7 summarizes single-tier, two-tier and n-tier computing.

Table 8-7: Summary of single-tier, two-tier and n-tier computing

Model	Description	Example
Single-tier	All three layers are combined into one application or database.	A Microsoft Access database available only on a local system. A user simply opens Access, then manipulates the database.
Two-tier	The client is responsible for presentation and business logic, and a server houses only the data. Called a client-server relationship. Any change to the database requires client upgrade.	A proprietary client connects to a database server to process information. For example, using Microsoft Access to query a remote database.
N-tier	The business logic, data and presentation are completely separated. An upgrade in one of the layers does not necessarily mean the others are affected.	Using a Web browser to visit a Web site that is connected to a remote database. The Web browser downloads the necessary forms and is responsible for presentation. The Web server is responsible for providing the business logic and programming. The remote database provides the data. Many times, multiple Web servers and databases are used.

CIW Online Resources – Course Mastery

Visit CIW Online at *http://education.Certification-Partners.com/CIW* to take the Course Mastery review of this lesson or lesson segment.

SDA Lesson 8 - Part B

Case Study

Choose Your CGI

Darius is the project manager of a Web development team for a mid-size corporation. The team needs to choose a CGI technology for the company's new primary Web site. Darius must write the recommendation that upper management will review in deciding whether to approve funds.

In creating a short summary of the project, Darius asked his team members to help answer the following questions:

- Do any developers in the company know common CGI technologies?

- What operating systems are currently in use in the company? (by percentage, such as 50 percent Windows, 30 percent Linux, 20 percent Solaris)

- What operating systems are ideal for this project?

- What Web servers are ideal for this project?

Darius learned that the company's computer environment was almost completely Windows-based. Also, several members of the Web development team knew how to use VBScript and had experience using Active Server Pages (ASP). Although ASP is an older Microsoft technology (.NET is newer and more versatile), the Web development team recommended ASP as the best choice.

As Darius' team made their choice, they considered the importance of using client-side technologies such as JavaScript. However, they also considered that some browsers do not support JavaScript, and that some users may deactivate JavaScript in their browsers, which could cause Web pages to render differently and disappoint some site visitors. After some deliberation, Darius and his team decided to use server-side technology (specifically ASP) for all applications.

*   *   *

As a class, consider this scenario and discuss the following points:

- Would Darius' team have chosen the same CGI technology if the computer environment had been mostly Linux? What might they have chosen instead?

- If Darius' team had chosen a client-side technology, what steps could they have taken to improve accessibility?

Lesson Summary

Application project

This lesson taught you more about several Web technologies, including programming languages, HTML5 APIs, and the W3C DOM. Visit the following sites to learn more about these technologies:

- World Wide Web Consortium (*www.w3.org*)

- W3 Schools (*www.w3schools.com*)

- PHP (*www.php.net*)

- Perl (*www.activestate.com* and *www.perl.com*)

- Active Server Pages (ASP) and .NET (*www.microsoft.com*)

- Java (*www.java.com*)

Skills review

In this lesson, you studied Web-based technologies that extend your HTML pages, including server-side and client-side scripts. You wrote some simple JavaScript code to make a Web page interactive, and you learned how DHTML can also add interactivity to your Web pages. You learned the purpose of the DOM and the importance of DOM Web browser support.

You also experimented with HTML5 APIs that included canvas, offline Web applications, geolocation, and drag-and-drop. Finally, you learned about Web application frameworks, which contain reusable common programming code that developers can use to develop Web pages easily.

Now that you have completed this lesson, you should be able to:

✓ 2.1.6: Define the Document Object Model (DOM) and its relationship to Dynamic HTML (DHTML).

✓ 2.1.9: Add third-party applications to your Web page (e.g., Google gadgets for the Web).

✓ 2.10.8: Describe various HTML5 Application Programming Interfaces (APIs), including canvas, geolocation, offline Web application, drag-and-drop.

✓ 2.10.9: Demonstrate basic HTML5 API functionality using JavaScript and HTML5 elements.

✓ 2.17.1: Compare popular client-side and server-side programming languages, including JavaScript, Java, PHP, Python, .Net, C, C++, Visual Basic, C#.

✓ 2.17.2: Define Common Gateway Interface (CGI) methods, including .Net, Django, Python, JavaServer Pages (JSP), Server-Side JavaScript (SSJS), Active Server Pages (ASP), PHP Hypertext Preprocessor (PHP), Ajax.

✓ 2.17.5: Identify the value of n-tier applications and associated techniques in processing online transactions.

✓ 2.19.1: Identify ways to use additional technologies to provide custom features to an end user (e.g., using JavaScript to detect Web browser type, using cookies).

CIW Practice Exams

Visit CIW Online at *http://education.Certification-Partners.com/CIW* to take the Practice Exams assessment covering the objectives in this lesson.

SDA Objective 2.01 Review

SDA Objective 2.10 Review

SDA Objective 2.17 Review

SDA Objective 2.18 Review

SDA Objective 2.19 Review

Note that some objectives may be only partially covered in this lesson.

Lesson 8 Review

1. In programming, what is the term for a space of memory used to store information for later use?

   _____

2. How can the removal of browser plug-ins affect mobile devices?

   _____

   _____

   _____

3. What programming language is platform-independent and object-oriented, and can be used to create applications called servlets?

   _____

4. What does Dynamic HTML do?

   _____

   _____

5. What is the term for the API used to standardize the way that JavaScript applications can refer to HTML documents?

   _____

6. How can HTML be extended to create mobile applications for smartphones and tablets?

   _____

   _____

7. Describe a Web application framework, which developers can use to develop dynamic Web pages rapidly.

   _____

   _____

   _____

   _____

Lesson 9:
GUI HTML Editors and Mobile Web Sites

Objectives

By the end of this lesson, you will be able to:

✎ 2.1.10: Identify ways that a Web browser can become an application delivery platform, including strengths and weaknesses of the browser.

✎ 2.7.7: Identify the challenges of designing Web sites for mobile devices (e.g., smartphones, tablets, game consoles).

✎ 2.11.1: Evaluate a GUI HTML editor according to the W3C Authoring Tool Accessibility Guidelines.

✎ 2.11.2: Validate HTML code.

✎ 2.11.3: Use font and page appearance options in a GUI HTML editor.

✎ 2.11.4: View source code and preview Web pages in a browser.

✎ 2.11.5: Create HTML tables using a GUI HTML editor.

✎ 2.11.6: Publish (i.e., upload) Web pages and sites to a Web server.

✎ 2.11.7 Evaluate various types of HTML editors that can edit files in mobile devices and cloud services.

✎ 2.11.8 Distinguish between mobile apps and mobile Web sites.

✎ 2.21.5: Identify ways to create pages for traditional and mobile device browsers (e.g., validating code, appropriate resolutions, supported interpreters, extensive user testing).

Pre-Assessment Questions

1. Which type of editing application allows Web developers to automate tasks and integrate other applications into workflow?

    a. Page editors
    b. Text editors
    c. Site management editors
    d. WYSIWYG editors

2. Which of the following features of a GUI editor offers the quickest way to create a new Web page?

    a. Templates and wizards
    b. Importing HTML pages
    c. Icon bars
    d. Table creation

3. To what extent do GUI editors generally allow developers to modify HTML code manually?

    _____

    _____

Introduction to GUI HTML Editors

What You See Is What You Get (WYSIWYG) (pronounced whiz-ee-wig) A user-friendly editing format in which the file being edited is displayed as it will appear in the browser.

You can create Web pages using a graphical user interface (GUI) HTML editor, also called a **What You See Is What You Get (WYSIWYG)** editor. These editors allow Web authors to create Web pages without typing the requisite HTML code. Many WYSIWYG editors exist, such as Adobe Dreamweaver, Microsoft Expression Web and the open-source KompoZer (*www.kompozer.net*).

In this lesson, you will use KompoZer as your GUI editor. KompoZer complies with W3C Web standards and creates pages as HTML 4.01 Transitional by default. However, you can create HTML5 templates to ensure the <!DOCTYPE> declaration supports HTML5. KompoZer is better used for Web page creation, not Web site management. This fact greatly simplifies the program because it focuses on the creation of one page at a time, which is similar to the way you approached HTML coding in previous lessons. When the pages are created, you can then join them using hyperlinks. KompoZer offers no comprehensive site management tools, and site management is beyond the scope of this course.

To learn about site management concepts and tools, it is recommended that you pursue the CIW Web Design Specialist course.

This lesson will examine the basic capabilities of a GUI HTML editor, including procedures for creating text styles, icon bars, inline images, hyperlinks and tables.

CIW Online Resources – Movie Clips

Visit CIW Online at http://education.Certification-Partners.com/CIW to watch a movie clip about this topic.

Lesson 9: GUI HTML Editors and Mobile Web Sites

Types of GUI Editors

As mentioned, there are two types of GUI editors:

- Page editors

- Site management editors

Both are WYSIWYG programs.

Page editors

GUI page editors allow you to create a Web page using your mouse and a toolbar. Functionality is usually limited to creating individual Web pages. Software programs that provide only page editor functionality include:

- Virtual Mechanics WebDwarf (*www.virtualmechanics.com/products/dwarf*).

- Mozilla SeaMonkey (*www.seamonkey-project.org*).

Site management editors

GUI Web site management editors provide both Web page creation and site management functionality. They allow teams of designers and developers to work in an integrated environment to design, build and manage Web site and Internet applications. In addition to creating the Web pages, team members can manage the entire Web site with this type of application, both during and after development. Site management includes task automation and workflow integration with other programs (such as Microsoft Office and Web applications) in a production environment.

Software programs that provide these functions include:

- Adobe Dreamweaver.

- Microsoft Expression Web.

In this lesson, you will use a GUI page editor to create pages similar to those you created using a text editor earlier in this course. First, however, you will learn about some of the features common to all GUI editors, and about accessibility guidelines for GUI editor applications.

GUI HTML Editor Functionality

GUI HTML editors allow you to create Web pages. In most cases, you enter and edit text similar to the way you would in a word-processing application. Images, tables, links, bookmarks and so forth can be created easily because the application writes the HTML code automatically.

The following features are offered by most GUI editors:

- **Templates and Wizards** — allow you to create custom Web pages quickly by selecting from a series of choices.

- **Text Style options** — allow you to format text in different font styles, alter text size and color, and apply formats such as centering, boldface and italics. Remember that some visitors to your site may not have all the fonts installed on their systems that you want to use on your Web pages. Choose your fonts carefully, or else your page may not render as expected to some visitors.

- **Icon bars** — offer easily identifiable graphic icons to provide the same functions found in text-based menus.

- **Image features** — allow you to easily insert graphic images into a Web page.

- **Hypertext Links features** — allow you to create hypertext links to pages and files within your Web site, and to pages and files on the World Wide Web. Once the link has been created, the editor displays the target page.

- **Import HTML Pages features** — allow you to open pages from the World Wide Web and, when permissible, save them to a Web site or local file system. The editor can also import all images on a page into a Web site or file system.

- **Table Creation features** — allow you to add tables to arrange data or organize a page layout.

- **Spelling check** — Most GUI editors provide an automatic spelling checker, similar to those found in word-processing applications such as Microsoft Word and Apache OpenOffice (*www.openoffice.org*). However, understand that a mere spelling check cannot ensure that your Web pages project the proper message. Your page content should be edited by a knowledgeable professional who understands your organization's message and the languages your site uses.

- **Publish Documents features** — allow you to click a button to post pages to a Web server. These features automatically copy files from a local hard drive to a directory on an ISP's server.

CIW Online Resources – Online Exercise

Visit CIW Online at *http://education.Certification-Partners.com/CIW* to complete an interactive exercise that will reinforce what you have learned about this topic.

Exercise 9-1: Reviewing the key features of a GUI editor

W3C Authoring Tool Accessibility Guidelines

OBJECTIVE
2.11.1: W3C Authoring Tool Accessibility Guidelines

The W3C Authoring Tool Accessibility Guidelines Recommendation outlines seven points that help determine the suitability of a GUI editor for developers with disabilities. All seven points focus on the following issues:

- The ability of the GUI editor to generate proper code

- The usability of the GUI editor by a disabled person creating a Web page

The seven points each contain checkpoints (i.e., subpoints). Each checkpoint offers specific examples of usability techniques that the GUI editor must support. You can read the W3C Authoring Tool Accessibility Guidelines (ATAG) Recommendation at *www.w3.org/TR/ATAG20/*.Table 9-1 summarizes the major points of this Recommendation.

Table 9-1: W3C Authoring Tool Accessibility Guidelines Recommendation summary

Guideline	Description	Subheadings
A. Make the authoring tool user interface accessible	The authoring tool itself must be accessible to people with disabilities, including the editing views and alternative text for toolbar icons.	**A.1.** Authoring tool user interfaces must follow applicable accessibility guidelines, such as the ATAG. **A.2.** Editing views must be perceivable, such as including alternative content and larger fonts. **A.3.** Editing views must be operable, such as providing keyboard access for GUI HTML editors. **A.4.** Editing views must be understandable, which includes the ability to help authors avoid and correct mistakes; the user interface must be well-documented.
B. Support the production of accessible content	The authoring tool must support procedures that enable the creation of accessible Web pages. In other words, if the tool does not allow you to create code that helps disabled users browse the site, then the tool is not compliant.	**B.1.** Fully automatic processes must produce accessible content. **B.2.** Authors must be supported in producing accessible content, such as pre-authored content, accessibility tools, author forums and FAQs provided by the developer. **B.3.** Authors must be supported in improving the accessibility of existing content. **B.4.** Authoring tools must promote and integrate their accessibility features.

As you design your Web pages, make sure that you consider the following points:

- Some users may be unable to use a mouse to navigate between links. Make sure that your pages allow users to tab to new links.

- You may need to provide larger text on your Web pages for visually impaired users.

Creating Web Pages with a GUI Editor

The labs in this lesson will familiarize you with the toolbar, menus and functions of a GUI Web page editor, KompoZer. Most of these features are similar in any GUI editor you use. However, the interface will differ among applications.

In the following series of labs, you will create a Web page with a GUI page editor. Suppose you want to apply for an internship with a technology training company. The company's internship requirements include beginning networking and HTML experience. To prove your skills, you decide to create your résumé in HTML.

 Lab 9-1: Creating a Web page with a GUI editor

In this lab, you will create a Web page using the KompoZer GUI page editor with an HTML5 template. Similar to a résumé, this Web page will promote your skills to potential employers.

OBJECTIVE
2.11.3: Formatting in
GUI HTML editor

1. **Windows Explorer:** Create a folder named **Promo** on your Desktop.

2. **Windows Explorer:** Copy the **C:\CIW\Site_Dev\Lab Files\Lesson09** folder to your Desktop.

3. Open the Desktop **Lesson09\Lab_9-1** folder and extract the **KompoZer-0.7.10-win32.zip** files to a **KompoZer-0.7.10-win32** folder on your Desktop.

4. Open the **KompoZer-0.7.10-win32\KompoZer 0.7.10** folder and double-click **kompozer.exe** to open the application. Close the **KompoZer Tips** dialog box that appears.

5. **KompoZer:** You must use an HTML5 template to create an HTML5 <!DOCTYPE> declaration in KompoZer. Otherwise, it will default to an HTML 4.01 version. To perform this task, click the **Open** button on the toolbar (or select **File | Open File**). The Open HTML File dialog box will appear.

6. In the Open HTML File dialog box, locate and select the **Desktop/Lesson09/Lab_9-1/html5_template.html** file, as shown in Figure 9-1. Click the **Open** button.

Figure 9-1: Selecting HTML5 template in KompoZer

7. You will need to save the file under a different name so you do not overwrite the html5_template.html file. Select **File | Save As**. The Page Title dialog box will appear.

8. In the Page Title dialog box, enter a title for your Web page. For example, enter your name, followed by — *Internet Certified*. This title will appear in the browser window title bar and the Bookmarks or Favorites folders of Web browsers. Click **OK**.

9. The Save Page As dialog box will appear. This dialog box allows you to name the HTML file. Name your file *default.html*, and navigate to the **Promo** directory you created in Step 1. Click the **Save** button to save the file to the Promo folder.

10. KompoZer: You are now ready to create an HTML page in a GUI editor. Select **Heading 1** from the paragraph format drop-down menu, as shown in Figure 9-2.

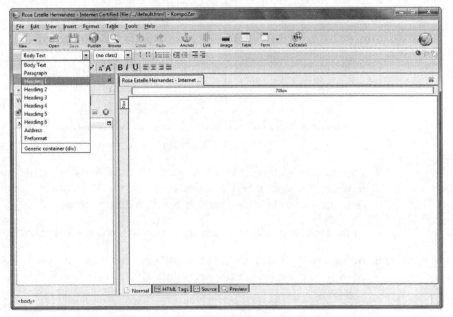

Figure 9-2: KompoZer paragraph formatting

11. Type your first, middle and last name. Center it by selecting **Format | Align | Center** (or by clicking the **Align Center** button on the toolbar).

    Note: If you make a mistake, you can use the CTRL+Z key combination to undo your previous actions. Press CTRL+Y to redo any changes that you have undone and want to reinstate.

12. Move the cursor to the line below your name (similar to a word processor, place the cursor at the end of your name and press the **ENTER** key). The paragraph format should return to Body Text, as displayed in the drop-down menu. If not, select **Body Text** from the paragraph format drop-down menu.

13. Enter the text ***Internet Certified and Ready to Succeed!*** Select this text and make it boldface by clicking the **Bold** button on the toolbar (or by pressing CTRL+B). Then, center the text.

    *Note: To avoid typing, you can copy and paste the Web page text from the **GUI_HTML_editor.txt** file located in the **C:\CIW\Site_Dev\Lab Files\Lesson09** directory.*

14. Save the **default.html** file. Except for the name, your screen should closely resemble Figure 9-3.

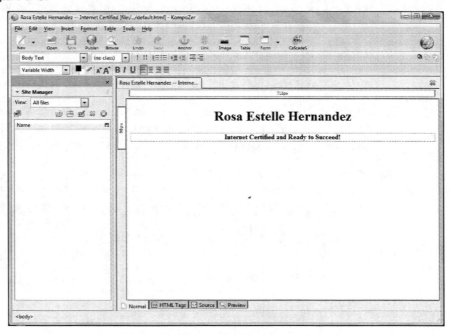

Figure 9-3: Creating Web page using GUI HTML editor

15. To view the Web page in a browser, click the **Browse** button on the KompoZer toolbar, or select **File | Browse Page**. In the External Protocol Request dialog box that appears, click the **Launch Application** button.

    Note: Make sure that you always save any changes before clicking the Browse button.

16. **Browser:** Your default browser will open and display your Web page. You can now read the entire title in the browser's Title bar. When finished, close the browser window.

Note: At the time of this writing, no open-source GUI HTML editors supported HTML5, including KompoZer. That means the built-in Preview browser in KompoZer is not HTML5-compliant. To ensure your Web page renders properly in HTML5, you should always preview your site in your computer's default HTML5-compliant browser, such as Chrome. At the end of these labs, you will update the KompoZer source code to HTML5.

In this lab, you began creating a résumé using a GUI Web page editor.

In the following lab, you will use a GUI page editor to modify font and background colors on a Web page. Suppose that as you are creating your résumé, you want to experiment with various color schemes. You know that color combinations can convey different moods, tones and messages. What color combinations would convey the best message for your résumé? Is a different tone appropriate when applying for an internship, rather than an entry-level position or a contract project? If you were submitting this résumé to five different companies, would you modify the résumé's look for each company?

 Lab 9-2: Changing font and background color with a GUI editor

OBJECTIVE
2.11.3: Formatting in
GUI HTML editor

In this lab, you will use the GUI page editor to change your Web page's font and background color. Continue to use the *default.html* file.

1. **KompoZer:** Select **Format | Page Colors And Background**. The Page Colors And Background dialog box will appear.

2. Select the **Use Custom Colors** radio button. Click the **Background** button, and select a color from the Block Background Color dialog box that appears.

3. Click **OK** to return to the Page Colors And Background dialog box.

4. Click the **Normal Text** button, and select a text color from the Text Color dialog box that appears. When you are satisfied with your choice, click **OK** twice to return to your page in the KompoZer window.

5. Save the **default.html** file, and view your changes in the browser.

6. As a class, discuss the following questions:

   • Thus far, you have used a few interfaces and commands. Are these interfaces and commands easy to access if you are disabled? Why or why not?

   • View the source code you have created by clicking the **Source** tab at the bottom of the KompoZer window. What type of code is being written? HTML 4.01? XHTML? HTML5? Is this code standard? Which standard?

In this lab, you modified the font and background colors on your résumé. You also learned more about the type of HTML that is generated by this GUI page editor.

In the following lab, you will use a GUI page editor to add a horizontal rule to a Web page. Suppose that as you are creating your résumé, you want to experiment with graphical features on the page. You know that graphics should be used sparingly because they can distract from the important information on your page. However, you want to introduce some visual interest to the page and add an organizational element for emphasis. A horizontal rule provides a subtle graphic enhancement that will emphasize your name at the top of your résumé.

 ## Lab 9-3: Adding a horizontal rule to a Web page with a GUI editor

OBJECTIVE
2.11.3: Formatting in GUI HTML editor

In this lab, you will use a GUI page editor to add a horizontal rule to a Web page. Continue to use the *default.html* file.

1. **KompoZer:** Place your cursor after the text *Internet Certified and Ready to Succeed!*, then press **ENTER** twice to create a double return (two blank lines).

2. Select **Insert | Horizontal Line** to insert a horizontal rule. After creating a horizontal line, your screen should resemble Figure 9-4.

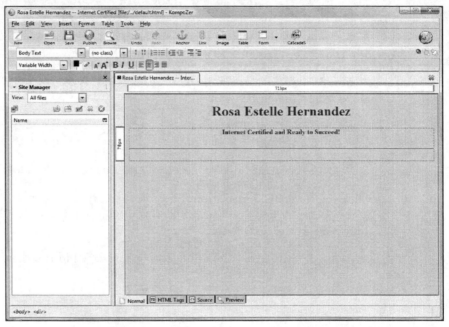

Figure 9-4: Adding horizontal rule using GUI HTML editor

3. Save the **default.html** file, and view your changes in the browser.

In this lab, you added a horizontal line to a Web page using a GUI page editor.

In the following lab, you will use a GUI page editor to create ordered and unordered lists on a Web page. Suppose that as you are creating your résumé, you consider that adding numbered and bulleted lists will help emphasize your achievements, as well as enhance the readability of the page. What types of information work well with numbered lists? What types of information are better as bullet points?

Lab 9-4: Creating bulleted and numbered lists with a GUI editor

OBJECTIVE
2.11.3: Formatting in
GUI HTML editor

In this lab, you will use a GUI page editor to create an unordered list and an ordered list on your Web page. Continue to use the *default.html* file.

1. **KompoZer:** Place the cursor on the blank line below the horizontal rule.

2. Type the word *Certifications*, and apply bold and italic formatting.

3. Left-justify the text **Certifications** by selecting **Format | Align | Left** (or by clicking the **Align Left** button on the toolbar).

4. Press **ENTER** to create a new line beneath the text that reads **Certifications**. Your cursor should be on the new blank line.

5. Enter the following words below **Certifications** as body text, and press **ENTER** after each line of text to create separate lines:

   CIW Internet Business Associate

   CIW Site Development Associate

   CIW Network Technology Associate

   CIW Web Foundations Associate

6. Select the four lines of text you just entered, then click the **Bulleted List** button on the toolbar to automatically insert bullet points. Alternatively, you can select the text, then select **Format | List | Bulleted**.

7. Create a new line, but make sure the new line is not bulleted. To exit the bulleted list mode, press **ENTER** and deselect the **Bulleted List** button, if necessary.

8. Left-justify the new line, if necessary.

9. On the new line, type the words *Internet Skills*, and apply bold and italic formatting.

   Note: To avoid typing in the next step, you can copy and paste Web page text from the GUI_HTML_editor.txt file located in the C:\CIW\Site_Dev\Lab Files\Lesson09 directory.

10. Create another new line beneath **Internet Skills**. Enter the following text on separate lines as shown:

    Web browsers, mobile devices, SMS, e-mail, FTP, social networking, e-commerce

    Web page authoring in HTML5, CSS, and simple JavaScript

    Basic networking components, protocols and server configuration

    Basic security concepts and virus protection

    Project management skills for individual and team job tasks

11. Select the five lines of text you just entered, then click the **Numbered List** button on the toolbar to automatically insert numbering. Each line should now be numbered,

and your screen should resemble Figure 9-5. Eliminate any extra space between the words **Internet Skills** and the numbered list, if necessary.

Figure 9-5: Bulleted list and numbered list in GUI HTML editor

12. Save the **default.html** file, and view your changes in the browser.

    Note: The GUI_HTML_editor.txt file located in the \Site_Dev\Lab Files\Lesson09\ folder contains the skills list you used in this lab, which you can paste into your Web page. You will learn these skills by completing the CIW Web Foundations course series. You can use this list for your personal résumé when searching for a job. You can earn the CIW Web Foundations Associate certification by taking and passing the CIW Web Foundations Associate certification exam. You can earn the CIW Site Development Associate certification by taking and passing the CIW Site Development Associate certification exam. For more information about CIW exams, visit www.CIWcertified.com.

In this lab, you created an unordered list and an ordered list on your Web page.

In the following lab, you will use a GUI page editor to create external hyperlinks on a Web page. Suppose that as you are creating your résumé, you consider that adding some hyperlinks to relevant Web sites could substantiate your credentials. You also consider that any sites to which you link from your résumé should be professional, reputable and relevant to your résumé information. Every reference should serve the purpose of providing useful information.

Lab 9-5: Creating external hyperlinks with a GUI editor

OBJECTIVE
2.11.3: Formatting in GUI HTML editor

In this lab, you will use a GUI editor to create a hyperlink from your Web page to an external Web site. Continue to use the *default.html* file.

1. **KompoZer:** Select the words **CIW Web Foundations Associate** in the bulleted list.

2. Select **Insert | Link** (or click the **Link** button on the toolbar; or right-click the selected text and select **Create Link**) to open the Link Properties dialog box.

3. Enter ***http://www.CIWcertified.com*** into the Link Location field, as shown in Figure 9-6. You can also include a deep link to the certification, which means a specific page within the CIW Web site. For CIW Web Foundations Associate, the address would be *http://www.ciwcertified.com/Certifications/Web_Foundations_Series/associate.php*.

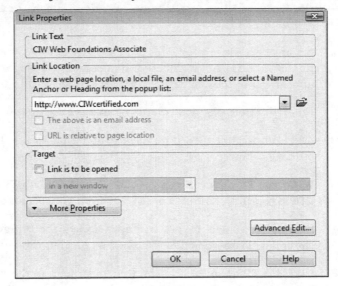

Figure 9-6: Creating hyperlink in GUI HTML editor

4. Click **OK** to return to your Web page. Notice that the words **CIW Web Foundations Associate** now appear in underlined blue font, indicating that the text is a hyperlink.

5. Highlight the other certifications in the bulleted list. Create a deep link to each of them within the CIW Web site.

6. Save the **default.html** file.

7. Test the hyperlinks by viewing your page in a browser, then clicking the hyperlinks.

8. **Browser:** When you are finished testing your hyperlinks, return to **KompoZer**.

In this lab, you created external hyperlinks in your Web page document.

In the following lab, you will use a GUI page editor to add an image to a Web page. Suppose you have already passed the CIW Web Foundations Associate certification exam. You would then be a certified CIW Web Foundations Associate. CIW provides access to an official graphical logo after you earn the CIW Web Foundations Associate certification. As you create your résumé, you might want to include the official CIW Web Foundations Associate logo to tout your professional credential. Displaying this logo on your résumé adds visual interest and shows that you have industry-standard skills that employers want. The logo image you will add to your page in the next lab is similar to the one you would receive as a CIW Web Foundations Associate.

Tech Tip

Remember that in any résumé document you submit to an organization for a professional position of any type, you should claim only skills, experience and credentials that you do in fact possess or have earned.

Lab 9-6: Adding an image to a Web page with a GUI editor

OBJECTIVE
2.11.3: Formatting in
GUI HTML editor

In this lab, you will use a GUI editor to add an image to your Web page. Continue to use the *default.html* file.

1. **KompoZer:** Place your cursor on a blank line below the numbered list. Be sure that this new line is not numbered. If necessary, press **ENTER** to see if a new number appears. If it does, click the **Numbered List** button to stop the numbering.

   *Note: Alternatively, you can also click the **Source** tab and edit the code manually.*

2. Add a horizontal rule. If necessary, add a blank line below the rule and place your cursor on it.

3. **Windows Explorer:** From **C:\CIW\Site_Dev\Lab Files\Lesson09**, copy the **CIWlogo.gif** file to the **Promo** folder on your Desktop.

4. **KompoZer:** Select **Insert | Image** (or click the **Image** button on the toolbar) to open the Image Properties dialog box. The Location tab is selected by default.

5. Click the **Choose File** button (the folder icon to the right of the Image Location text box). The Select Image File dialog box will appear. Navigate to the **Promo** folder, click the **CIWlogo.gif** file, then click the **Open** button.

6. The Image Properties dialog box will appear, with the CIWlogo.gif image you selected now entered into the Image Location field. Notice that the **Alternate Text** radio button is selected. The field associated with this radio button allows you to enter text that describes the image to text-only browsers, such as Lynx. Enter the words *CIW Logo* into the Alternate Text field, then click **OK** to insert the image into your document.

7. After inserting the image, center it on the Web page.

8. Save your changes to the **default.html** file.

9. View your page in the browser to review your work. Your screen should resemble Figure 9-7.

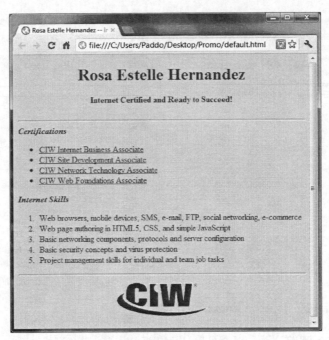

Figure 9-7: Image displayed in Web browser

10. Return to **KompoZer**.

In this lab, you added an image to your Web page document.

In the following lab, you will use a GUI page editor to create a table in a Web page. Suppose you want to add some structure to your résumé Web page. You consider that an HTML table can help organize the information on your page into a balanced, easy-to-read page design.

Lab 9-7: Creating an HTML table with a GUI editor

OBJECTIVE
2.11.5: Tables in GUI
HTML editor

In this lab, you will use a GUI editor to create a basic table on your Web page. Continue to use the *default.html* file.

1. **KompoZer:** Place your cursor directly before the word **Certifications** on your Web page. Press **ENTER** to create a blank line. Place your cursor on this new blank line.

2. Select **Insert | Table** (or click the **Table** button on the toolbar). The Insert Table dialog box will appear.

3. Click the **Precisely** tab. Verify that both the Rows and Columns fields show the value **2**. If the values are different, change them to **2**.

4. Verify that the Width field shows a value of **100**. Display the drop-down menu to the right of the Width field and select **% of window**.

5. Click the **Advanced Edit** button.

6. Verify that the Cellspacing and Cellpadding values are both **2**. If they are not, change both values to **2**.

7. Change the Border value to 2 by clicking the word **Border**, then entering **2** in the Value field at the bottom of the Advanced Property Editor dialog box.

8. Click **OK** to return to the Insert Table dialog box. The Insert Table dialog box should resemble Figure 9-8.

Figure 9-8: Creating table using GUI HTML editor

9. Click **OK** to insert the table.

10. Place your cursor in the table's upper-left cell. Then, right-click your mouse and select **Table Select | Row**. This action will select the first row of the table. You can now format this row as a table header.

11. With the entire first row still selected, right-click the selection and click **Table Cell Properties**. The Table Properties dialog box will appear.

12. The **Cells** tab should already be selected. Select the **Cell Style** check box, and change the style to **Header** using the drop-down menu. Click **OK**.

13. Cut the word **Certifications** from your Web page and paste it into the table's upper-left cell.

14. Cut the words **Internet Skills** from the page and paste them into the table's upper-right cell.

15. Cut the bulleted CIW certification hyperlinks and paste them into the table's lower-left cell. Keep the bulleting. Ensure that the certifications occupy the same cell; do not create a new table row for each certification.

16. Cut all of the numbered list items (e.g., *Web browsers, mobile devices, SMS, e-mail, FTP, social networking, etc.*) and paste them into the table's lower-right cell. Keep the numbering. Ensure that all numbered items are placed in the same cell.

17. Place your cursor in the top-right cell of the table. Right-click and select **Table Cell Properties** to display the Table Properties dialog box.

18. In the Size section, select the **Width** check box, and enter **50** in the field. Change the value in the drop-down menu from Pixels to **% of Table**. When finished, click **OK** to return to your page. Notice that each column occupies exactly half of the table.

19. Delete all blank lines that remain above and below the table between the two horizontal rules.

Note: When deleting extra spaces and characters, try using both the **DELETE** *and* **BACKSPACE** *keys. Be careful not to delete the image or the horizontal rules. If you do, press* **CTRL+Z** *to undo any changes. Remember that* **CTRL+Y** *will redo any changes you undo. If you prefer using the mouse to undo and redo, select* **Edit | Undo** *and* **Edit | Redo.**

20. If you want, create additional spaces between the table data and the table borders, either by pressing the **ENTER** key or by modifying the cell padding values.

21. When you are finished, save the **default.html** file, then view your page in a browser. Your screen should resemble Figure 9-9.

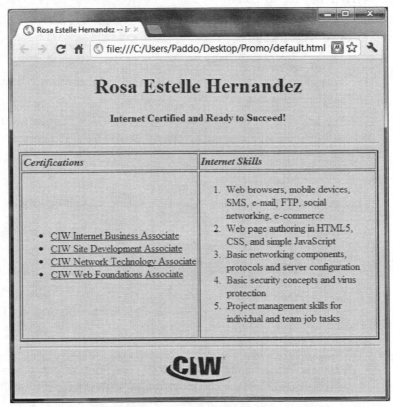

Figure 9-9: Table displayed in Web browser

22. If you want to make changes to your page, then exit the browser and return to KompoZer. Modify the page as necessary to achieve the results you want. Remember to save the file each time you change it to see an accurate representation in the Web browser.

23. Verify that your code renders as expected in at least one more browser.

In this lab, you created an HTML table on a Web page and formatted information in the table. The preceding series of labs introduced you to the basic features of a GUI HTML editor.

HTML Text Editors vs. GUI Editors

The following sections describe some of the advantages and disadvantages of text editors and GUI editors. The type of editor you choose depends on your personal preferences and your specific Web project needs.

In most cases, you will use both types of HTML editors. You can create the majority of your Web site quickly with a GUI editor, then use a text editor (most GUI editors include one) to enter scripts for advanced functionality.

HTML text editors

Text editors such as Notepad, WordPad, Vi and Emacs present the following advantages for Web page authors:

- If you are considering learning a scripting language such as JavaScript or VBScript, you *must* learn to write code manually. If you want to add forms to your Web pages, it is also helpful to be proficient in HTML.

- If you know HTML code, you can maximize the benefit of GUI HTML editors by manually modifying code, independently from the editor.

- You can learn the fundamentals of HTML and update your pages to the latest version(s).

Now consider the following drawbacks of using text editors to create Web pages:

- Typing code can be time-consuming, especially if you must learn the latest changes to code standards from the W3C.

- People with disabilities may find manual entry too time-consuming and/or too difficult.

- A text editor may require too much attention if you need only a simple page.

GUI HTML editors

GUI HTML editors such as KompoZer, Sea Monkey Composer, Dreamweaver and Expression Web present the following advantages for Web page authors:

- GUI editors place code into files for you, which enables you to create pages quickly by simply clicking your mouse.

- Most GUI editors allow you to modify your code manually.

Now consider the following drawbacks of using GUI editors to create Web pages:

- Some GUI editors will alter or ignore any code you enter manually. For instance, you can manually add a paragraph tag <p/>, but the GUI editor may not recognize it. This situation can be frustrating if you want to format a Web page your own way.

- Many GUI editors have not kept pace with the evolution of HTML, and thus do not provide options for using some of the recently developed tags. You must upgrade your GUI editor if you want to begin using a later version of HTML.

- At the time of this writing, HTML5 was not supported by any open-source GUI or WYSIWYG HTML editors. Instead, an HTML5 template was required in KompoZer to produce the HTML5 <!DOCTYPE> declaration. Once the code is complete, it must be validated and updated as needed.

GUI editors often simply fail to load and edit code that contains newer tags. Be careful when making changes to your pages. Make backup copies of your pages first, then test each change in the GUI editor to make sure it understands the new code.

CIW Online Resources – Course Mastery

Visit CIW Online at *http://education.Certification-Partners.com/CIW* to take the Course Mastery review of this lesson or lesson segment.

SDA Lesson 9 - Part A

Previewing Pages and Validating Code

OBJECTIVE
2.11.4: Source code and page previewing

You have seen in the previous labs that it is necessary to preview your pages when using a GUI editor, despite the WYSIWYG development environment. Most GUI editors make it quite easy to:

- Preview pages in a browser.

- View source code.

- Validate code using built-in validators or a site such as *http://validator.w3.org.*

Many GUI editors allow you to choose the browser you use for previewing. By not limiting you to any single browser, the GUI editor helps you to test your pages in multiple browsers, or to focus your development on your favorite or company standard browser.

<!DOCTYPE> declaration options

Validation engines, such as the one provided by the W3C, first read the <!DOCTYPE> declaration in an HTML page before validating the code. The validation engine examines the code according to the standard specified in the <!DOCTYPE> declaration. As a result, your code may fail validation with one <!DOCTYPE> reference, but pass if you change the standard in your <!DOCTYPE> declaration.

For example, suppose you have written code in a page to the HTML 4.01 Transitional standard, and it has validated. Then one of your team members hears that the site will be updated to HTML5 in the coming months. In an effort to start the update project early, he changes the <!DOCTYPE> declaration on this page to refer to HTML5. Although your page once validated as HTML 4.01 Transitional, it may no longer validate. To get the page to validate now, you can either edit the page code to conform to the HTML5 standard as declared in the <!DOCTYPE>, or you can change the <!DOCTYPE> reference back to HTML 4.01, the standard to which the page code currently conforms.

OBJECTIVE
2.11.2: Validating HTML code

Validating HTML code

When validating code created by a GUI editor, consider the following points:

- Most GUI editors include their own native validation tools or offer menus that provide access to validators. For example, KompoZer provides the Validate HTML option, which you will use in the next lab.

- Some GUI editors have special features that help ensure accessibility in regard to validation.

In the following lab, you will validate Web page code generated by a GUI page editor. Suppose you want to ensure that your résumé page uses proper HTML5 code standards. You can validate your résumé page code using the W3C validator service. You will not use the built-in GUI editor's validator. Validating your code is an important step, and using clean validated code in your résumé demonstrates your skill and commitment as a Web developer.

Lab 9-8: Validating and updating HTML code generated by a GUI editor

OBJECTIVE
2.11.2: Validating
HTML code

In this lab, you will validate the HTML code created by KompoZer. Then you will edit your Web site to conform to HTML5 by adding a CSS file.

1. **KompoZer:** Verify that you have saved all changes to your résumé document, default.html.

2. Exit KompoZer.

3. **Browser:** Open the W3C Markup Validation Service at ***http://validator.w3.org/***. Load **default.html** into the validator.

4. What results were returned from the validation process? What version of HTML is identified? Your results should appear similar to Figure 9-10.

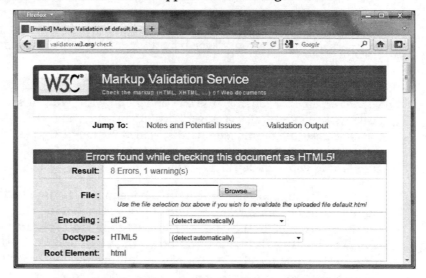

Figure 9-10: Errors found while checking document as HTML5

5. As a class, discuss the following questions:

   - What modifications does this code need in order to validate as HTML5?

   - How long would it take to upgrade this code?

   - What were the benefits of using a GUI editor to create your résumé Web page?

   - What were the drawbacks?

6. Using the results from the validator, create a list of the errors along with a solution for each. Most, if not all, errors can be corrected by transferring styles to an external CSS sheet or inline CSS.

   The common validation errors for this lab are HTML 4.01 style attributes. These style attributes were inserted directly into the HTML elements. In HTML5, these styles are transferred to CSS. The style attributes that must be updated and transferred will be similar to the following list and the list shown in Figure 9-11:

- Hyperlink styles (*vlink, alink, link*)

- Table styles (*cellpadding, cellspacing*)

- Text and Image alignment styles (*align, valign*)

- Thickness value of the table's *border* attribute

Figure 9-11: Validation errors that need fixing

7. **Editor:** Open **default.html** in a text editor, such as Notepad. The HTML code created from the HTML GUI editor will resemble the code shown in Figure 9-12.

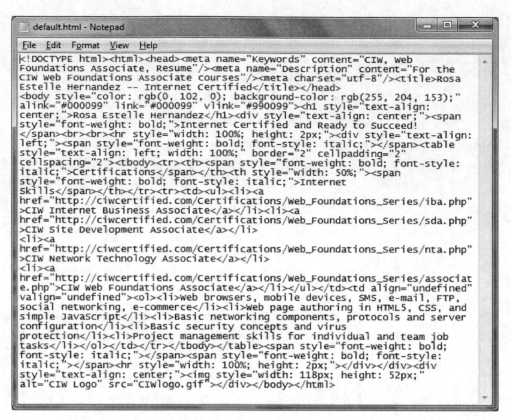

Figure 9-12: Example code generated from HTML GUI editor

8. **Editor:** Create a new file named **default.css.** Link the file to your HTML document.

9. **Editor:** Transfer the necessary styles from **default.html** to **default.css**.

10. **Browser:** Validate **default.html** using the **W3C Markup Validation Service** until it validates as HTML5. Your code may resemble Figure 9-13.

Figure 9-13: Example code when upgraded to HTML5

11. **Browser:** Validate **default.css** using the W3C CSS Validation Service at *http://jigsaw.w3.org/css-validator/* and fix any errors until it validates.

12. **KompoZer:** Open **default.html** in KompoZer. As a class, discuss the following questions:

- Can you access the default.css file using KompoZer?

- Can you modify the default.css file using KompoZer?

- Can you simultaneously work with the HTML and CSS files?

- Would it be easier to transfer styles to CSS using KompoZer instead of a text editor?

- Are there additional styles that could be transferred from default.html to default.css, even though the documents were already validated?

- Does CSS create a lot of additional work? If so, why does the W3C enforce it? Does it make more sense for larger sites with dozens or hundreds of Web pages?

13. **KompoZer:** Save and close your files.

14. Browser: Validate the files, make any necessary changes, and view the site in your browser.

In this lab, you validated and fixed HTML code generated from a GUI editor. You updated the code to HTML5 by transferring styles to CSS.

OBJECTIVE
2.11.6: Publishing
Web sites

File Transfer Protocol (FTP)
An Internet protocol used to transfer files between computers; allows file transfer without corruption or alteration.

Web Site Publishing

The final step in Web site development is publishing your site to the World Wide Web. You can publish your site in several ways, depending on the tools used to create it. Most GUI HTML editors provide a Publish feature that allows you to easily post your Web page files to your designated Web host. You can also use a **File Transfer Protocol (FTP)** client, such as FileZilla (*http://filezilla-project.org/*) or Ipswitch WS_FTP Professional (*www.ipswitch.com*).

FTP is the protocol most often used to transfer files between two computers, or a server and a computer, depending on the configuration. Transferring files over the Internet requires an FTP client to send the files and a destination FTP server to receive them. FTP can also be used to transfer files to an HTTP server, provided that the HTTP server is also running FTP. However, before you can transfer your Web site files, you must decide where your site will be hosted.

Publishing to a test Web server

Professional Web developers post the final version of the Web site files to a test Web server before moving them to the production server for the following reasons:

- To verify that the Web server can process any CGI and database access requests.

- To locate and repair any dead links.

- To allow members of the development team and other stakeholders to preview the site. You will find that many changes are needed before your "final" code is ready for publication.

Test server configuration

Your test server must be as nearly identical to the production server as possible. The test server should have:

- **The same operating system version** — If your production server is a Linux system or a Windows Server, for example, then your production system should be the same model.

- **The same type and version of Web server software** — Even if your test system uses a software type or version very similar to the production system, this test system is not adequate. For example, if your production Web server uses Apache Server 2.2 and your test server is using Apache Server 2.4, then your testing server will not provide a true test of your site.

- **The same CGI interpreter software** — If your production server uses PHP 5.4.0, then your test server should use PHP version 5.4.0.

 Test servers are often called staging servers.

Publishing with KompoZer

If you want to publish files directly from KompoZer, you simply select File | Publish, then enter the appropriate information. Earlier in this course, you learned about the information required for publishing a Web site. Figure 9-14 shows example information that you might enter in the Settings tab of the Publish Page dialog box in KompoZer, such as authentication information and the name of the Web server to which you are sending the files.

Figure 9-14: Specifying ISP and authentication information to publish Web pages

Discuss the multitude of Web publishing options available for students, such as their local ISP, large hosting companies such as GoDaddy.com, and various cloud service providers. In addition to the destination server's name (or IP address) and authentication information, you must also specify the location on the remote server that you want your files placed. In Figure 9-15, the résumé file is named default.html and will be placed in the /html/resume_files/ directory on the remote Web server.

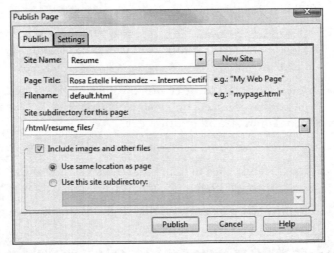

Figure 9-15: Specifying file names and directory location for publishing

OBJECTIVE
2.21.5: Designing for
traditional vs.
mobile browsers

Developing Web Pages for Mobile Devices

With the increasingly widespread use of mobile devices, such as smartphones and tablets, it is important that you consider how your Web site (or the mobile version of your Web site) will display on these devices. As of 2012, it was estimated that almost 80 percent of the world's population used mobile phones. Half of all mobile phones sold in the United States were smartphones. These trends will continue until nearly everyone has an Internet connection on a mobile device.

OBJECTIVE
2.7.7: Design
challenges for
mobile devices

There are several key points you should consider in order to optimize your Web site for viewing on mobile devices:

- **Keep your Web pages simple and uncluttered** — Mobile devices have smaller screens than desktop or laptop monitors, and Internet connectivity is often slower. It is important that your site visitors have easy access to important information without getting bogged down by unnecessary clutter. Use white space to help give the site an uncluttered look, and keep the use of images to a minimum.

OBJECTIVE
2.11.7: Mobile and
cloud HTML editors

- **Prioritize your content** — When users are viewing a Web site with a mobile device, they are often looking for very specific information. For example, users who are viewing a store's mobile Web site may be looking for the nearest store to their current location, as opposed to simply browsing the site. Therefore, include only content that is absolutely necessary for the viewer. For this reason, most mobile Web sites should not contain any banner ads or other types of advertisements.

- **Optimize your site to a smaller screen size** — Although screen sizes vary among mobile devices, the most common size for traditional feature phones is 240x320 pixels. Smartphones typically use 320x480 pixels, with some rendering 480x800. You should tailor your mobile Web site to make sure your site is easily viewable by the majority of mobile device users.

As you develop a Web site designed for mobile devices, keep the following considerations in mind:

- Use clean, valid markup, and use CSS to separate the presentation from the content. Most mobile site visitors want access to content and links and may have CSS disabled.

- Always use the *alt* attribute in your <img> tags because images may be difficult to see (or will be disabled) on some mobile devices. Besides, it will not validate as HTML5 if you do not add alternative text.

- Ensure that you label form fields so that they are easily identifiable.

- Use heading tags to help build the structure of the page and to style text. Use tags <h1> through <h4> only; smaller heading tags will be too difficult to see.

- Reduce margins and padding to give yourself more usable space in which to display content.

- Provide easy-to-use navigation options and links.

- Ensure that your content is easy to read on a mobile-device screen.

Figures 9-16 and 9-17 show the home page of the traditional Web site and the mobile Web site, respectively, for eBay.

Figure 9-16: eBay traditional Web site

Figure 9-17: eBay mobile Web site viewed in traditional Web browser

As you can see from the two figures, the mobile version of the Web site is very simplistic compared to the traditional site. What are the differences between the two sites?

Companies should consider creating both a traditional and a mobile version of their Web sites to accommodate both desktop and mobile users. There are pros and cons of providing mobile sites:

- Pros — Easier navigation and an optimized user experience due to focused site content.

- Cons — Limited advertising space, minimalistic design; Web sites that rely heavily on graphics usually need to be redesigned.

CIW Online Resources – Movie Clips

Visit CIW Online at http://education.Certification-Partners.com/CIW to watch a movie clip about this topic.

Lesson 9: Designing Pages for Mobile Devices

CIW Online Resources – Online Exercise

Visit CIW Online at *http://education.Certification-Partners.com/CIW* to complete an interactive exercise that will reinforce what you have learned about this topic.

Exercise 9-2: Developing Web pages for viewing on mobile devices

OBJECTIVE
2.11.8: Mobile apps vs. mobile sites

Mobile Apps vs. Mobile Web Sites

There are many arguments regarding the better approach for mobile devices: mobile apps or mobile Web sites. Mobile apps are stand-alone applications that are downloaded from a vendor's software repository onto a mobile device. Apple iTunes and Google Play are two leading providers of apps for the Apple and Android mobile devices, respectively. As you have learned, mobile Web sites are usually stripped-down versions of traditional Web sites.

For HTML5 developers, the difference is fading between mobile apps and mobile Web sites. Opportunities exist in both arenas because HTML5, CSS and JavaScript are now being used to create both mobile apps and mobile Web sites.

Figure 9-18 shows the Habitat for Humanity Web site (*www.habitat.org*) in an iPad simulator (*http://ipadpeek.com*).

Figure 9-18: Habitat site viewed in iPad simulator

Figure 9-19 shows the Habitat site in an iPhone/iPod Touch simulator (*http://iphone4simulator.com/*).

Figure 9-19: Habitat site viewed in iPhone/iPod Touch simulator

As you can see, the Habitat site was not available as a mobile Web site at the time of this writing. Only part of the Web site appears in the small screen. Instead, the organization has created a mobile app that is available for download on Apple iTunes (for Apple mobile devices) and Google Play (for Android devices). The Google Play download site for the app is shown in Figure 9-20:

Figure 9-20: Habitat Android app download site from Google Play

Why do you think the Habitat for Humanity organization has not created a mobile Web site at the time of this writing? What are the advantages and disadvantages of mobile Web sites?

The advance of the HTML5 specification and its Application Programming Interfaces (APIs) have allowed Web developers to create more immersive experiences for mobile Web site users. Until recently, mobile apps were the only way to provide these experiences and more complex programs.

One important advantage that mobile Web sites have over mobile apps is cross-platform usability. Mobile Web sites can be viewed from almost any mobile device, regardless of its operating system or browser. Web information can be accessed without waiting for an app to download and install from a vendor's software repository.

On the other hand, mobile apps are designed and built for specific mobile operating systems. The programming languages used to create the apps are optimized for the device, which often enables them to run more quickly. No Web browser is required.

In conclusion, mobile apps and mobile Web sites will continue to co-exist. The majority of companies will create both to reach a larger audience. They will also need a traditional Web site, so HTML5 developers will have no shortage of work.

OBJECTIVE
2.11.7: Mobile and cloud HTML editors

Converting a Web site for Mobile Users

Many services are available to convert traditional sites to mobile sites. You must consider what types of mobile devices to support. Most services will convert traditional Web sites to support the major types of mobile operating systems used in smartphones and tablets. However, many users still have older phones, so ensure the conversion service provides support for whatever mobile devices your customers will be using to access your site.

Following is a list of sites that you can use to convert Web pages for mobile devices:

- bMobilized (*http://bmobilized.com*)
- ConvertWebSite.com (*www.convertwebsite.com*)
- Mobify (*www.mobify.com*)
- MobileAppAmerica (*www.mobileappamerica.com*)
- mobiSiteGalore (*www.mobisitegalore.com*)
- MobStac (*http://mobstac.com*)
- MoFuse (*http://mofuse.com*)
- onbile (*www.onbile.com*)

Testing a mobile Web site

Testing your mobile Web site on as many mobile devices as possible is critical because of the variety of devices that visitors will be using to access your site. It is also important to validate your markup code to HTML5, which was created in part to provide support for mobile devices.

Following is a list of sites that you can use to test Web pages that you design for mobile devices:

- W3C mobileOK Checker (*http://validator.w3.org/mobile*)
- Ready.mobi (*http://ready.mobi/launch.jsp*)
- dotMobi Emulator (*http://mtld.mobi/emulator.php*)

- iPhoney (*www.marketcircle.com/iphoney*)

- iPadPeek.com (*http://ipadpeek.com*)

- BlackBerry Simulators
  (*http://us.blackberry.com/developers/resources/simulators.jsp*)

Working with Web 2.0

Web 2.0
A concept referring to the changing trends in the use of WWW technology and Web design that have led to the development of information-sharing and collaboration capabilities.

The evolution of Web technologies has given rise to the term "Web 2.0." **Web 2.0** is a common term that refers to the changing trends in the use of World Wide Web technology and Web design since the early days of the Web when most Web pages were static, when users simply retrieved information, and when Internet connections were slow. Web use before the "bursting of the dot-com bubble" in 2001 is now referred to as "Web 1.0."

Web 2.0 is a paradigm shift in the way the Internet is used compared with the Web 1.0 day. Web 2.0 involves a more open approach to the Internet that concentrates on developing the information-sharing and collaboration capabilities of the Web. Web 2.0 has enabled users to provide a significant amount of information on the Web, and there are no longer any restrictions on what they produce.

Web 2.0 has also led to the development of Web-based communities and hosted services, such as social networking sites, video-sharing sites, wikis, blogs, RSS feeds, podcasts and so forth. The Web is now a resource through which users have the ability to generate and distribute content, as well as to update and modify it.

OBJECTIVE
2.17.2: CGI methods

Ajax
A programming methodology that uses a number of existing technologies together and enables Web applications to make incremental updates to the user interface without the need to reload the browser page.

XMLHttpRequest
An Application Programming Interface (API) that is used to transfer XML and other text data between a Web server and browser.

Ajax (Asynchronous JavaScript and XML) is a Web 2.0 programming methodology that enables Web applications to interact with users in much the same way they do with desktop applications. Ajax allows you to create interactive Web applications using XHTML, CSS, the Document Object Model (DOM), JavaScript and **XMLHttpRequest**.

With the advent of Web 2.0 technologies and Ajax, you can use the Web to perform many tasks including using Web browsers as application delivery platforms, adding third-party applications to your Web page, and accessing and using Web feeds and podcasts.

 A more detailed discussion of Web 2.0 is presented in the CIW Internet Business Associate course.

CIW Online Resources – Movie Clips

Visit CIW Online at http://education.Certification-Partners.com/CIW to watch a movie clip about this topic.

Lesson 9: Working with Web 2.0

Browsers as application delivery platforms

You were introduced to cloud computing and Software as a Service (SaaS) in a previous lesson. Application delivery platform is another term that refers to the way Web browsers are used to access hosted applications and services that enable you to perform computing tasks without the need to download and install any software.

Recall that in cloud computing, software, infrastructure and platform services are hosted by a remote data center and provided to organizations or individuals over the Internet. A Web browser is the only locally installed application necessary to access these applications. Even though only a Web browser is used, the cloud-based applications are nevertheless meant to be as robust and as sophisticated as those installed on your local system.

 A more detailed discussion of cloud computing is presented in the CIW Internet Business Associate course.

OBJECTIVE
2.1.10: Web browser
as application
delivery platform

Software as a Service (SaaS) is another term used to describe cloud computing because:

- The software responsible for providing the service cannot be downloaded and owned by the end user. It is available as a solution only on a remote basis.

- The software becomes available as a service either for free or for a fee. Many times, the service is available free for a certain period of time. Two versions of a service are often made available: The first version is usually a free service that is limited in some way or contains advertisements. The second version is an enhanced or "professional" service that contains no advertisements and is often full-featured. In some cases, the full-featured version is available either for a fee or in exchange for user profile information.

Meebo (*www.meebo.com*) is an example of a Web application delivery platform. Meebo is a free, Ajax-based instant messaging program that combines existing IM services onto one Web interface. Meebo supports AOL Instant Messenger, Yahoo!, MSN, Google Talk, Gmail, MySpace Instant Messenger, Facebook, Chat and others. Meebo enables users to engage in instant messaging without the need to download and install any IM software. The Meebo home page is shown in Figure 9-21.

Figure 9-21: Meebo Messenger

Other Web environments that can serve as application delivery platforms include:

- Aptana (*www.aptana.com*).
- Bindows (*www.bindows.net*).
- Laszlo Webtop (*www.laszlosystems.com*).
- OpenLaszlo (*www.openlaszlo.org*).

Advantages to using browsers as application delivery platforms

Following are some advantages to using browsers as application delivery platforms:

- **Flexibility** — Using powerful cloud computing software, a single person can run a sophisticated business. Yet a large enterprise can use a very similar product as well.

- **Scalability** — As an enterprise grows, it can simply rely on its cloud computing partner to increase capability instead of hiring additional employees and obtaining new hardware.

- **Cost reduction** — Companies that use cloud computing software can hire fewer employees and purchase less hardware.

Disadvantages to using browsers as application delivery platforms

Following are some drawbacks to using browsers as application delivery platforms:

- **Connectivity** — If Internet access is cut off to a particular company or division for some reason, then the cloud-based service will no longer be available. Workers would be entirely dependent upon accessing remote applications. Furthermore, if the company or end user tends to store information only on the remote servers, then this information is no longer available as well.

- **Speed** — If Internet access somehow becomes impaired, then users will not be able to use or obtain information.

- **Lockout** — If the cloud-based organization decides to limit access to its services, you may no longer be able to access information stored remotely.

Personalizing a Web page with third-party applications

OBJECTIVE
2.1.9: Third-party
applications on
Web pages

You can personalize your Web pages by adding third-party applications to them. Third-party applications can dramatically increase the functionality and usability of your Web page without the need for you to create the programs yourself. However, be aware that adding such applications may slow page rendering speeds and can easily be overused.

iGoogle (*www.google.com/ig*) is an example of a service that offers many third-party applications that you can add to your Web page. This service allows you to create your own home page on iGoogle or on any other site.

Gadgets are mini-applications created with HTML and JavaScript. They can be created with the Google Gadgets Editor (*http://code.google.com/apis/gadgets/docs/basic.html*). They are a good example of how apps can be created for mobile phones.

In the following lab, you will add third-party applications to a Web page. Suppose your project manager has asked you to customize a browser home page for each member of the project team so that they can track individual projects. You discovered Google Gadgets and realized that many applications that you would like to add to enhance the pages already exist and can be easily incorporated.

 Lab 9-9: Personalizing a Web page with Google Gadgets

In this lab, you will add third-party applications to a Web page via Google Gadgets.

1. Open a browser and go to **www.google.com** to display the Google home page.

2. Locate and click the **iGoogle** link. The iGoogle page will appear, as shown in Figure 9-22. You can use iGoogle to add Web feeds and Google Gadgets (mini-applications that can deliver services, such as calendars, e-mail, weather, photos and personalized news) anywhere on a Web page.

Figure 9-22: iGoogle page

3. Scroll through the page and notice the default Gadgets: Weather, Date & Time, YouTube and CNN.com. Links to the default Gadgets also appear in the navigation box on the left side of the screen (the area that appears under the Home link).

4. In the "Create your own homepage in under 30 seconds" box, select several interests of your choice, enter your ZIP code, then click the **See Your Page** button. Depending on the interests you selected and location you specified, your iGoogle home page may resemble Figure 9-23.

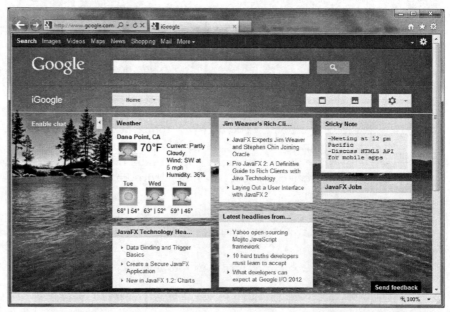

Figure 9-23: Personalized iGoogle page

5. Scroll through the page and observe the Gadgets that were added based on your selections.

6. In the iGoogle page, maximize the **Weather** gadget. Notice that it expands to show detailed information about the weather in your location. It should include an air quality chart, airport weather information and a map of the area from Google Maps.

7. Minimize the **Weather** gadget to return to the iGoogle home page.

8. Click the **Add Gadgets** button to display a list of Gadgets you can add to your iGoogle page. Scroll through the list of Gadgets to familiarize yourself with the available applications.

9. Click the **Change Theme** button to display a list of available themes. When you are finished exploring the themes, close the "Select a theme for your page" window and return to the iGoogle page.

10. Click the **Classic Home** link in the lower-left corner of the window to display the default Google home page.

11. Close the browser.

In this lab, you used Google Gadgets to personalize a Web page.

Web feeds

Web feed
A data format for delivering Web content that is updated frequently.

A **Web feed** is a data format for delivering Web content that is updated frequently, such as blog entries and news headlines. Web feed formats allow you to view headlines and updates from your favorite Web sites without the need to open your Web browser or visit any Web sites. There are two popular feed formats:

- **RSS (Really Simple Syndication, RDF Site Summary or Rich Site Summary)** — Currently at version 2.0, RSS is the "original" family of Web feeds. RSS 2.0 has the widest acceptance of any feed format.

- **Atom** — Currently at version 1.0, Atom is a relatively recent development but is much more robust and feature-rich than RSS. Atom is designed solely for the syndication of entire news articles.

Atom vs. RSS

Unlike RSS, Atom provides not only the document's content, but also metadata about the document:

- What it is called

- Who created it

- When it was created

- Where it is located

 A more detailed discussion of Web feeds is presented in the CIW Internet Business Associate course.

Podcasts

podcast
The use of audio or video digital-media files that are distributed through Web feeds to subscribed users.

A **podcast** is similar to an RSS feed in that the user can download syndicated audio or video digital-media files to computers or portable media players, such as Apple iPods. To create a podcast, you can produce your own audio files (e.g., MP3, Ogg Vorbis or WAV files) and publish them online. You can then index the files so that an RSS reader can subscribe to them. Podcasts can also consist of rebroadcasts of radio or television content, educational tutorials, and other audio content.

A podcast differs from other digital formats, such as streaming media, in that the podcast files can be syndicated, subscribed to and downloaded automatically as you add new content. Users who want to subscribe to a podcast's syndicated media need to acquire feed aggregator software, such as Apple iTunes player (*www.apple.com/itunes*). Most users use MP3 players or computers that have media player software installed to listen to podcasts.

CIW Online Resources – Online Exercise

Visit CIW Online at *http://education.Certification-Partners.com/CIW* to complete an interactive exercise that will reinforce what you have learned about this topic.

Exercise 9-3: Advanced Web Technologies

CIW Online Resources – Course Mastery

Visit CIW Online at *http://education.Certification-Partners.com/CIW* to take the Course Mastery review of this lesson or lesson segment.

SDA Lesson 9 - Part B

Case Study

The Best GUI Editor

Patrick needs to create a Web site for a small company he is launching. He needs to develop and post the site as quickly as possible, so he decides to use a GUI Web page editor to create the site. When comparing the GUI editor applications he could use, Patrick considers the following issues:

- **The type of code that the editor creates** — Patrick must decide between HTML 4.01 and HTML5 standards, including W3C compliance. He needs a program to produce code that will validate to standards with as little manual modification as possible.

- **Accessibility** — Patrick has tendonitis and sometimes experiences difficulty using the computer's mouse. The program must accommodate his physical limitations.

- **Ability to insert customized code** — Patrick wants to include processes that require JavaScript, PHP and SQL statements, but he does not know those languages.

- **Publishing capabilities** — Patrick needs a program that can publish his pages to a remote Web server when he has finished creating them.

- **Cost** — Patrick wants a quality product, but he is running a small business. He does not want to spend much more than U.S. $150.00.

- **Validation features** — Patrick believes that validating Web page code to standards is important, and he plans to validate his code frequently during development.

- **Language support** — Patrick's company has an affiliate in Japan.

After considering all these issues, Patrick researches four GUI editor vendors offering various editor products. He visits the vendors' Web sites for specific information about compliance, accessibility and flexibility. He then creates a short list of GUI editors that best meet his needs.

After comparing costs, features, and support, Patrick chooses Microsoft Expression Studio Web Professional (*www.microsoft.com/expression/products/ StudioWebPro_Overview.aspx*). The product is within his budget; includes accessibility features; and supports multiple languages, including Japanese. It also allows file uploads to a remote Web server. It is not an open-source product, but it does offer validation support. Patrick knows he can also obtain free third-party validation tools that are current and easy to use.

*   *   *

As a class, consider the issues Patrick reviewed when choosing a GUI editor, and answer the following questions.

- Which do you think are most important features in a GUI editor product?

- Which features would you expect in a GUI editor that requires you to purchase a license, in contrast to the features you would expect from a GUI editor that is available for free? Why?

Lesson Summary

Application project

As you learned in this lesson, using a GUI HTML editor to develop Web pages can save you time. How could your company's intranet or Internet site be expanded using a GUI HTML editor? How could the GUI editor help save time and energy on these tasks? Could employees with little or no HTML experience contribute?

View the Web page you created in this lesson's labs with both Mozilla Firefox and Windows Internet Explorer. Does the table appear the same in each browser? How is it different? Using your HTML knowledge, how could you manually modify the table's HTML code to ensure that the table appears the same in each browser?

When time permits, create a complete Web page résumé that details your skills, associations and work experience. After you earn your CIW Web Foundations Associate certification, you can submit your résumé to an Internet job search company, such as Monster.com (*www.monster.com*) or Yahoo! Careers (*http://careers.yahoo.com*), or you can post it on your own Web site.

Skills review

In this lesson, you were introduced to GUI HTML editors and mobile Web site development. You used a GUI editor to develop a Web page, and you experienced the power and control that a GUI editor provides over a development project. You explored the GUI editor's features, including text style, horizontal rules, inline images, hypertext links, table creation and code validation. You considered the advantages and disadvantages of using such a tool to develop your Web pages and then upgraded the GUI editor's output to HTML5. The upgrade included transferring styles from the HTML document to a newly created CSS file. Finally, you learned about mobile Web site development and Web browsers as application delivery platforms.

Now that you have completed this lesson, you should be able to:

✓ 2.1.10: Identify ways that a Web browser can become an application delivery platform, including strengths and weaknesses of the browser.

✓ 2.7.7: Identify the challenges of designing Web sites for mobile devices (e.g., smartphones, tablets, game consoles).

✓ 2.11.1: Evaluate a GUI HTML editor according to the W3C Authoring Tool Accessibility Guidelines.

✓ 2.11.2: Validate HTML code.

✓ 2.11.3: Use font and page appearance options in a GUI HTML editor.

✓ 2.11.4: View source code and preview Web pages in a browser.

✓ 2.11.5: Create HTML tables using a GUI HTML editor.

✓ 2.11.6: Publish (i.e., upload) Web pages and sites to a Web server.

✓ 2.11.7 Evaluate various types of HTML editors that can edit files in mobile devices and cloud services.

✓ 2.11.8 Distinguish between mobile apps and mobile Web sites.

✓ 2.21.5: Identify ways to create pages for traditional and mobile device browsers (e.g., validating code, appropriate resolutions, supported interpreters, extensive user testing).

CIW Practice Exams

Visit CIW Online at *http://education.Certification-Partners.com/CIW* to take the Practice Exams assessment covering the objectives in this lesson.

SDA Objective 2.01 Review

SDA Objective 2.11 Review

SDA Objective 2.21 Review

Note that some objectives may be only partially covered in this lesson.

Lesson 9 Review

1. What is another common term for a graphical user interface (GUI) HTML editor?

    _____

2. What two types of HTML GUI editors are available?

    _____

3. List several HTML GUI editor applications currently available on the market.

    _____

4. What type of application offers an interface similar to an HTML GUI editor?

    _____

5. Name a disadvantage of creating Web pages using an HTML text editor that is resolved by using a GUI editor.

    _____

    _____

6. Name two design techniques you should consider when designing Web pages for mobile devices.

    _____

    _____

7. Explain the difference between mobile Web sites and mobile apps. Which is better?

    _____

    _____

    _____

    _____

Lesson 10: Web Site Development for Business

Objectives

By the end of this lesson, you will be able to:

- 2.10.1: Identify the uses and benefits of various document and multimedia file formats, including PDF, RTF, PostScript, EPS, MOV, MPEG, streaming media, non-streaming media.

- 2.10.2: Define the following Web-related mechanisms for audience development (i.e., attracting and retaining an audience): push technology, pull technology, visitor tracking.

- 2.10.3: Evaluate the benefits and drawbacks of proprietary technologies such as Adobe Flash and Microsoft Silverlight.

- 2.12.2: Estimate download time for Web pages.

- 2.12.4: Document results of Web site functionality testing.

- 2.16.1: Define e-commerce terms and concepts, including business-to-business (B2B), business-to-consumer (B2C), Electronic Funds Transfer (EFT), merchant systems, relationship management, customer self-service, Internet marketing, 3-D Secure.

- 2.16.3: Identify payment models used in e-commerce, including payment gateways.

- 2.16.4: Identify issues related to working in a global environment, including different currencies, multi-lingual issues, international shipping, legal and regulatory issues.

- 2.16.5: Identify the importance of SSL/TLS to a transaction that contains sensitive information.

- 2.16.6: Identify the importance of online indexing and cataloging.

- 2.16.7: Define search engine optimization (SEO) and related key terms (e.g., Internet marketing, organic vs. non-organic [pay-per-click], Web analytics).

☞ 2.17.2: Define Common Gateway Interface (CGI) methods, including .Net, Django, Python, JavaServer Pages (JSP), Server-Side JavaScript (SSJS), Active Server Pages (ASP), PHP Hypertext Preprocessor (PHP), Ajax.

☞ 2.17.3: Define database connectivity technologies (e.g., Open Database Connectivity [ODBC], Java Database Connectivity [JDBC]), and explain the importance of connecting databases with Web sites and other Internet-based services.

☞ 2.19.2: Manage branding issues when developing a site (e.g., logo placement and sizing).

☞ 2.21.3: Create Web pages that rank highly for search engines that use spiders and screen readers.

☞ 2.21.4: Consult respected Web development resources, including books, trade journals, online sources, qualified individuals, user groups.

Pre-Assessment Questions

1. How can a Web site help differentiate a company from its competitors and make the company more competitive?

   _____

   _____

2. Which of the following relies upon digital certificates embedded within a Web browser in order to authenticate hosts, encrypt transmissions and ensure data confidentiality?

   a. 3-D Secure
   b. EDI
   c. SSL/TLS
   d. B2B/B2C

3. Which term is used to describe the rate of data transfer over a network connection, measured in bits per second?

   a. Accessibility
   b. Download
   c. Bandwidth
   d. Spam

Developing a Business Web Site

demographics
The study of groups of people. Specifically, the practice of gathering statistical data by studying populations based on characteristics such as age, income and education.

The Web is the primary medium that many customers (and potential customers) use to find information about the products or services they want. Providing a Web site is an essential step for any business today, and the Web site can serve as the business's primary means of advertising and marketing. Besides using it as a way to sell services, companies can also use the Web to gather vital **demographic** information to help further tailor products.

As a designer and developer, it is your responsibility to ensure that the Web presence you are creating complements your organization.

A business that is just starting up, or one that is changing or expanding its offerings, must perform some key steps:

- Identify a market need or opportunity.

- Identify a unique product or service to address that need or opportunity.

- Define the target market.

- Gather essential user information to help improve the company's product or ability to market and sell.

- Determine how the business can best communicate with the target market.

- Establish a brand for the product or service.

- Determine how to advertise the product or service, including developing a Web site and a social media presence.

Once the business has completed the first four steps, establishing a brand for the product or service and creating a Web site and a social media presence are key steps to building and maintaining demand for the product or service, and helping the business to succeed.

Whether you become a Web developer or not, you can help any business that you work for, start up or acquire by understanding the importance of the business's branding, marketing and Web site.

CIW Online Resources – Movie Clips

Visit CIW Online at http://education.Certification-Partners.com/CIW to watch a movie clip about this topic.

Lesson 10: Web Site Development for Business

Branding concepts

OBJECTIVE
2.19.2: Branding issues

brand
A concept or collection of symbols associated with a product, service or person.

A **brand** is a concept or collection of symbols associated with a product, service or person. Brands can be expressed in the form of pictures, icons, logos and other graphical representations of the item that the brand is intended to represent. The brand that a business establishes for itself can be extremely helpful in increasing the public's awareness of its product or service, and can help sustain and increase the growth of the business.

Branding is the process by which a business uses its brand to enable people to remember its product or service over a competitor's product or service. A Web site is a primary means of establishing and maintaining a company's brand.

Following are some branding concepts to consider when deciding on a brand:

- **The brand should be simple** — Easy-to-remember logos or graphics make very good brands. People tend to remember simple things and ignore or forget complex things.

- **The brand should be different** — A business's brand will be easier to recollect if it is different from those of competing products or services. A truism of marketing is that a brand helps differentiate a company's product. An effective Web site can help with product differentiation.

- **The brand should be safe** — A business must ensure that its logo, icon or picture does not inadvertently offend its target market. Decision-makers must be aware of cultural, regional or national attitudes before deciding on a particular brand. However, you can still create an "edgy" brand as long as it will be perceived as acceptable by the company's key demographic.

- **The brand should make a promise** — The brand needs to clearly express to customers the most important benefits of the business's product or service.

- **The brand should reflect the company's attributes** — The brand needs to describe what the customer will experience when he or she buys that business's product or service (e.g., quality, a unique experience, customer service and so forth).

- **The brand should reflect the company's personality** — The brand needs to reflect the way the customer will feel when they purchase that business's product or service. The customer's emotional connection to the business's brand is a critical component to establishing repeat business.

- **The brand should appeal to the intended audience** — A brand is often chosen because it helps customers self-identify and decide to purchase a particular product or service.

Branding standards and creative design will be discussed in more detail later in this lesson.

You must first have a clearly established brand before you can begin to create a compelling Web page. Consider this before you try to choose colors, determine a navigation scheme, etc. You may want to rush right into a discussion of search engine optimization (SEO), but first you must focus on the company brand. You will study SEO — which is the practice of modifying a Web page's content so it ranks highly in search engine results -- later in this lesson.

OBJECTIVE
2.21.4: Respected
Web development
resources

Development and design

If you are involved in developing a business's Web site, there are many resources available to help you. You can find Web development training, tips, tricks and advice from various resources, including courses such as the one you are taking, online tutorials, user groups, professional trade journals, scholarly writings, reference books and so forth.

A Web site is part of a business's marketing effort and is the company's first form of advertising. Marketing is essentially presenting the business's product to potential customers in such a way that they want to buy it, and they want to buy it from that company instead of from someone else.

Sample resources

Selected resources to consider for learning more about Web design and development include the following:

- **Design & Publishing Center** (*www.graphic-design.com*)

- **Website Magazine** (*www.websitemagazine.com*)

- **A List Apart** (*www.alistapart.com*)

- **CYMK Magazine** (*www.cmykmag.com*)

- **Computer Graphics World** (*www.cgw.com*)

- **Web Designer Magazine** (*www.webdesignermag.co.uk*)

- **Layers Magazine** (*www.layersmagazine.com*)

- **WebDevForums.com** (*www.webdevforums.com*)

- **W3Schools** (*www.w3schools.com*)

As you review resources, use the following questions to help determine whether the site is reputable:

- Has the site been updated recently? Is the magazine still in publication?

- Is the site or magazine created by people who are recognized experts? Find out the names of contributors and editors, then conduct additional searches.

- Does the resource tend to push one product over all others? In some cases, vendor-specific sites may be excellent resources; but always be careful to temper vendor-specific solutions with skills-based approaches to Web design.

Keep it simple

spider
An automated program created by search engine companies that scans Web pages and other resources so that the search engine can process data to be used in search results.

Most customers do not read Web pages. They scan them, picking out individual words and phrases. To help people and automated scanning programs such as search engine **spiders** find information quickly, you should structure page text so that it is easy for customers to scan. Highlighted keywords, meaningful subheadings and bulleted lists are ways to capture customers' attention and help them find the information they are seeking.

To capture a customer's interest, you should convey the business's central message in the first two paragraphs of the page, and makes sure that all subheadings, paragraphs and bullet points start with appropriate keywords that users will notice as they scan the page.

Effectively designed pages:

- Feature crisp, concise text (limiting the word count to half of what would be used in conventional writing).

- Include one idea per paragraph.

- Include search engine keywords in the main portions of text.

- Convey the central message using the inverted-pyramid writing style (i.e., the conclusion is presented at the top of the page, followed by supporting information).

Although a stunning Web site may attract customers initially, a Web site that is simple to use will help keep them coming back. Navigating a Web site should be easy. Each page should include a navigation bar directing visitors to major parts of the site. The site should provide multiple ways to navigate back to the home page so that customers can start over if they get lost.

E-Commerce Considerations

OBJECTIVE
2.16.1: E-commerce terms

electronic commerce (e-commerce)
The integration of communications, data management and security capabilities to allow organizations and consumers to exchange information related to the sale of good and services.

business-to-consumer (B2C)
An e-commerce model in which a Web-based business sells products and/or services to consumers or end users.

business-to-business (B2B)
An e-commerce model in which a Web-based business sells products and/or services to other businesses.

consumer-to-consumer (C2C)
An e-commerce model in which individual consumers sell products or services to other consumers.

Internet-based and Web-based technologies have allowed the continued growth of **electronic commerce (e-commerce)**. Each year, more goods are being created, bought and sold using Internet technologies, and traditional businesses continue to use Web-based technologies to work more efficiently and tap new markets.

When developing a Web site, you must consider e-commerce aspects. This section will explain some basic, yet important, e-commerce concepts.

There are three major e-commerce models that are widely implemented:

- **Business-to-consumer (B2C)** — A model in which a Web-based business sells products and/or services to consumers or end users.

- **Business-to-business (B2B)** — A model in which a Web-based business sells products and/or services to other businesses.

- **Consumer-to-consumer (C2C)** — A model in which individual consumers sell products or services to other consumers.

A shopping portal such as Buy.com (*www.buy.com*) or Google Shopping (*www.google.com/shopping*) can introduce you to B2C outlets. A network such as B2BToday.com (*www.b2btoday.com*) can provide leads to B2B professionals. And any search engine can help you find a business selling a specific product or service you are looking for.

C2C sites generally have interfaces that are very intuitive and easy to navigate. Because the sites function as intermediaries designed to match sellers with buyers, they rely on repeat visits on a massive scale to succeed. For this reason, C2C sites need to be as user-friendly as possible. Consider the Craigslist home page, shown in Figure 10-1.

Figure 10-1: Craigslist home page

Notice that the site design is extremely basic, but you can immediately determine what links you need to click to access the classified ads for a particular city, state or country.

CIW Online Resources – Online Exercise

Visit CIW Online at *http://education.Certification-Partners.com/CIW* to complete an interactive exercise that will reinforce what you have learned about this topic.

Exercise 10-1: E-commerce models

OBJECTIVE
2.16.7: SEO

Internet Marketing and Search Engine Optimization (SEO)

As a member of a Web team, you must consider marketing issues because they affect the design, content and performance of your Web site. Internet marketing applies traditional marketing concepts to Web-based and Internet technologies. Table 10-1 discusses marketing issues and terms with which you should be familiar.

Table 10-1: Marketing terms

Term	Description
Branding	The creation of a distinctive identity and place in the market for a product or organization. Allows consumers to readily identify a product and its purpose. The look and feel of your Web site is often part of a marketing department's branding.
Target market	The specific sector in a market (i.e., the audience) that a product or service addresses. The target may be broad or it may be a niche market. For example, Microsoft and Ubuntu target several markets, including the market for Web and database servers for e-commerce.
Demographics	The study of groups of people. Includes categorizing populations by interests, ethnicities, cultures and subcultures. Involves studying trends and needs associated with a particular group (for example, computer users between the ages of 18 and 49).
Niche	A smaller, specialized portion of the market. An example of a niche market in IT might be companies that provide clustering (multiple systems acting as a single host) for computer systems. Such companies service a much smaller market than computer users or Web database servers.
Mind share	The effect of marketing efforts influencing a particular target market or demographic. Mind share includes commercial phrases, catch words and sound bites that provoke recognition of the product, service or company by the public.
Target date	The projected point in time that a product or service will be released.
Aggregator	A business (usually Web-based) that markets and sells goods and services that it does not own or store. The aggregator allows other vendors to compete using its site, and then takes a percentage of the business. In essence, the site acts as a portal for an entire industry niche.

Internet marketing consists of the following practices:

- **Search engine optimization (SEO)** — the use of specific techniques to increase a page's or site's rank on a search engine (such as Google, Yahoo! or Bing). Such techniques are said to be "organic" because they do not include paid advertisements of any kind. SEO experts edit pages and sites to enable search engines to recognize the inherent value of the content and services on the site.

- **Pay per click (PPC)** — an Internet marketing technique in which you pay for high search engine results by advertising on keywords that describe your product or service. You pay your site hosts only when your ads are clicked by the user.

- **Web analytics** — The practice of collecting data and studying user behavior in an attempt to increase market share and sales.

You will learn more about each of these practices in the sections that follow.

Search engine optimization (SEO)

search engine optimization (SEO)
The process of improving the volume and quality of traffic to a Web site by structuring content to improve search engine ranking. A specific activity of Internet marketing.

Search engine optimization (SEO) involves learning how a particular search engine ranks a Web site. You can use this knowledge to customize a site's Web pages so that the site is ranked as highly as possible in a search engine's results. If a page is ranked highly on search engines, that page is more likely to create situations in which potential customers purchase goods or services.

 SEO is a specific activity of Internet marketing.

SEO experts must learn about and consider the factors that search engines take into account as they rank sites, then try to create and edit Web pages accordingly. Increasing traffic or even ranking is not enough. SEO experts are expected to lead users to a specific result, or conversion. To do this, SEO experts can use data provided by the search engine providers themselves.

Search engine providers, such as Google, Yahoo! and MSN, often provide search patterns for profit. That is, the providers accumulate data on all of the searches that users conduct on their search engines, and then determine the correlation between the keywords used and the results found. The providers then make this data available for sale. SEO experts can use this data to determine the most relevant keywords associated with a particular product or service, and ensure that the keywords are used in a site's pages.

Pay per click (PPC)

pay per click (PPC)
An Internet marketing technique that enables you to list your site high in search engine rankings by advertising on keywords that describe your product or service.

Pay per click (PPC) is an Internet marketing technique that enables you to list your site high in search engine rankings by advertising on keywords that describe your product or service. Using PPC, you place your ad with established services that provide you with keywords to help your site's ranking. PPC is not considered an "organic" solution. Instead of optimizing pages to help make them appear naturally more relevant, you simply pay to have your page listed as highly as possible.

PPC is a good way to reach your target market and generate high-quality sales leads. Most Internet marketing campaigns combine SEO and PPC strategies.

Web analytics

Web analytics
The practice of collecting data and studying user behavior in an attempt to increase market share and sales.

There are two types of **Web analytics**:

- **On-site analytics** — studying visitor behavior once that visitor has accessed your site. You can use trend-analysis software, such as WebTrends (*www.webtrends.com*) and Webalizer (*www.webalizer.org*) to review log files and determine the number of hits (i.e., page views) your page received, the length of each stay, and demographic information about the visitors.

- **Off-site analytics** — determining your potential audience and how well your site has addressed and penetrated a specific market. It includes identifying the size of your market, identifying competitors, determining your market penetration, conducting surveys, and consulting market research sources.

In the following lab, you will visit several pay-per-click services to see how they compare to one another. Suppose you are the marketing manager for your company and you are looking for ways to increase the number of visitors to your site. You can use pay per click to achieve a high search engine ranking and drive more customers to your Web site.

 Lab 10-1: Comparing pay-per-click (PPC) services

In this lab, you will compare pay-per-click services.

1. Open a browser and visit the following pay-per-click services:

   - Google Adwords (*https://adwords.google.com*)

   - Microsoft Advertising AdCenter (*https://adcenter.microsoft.com*)

   - Yahoo! Advertising Solutions (*http://searchmarketing.yahoo.com/arp/kpsrch.php*)

   - Adknowledge Miva (*www.miva.com/*)

   - Search123 (*www.search123.uk.com*)

2. Compare each of the above services by studying the pay-per-click features listed in the following table. These features will help you determine the best service for your particular needs.

Feature	Description
Price per keyword	Make sure you compare prices carefully. If a particular PPC service is more effective or provides better services, paying extra may be worth it.
Keyword generation service	How does the service help you generate keywords? Does the service provide an engine, wizard or other interface for this purpose?
Bidding options	Many sites will prompt you to bid for keywords. Other sites will have fixed prices. You must determine which is appropriate for your business.
Interface quality	Ease of use is vital, because you may waste time trying to learn a difficult interface. You may also become discouraged if the interface is overly complex.
Account fee	Many sites require a fee to open an account.
Monthly minimum	Some services will charge you if you do not generate a minimum number of keyword hits per month.
Software download	Most sites are Web-based. But some services require you to install a software application.
Additional features	Write down additional features that you think will help your particular situation. These particular features might mean the difference between success and failure of your keyword campaign.
Promotions	Many PPC services have promotions that might save you money. However, make sure that these promotions do not cost you more money in the long run.

3. Close your browser.

In this lab, you compared PPC services to determine which may be the most beneficial for your particular situation. How do the services compare with each other?

CIW Online Resources – Online Exercise

Visit CIW Online at *http://education.Certification-Partners.com/CIW* to complete an interactive exercise that will reinforce what you have learned about this topic.

Exercise 10-2: Reviewing Internet marketing practices

OBJECTIVE
2.16.1: E-commerce terms

2.16.3: E-commerce payment models

3-D Secure
An XML-based protocol used by credit card companies to add security to online credit and debit card transactions.

OBJECTIVE
2.16.5: SSL/TLS transactions

Secure Sockets Layer (SSL)
A protocol that provides authentication and encryption, used by most servers for secure exchanges over the Internet. Superseded by Transport Layer Security (TLS).

Transport Layer Security (TLS)
A protocol based on SSL 3.0 that provides authentication and encryption, used by most servers for secure exchanges over the Internet.

Request for Comments (RFC)
A document published by the IETF that details information about standardized Internet protocols and those in various development stages.

E-Commerce Payment Technologies

Organizations need standard methods for exchanging funds just as much as they need standards for exchanging information. Several e-commerce payment technologies are in common use, either as transaction methods or as tools to secure transactions:

- **Electronic Funds Transfer (EFT)** — Electronic Funds Transfer) is a generic term that describes the ability to transfer funds using computers, rather than using paper. Banks use EFT to save time and ensure that monetary exchange between individuals and businesses is as secure as possible. Other large organizations use EFT as well.

- **Payment gateways** — A payment gateway is a system, either hardware-based or software-based, that mediates between a merchant (i.e., an e-commerce-enabled Web site) and an acquirer (e.g., the merchant's bank). End users do not configure their systems to become payment gateways. Once the merchant receives payment from a customer, the merchant uses the payment gateway to transmit credit card information to the bank.

- **3-D Secure** — 3-D Secure is an XML-based protocol used by credit card companies to add security to online credit and debit card transactions. It is often listed as "Verified by VISA" or "MasterCard Secure Code." 3-D Secure has replaced the Secure Electronic Transactions (SET) protocol.

Secure Sockets Layer (SSL) / Transport Layer Security (TLS)

Neither SSL nor TLS are transaction methods; rather, they are tools used to secure transactions. **Secure Sockets Layer (SSL)** and **Transport Layer Security (TLS)** are methods used to encrypt data transmissions. They act as the foundation for many e-commerce protocols, including 3-D Secure. You can view the SSL 3.0 specification at *www.freesoft.org/CIE/Topics/ssl-draft/3-SPEC.HTM*.

TLS is quite similar to SSL, but TLS is an open standard that is updated frequently. You can read about TLS in the **Request for Comments (RFC)** document 2246 (RFC 2246). TLS has rapidly become the accepted standard, although it is often called SSL or SSL/TLS.

SSL and TLS are protocols that are included within transaction methods to secure transactions. SSL/TLS secures transactions through encryption. Encryption can provide authentication, data confidentiality and data integrity. Many other encryption methods exist, but SSL/TLS is arguably the most universally applied.

SSL/TLS and Public Key Infrastructure (PKI)

You need a certificate to enable host authentication before you can begin an SSL session. So before an organization can use SSL/TLS to enable encryption, it must participate in Public Key Infrastructure (PKI), which is a collection of individuals, networks and computers that together have the ability to authoritatively confirm the identity of a person, host or organization. PKI makes it possible for two parties that have never met each other to trust each other. Once trust is established, encryption can begin. PKI involves two elements with which you should be familiar:

- **Digital certificate** — a signed public key that verifies a set of credentials associated with the public key of a certificate authority (CA). All SSL/TLS sessions require a valid certificate, which acts as a trusted third party to allow unknown parties to authenticate with each other and begin encryption.

- **Certificate authority (CA)** — a trusted third party that verifies the identity of the person or company that has submitted a certification request (CR). A CA is an organization that issues digital certificates and helps to ensure the identity of a person, host or process. A CA is more than just a computer that issues digital certificates; a CA is an entire organization.

In the following lab, you will review an SSL/TLS session. Suppose your project manager has asked you to describe the SSL/TLS process to members of another department. They understand that it somehow enables encryption and is related to the ability to authenticate hosts. You can demonstrate an example of the way that certificates are automatically exchanged and encryption is made possible.

Lab 10-2: Reviewing an SSL/TLS session

In this lab, you will use Firefox (version 10 or higher) to learn how an SSL/TLS session is built using certificates. Other browsers, such as Internet Explorer version 9 or Chrome, will use different commands to access the same information.

1. Open **Firefox** and go to *www.yahoo.com*.

2. **Browser:** Click the **Site Identity Button** to the left of the address bar (it appears as the Yahoo! logo).

3. Read the information in the Site Identity window. Notice that the Web page does not have identity information and is not encrypted. Click **More Information** to view the security details in the **Page Info** window.

4. Close the **Page Info** window to return to the Yahoo! home page.

5. Go to *https://login.yahoo.com*. Notice that the URL begins with *https* rather than *http*.

6. An alert message box may appear (depending on your browser's security settings) informing you that you have requested a secure document, which opens an SSL/TLS session. If the message appears, click **OK**.

7. When the Yahoo! sign-in Web page appears, click the **Site Identity Button**, then click **More Information**. Notice that the information has changed due to an SSL/TLS session, as shown in Figure 10-2.

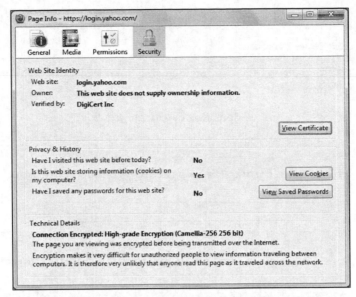

Figure 10-2: Viewing security information during SSL/TLS session

8. **Page Info:** Click the **View Certificate** button. The Certificate Viewer dialog box will appear, as shown in Figure 10-3.

Figure 10-3: Viewing certificate information

Tech Note: The fingerprints listed in the dialog box refer to the series of bytes that make up the SHA1 and MD5 hash functions used to encrypt public keys. The SHA1 fingerprint is a 160-bit hash function, and the MD5 fingerprint is a 128-bit hash function.

9. **Certificate Viewer:** Select the **Details** tab to learn more about the certificate.

10. Close the **Certificate Viewer** dialog box and the **Page Info** window.

11. Close **Firefox**.

12. As a class, discuss the following questions, and write your answers in the spaces provided.

What services does this certificate provide?

_____

How can certificates help secure e-commerce transactions?

_____

_____

In this lab, you learned about the ways that SSL/TLS functions to secure Web-based transactions.

Working in a Global Environment

OBJECTIVE
2.16.4: Global
business issues

E-commerce requires you to understand global issues. Remember that by placing a business on the Web, the audience is expanded to include anyone in the world with a browser and Internet access. Therefore, you must consider the level to which you will accommodate potential customers from countries outside yours. You should be aware of the following items:

- **Currency differences** — E-commerce sites such as eBay and global businesses such as IBM facilitate business with people in many different countries. These businesses must be able to automatically calculate exchange rates for the day of the transaction (often called currency conversion). They must also calculate taxes and tariffs on goods, which incur additional costs.

customs
National
departments
responsible for
controlling items
entering and
leaving the country.

- **International shipping** — When shipping goods internationally, you must consider searches by **customs**, costs incurred by customs, delays caused by customs, and all tariffs. A product you sell legally in one country may be illegal in another or heavily regulated.

- **Language concerns** — Consider the language(s) used by the target audience and the characters necessary (e.g., alphanumeric, mathematical or currency symbols). You may be assigned to create a page for a language that requires a particular character set. To solve this problem, specify Unicode support for all of your site's Web pages. The Unicode Technical Committee (UTC) maintains the Unicode standard. The UTC is a subcommittee of the Unicode Consortium (*www.unicode.org*).

- **Relationship management** — Every business wants to establish solid relationships with all parties involved. Two important concepts that can help you ensure success are trust-building and customer self-service. Trust is built through quality customer service and frequent contact. Customer self-service includes the ability to track orders, customize orders (such as modify or cancel an order, change a shipping address, etc.) and choose products without the help of a live person.

In the following lab, you will use currency-conversion tables. Suppose your Web development team is designing a B2B e-commerce solution that will allow your company to automatically receive orders and process purchases from your customer companies in

United Kingdom and other parts of Europe. Your project manager has asked you to research currency-conversion tools that you could incorporate into your B2B site. You can demonstrate an example tool that allows users to easily convert currencies.

 Lab 10-3: Converting currency values

In this lab, you will convert currency values using a popular online tool.

1. Open a browser and access ***www.xe.com/ucc***. You will see the XE – Universal Currency Converter page.

2. Convert **500 U.S. Dollars** into **U.K. Pounds**. How many pounds will you get?

3. Convert **500 U.K. Pounds** into **Euros**. How many euros will you get?

4. Convert **500 Euros** into **Rubles**. How many rubles will you get?

5. Conduct additional exchanges for other currencies.

6. Close your browser.

7. As a class, discuss the following questions:

    *   If you ran an e-commerce site, would you want to perform these types of conversions yourself, or have them performed automatically by the site? Why?

    *   How can you adjust your prices when currency fluctuations occur?

    *   Try repeating this lab at a later date. By how much have currency values changed? How would this affect your business with a European customer who is purchasing US$100 worth of product from you? What about a U.K. customer who is purchasing US$10,000 worth of product?

In this lab, you learned how to convert currency values quickly and easily using an online tool.

Databases and Web Pages

Web sites can use databases to store information about the products a company is ready to sell. These databases can be connected to Web pages so that employees can readily check on company inventory. Web pages can also be used to obtain information from end users and store it in databases. To accomplish this, you can use HTML code to create a user-input form.

A form allows end users to enter information into a Web page that sends the information to an organization or business. There are various types of forms. When an end user enters information into a form and clicks OK or Send, the page sends the user's information to a database in which the information can be processed. Information might include opinions or user preferences, bids in eBay auctions (*www.ebay.com*), or credit card information to make purchases from a company such as Amazon.com (*www.amazon.com*).

OBJECTIVE
2.17.2: CGI methods

Web pages and CGI

A user-input form must contain code that references a Web server. This code is called an application, or a Web server application. This application helps convey the information provided by the end user to the Web server, or to a database server that can store and/or process the information. Such applications are called Common Gateway Interface (CGI) applications because they enable information to pass in and out of a server. Various CGI implementations exist. CGI implementations use various computer languages and technologies, including those discussed in Table 10-2.

Table 10-2 Popular CGI technologies

CGI Technology	Description	Additional Information
Perl	A traditional CGI technology that is platform-independent (i.e., you can install it on any server-based operating system). Once you install the Perl interpreter on the system, you can use Perl-based CGI applications. Available at *www.cpan.org* and *www.activestate.com.*	Because of its relative longevity, Perl is well known and is supported by many operating systems. It is renowned for creating stable applications. As a universal technology, you can install the Perl interpreter on almost any operating system (e.g., Linux, Solaris, Windows).
PHP Hypertext Preprocessor (PHP)	A newer CGI technology that will run on multiple platforms. Once you install the PHP interpreter on the system, you can create applications. Available at *www.php.org.*	Although it is a newer technology, PHP has become quite popular due to its relative simplicity and ability to create powerful applications. A universal technology.
Active Server Pages (ASP)	An older, proprietary CGI technology available only on Microsoft-specific systems or systems with a special interpreter installed (e.g., the ChiliSoft ASP interpreter). The ASP interpreter is installed on all Microsoft Internet Information Services (IIS) systems. Developers can create ASP scripts using VBScript or JavaScript. To learn more about ASP, visit *www.microsoft.com.*	ASP is powerful because it is specially designed to work with the underlying operating system. ASP requires developers to learn VBScript and/or JavaScript.
.NET	Microsoft's standard development platform. A proprietary set of technologies and languages available mostly on Windows systems and installed on all IIS systems. .NET allows you to use various languages, including C# (a replacement for Java), JavaScript, VBScript or Visual Basic. To learn more about .NET, visit *www.microsoft.com.*	.NET is Microsoft's latest effort to interconnect all Internet-based servers. A more powerful option than the older ASP approach. .NET provides additional database connectivity, and allows you to use more powerful languages (e.g., C#), although C# is more difficult to learn than VBScript, Perl or PHP.
JavaServer Pages (JSP)	A universal CGI technology that uses the Java interpreter, allowing developers to create CGI using the Java language. Download Java at *www.java.com.* To learn more about JSP, visit *http://java.sun.com/.*	Like Perl and PHP, JSP is a universal technology. Although Java is more difficult to learn than PHP or Perl, it is also a more powerful language and creates more stable applications.
ColdFusion	A proprietary CGI technology designed to be easier to install and use than other interpreters and languages. To learn more about ColdFusion, visit *www.adobe.com/products/coldfusion/.*	ColdFusion purportedly does more work using less code, which generally makes your applications easier to develop and use. Although ColdFusion is a proprietary technology, you can install it on various operating systems (e.g., Linux, Windows, Solaris).

Table 10-2 Popular CGI technologies (cont'd)

CGI Technology	Description	Additional Information
Python	An open-source CGI technology that emphasizes code readability by employing minimalistic code syntax and semantics. Python is an object-oriented programming language that can be easily integrated with other languages. To learn more about Python, visit *www.python.org*.	Python runs on Windows, Linux/UNIX, Mac OS X, OS/2, Amiga, palm handhelds and Nokia mobile phones. Python has also been ported to the Java and .NET virtual machines. Python uses white space as block delimiters, which is unusual among popular programming languages.
Django	An open-source Web framework written to help developers use the Python language. It is meant to be a fast-development platform. To learn more about Django, visit *www.djangoproject.com*.	Django makes the creation of complex, database-driven Web sites easier by emphasizing the use of components that can be reused. It also emphasizes the DRY (Don't Repeat Yourself) principle, which seeks to eliminate any duplication so that modifying an element of a program will not affect other logically unrelated elements.
Ajax	A CGI programming methodology that enables Web applications to interact with users in much the same way they do with desktop applications. You can use Ajax to create dynamic and interactive Web pages without the need to refresh or reload the page. To learn more about Ajax, visit *http://en.wikipedia.org/wiki/Ajax_(programming)/*.	Ajax uses a number of existing technologies together (HTML, CSS, the Document Object Model [DOM], JavaScript and XMLHttpRequest), and enables Web applications to make incremental updates to the user interface without the need to reload the page in the browser.
Ruby	An object-oriented programming language based on Perl and **Smalltalk**. It has powerful capabilities, but is easier to use than many other languages, including Java and C#. To learn more about Ruby, visit *www.ruby-lang.org*.	Includes the Ruby On Rails framework, which makes it possible to use Ruby to rapidly develop applications.

Smalltalk
A programming language that pioneered object-oriented programming. Not popularly used in Web development.

Tech Tip Other CGI technologies are also available. You do not need to understand the details of these technologies for the CIW Web Foundations Associate exam, but know that CGI is necessary to enable a Web form for communication between an end user and a Web server.

CIW Online Resources – Online Exercise

Visit CIW Online at *http://education.Certification-Partners.com/CIW* to complete an interactive exercise that will reinforce what you have learned about this topic.

Exercise 10-3: CGI technology and the languages used to create CGI

Support for mobile devices

As you create Web pages, consider that more and more people are viewing Web pages using smartphones and mobile devices instead of standard browsers.

It is vital that you take the time to ensure that your pages render well on various devices, including traditional desktop computers as well as a variety of mobile devices.

Optimizing the Impact of the Web Page

As mentioned previously, the practice of search engine optimization (SEO) involves making changes to a Web site's content so that the site ranks as highly as possible in search engine results. A high ranking on a search engine results page can help increase the number of visits (i.e., hits) per month, ensuring more visibility for your product or page.

SEO techniques are designed to get Web pages to conform to the expectations of search engine applications. These applications, often called bots, automatically scan Web pages and index them. Search engine companies then analyze these Web pages and rank them according to relevance.

When a Web user visits Google or Yahoo!, these search engines are supposed to return the most relevant Web pages for the user's search. Search engine companies consider many factors, including but not limited to:

- How many hyperlinks from other sites point to a page.

- How informative a page is.

- How well a page's code is structured.

- How often the content on the page is updated.

Many other techniques that may appear to be completely unrelated to SEO are in fact foundational for anyone conducting search engine optimization. Such activities include:

- Using properly validated HTML code.

- Applying Cascading Style Sheets (CSS).

- Structuring pages correctly.

Front-End Issues

Front-end issues are essentially interface issues. The back end is usually the Web server, the network and databases. A Web page front end acts as an interface for information. You can structure the information in tables, forms and other less-formal ways. A properly created Web page should:

- Be accessible by all users, including those with disabilities (e.g., hearing or sight impairment).

- Incorporate attractive images and graphical elements.

- Contain constantly updated hyperlinks and content.

- Use tables wisely (ideally, tables should be used to place information in tabular format, not to structure entire Web pages).

- Present carefully designed forms.

- Securely attach pages to databases.

- Use the most current technologies appropriate for the page.

- Use images sparingly. Images can clutter the page and create bandwidth problems. You will learn more about bandwidth shortly.

- Be easily navigable and without dead ends.

- Include alternative navigation links. For example, when defining an image map for a Web site, you should provide standard hypertext links to the site as well. This feature helps accommodate visitors who have deactivated image downloading in their browsers. Also, many developers use image maps to define an entire page. Although attractive, this strategy can effectively exclude such a page from search engine spiders unless you provide alternative text information.

The Web presents several obstacles to user accessibility, including the fact that you have no control over the ways in which users will access and view your pages. You do not know which browsers they will use, nor can you direct them to certain areas of the pages or site. Furthermore, you have no control over the speed with which users will be downloading your pages.

Site maps

As you learned in a previous lesson, a site map can be an important part of Web page accessibility. It allows visitors to view a summary of your Web site's structure. A site map should show the locations of all site sections, usually beginning with the index page on top. Useful site maps include the following:

- **Topical hierarchy** — A site map should clearly outline the site's sections in a visual, hierarchical format. However, do not provide only a graphic as a site map. Alternative browsers may not render the graphic, and alternative image text may not describe the graphic's content adequately for users who cannot see it.

- **Aptly named site sections** — Make sure that each section of your site is named accurately to enable users to find the pages they need.

- **Search capability** — Visitors might not find the exact information they seek even after consulting your site map. You can include a search engine text box on the site map page (or a link to your site's search engine) so that visitors can search for the resource they want.

A useful site map is the product of proper site planning. If you begin creating your site map after you have finished creating the site, then you have skipped some steps in proper site planning.

OBJECTIVE
2.19.2: Branding issues

Creative design and branding standards

As discussed, a Web page is often part of a larger marketing and sales strategy. In fact, Web sites have become a means for creating and ensuring brand recognition and mind share. In short, Web sites have become an important marketing tool. You must design your Web pages according to marketing demands. To do this, you should understand the motivations of a marketing specialist.

A marketing specialist's primary goal is to establish name and brand recognition. For example, many people can immediately identify the hood ornament symbol of a Mercedes-Benz, and many people are equally familiar with the McDonald's "golden arches." Both are examples of name and brand recognition.

A term closely related to name recognition is mind share. One way for an organization or company to increase business and gain recognition is to adopt catch words, phrases and other sound bites that help the general public identify a product, person or service. Examples of mind share include Intel Corporation's "Intel Inside" and Microsoft Corporation's "Where do you want to go today?" Such commercial phrases help to keep a company's name in the minds of the public. The Habitat for Humanity Web site (*www.habitat.org*), shown in Figure 10-4, was created with name recognition in mind.

Figure 10-4: Habitat for Humanity home page

The primary way to achieve such recognition is to clearly define and execute a branding standard, which is a set of comprehensive marketing goals and strategies. Most organizations devise a branding standard through well-coordinated meetings and carefully devised plans.

The primary goal of a Web developer is to help the company reinforce its branding standard. As you design page layout and create graphical content, remember that your site is part of a larger context. The look and feel of your Web site should be consistent with the design principles, color schemes, graphics and logos found in existing company stationery, posters and advertisements. If your company uses a particular sound bite or catch phrase, find a way to cleverly incorporate it into your site. If you can apply effective design principles to your company's marketing strategy, your site will be more successful.

Design and branding standards meetings

You will probably need to meet with various departments and individuals to ensure that your Web site complements the company's branding strategy as effectively as possible. Such meetings generally focus on the following:

*   Target markets

*   Market messages

*   Media choices

- Color combinations

- Sales strategies

- Technologies you want to use

A thorough discussion of the ways that your Web pages fulfill branding standards is beyond the scope of this course. However, you should understand that as you write HTML code, you will probably do so to fulfill very specific organizational goals.

Audience development techniques

OBJECTIVE
2.10.2: Audience development mechanisms

You may be asked for your input regarding ways to develop an audience for your Web site. You might discuss the following methods:

- Providing standard Web site features, including properly placed video, audio and active content (e.g., Adobe Flash programs, Microsoft Silverlight applications, Java applets).

OBJECTIVE
2.10.3: Proprietary technologies

- Providing unique Web site features, which include ideas generated by you and your Web team, and input from other areas of the company (marketing, sales, upper management).

- Using logos and other images traditionally used by the company.

- Coordinating your efforts with traditional marketing strategies. You should work with the marketing department to ensure that your Web site's look and feel complements the company's marketing slicks and traditional paper items (e.g., letterhead, envelopes, notepads).

- Tracking user visits, which can indicate the popular parts of your site, and can help you to improve the unpopular parts.

- Analyzing and interpreting statistics to help increase Web site efficiency. For example, consider ways to increase visitor time at site locations where revenue is generated.

- Working with the sales and marketing teams to obtain input from customers about desired Web site features.

Table 10-3 explains additional techniques that can help develop your audience.

mailing list server
An e-mail server that regularly sends e-mail messages to a specified list of users.

spam
Unsolicited and unwanted e-mail messages; the online equivalent of junk mail.

Table 10-3: Audience development techniques

Technique	Description	Benefit
Push technology	Any technology that automatically provides information to a customer list. In legitimate cases, the customer initially makes a request to be placed on the list. Customers receive information until they ask to be removed. One example of push technology is a **mailing list server**. Illegitimate examples of push technology include **spam**.	Customers automatically receive new information about a product or service. This technique is often sales-based and marketing-based because many organizations push information to customers and potential customers.
Pull technology	Any technology that provides information to a customer only upon request. A more standard way to disseminate information from a server. For example, whenever you download a file from a Web site or collect your e-mail, you are using pull technology.	Because the customer asks for information and content, this technique is demand-based and immediate.

cookie
A text file that contains information sent between a server and a client to help maintain state and track user activities. Cookies can reside in memory or on a hard drive.

Table 10-3: Audience development techniques (cont'd)

Technique	Description	Benefit
Visitor tracking	Any technology that provides the following information: -The number of visitors that connected to the site or specific pages -The length of time visitors remained at the site or specific pages -The frequency with which a specific visitor returns to the site For example, Web sites use **cookies** to help determine how often end users visit the site. You can also track users by viewing log files.	This technique provides feedback that you can use to update site content, revise site navigation, review product offerings, market to all or specific customers, and so forth.

Portals

A portal is a Web site that acts as a centralized access point for other sites. There are two types of portal: vertical and horizontal.

- **Vertical** — a portal dedicated to one specific interest or field (e.g., women's health, network security, sports or politics), also called a "vortal." Each linked site on a vertical portal maintains a topical focus. Examples include CNET (*www.cnet.com*), Slashdot (*http://slashdot.org/*) and RealEstate.com (*www.realestate.com*). Intranets and extranets are also examples of vertical portals because they provide links to external sites and are dedicated to a specific topic: the businesses that host them. Intranets are sometimes known as corporate portals.

- **Horizontal** — a portal that provides links to various Web sites with no particular focus. Examples include Google (*www.google.com)* and Yahoo! (*www.yahoo.com*). Each of these sites contains links to other sites, but linked sites represent diverse interests (e.g., travel, news, shopping), rather than one focus.

Portals can provide various services, including e-mail accounts, chat services, message forums, stock information and access to newsgroups. Many portals also provide search engines.

A portal is also known as a gateway.

Portal benefits

A portal can benefit both end users and businesses. A portal benefits end users because it directs them to the best sites for a particular topic, and helps users find information and products faster. A portal benefits businesses because it can create a stream of customers who generate revenue. A business can also use a portal to help position its brand, improve brand recognition in a market, and strengthen the brand by comparing it with competitors.

CIW Online Resources – Online Exercise

Visit CIW Online at *http://education.Certification-Partners.com/CIW* to complete an interactive exercise that will reinforce what you have learned about this topic.

Exercise 10-4: Web portals

Wiki sites

A wiki is a Web site that allows all visitors to collaborate in its construction. You can use a wiki to create an information repository or portal. A wiki uses specialized Web-based software (called wiki software) that allows any visitor to update the site using a Web browser.

 The word wiki is coined from the Hawaiian phrase "wiki wiki," which means "very quick."

Wiki software cooperates with a Web server to generate pages in HTML so that a Web browser can render them. However, most wiki pages are written in simplified markup language called LaTeX (*www.latex-project.org*) that accommodates the fast-paced nature of a wiki site.

Specific pages of a wiki can be locked down while leaving others available for public or permitted editing. The first wiki ever established was the Portland Pattern Repository (*http://c2.com/ppr*). Following are examples of current wiki sites:

- Wikipedia (*www.wikipedia.org*)

- LinuxQuestions.org (*http://wiki.linuxquestions.org/wiki/Main_Page*)

- BerliOS (*http://en.wikipedia.org/wiki/BerliOS*)

- MemoryAlpha (*http://en.wikipedia.org/wiki/Memory_Alpha*)

Many purveyors of wiki software exist, including the following:

- Wiki Base (*http://c2.com/cgi/wiki?WikiBase*)

- Wiki Choicetree (*http://c2.com/cgi/wiki?WikiChoicetree*)

- JSPWiki (*www.jspwiki.org*)

OBJECTIVE
2.7.3: Accessibility standards and compliance

2.12.4: Documenting test results

Documenting changes

As you make changes to your Web site, make sure that you keep a written record of all changes. The practice of documenting changes to a site is called change management. Documenting change is essential because it allows you to:

- Remember which changes have been made to the HTML code and/or pages on the site.

- Ensure that you publish all security updates to the Web server.

- Provide evidence of good-faith efforts to ensure accessibility.

- Verify that you have fulfilled requests from departments in your organization.

OBJECTIVE
2.10.1: Document and multimedia file formats

File Formats and Active Content

Web servers provide more than just pages created in markup languages. You will populate your pages with various content formats, including Portable Document Format (PDF) documents, images and media files.

Common file formats and MIME types

All of the file formats you will use on your Web pages have a specific MIME type (a protocol that enables operating systems to map file name extensions to corresponding applications). The Internet Assigned Numbers Authority (IANA) is responsible for standardizing MIME types. Table 10-4 lists common file formats used in Web pages.

Table 10-4: Common file formats

File Format	File Name Extension	Description	MIME Type
HTML	.html or .htm	HTML files.	text/html
XHTML	.html or .htm	XHTML files.	application/xhtml+html
Joint Photographic Experts Group (JPEG)	.jpeg or .jpg	A standard Web page image format. Provides variable image quality and compression algorithms to help reduce file size.	image/jpeg
Graphics Interchange Format (GIF)	.gif	A standard Web page image format. Does not provide native compression. Two types of GIF exist: -GIF87a (standard) -GIF89a (animated GIF) Animated GIFs show a series of embedded images, simulating motion. GIF files can also be interlaced for gradual display during a slow download.	image/gif
Portable Network Graphics (PNG)	.png	The newest standard Web page image format. Supports compression, and various quality levels and file sizes (the higher the image quality, the larger the file size). PNGs can also be animated.	image/png
Text	.txt	Standard (ASCII) text files.	text/plain
Cascading Style Sheets (CSS)	.css	CSS formatting is defined in text files, which can be attached to HTML documents to apply the defined styles.	text/css
Rich Text Format (RTF)	.rtf	Documents that contain simple formatting (e.g., underlining, bold, and font faces and sizes).	text/rtf
PostScript	.ps	A language designed to describe page formatting for text and graphics. Developed by Adobe, but has become an open standard.	application/postscript
Portable Document Format (PDF)	.pdf	Adobe Acrobat proprietary format, based on PostScript technology. Can retain sophisticated formatting and graphics.	application/pdf
Zip	.zip	Files compressed using the zip/unzip family of file applications.	application/zip
Pretty Good Privacy (PGP) / GNU Privacy Guard (GPG)	.pgp .gpg	Files encrypted by PGP/GPG.	application/pgp-encrypted application/gpg-encrypted

Table 10-4: Common file formats (cont'd)

File Format	File Name Extension	Description	MIME Type
Moving Pictures Experts Group (MPEG) – audio	.mpeg	MPEG streaming audio.	audio/mpeg
MPEG – video	.mpeg	MPEG streaming video.	video/mpeg
MPEG Audio Layer 3 (MP3)	.mp3	MP3 audio file format.	audio/mp3
Ogg-Vorbis	.ogg	Ogg-Vorbis audio file format.	application/ogg
WAV	.wav	Native digital audio format of Windows operating systems.	audio/wav audio/x-wav
RealPlayer	.ram, .ra	Audio and video files in the RealPlayer format (*www.real.com*).	audio/ram audio/pn-realaudio ram audio/x-realaudio ra
Word	.doc	Microsoft Word documents.	application/msword
Excel	.xls	Microsoft Excel documents (spreadsheets).	application/vnd.ms-excel
PowerPoint	.ppt	Microsoft PowerPoint documents (presentation slide shows).	application/vnd.ms-powerpoint
Unrecognized images	N/A	For any images and streaming media not currently standardized by IANA.	application/octet-stream

For a full list of MIME types from the official source, visit the IANA site at *www.iana.org/assignments/media-types*.

Proprietary formats and evaluating their use

OBJECTIVE
2.10.3: Proprietary technologies

Many of the file types previously discussed are standard and do not require your system to have special plug-ins. Proprietary formats may require special plug-ins, but can enhance the look and feel of your Web site. Table 10-5 provides an overview of drawbacks to consider in relation to proprietary file formats.

Table 10-5: Issues with proprietary file formats

Issue	Description
Difficulty/ inconvenience	Some plug-ins and software may be unduly difficult to obtain. If your development team agrees that a required plug-in or software is not too difficult for end users to obtain, then you can proceed using a proprietary technology without impacting your pages' accessibility and potential audience.
Cost	Some proprietary file formats (e.g., Microsoft Word) require software that must be purchased. You should consider free or open-source alternatives for file formats.
Audience limitation	As previously discussed, some formats limit a disabled person's ability to obtain information. For example, if you plan on posting essential information in a PDF document, you should provide equivalent information in standard text format elsewhere on the site because sight-assistance tools may not be able to convert the PDF document to audible content.

Back-End Issues

Server resources that process and store user input are referred to as the back end of a Web site. Because you are using your Web documents to communicate over a network, you should ensure that they operate as efficiently as possible. You have already learned the importance of the front-end interface. Now, you should consider some back-end issues.

Database connectivity

Most Web sites do more than simply present text, a few image files and a couple of documents. Fully functional Web sites also include database connectivity. Databases provide the ability to:

- Present stored information to customers, and allow them to search and retrieve.

- Receive information from customers and save it for later retrieval.

Many companies use database-enabled sites. Amazon.com, eBay and IBM are only a few examples.

Types of databases

There are several database types:

- **Flat file** — Information is stored in a single table, often in a simple text file. The Windows registry is an example of a flat-file database.

- **Non-relational** — Information is stored statically. Information can be searched, but cannot be reorganized or placed into another database.

- **Relational** — Information can be sorted, altered and placed into other databases for retrieval.

- **Object-oriented** — A newer form with the capabilities of a relational database, plus greater storage and search efficiency.

This section will focus on relational databases because they are the most common.

Relational databases

A relational database stores information in tables. These tables contain fields that allow data in the tables to be cross-referenced and joined in various ways. You or your database administrators define the categories and descriptions in the tables. Information in these tables can also be updated (e.g., added to or deleted). When you conduct a search in a site such as eBay to retrieve information about a type of item you want to buy, for example, you are using a Web-enabled relational database.

A relational database can consist of a single file or it can be distributed among several database servers. After you have organized a database, you can access its information in various ways. For example, if you have a database of employee information, you can query the database for an alphabetical list of employee names, or you can sort the employees by age, employee number, date of hire and so forth.

Table 10-6 lists examples of relational database vendors.

Table 10-6: Relational database vendors

Vendor	Description
Oracle	You can learn more about the latest Oracle products at *www.oracle.com*.
IBM	IBM's database product is called DB2. You can learn more about IBM products at *www.ibm.com*.
Microsoft	Microsoft offers a database server product called SQL Server. You can learn more about Microsoft products at *www.microsoft.com*.
MySQL	MySQL is an open-source database that will run on Linux, UNIX and Windows systems. You can learn more about MySQL at *www.mysql.com*.
PostgreSQL	PostgreSQL is another open-source database product that is often considered to be more powerful and stable. You can learn more about PostgreSQL at *www.postgresql.org*.

Structured Query Language (SQL)

Structured Query Language (SQL)
A language used to create and maintain professional, high-performance corporate databases.

After you have created several data tables, you can query them to glean information. Generally, if you want to query a relational database, you use **Structured Query Language (SQL)**. For example, using SQL, you can allow end users to determine the number of projects that Sandi Stanger finished by a certain date. You can also obtain a record that provides this information along with her employee ID number and hire date.

You can also create a Web page that allows end users to conduct these queries through the page. You simply program the Web server pages to access server-side applications. These applications can receive parameters provided by end users, then use these parameters to query databases so that the end users obtain the information they want.

Database connection methods

You can connect to database files by using the Microsoft Open Database Connectivity (ODBC) interface or its Java counterpart, Java Database Connectivity (JDBC).

- **Open Database Connectivity (ODBC)** — ODBC's primary purpose is to allow an operating system to register a database. ODBC supports SQL and all major database vendors. Once the database is registered, the operating system and its components (such as a Web server) can easily read and update the database. ODBC was developed by Microsoft and is proprietary to Windows-based operating systems.

- **Java Database Connectivity (JDBC)** — JDBC was developed by Sun Microsystems. Unlike ODBC, JDBC is not limited to Microsoft operating systems. Like ODBC, JDBC supports major vendors (e.g., IBM and Oracle), and it also supports SQL. JDBC can be run on various systems, including Windows and UNIX. For more information, visit the Java Database Technologies page at *http://java.sun.com/javase/technologies/database/index.jsp*.

OBJECTIVE
2.17.3: Database connectivity technologies.

2.16.6: Online indexing and catalogs

Indexing and cataloging

Another Web site feature related to databases is the ability to index and catalog a site. More complex sites provide an internal search engine that allows visitors to conduct searches for site elements. Most Web servers, including Apache Server (*www.apache.org*) and Microsoft Internet Information Services (IIS) provide indexing features.

OBJECTIVE
2.12.2: Estimating
download times

Bandwidth and Download Time

HTML pages require a relatively small amount of space on a hard drive. Because their file size is small, they are also easy to download over a network. However, as suggested by Figure 10-5, when you download an HTML page that refers to several graphics, you will generally download each graphic as well.

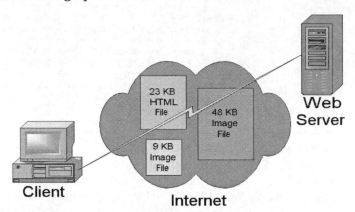

Figure 10-5: Web page files downloading over network

bandwidth
The amount of information, sometimes called traffic, that can be carried on a network at one time. The total capacity of a line. Also, the rate of data transfer over a network connection; measured in bits per second.

Image files can be quite large. For example, a simple JPEG image of your house or apartment could easily exceed 1 MB. A file this large usually takes some time to download over a network.

Although both JPEG and GIF image formats support compression, remember that any file downloaded over a network requires **bandwidth**. To download a large file in a short amount of time, you need more bandwidth. If you cannot get more bandwidth, you need more time to download the file.

A graphic that accompanies an HTML page can take an unacceptably long time to finish downloading, especially if the user has an older 56-Kbps dial-up modem. Even at **T1** and broadband speeds, a large file or graphic can cause a frustrating wait.

T1
A digital carrier that transmits data at a speed of 1.544 Mbps.

Therefore, make sure that your Web pages do not reference several large files. You should also avoid using too many small image files. It is difficult to determine an acceptable download size for files associated with an HTML page. However, you must consider the total size of your page, including all images, plug-ins and other programs. As a general rule, your pages should not exceed 100 KB without a very good reason.

Determining download time for a Web page

To calculate download time for a Web page, follow these steps.

Step 1: Check the size of the HTML file and any associated images, files or programs. For example, your page may consist of 11 files that total 84 kilobytes (KB).

Step 2: Determine the speed of your network connection, which is generally measured in kilobits per second (Kbps). Some of the more common connection speeds are:

- 14.4 Kbps (slow modem speed).

- 28.8 Kbps (typical modem speed).

- 33.6 Kbps (typical modem speed).

- 56 Kbps (typical modem speed).

- 128 Kbps (upper-limit speed of ISDN connection).

- 512 Kbps (typical broadband speed — DSL or cable modem).

- 1.544 Mbps (full T1, enterprise-grade network line).

For this example, we will use 56 Kbps.

Step 3: The connection speed and the file size must be converted into a common unit of measure for division: either bytes or bits. Consider that 1 byte equals 8 bits. The connection speed is already defined in bits: 56 kilobits = 56,000 bits. To convert the file size into bits, you should first convert it into bytes (84 kilobytes = 84,000 bytes). Then convert the bytes into bits by multiplying 84,000 by 8 (1 byte = 8 bits), which results in 672,000 bits.

Step 4: Divide the file size (672,000 bits) by the connection speed (56,000 bits per second). The bits cancel out, and the result is 12 seconds. This result is the amount of time theoretically required to download the Web page.

Remember that the result derived from these four steps is a theoretical measurement. It does not consider certain factors, such as the fact that 56-Kbps modems rarely operate above 50 Kbps. Nor does it consider network overhead, noisy phone lines or network congestion. Therefore, the best way to determine how quickly users can download your HTML pages is to test them in real-world settings. For example, test your Web site by accessing it through a dial-up (i.e., telephone-line modem) connection. This method will provide a much more reliable estimate.

Some sources refer to "bits per second" as "characters per second," although these terms are not technically equivalent. It is recommended that you use bits/kilobits/megabits/gigabits per second as the units of measure when discussing bandwidth and connection speeds.

CIW Online Resources – Online Exercise

Visit CIW Online at *http://education.Certification-Partners.com/CIW* to complete an interactive exercise that will reinforce what you have learned about this topic.

Exercise 10-5: Determining download time for a Web page

Naming Web Page Files

As you create your Web pages, you may need to restrict the length of file names. You should also consider naming your HTML pages to correspond to their content. For example, if the page is a sales form, you could name it *salesform.htm.*

You can give your Web page files (i.e., HTML files) any name you want. However, you must identify each file as the appropriate file type by appending either the *.htm* or *.html* extension to the end of the file name. Some server administrators prefer that you use the .html file name extension. Others may prefer the .htm extension. When in doubt, ask your service provider or Web server administrator which standard you should follow.

More technologically complex pages may require file name extensions other than .htm or .html. For example, Active Server Pages (ASP) files require the .asp extension, and JavaServer Pages (JSP) files require the .jsp extension.

Default files and the HTTP server

You should remember that your pages will probably reside on a Web server (also called an HTTP server). Usually, an HTTP server looks for a default page, which is a specially named file. The server will present this page automatically each time a user enters the minimum amount of information required to connect to the site. Rather than having to enter the page address *www.company.com/index.html*, a user need only enter *www.company.com*. The server supplies the default page *index.html* automatically.

Default document names differ from server to server. Microsoft Internet Information Services (IIS) looks for the *default.htm* file. Apache HTTP server looks for the *index.html* file. You can change the name of the default document, but you should be aware that every Web server is preconfigured to a default document name. Following are some common default page names:

- index.htm
- index.html
- index.asp
- index.jsp

- default.htm
- default.html
- default.asp
- default.jsp

- welcome.htm
- welcome.html
- welcome.asp
- welcome.jsp

- home.htm
- home.html
- home.asp
- home.jsp

Consult the Web server documentation, your site administrator or your Internet Service Provider (ISP) to ensure that your default file name functions properly on your Web server.

HTTP 404 – File Not Found error

An HTTP 404 – File Not Found error indicates that you have requested a file that does not exist on the specified Web server. This server-generated error indicates that the server is functioning, but the specific file you requested from that server cannot be located because the file may have been renamed or removed from the site.

You will also receive this error if you request a site's default document by the wrong name. For example, the default document name for the Yahoo! Web site is *www.yahoo.com/index.html*. If you request *www.yahoo.com/default.html*, you will receive a 404 error.

Many Web browsers, including Windows Internet Explorer, will automatically generate a custom page when an end user requests a non-existent page. Increasingly, Web site administrators create a custom page that will appear whenever a user requests a non-existent page. Figure 10-6 shows a custom 404 error page.

Figure 10-6: HTTP 404 – File Not Found error

CIW Online Resources – Course Mastery

Visit CIW Online at *http://education.Certification-Partners.com/CIW* to take the Course Mastery review of this lesson or lesson segment.

SDA Lesson 10 - Part B

Case Study
Planning the Site at Both Ends

Puja is part of a Web development team. Planning so far has focused on the "look and feel" of the Web site, and has included discussions about color schemes and image choices. Puja makes the following list of additional items that need to be discussed in relation to the site:

- Markup languages to use (e.g., the HTML version)

- Development environments to use (e.g., simple text editor, GUI editors such as Dreamweaver)

- CGI choices

- Database connectivity

- Now, Puja has been asked to determine the ideal Web server platform for this site. She has been given the following information:

- Her company uses Sun Solaris almost exclusively. Sun Solaris is a version of UNIX. UNIX systems have supported languages such as Java and Perl for years.

- The company has a team of developers who know scripting languages such as JavaScript and Perl.

- Several of the developers are accustomed to using Apache Server, an open-source Web server that can run on any operating system but is traditionally used on UNIX.

After considering this information, Puja decides to use Apache Server, which supports Perl.

*   *   *

As a class, discuss the factors that you should consider when choosing a server platform, including:

- Existing operating systems.

- Development resources.

- Cost of operating systems and/or Web server software.

Lesson Summary

Application project

Calculate the amount of time it will take a user to download a 70-KB home page if he or she is still using an older 56-Kbps modem. Do you think this time requirement is acceptable to a waiting user?

If you have used a Web site to shop or make purchases, either for your personal use or your business, consider the customer service experiences you have had. Which Web businesses were easy to do business with? What made your transactions easy? Which businesses gave you problems? Are there some businesses you return to frequently because they have earned your trust as a consumer? Which ones, and why? Are there some businesses that you return to despite customer service problems you have had? Which ones, and why? How can you use these experiences to improve the customer service offered by your own e-commerce site?

Skills review

In this lesson, you learned about developing a business Web site. You learned about business-to-business, business-to-consumer and consumer-to-consumer e-commerce models, and you studied their enabling technologies including EDI, OBI, 3-D Secure and SSL/TLS. You also learned about Internet marketing and its associated technologies of search engine optimization (SEO), pay per click (PPC) and Web analytics. You also studied front-end and back-end issues. You received a brief overview of global commerce issues, and the ways that Web technologies can be used to improve customer relationships.

You know that Web pages are connected to databases using technologies such as CGI and ODBC. Before you develop a Web page or site, you must consider important variables such as the interface, business considerations, bandwidth and the names of your Web page files.

Now that you have completed this lesson, you should be able to:

✓ 2.10.1: Identify the uses and benefits of various document and multimedia file formats, including PDF, RTF, PostScript, EPS, MOV, MPEG, streaming media, non-streaming media.

✓ 2.10.2: Define the following Web-related mechanisms for audience development (i.e., attracting and retaining an audience): push technology, pull technology, visitor tracking.

✓ 2.10.3: Evaluate the benefits and drawbacks of proprietary technologies such as Adobe Flash and Microsoft Silverlight.

✓ 2.12.2: Estimate download time for Web pages.

✓ 2.12.4: Document results of Web site functionality testing.

✓ 2.16.1: Define e-commerce terms and concepts, including business-to-business (B2B), business-to-consumer (B2C), Electronic Funds Transfer (EFT), merchant systems, relationship management, customer self-service, Internet marketing, 3-D Secure.

✓ 2.16.3: Identify payment models used in e-commerce, including payment gateways.

✓ 2.16.4: Identify issues related to working in a global environment, including different currencies, multi-lingual issues, international shipping, legal and regulatory issues.

✓ 2.16.5: Identify the importance of SSL/TLS to a transaction that contains sensitive information.

✓ 2.16.6: Identify the importance of online indexing and cataloging.

✓ 2.16.7: Define search engine optimization (SEO) and related key terms (e.g., Internet marketing, organic vs. non-organic [pay-per-click], Web analytics).

✓ 2.17.2: Define Common Gateway Interface (CGI) methods, including .Net, Django, Python, JavaServer Pages (JSP), Server-Side JavaScript (SSJS), Active Server Pages (ASP), PHP Hypertext Preprocessor (PHP), Ajax.

✓ 2.17.3: Define database connectivity technologies (e.g., Open Database Connectivity [ODBC], Java Database Connectivity [JDBC]), and explain the importance of connecting databases with Web sites and other Internet-based services.

✓ 2.19.2: Manage branding issues when developing a site (e.g., logo placement and sizing).

✓ 2.21.3: Create Web pages that rank highly for search engines that use spiders and screen readers.

✓ 2.21.4: Consult respected Web development resources, including books, trade journals, online sources, qualified individuals, user groups.

CIW Practice Exams

Visit CIW Online at *http://education.Certification-Partners.com/CIW* to take the Practice Exams assessment covering the objectives in this lesson.

SDA Objective 2.07 Review	SDA Objective 2.17 Review
SDA Objective 2.10 Review	SDA Objective 2.19 Review
SDA Objective 2.12 Review	SDA Objective 2.21 Review
SDA Objective 2.16 Review	

Note that some objectives may be only partially covered in this lesson.

Lesson 10 Review

1. User-friendly Web page interfaces, such as a pleasing layout and accessible navigation, are considered to be what type of issues?

    _____

2. What is Internet marketing, and of what three components does it consist?

    _____

    _____

    _____

3. What technologies discussed in this lesson help e-commerce companies exchange funds?

    _____

    _____

    _____

4. Calculate the time required, in seconds, to download a 14,000-byte Web page using a 56-Kbps modem.

    _____

    _____

5. If you request a file that does not exist on a Web server, what types of messages will you receive? (Name or describe at least two.)

    _____

    _____

    _____

Appendixes

All appendixes located on CIW Online (http://education.certification-partners.com/ciw/)

Glossary

3-D Secure — An XML-based protocol used by credit card companies to add security to online credit and debit card transactions.

Ajax — A programming methodology that uses a number of existing technologies together and enables Web applications to make incremental updates to the user interface without the need to reload the browser page.

application cache — A directory on a computer where applications, such as Internet apps, can be stored and run without access to the original application.

Application Programming Interface (API) — A set of universal commands, calls and functions that allows developers to communicate with an application or operating system.

bandwidth — The amount of information, sometimes called traffic, that can be carried on a network at one time. The total capacity of a line. Also, the rate of data transfer over a network connection; measured in bits per second.

block-level element — A markup element that affects at least an entire paragraph.

brand — A concept or collection of symbols associated with a product, service or person.

business-to-business (B2B) — An e-commerce model in which a Web-based business sells products and/or services to other businesses.

business-to-consumer (B2C) — An e-commerce model in which a Web-based business sells products and/or services to consumers or end users.

canvas — An HTML5 Application Programming Interface (API) used for rendering visual images on the fly by providing scripts with a bitmap canvas.

Cascading Style Sheets (CSS) — A technology that allows greater style definition and formatting control of HTML elements. Formatting can be placed within the HTML or called remotely from an external style sheet.
character set — The group of symbols used to render text on a page.

client — An individual computer connected to a network. Also, a system or application (such as a Web browser or user agent) that requests a service from another computer (the server) and is used to access files or documents.

client-side script — Code embedded into an HTML page and downloaded by a user; resides on the client and helps process Web form input. Common client-side scripting languages include JavaScript and VBScript.

cloud computing — Software, infrastructure and platform services that are hosted by a remote data center and provided to organizations or individuals over the Internet.

Common Gateway Interface (CGI) — A program that processes data submitted by the user. Allows a Web server to pass control to a software application, based on user request. The application receives and organizes data, then returns it in a consistent format.

consumer-to-consumer (C2C) — An e-commerce model in which individual consumers sell products or services to other consumers.

cookie — A text file that contains information sent between a server and a client to help maintain state and track user activities. Cookies can reside in memory or on a hard drive.

customs — National departments responsible for controlling items entering and leaving the country.

demographics — The study of groups of people. Specifically, the practice of gathering statistical data by studying populations based on characteristics such as age, income and education.

dithering — The ability for a computer to approximate a color by combining the RGB values.

document type declaration (<!DOCTYPE>) — A declaration of document or code type embedded within an HTML, XHTML, XML or SGML document; identifies the version and markup language used. Denoted by the <!DOCTYPE> declaration at the beginning of the document.

Document Type Definition (DTD) — A set of rules contained in a simple text file that defines the structure, syntax and vocabulary as it relates to tags and attributes for a corresponding document.

drag-and-drop — Functionality that allows a user to grab an object and move it to a different location on a computer screen.

drop zone — An area of a Web page that has been defined as a place where dragged items can be placed.

Dynamic HTML (DHTML) — An umbrella term that describes the combination of HTML, script, styles and the Document Object Model (DOM) to provides Web page interactivity.

electronic commerce (e commerce) — The integration of communications, data management and security capabilities to allow organizations and consumers to exchange information related to the sale of good and services.

emulator — A type of software that imitates a computer then allows non-native software to run in a foreign environment. Sometimes also a hardware device.

Extensible Markup Language (XML) — A markup language that describes document content instead of adding structure or formatting to document content. A simplified version of SGML.

File Transfer Protocol (FTP) — An Internet protocol used to transfer files between computers; allows file transfer without corruption or alteration.

fixed-width font — A font in which every character, including the space character, has equal width. In proportional-width fonts, letters such as I and J have less width than M or B.

geolocation — The ability to determine a user's location. Web sites can use this information to enhance the user experience and provide location-based services.

graphical user interface (GUI) — A program that provides visual navigation with menus and screen icons, and performs automated functions when users click command buttons.

hexadecimal — A base-16 number system that allows large numbers to be displayed by fewer characters than if the number were displayed in the regular base-10 system. In hexadecimal, the number 10 is represented as the letter A, 15 is represented as F, and 16 is represented as 10.

hyperlinks — Embedded instructions within a text file that link it to another point in the file or to a separate file.

Hypertext Markup Language (HTML) — The traditional authoring language used to develop Web pages for many applications.

image map — A Web page image with clickable regions that are defined as "hot spot" hyperlinks to other pages or page sections.

inline images — Images rendered in a Web page.

link rot — The phenomenon in which hyperlinks on a Web site gradually become invalid as referenced Web page content, links and page locations change.

mailing list server — An e-mail server that regularly sends e-mail messages to a specified list of users.

manifest — A list of the files that are needed for the Web application to work offline.

markup language — A series of commands used to format, organize and describe information on a Web page.

metalanguage — A language used for defining other languages.

Multipurpose Internet Mail Extensions (MIME) — A protocol that enables operating systems to map file name extensions to corresponding applications. Also used by applications to automatically process files downloaded from the Internet.

object-based — Similar to object-oriented programming languages, but does not allow for inheritance from one class to another.

offline Web application — Permits the user to continue working with Web sites and Web documents even when a network connection is unavailable.

on the fly — Dynamically created Web page content, as opposed to pre-defined, static content.

pay per click (PPC) — An Internet marketing technique that enables you to list your site high in search engine rankings by advertising on keywords that describe your product or service.

podcast — The use of audio or video digital-media files that are distributed through Web feeds to subscribed users.

Request for Comments (RFC) — A document published by the IETF that details information about standardized Internet protocols and those in various development stages.

rule — In a style sheet, a format instruction that consists of a specified selector and the properties and values applied to it.

sans-serif — A font style that does not use decorative strokes at the tips of characters. Includes the Arial font family.

search engine optimization (SEO) — The process of improving the volume and quality of traffic to a Web site by structuring content to improve search engine ranking. A specific activity of Internet marketing.

Secure Sockets Layer (SSL) — A protocol that provides authentication and encryption, used by most servers for secure exchanges over the Internet. Superseded by Transport Layer Security (TLS).

selector — In a style sheet, any element to which designated styles are applied.

serif — A font style that uses characters with small decorative additions at the outermost points of the characters, called strokes. Includes the Times and Times New Roman fonts.

server-side script — Code that resides on a server to help process Web form input. Server-side CGI scripts are commonly written in Perl.

site map — A brief, hierarchical representation of a Web site that enables visitors to quickly identify areas of the site and navigate to them.

Smalltalk — A programming language that pioneered object-oriented programming. Not popularly used in Web development.

Software as a Service (SaaS) — Software that is hosted centrally on the Internet and accessed by users with a Web browser.

spam — Unsolicited and unwanted e-mail messages; the online equivalent of junk mail.

Standard Generalized Markup Language (SGML) — A metalanguage used to create other languages, including HTML and XHTML.

Structured Query Language (SQL) — A language used to create and maintain professional, high-performance corporate databases.

T1 — A digital carrier that transmits data at a speed of 1.544 Mbps.

text-level element — A markup element that affects single characters or words.

Transport Layer Security (TLS) — A protocol based on SSL 3.0 that provides authentication and encryption, used by most servers for secure exchanges over the Internet.

troll — A Web user who publishes negative comments or submits feedback simply to annoy or anger.

trouble ticket — A record of a problem related to a service provided by an ISP or cloud service provider. Used to record receipt of a complaint and track resolution of the problem.

Unicode — A universal character set designed to support all written languages, as well as scholarly disciplines (e.g., mathematics).

user agent — Any application, such as a Web browser, mobile phone, smartphone or help engine, that renders HTML for display to users.

Web 2.0 — A concept referring to the changing trends in the use of WWW technology and Web design that have led to the development of information-sharing and collaboration capabilities.

Web analytics — The practice of collecting data and studying user behavior in an attempt to increase market share and sales.

Web application framework — A set of software tools or code that is commonly used in the creation and management of online applications.

Web feed — A data format for delivering Web content that is updated frequently.

What You See Is What You Get (WYSIWYG) — (pronounced whiz-ee-wig) A user-friendly editing format in which the file being edited is displayed as it will appear in the browser.

wireframing — The process of developing an outline for a Web presence.

XMLHttpRequest — An Application Programming Interface (API) that is used to transfer XML and other text data between a Web server and browser.

Index

macro, 8-10
MAGpie, 1-20
mailing list server, 10-21
managing a site, 1-31
map, image, 7-14
market messages, 10-20
marketing strategy, 10-19
marketing, Internet, 10-7
markup code validation, 1-12
markup language, 1-4
markup tags, 2-3
markup, universal, 1-12, 2-28
Massachusetts Institute of Technology, 1-8
maxlength attribute, 6-13
Mbps, 10-28
media choices, 10-20
meetings, design and branding, 10-20
meetings, leadership, 1-28
message of site, 1-23
metalanguage, 1-7
method attribute, 6-9
Microsoft, 8-8, 10-26
Microsoft Expression Web, 1-6, 9-4
Microsoft Internet Information Server (IIS), 10-29
Microsoft Silverlight, 7-24
MIME, 1-5, 7-4
MIME type, 10-23
mind share, 10-8, 10-19
mobile apps, 9-28
mobile devices, designing for, 9-25
mobile Web sites, 9-28
modem speed, 10-28
Moving Pictures Experts Group (MPEG), 10-24
Mozilla Firefox, 1-30
Mozilla SeaMonkey, 1-6
MP3, 10-24
MP4 video format, 7-4
MPEG, 10-24
MPEG 4, 7-4
multiple attribute, 6-25
multiple declarations, CSS, 3-5
multiple selections, 6-10
multiple-option select list, 6-25
multiple-select list, 6-10
Multipurpose Internet Mail Extensions (MIME), 1-5, 7-4
MySQL, 8-40, 10-26
name attribute, 4-12, 6-5, 6-13
name attribute, <map> tag, 7-15
name recognition, 10-19
name=value pair, 6-5
naming Web page files, 10-28
NDA, 1-35
nesting tags, 2-18
network congestion, 10-28
network overhead, 10-28
niche, market, 10-8
non-breaking space, 3-21
Non-Disclosure Agreement (NDA), 1-35
non-graphical browsers, 3-12
non-interlaced image, 7-23
non-keyboard character, 3-20
non-relational database, 10-25
n-tier database, 8-32, 8-33
numbered list, 2-25
object, 8-7
object-based language, 8-10
object-oriented database, 10-25
object-oriented language, 8-7

ODBC, 10-26
offline Web application, 8-22
off-site analytics, 10-9
Ogg video format, 7-4
Ogg-Vorbis, 10-24
on-site analytics, 10-9
Open Database Connectivity (ODBC), 10-26
opening tag, 2-4
Opera, 1-30
Oracle, 10-26
order tracking, 10-14
ordered list, 2-25
outsourcing, 1-35
padding CSS property, 5-5
page colors and backgrounds, 3-23
page creation skills, 1-4
page design issues, 3-28
page editor, GUI, 9-3
page layout, 3-29
Paint Shop Pro, 7-13
paragraph breaks, 2-14
paragraph formatting, 2-14
partial URL, 4-3
password field, 6-11
path name, relative, 3-32
paths, 4-4
pay per click (PPC), 10-8, 10-9
payment gateway, 10-11
payment technologies, e-commerce, 10-10
PDF, 10-23
Perl, 6-6, 8-6, 8-40, 10-15
permissions and CGI, 8-31
PGP, 10-24
photographs, 3-11
PHP, 6-6, 8-39
PHP Hypertext Preprocessor (PHP), 8-5, 10-16
phrase elements, 2-23
pixel, 3-19, 7-27
pixels per inch (ppi), 7-28
PKI, 10-11
plagiarism, 1-33
Play, Google, 9-29
plus signs, 6-5
PNG, 3-12, 7-13, 7-21, 7-23, 10-23
PNG format, layers, 7-27
PNG, animated, 7-23
podcast, 9-35
polygon, 7-15, 7-17
polymorphism, 8-7
pop-up windows, 8-10
Portable Document Format (PDF), 10-23
Portable Network Graphics (PNG), 3-12, 10-23
portal, 10-21
post, 6-9
poster attribute, video, 7-3
PostgreSQL, 10-26
PostScript, 10-23
PowerPoint file format, 10-24
PPC, 10-8, 10-9
ppi, 7-28
Practical Extraction and Report Language (Perl), 8-5
preformatted text, 2-20
presentation, oral, 1-27
Pretty Good Privacy (PGP), 10-24
primitive formatting, 2-20
print command, 8-3
procedural language, 8-6
programming concepts, basic, 8-3
programming statements, 8-4

Certified Internet
Web Professional

www.CIWcertified.com

ISBN 0-7423-3134-2

DELIGHTFUL DIP

1 (8.5-ounce) can artichoke hearts
1 (13.5-ounce) can chopped spinach
2 cups light sour cream
1/4 cup fat-free mayonnaise
1 (1.5-ounce) package dry onion soup mix
1 tablespoon grated parmesan or romano cheese

Drain artichokes and spinach, reserving 1 tablespoon of liquid from each. Combine sour cream, mayonnaise, soup mix and reserved liquid in a large bowl. Finely chop artichoke hearts and combine with spinach, add to sour cream mixture. Mix well. Chill at least 1 hour. (Chilling overnight will give the dip a better flavor). Garnish with cheese and serve with bread, crackers or fresh veggies.

Lisa Bender
Home Office

TACO DIP

1 (8-ounce) package cream cheese
1 (8-ounce) carton sour cream
1 packet taco seasoning mix
Chopped lettuce
Black olives
Grated cheese
Tortilla chips

Combine cream cheese, sour cream and seasoning mix; stir until smooth. Spread on round platter. Top with chopped lettuce, black olives and your choice of grated cheese. Dip with your favorite tortilla chips, or whatever you dip with!

Mary Getchell
Asheville

CHILI CON QUESO

1 small onion, finely chopped
1 jalapeno pepper, finely chopped
1 (14 1/2-ounce) can tomatoes, blended
1 1/2 cups water
3 chicken bouillon cubes
1/2 teaspoon garlic powder
2 to 3 teaspoons cumin
1 pound cheddar cheese, cubed
1/4 cup cornstarch, dissolved in 1/4 cup water

Saute onion and pepper in a little margarine until tender. Add tomatoes, water, bouillon cubes, garlic powder and cumin; cook over medium heat until just boiling. Add cheese and stir until melted. Gradually add cornstarch mixture, constantly stirring. This will thicken more as it cools. Serve warm with tortilla chips.

Janet Bright
Hendersonville

YOGURT DIP

1 cup plain yogurt
3 green onions, chopped
1/2 teaspoon chili powder
1/2 teaspoon garlic powder
1/2 teaspoon pepper

Combine the yogurt, onions, chili powder, garlic powder and pepper; mix well. Refrigerate several hours before serving with fresh vegetables.

Mary Jane Matthews
Waynesville

CREAMY CARAMEL DIP

1 (8-ounce) package cream cheese, softened
3/4 cup brown sugar
1 cup sour cream
2 teaspoons vanilla extract
2 teaspoons lemon juice
1 cup cold milk
1 (3.4-ounce) box vanilla instant pudding mix

Mix cream cheese and brown sugar together until smooth. Add sour cream, vanilla, lemon juice, milk and pudding mix. Beat well after each addition. Cover and chill for one hour. Serve with fresh fruit such as apples, pineapple or strawberries.

Debe Jones
Home Office

SURPRISE CHEDDAR CHEESE PUFFS

2 cups grated sharp cheddar cheese
1 stick butter, room temperature
1 cup flour
1/2 teaspoon salt
1/2 teaspoon paprika
48 small green, stuffed olives, well drained

Blend grated cheese and butter. Stir in flour, salt and paprika (may be done in a food processor). Mold 1 teaspoon of the mixture around each olive. Chill the puffs until firm - about 30 minutes. Arrange the puffs on ungreased cookie sheets. Bake in preheated 400° oven for about 15 minutes or until browned.

Mary Jane Matthews
Waynesville

"You can freeze the puffs for up to 10 days. Bake them, still frozen, until brown."

Spinach Balls

1 (10-ounce) package frozen chopped spinach
2 cloves garlic, chopped or minced
1 stick margarine, melted
1 cup bread crumbs
3/4 cup grated parmesan cheese
Salt and pepper, to taste
1 egg, beaten

Cook spinach; drain thoroughly. Mix the spinach, garlic, margarine, bread crumbs, cheese, salt and pepper in a bowl. Add the egg and mix well. Place teaspoon size balls on a cookie sheet. Bake in preheated 350° oven for 40 minutes or until golden brown.

Tracey Thompson
Home Office

"It wouldn't be a covered dish celebration without Tracey's spinach balls!"

Sausage Balls

2 cups biscuit baking mix
1 pound sausage
1 cup grated cheddar cheese

Stir the biscuit mix, sausage and cheese together. Form into 1-inch balls. Place on a greased cookie sheet. Bake in preheated 375° oven for 12 to 15 minutes.

Melissa Edmisten
Home Office

"You may freeze and reheat at a later time."

CHEESEBALL

2 (3-ounce) packages sliced pressed beef
2 (8-ounce) packages cream cheese, softened
1 medium onion, diced
2 tablespoons Worcestershire sauce

Chop beef into small pieces; reserve enough to roll cheeseball in. Combine cream cheese, beef, onions and Worcestershire sauce. Mix well. Form into a ball. Garnish with remaining beef; chill. Serve with crackers.

Teresa Presnell
Original Store

RUMAKI

1 (8-ounce) can whole water chestnuts
1 (5-ounce) bottle soy sauce
Brown sugar
1 pound sliced bacon
Toothpicks

Drain water chestnuts and place in bowl. Add soy sauce. Marinate for 4 hours. Place small amount of brown sugar in center of 1 slice of bacon. Place a water chestnut on top of sugar. Wrap bacon ends around chestnut and secure with a toothpick. Bake in preheated 275° oven until bacon is done. For microwave, cook bacon partially before adding sugar and water chestnuts. Return to microwave for 1 to 2 minutes, until bacon is done.

Kelly Mast
Original Store and Boone

SALMON LOG

1 (15-ounce) can pink salmon, drained and flaked
1 (8-ounce) package cream cheese, softened
1 tablespoon lemon juice
2 teaspoons minced onion
1 teaspoon horseradish
1/2 teaspoon salt
1/4 teaspoon Worcestershire sauce
1/2 cup chopped pecans
3 tablespoons parsley flakes

Combine salmon and cheese, mixing well. Stir in lemon juice, onion, horseradish, salt and Worcestershire sauce. Shape into a 12-inch log; chill. Combine pecans and parsley on a flat surface and roll chilled log until well coated. Serve with crackers.

Debe Jones
Home Office

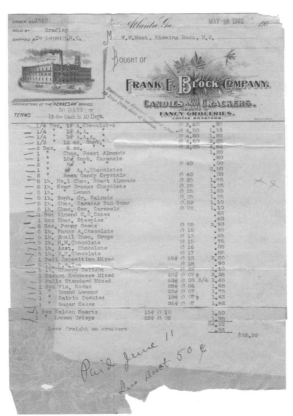

The Mast Store carried items for every day life...as well as those to satisfy a sweet tooth.

CARE OF DISHES

Dishwashing need not be an unpleasant task if these four rules are observed:
1. Use hot soapy water.
2. Change the water frequently.
3. Have the dishes free from crumbs and scraps before beginning to wash them.
4. Wash kettles and other cooking utensils first.

Directions for Dishwashing.

Preparation

1. Collect all dishes to be washed.
2. Scrape them, putting scraps in an earthenware or enameled dish: wipe frying pans and other greasy dishes with pieces of soft paper. This paper may be used for kindling.
3. Fill greasy pots and pans with hot water to which a teaspoonful of salt soda has been added, and let them stand. Soak dishes that have contained batter, dough, eggs, or any scratchy material in cold water; dishes that have been used to cook sugar, in hot water.
4. Put all dishes of a kind together; plates in piles, knives, forks, and spoons laid with handles one way, etc. Place nearest to you the dishes to be washed first.
5. Have a clean dry place clear for clean dishes.
6. Make ready two pans, one half full of hot soapy water, and the other half full of clear hot water.

Washing

7. Wash the dishes in the following order:
   a. Large kettles and cooking utensils.
   b. Smaller articles of kitchenware.
   c. (With clean water and dishcloth) glassware.
   d. Silver.
   e. Cups and saucers.
   f. Plates.
   g. Platters, vegetable dishes, etc.

General instructions.

8. Wash all dishes, including kettles, inside and out, in soapy water; rinse in clear water, drain, and wipe dry.
9. Use Sapolio* to remove food that sticks or is burnt on.
10. Use a wire dishcloth on ironware, a scrubbing-brush, if necessary, on enameled ware, tin ware, and wire strainers. Clean seams in tin ware and enameled ware with a wooden skewer.

*An early brand of soap.

Special instructions.

11. Do not put knife handles in water. Water discolors and cracks ivory and bone handles, and may loosen wooden ones. After washing knives, scour them with bath brick.

12. Do not wash breadboard or rolling pin at an iron sink. The iron will leave marks on them. Wash them at the table.

13. Be careful not to wet the cogs of a Dover eggbeater. Wash the lower part, and wipe off the handle with a damp cloth. Water washes the oil from the cogs, thus making the batter hard to turn.

14. Dry the seams of a double boiler carefully.

15. Do not waste time polishing tins. It is sufficient to have them clean and dry.

16. Dip glasses into hot water, so that they will be wet inside and outside at the same time. Unequal expansion of the glass, caused by one part being heated suddenly, is what breaks them.

17. Silver and glass are brightest if wiped directly from clean, hot suds, without being rinsed. A damp towel makes dull spoons and glasses.

18. Scald; i.e. rinse with boiling water all vessels that have contained milk.

19. Wash teapot and coffeepot in clean hot water without soap, and wipe dry. Clean the spout carefully. Let them stand for a while with covers off.

20. Wash dishpan and rinsing-pan, and wipe dry with a towel, not with the dishcloth.

My grandmother, Callie Greene Duffield, graduated from Watauga Academy in 1917. She was a school teacher here in the mountains and from what I have been told, she rode the E.T. & W.N.C. Railroad (affectionately known as "Tweetsie") to work. These tips and others you'll find sprinkled throughout this cookbook come from a textbook she used called Elements of the Theory and Practice of Cookery. In addition to finding the typical notes that would be helpful for her lessons, I also found recipes that she used written on blank pages, old newspaper clippings from the recipe section, and miscellaneous unidentified family photos. I hope that you enjoy them and maybe even find a few useful. The book was copyrighted in 1901 and reprinted several times with the most recent one being in 1913.

       Sheri Moretz

A clean kitchen is a must.

Sandwiches, Soups & Salads

Another General Store in Valle Crucis

In 1909, a new general store was built in Valle Crucis ..... just 2/10s of a mile from the Mast Store. This new store was constructed of locally-harvested lumber including the now extinct American Chestnut and was owned by R. L. Lowe and Company. When it first opened, it was called the Watauga Supply Co. Just a year later, Squire Taylor (his former home is now called the Inn at the Taylor House) and Dr. Henry Perry purchased the store and renamed it Valle Crucis Company.

The Mast Store and the Farthing Store, as the Valle Crucis Company ultimately became known, carried much the same goods with some variation. For instance, the Mast Store had a catalog where you could pick out your own ready-made suit and the Farthing Store had a

The Mast Store Annex as it appeared around 1927.

catalog where you could give your measurements and have a suit specially made just for you. Or if you needed a hay baler, you might find different brands at each of the stores.

It might seem odd to have two general stores so close to each other in such a small community, but with transportation not being as readily available as it is today, folks couldn't travel as far to get staples for the home. These stores were "destinations" because they were large enough to have a wide selection of goods - plus with being so close, if you didn't find it at one, you could walk to the other.

General stores didn't have a set closing time unless it was stated as "when the last person leaves." Friends and neighbors would gather at the store after a long day's work to pick up a few things and to tell a few "whoppers" around the stove. According to Mary Farthing Mast, whose family used to own the Valle Crucis Company, "People talk about women being gossips; they should have been down at the store when the men gathered."

Today, the stove is gone from the Annex, but if you use your imagination just a bit back in the left hand corner, you can almost hear some of those "fish stories".

CORN CHOWDER

12 slices bacon
2 medium onions, chopped
4 medium potatoes, peeled and cubed
1 cup water
4 cups milk
2 (17-ounce) cans creamed corn
1 teaspoon salt
Dash of pepper
1 clove garlic, minced

Fry bacon until crisp; reserve 2 tablespoons drippings. Set bacon aside to drain; saute onions in drippings. Add potatoes and water, and pour into medium sauce pan. Simmer for 20 minutes. Stir in milk, corn, salt, pepper and garlic. Cook over medium heat, stirring occasionally, until potatoes are tender. Crumble bacon into chowder and serve.

Allen Mast
Original Store

CHICKEN ARTICHOKE SOUP

2 to 4 chicken breasts
2 cups chopped carrots
2 cups chopped celery
1/2 stick butter
1 package long grain wild rice (do not use seasoning packet)
2 cups chopped artichoke hearts

Cook chicken breasts in 1 quart of water until done. Remove chicken and when cool, shred. Save broth. (You may add chicken bouillon cubes and extra water, if more broth is needed.) Saute carrots and celery in butter in soup stock pot. Add extra broth and rice. Simmer till done, then add the chopped artichokes.

Myrna Newkirk
Hendersonville

CHICKEN BRUNSWICK STEW

1 whole chicken
1 (15 1/4-ounce) can whole corn, undrained
2 (14 3/4-ounce) cans cream-style corn
1 (10-ounce) package frozen tiny lima beans
4 large carrots, sliced in rounds
3 large potatoes, diced
2 (28-ounce) cans whole tomatoes, cut up
1 large onion, diced
4 chicken bouillon cubes
1/2 teaspoon black pepper
1/2 teaspoon parsley
1/2 teaspoon basil
1/2 teaspoon thyme

In a big pot, cover chicken with water and simmer until tender, skimming foam and fat off top. Remove chicken from broth, debone and cut into small pieces. To broth, add chicken, whole corn, cream-style corn, lima beans, carrots, potatoes, tomatoes and onion. Add bouillon cubes, pepper, parsley, basil and thyme. Cover and simmer, stirring occasionally, until vegetables are done and chicken has "shredded". Add additional water or chicken broth if necessary, but stew should be slightly thick.

Janet Bright
Hendersonville

Photo by W.R. Trivett used with permission from Ralph Lentz.

CREAM OF BROCCOLI SOUP

8 ounces fresh broccoli, chopped fine (use blender)
1 quart water
1 pint milk
1 pint half and half
pinch pepper
4 chicken bouillon cubes
1/4 teaspoon baking soda
1 1/2 sticks margarine
2/3 cup flour

In large pot combine broccoli, water, milk, half and half, pepper, bouillon cubes and soda, and bring to a boil. In skillet melt butter, add flour and stir until smooth. After soup boils, stir in flour mixture. Cook slowly until it thickens, 5 to 8 minutes.

The Old Mast Store Deli
Valle Crucis

"Note: vegetable bouillon cubes can be substituted for the chicken bouillon cubes."

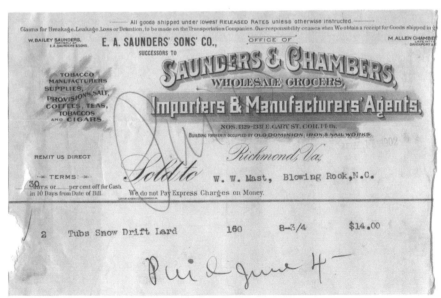

Several "Accounting Ledgers," kept in old wallpaper sample books, provide a look back at items carried in the store from 1898-1920.

FOUR CAN MINESTRONE

    4 ounces spaghetti, broken into short pieces
    3 cups water
    2 (10-3/4 ounce) cans vegetable soup
    1 (16-ounce) can pork and beans (throw out fat)
    1 (8-ounce) can tomato sauce
    Pinch of oregano
    Parmesan cheese

Cook spaghetti in boiling water until done; do not drain. Add soup, beans, tomato sauce and oregano. Heat thoroughly. Ladle into soup bowls and sprinkle with parmesan cheese.

Janet Bright
Hendersonville

ONION SOUP

    3 to 5 pounds yellow onions
    1/2 stick butter
    1/2 cup sugar
    2 quarts beef stock
    1 bottle vermouth
    Mozzarella cheese

In a soup stock pot, brown thinly sliced onions in butter and sugar for about 25 to 30 minutes. Add beef stock and vermouth. Simmer for 1 to 2 hours. Top with cut up mozzarella cheese. Microwave before serving to melt the cheese.

Myrna Newkirk
Hendersonville

"Freezes well."

PASTA FAGIOLI

1/2 pound ground beef
1 (15-ounce) can Italian-style stewed tomatoes, chopped
2 (10 1/2-ounce) cans beef broth
1 (15-ounce) can kidney beans with juice
1 (15-ounce) can navy beans, drained and rinsed
Salt and pepper, to taste
1 cup small elbow macaroni
Parmesan cheese, grated

Brown and drain ground beef; set aside. In Dutch oven, combine stewed tomatoes, broth, kidney beans, navy beans, ground beef, salt and pepper. Simmer 30 minutes. Cook macaroni according to package directions. Drain and add to the soup just prior to serving. Top each serving with grated parmesan cheese.

Della Goulter
Waynesville

"Serve with garlic bread or breadsticks and you have a complete meal."

How to have good tea.

1. Buy good tea; cheap tea is likely to be adulterated with used tea leaves and leaves of other plants.
2. Keep it in a closely covered glass jar or tin canister; if exposed to the air it loses flavor.
3. Use a china, or silver, or earthen teapot; never a tin one.
4. Have the water freshly drawn, and bring it quickly to the boiling point; water deprived of its air by standing or by boiling gives tea a flat taste.
5. Have the teapot hot and the water boiling at the moment the tea is made.
6. Steep it not over five minutes; never let it boil.

Elements of the Theory and Practice of Cookery. A textbook copyrighted in 1901 and reprinted several times with the most recent one being in 1913.

DELLA'S POTATO SOUP

1/4 cup chopped onion
1/4 cup chopped celery
4 tablespoons butter
4 (15-ounce) cans chicken broth
4 cups peeled, diced potatoes
Salt and pepper, to taste
2 cups half and half
Instant potato flakes
Bacon, cooked and crumbled
Green onion tops, chopped
Shredded cheddar cheese

Saute onion and celery in butter until tender. Add the chicken broth, potatoes, salt and pepper. Cook until potatoes are tender, but firm. Add half and half and potato flakes until desired thickness. Garnish with bacon, green onion and cheese prior to serving.

Della Goulter
Waynesville

POTATO SOUP

8 cups cubed potatoes
1/4 cup chopped onion
Salt and pepper, to taste
8 slices bacon
1/2 stick margarine
2 cups milk

Combine potatoes, onion, salt and pepper. Cover with water and cook until tender. Fry bacon and drain. Add margarine and milk to potatoes. Simmer 10 to 15 minutes. Crumble bacon and add to soup just before serving.

Jeanne Norris
Home Office

Potato Soup with Dumplings

6 medium potatoes, diced
2 large onions, diced
1 cup diced celery
1 teaspoon salt, or to taste
1/4 teaspoon pepper
3 cups water
3 cups milk
1 cup flour
1 egg
4 tablespoons butter

Place potatoes, onions, celery, salt, pepper and water in large saucepan; cover and bring to a boil. Cook about 15 minutes or until potatoes are done. Add milk and bring to a full boil again. While this is heating, measure the flour into a bowl and break in the egg. Stir with fork until thoroughly mixed. When soup is boiling vigorously, drop in the egg and flour mixture by spoonfuls. Add butter. Reduce heat to simmer and cook 10 to 15 minutes.

Janet Bright
Hendersonville

"Our milk was delivered to the back door twice a week. Occasionally we didn't drink it fast enough, and could count on Mom fixing potato soup for supper."

W. W. MAST'S STORE, VALLE CRUCIS, N. C.

An early postcard. W.W. Mast's home is in the foreground. Note the horse in front of the store.

TORTILLA SOUP

1 large onion, diced
3 (14 1/2-ounce) cans fat-free chicken broth
1 cup water
2 (14 1/2-ounce) cans tomatoes, cut up
3 (4-ounce) cans chopped mild green chilies
2 1/4 teaspoons cumin, divided
1 tablespoon chili powder
3/4 teaspoon black pepper, divided
1 pound ground beef or turkey
1 egg
1 slice bread, crumbled
Grated cheddar cheese
2 tortillas, cut into narrow strips, fried in oil

In large pot, saute onion until tender. Add chicken broth, water, tomatoes, chilies, 2 teaspoons cumin, chili powder and 1/2 teaspoon black pepper. Bring to a boil, lower temperature and simmer. In a bowl, mix ground meat, egg, 1/4 teaspoon cumin, 1/4 teaspoon black pepper and bread. Form small meatballs and cook in the simmering broth for 10 minutes, stirring occasionally. Ladle into bowls and top with grated cheese and tortilla strips. For a heartier dish, serve over cooked rice, 1/2 cup per serving.

Janet Bright
Hendersonville

"You can substitute lightly crushed tortilla chips for the homemade tortilla strips."

VEGETABLE SOUP

1 (14 1/2-ounce) can tomatoes
4 to 6 cups chopped vegetables, fresh or frozen
4 packages of vegetable broth (or 4 bouillon cubes)
Water
1 tablespoon basil leaves
1 tablespoon herb seasoning
Dash of garlic powder
2 teaspoons salt
Dash of pepper
2 tablespoons margarine
Handful of chopped onions

In a large soup pot mix tomatoes, vegetables, broth and enough water to fill pot to within 2 inches of the top. Add basil, herb seasoning, garlic powder, salt and pepper. Melt margarine in pan and saute onions; add to soup and let simmer to taste.

The Old Mast Store Deli
Valle Crucis

This photo by Tracey Thompson was taken on the Winter Solstice in 1999. The moon is at its closest point to Earth.

UNCLE ERNIE'S CHILI

"The main measuring device is my hand, which is medium of palm with not fat, but tending toward possibly stubby fingers. Adjust your measuring accordingly. My cook pot is about a gallon and a half, maybe two gallons (7 quarts). First, do the bean thing. Rinse and pour in about 3/4 bag of kidney beans, 1/3 bag black beans, 1/3 bag black-eyed peas, 1/3 bag pinto beans and a handful of lentils. The beans will be about two inches deep. Soak overnight and pour off the water in the morning. I don't know if it does, but this process is supposed to make the beans less gassy, if you know what I mean.

"Release the hounds: into bean pot, empty a 750-ml bottle of decent Zinfandel (about $6 to $8 a bottle; cheap stuff tastes cheap). Put in two (6-ounce) cans of tomato paste, 6 to 10 finely minced cloves of garlic, at least 3 diced medium sized onions, a good dollop of blackstrap molasses, 1 1/2 (50¢-sized) milk chocolate bars, 2 tablespoons salt, a bunch of freshly ground pepper, the juice of 2 limes and a few glugs of Tiger Sauce (apple cider vinegar can be substituted if you can't find Tiger Sauce). Put a big handful of cumin seeds in a pan, turn the oven to broil and lightly toast them. If you don't watch them, they'll burst into flame. Get them out as soon as you can smell them. Pour them all in; you can't use too much cumin seed. (You can get them in bulk from health food stores and they cost way less than when you get them in a bottle.)

"Finely dice some peppers - jalapenos (maybe 2 or 3), one of those long skinny green ones, and two dried peppers I can't remember the name of... habanero? A few squirts of hot pepper sauce wouldn't hurt. Fill the pot to about 3 or 4 inches from the top with water, cover and bring to a slow simmer. Let it simmer all day and all night.

"Next day, boil a small pot of water and dunk 10 home-grown roma tomatoes in the water. This makes them easier to peel. Quarter them and put them in the chili. Throw in about 20 raisins; a little burst of sweetness is a nice surprise now and then. In a cast iron skillet, fry a strip of bacon. Take a pound and a half of the most expensive beef you can afford, dice it up and cook it in the skillet with bacon. Toss in a squirt of Worcestershire sauce and grill the little squares to about medium done. Toss in the pot. Let simmer all day or until the beans are tender. About an hour before eating, throw in a couple handfuls of frozen white corn.

"For corn muffins, I just use small (8 1/2-ounce) corn muffin mix, but I throw in 2 medium handfuls of self-rising cornmeal and 3 tablespoons of brown sugar."

Submitted by Paul Saint Clair
Asheville
A Company Man

The man, the myth, the legend...A Company Man!

GORILLA GOULASH (AKA JOHN'S CHILI)

1 pound bacon, cut into 1-inch pieces
1 large onion, diced
1 green pepper, diced
4 ounces sliced pepperoni
3 pounds ground beef or ground turkey
2 (28-ounce) cans chopped tomatoes
2 teaspoons Worcestershire sauce
3 tablespoons chili powder
1/2 teaspoon cinnamon
1/4 teaspoon nutmeg
Hot pepper sauce, to taste
Salt and pepper, to taste
1 (15 1/2-ounce) can kidney beans, undrained
1/2 pound cubed cheddar cheese

Fry bacon until crisp and set aside to drain. Saute onions, green pepper and pepperoni in bacon grease; drain and set aside. Crumble and brown ground meat; pour off grease. Combine onions, green pepper, pepperoni, ground meat, tomatoes, Worcestershire sauce, chili powder, cinnamon, nutmeg, hot pepper sauce, salt and pepper in a large pot or Dutch oven. Simmer at least an hour, stirring occasionally. Add bacon and kidney beans; heat through. Just before serving, stir in cheese and heat until melted.

Janet Bright
Hendersonville

"When my three children and I first moved to North Carolina in 1976 to be with my future husband, he surprised us with his version of chili. It's not low calorie, but it sure is good!"

NO BEANS CHILI

1 medium onion, chopped
2 tablespoons chopped green pepper
1 tablespoon vegetable oil
1 pound ground beef
1 (6-ounce) can tomato paste
1 tablespoon vinegar
1 tablespoon chili powder
1 teaspoon salt
1/4 teaspoon pepper
2 cups water
Grated cheese

Saute onion and green pepper in oil in a Dutch oven. Add crumbled beef to pot and cook until browned. Stir in tomato paste, vinegar, chili powder, salt, pepper and water. Bring to a boil. Cover, reduce heat and simmer for 30 minutes. Garnish with grated cheese.

Teresa Presnell
Original Store

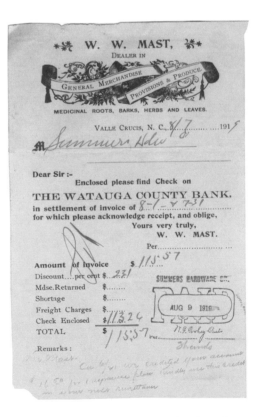

Mast General Store letterhead from 1919. The store, as noted under its logo, would accept medicinal roots, barks, herbs, and leaves (like ginseng, wild cherry, golden seal) in exchange for goods.

Killed Lettuce and Onions

Leaf lettuce
Onions, chopped or sliced, depending on their size
Salt
Apple cider vinegar
Water
Bacon drippings from 3 strips of bacon

Gather and wash enough leaf lettuce to fill a large glass or ceramic bowl. Drain and tear into smaller pieces. Chop onions and put over the top of the lettuce. (I like lots of onion, so put however much you want). Salt to taste. In a small pot, mix vinegar and water, using a little more vinegar than water (especially if you enjoy the tang of vinegar) and the bacon drippings. You should have enough to almost "cover" the wilted lettuce when it "kills" down. Bring these to a boil. Pour over lettuce and onions making sure to distribute as evenly as possible; toss slightly. Cover this with a plate or bowl lid to allow the lettuce to wilt.

Sheri Moretz
Home Office

"This is a good dish to go along with pinto beans and cornbread. Corn or vegetable oil can be substituted for bacon drippings, but your lettuce will not "kill" as well. I love going to Granny and Papaw Moretz's house in the early summer because I know the lettuce is coming in from the garden. Whenever Granny knows I'm coming, she makes a big 'ol bowl of lettuce and onions. It's my favorite dish, and no matter how many folks are at the table, it seems that I eat the most. I can make a meal out of it."

My grandmother is a Cook, by family name and by talent. This photo was taken at a Cook Family reunion in the early 1960s (before I was born). It was always a large gathering at the family homeplace in Silverstone.

Broccoli Salad

1 bunch of broccoli, including stalk
1/4 cup chopped red onion
1/2 cup raisins
6 bacon strips, cooked crisp and crumbled
3/4 cup mayonnaise-type salad dressing
1/2 cup sugar
2 tablespoons vinegar

Chop broccoli, including peeled stalk. Mix with onion, raisins and bacon in a large bowl. In a small bowl, combine salad dressing, sugar and vinegar. Pour over broccoli salad and toss well to coat.

Joyce Crandall
Hendersonville

"For variety try adding sunflower seeds, ham strips or swiss cheese."

Pea Salad

3 to 4 (15 1/4-ounce) cans of peas, drained
1/4 cup finely chopped onion
3/4 to 1 cup sweet pickle relish
4 to 6 hard boiled eggs, chopped
1 cup mayonnaise
2 tablespoons mustard
Salt and pepper, to taste

Pour peas into mixing bowl. Add onion, pickle relish and hard boiled eggs. Mix together the mayonnaise, mustard, salt, pepper and some pickle juice. Carefully add the mayonnaise mixture to the peas. This should look creamy. Chill overnight. Garnish with hard boiled eggs or sliced green peppers.

Greta Hollar
Home Office

Jennings Winter Garden Salad

1 head of cauliflower
1 bunch of broccoli
1/2 cup coarsely chopped onions
1/4 cup finely chopped green onions
1/4 cup chopped celery
1/2 cup thinly sliced carrots
1/4 cup imitation bacon bits
1 cup cubed cheddar cheese

Dressing:
1/2 cup mayonnaise
1/3 cup vinegar
1/3 cup salad oil
1/4 cup sugar
salt and pepper, to taste

Wash and break cauliflower and broccoli into small bite size pieces. Mix cauliflower, broccoli, onions, celery, carrots, bacon bits and cheddar cheese together in a bowl. Mix mayonnaise, vinegar, salad oil, sugar, salt and pepper in a jar and tightly cover. Shake well and let stand for 5 minutes. Pour dressing over vegetables, cover bowl and refrigerate 12 to 24 hours. Toss the salad 2 or 3 times while marinating.

Sarah Morgan Ernst
Original Store

CAULIFLOWER SALAD

1 head cauliflower, broken into pieces
1 medium onion, chopped
1/2 cup sour cream
1/2 cup mayonnaise
1/4 cup sugar
Lettuce, enough leaves to line large bowl
1 pound bacon, cooked and crumbled

Combine cauliflower and onion in bowl. In another bowl, mix together sour cream, mayonnaise and sugar; pour over cauliflower and onion, stir. Refrigerate overnight. Before serving, mix again; place in lettuce-lined bowl. Top with crumbled bacon.

Mary Getchell
Asheville

SPICY CAULIFLOWER

1/2 cup oil
1/2 cup white vinegar
2 teaspoons salt
1 teaspoon sugar
1/4 teaspoon hot pepper sauce
1 small cauliflower separated into florets
1 (2-ounce) jar sliced pimentos, undrained

In a large bowl mix oil, vinegar, salt, sugar and pepper sauce. Cut cauliflower florets in half lengthwise. Place in a bowl and stirring gently, mix cauliflower, pimentos and oil mixture until cauliflower is well coated. Cover and refrigerate over night, stirring occasionally. When ready to serve, remove from refrigerator and drain. Serve on toothpicks as an appetizer or on lettuce as a salad.

Melanee Lester
Waynesville

SOUR CREAM POTATO SALAD

6 cups diced and cooked potatoes
1 teaspoon salt
1/4 cup chopped green onions
1/2 cup chopped celery
1/2 cup chopped pickles
1/2 teaspoon pepper
4 hard-boiled eggs, chopped
1 teaspoon dry mustard
1/2 cup mayonnaise
1/4 cup vinegar
1 cup sour cream

Combine potatoes, salt, onion, celery, pickles, pepper and two chopped eggs. Mix dry mustard, mayonnaise, vinegar and sour cream in a small bowl. Combine with potato mixture. Garnish with 2 remaining eggs.

Connie Gioscio
Home Office

At the turn-of-the-century, the Mast Store operated a soda fountain in the rear of the Original Store in Valle Crucis. This may have been the supplier of the "charged water" to make the fizzy favorites.

Salad Olivier

2 whole cooked chicken breasts, chopped
1 onion, chopped
2 teaspoons salt
1/2 cup chopped dill pickle
4 new potatoes, boiled, peeled and sliced thin
1/8 teaspoon white pepper
3 hard-cooked eggs, sliced thin
3/4 cup mayonnaise
3/4 cup sour cream, mixed with mayonnaise
2 tablespoons capers, drained well
6 large green olives with pimentoes, sliced
Boston lettuce
Tomatoes

Mix together chicken, onion, salt, pickle, potatoes, pepper, eggs, mayonnaine, sour cream, capers and olives. Serve on Boston lettuce with tomatoes on side.

Susan Benson
Home Office

Mandarin Orange Salad

1 (10-ounce) package marshmallows
2 (8.7-ounce) cans mandarin oranges, drained
1 (15 1/4-ounce) can pineapple tidbits
1 (1-pint) carton fat-free sour cream
1 (3 1/2-ounce) can angel flake coconut
2 (1.5-ounce) boxes of raisins

Mix marshmallows, oranges, pineapple, sour cream, coconut and raisins. Refrigerate overnight and serve cold.

Connie Gioscio
Home Office

WATERGATE SALAD

1 (20-ounce) can crushed pineapple
1/2 (10 1/2-ounce) bag small marshmallows
1 (3.4-ounce) box pistachio instant pudding mix
1 (8-ounce) carton frozen nondairy whipped topping
1/2 cup chopped walnuts
Maraschino cherries

Drain pineapple over marshmallows in a medium bowl. Blend pudding mix and whipped topping in another bowl. Add nuts, pineapple and marshmallows to pudding mixture. Serve with cherries on top.

Judy Phillips
Original Store

CRANBERRY SALAD

1 (6-ounce) box cherry, strawberry or raspberry flavored gelatin
1/2 packet unflavored gelatin
2 cups hot water
1 (15 1/4-ounce) can crushed pineapple, drained (save juice)
2 (16-ounce) cans whole cranberry sauce
1 cup chopped pecans

Mix flavored gelatin with the package of unflavored gelatin. Combine 2 cups of hot water and 1 1/2 cups of juice from the pineapple and stir into gelatin. When gelatin is dissolved, stir in cranberry sauce. Continue to stir until the cranberry sauce dissolves. Add pineapple and nuts after the gelatin mixture cools. Pour into one large gelatin mold or 16 small molds. Refrigerate until ready to serve.

Jill Meares
Asheville

LUCY'S FRESH CRANBERRY SALAD

2 cups fresh cranberries
1 medium apple, washed, cored and chopped
1 orange, washed and quartered (with rind)
1/2 cup sugar
1/4 teaspoon salt
1 (3-ounce) box orange flavored gelatin
1 cup hot water
1/2 cup cold water
1/2 cup chopped celery

Pick over, wash and drain cranberries. Put cranberries, apple and orange in a food processor. Chop well. Pour into medium bowl; add sugar and salt to fruit. Set aside. In another bowl, dissolve gelatin in hot water. Add cold water and chill until thickened. Stir cranberry mixture and celery into gelatin, pour into mold and chill until set.

Lucy Mast Olson
Valle Crucis

Lucy Mast Olsen and her husband, Richard Olsen, operated the store for a short period after W.W. Mast retired.

STRAWBERRY SALAD

1 (6-ounce) box strawberry/banana flavored gelatin
1 cup boiling water
2 (10-ounce) packages frozen strawberries, thawed
1 (15 1/4-ounce) can crushed pineapple, drained
3 to 4 bananas, sliced
1 cup chopped pecans
1 (8-ounce) carton frozen nondairy whipped topping, thawed
1 (8-ounce) carton sour cream
1/4 teaspoon vanilla

Dissolve gelatin in 1 cup boiling water. Add the thawed strawberries to the gelatin. In another bowl, mix together the pineapple and sliced bananas. Then add the pecans and gelatin mixture. Pour half of this into a 13 x 9-inch glass dish. Chill until set. Mix together the whipped topping, sour cream and vanilla. Spread this mixture over the chilled gelatin. Pour the rest of the gelatin mixture over the top of the whipped topping and gelatin in the dish. Refrigerate until completely chilled.

Greta Hollar
Home Office

"Low-fat or fat-free sour cream or whipped topping and sugar-free gelatin may be substituted."

Greta (left) and her sister, Rebecca, enjoying a snack.

ROSY TOASTIES

8 slices of white bread
Enough American sliced cheese to cover 4 slices
1 egg
1/4 cup ketchup
1/4 cup water
Margarine as needed

Make 4 sandwiches with the bread and cheese. Trim crusts if desired; cut each sandwich into 2 triangles. Beat egg and mix in ketchup and water. Dip each sandwich half into egg mixture. Saute slowly in margarine until brown on both sides.

Janet Bright
Hendersonville

"Personal note by mother 45 years ago: 'Joe (my daddy) says good for cheese.' (He didn't really like cheese much.) We kids loved them, as do my children and grandchildren."

CUCUMBER SANDWICHES

1 (8-ounce) package cream cheese, softened
1 (1.5-ounce) packet Italian salad dressing mix
1 loaf mini rye bread
1 cucumber, thinly sliced
Fresh or dried dill, to sprinkle on top

Mix cream cheese and Italian dressing mix. Spread on sliced bread. Top with sliced cucumbers and sprinkle with dill.

Joyce M. Crandall
Hendersonville

"This is a simple but very tasty appetizer or tea sandwich."

SKILLET SQUASH SANDWICHES

1 yellow squash, sliced
1 zucchini, sliced
1/4 cup chopped green onion
1/2 to 1 clove garlic, minced
1 tablespoon olive oil
2 plum tomatoes, chopped
Salt and ground black pepper, to taste
1 tablespoon red wine vinegar
1/4 cup mayonnaise
1/2 cucumber, diced
Dried basil, to taste
Muenster or any good white cheese, sliced
Sandwich rolls

Saute squash, zucchini, green onion and garlic in oil. Add tomatoes, salt, pepper and vinegar. Cook, stirring occasionally, until tomatoes are thoroughly heated. In a bowl combine mayonnaise, cucumber and basil. Spoon on bottom half of sandwich rolls. Top with vegetables. Layer with slices of cheese and top of roll. Bake in preheated 400° oven until cheese melts. Make sure top of roll doesn't get too dark.

Eron Schell
Annex

"Even my meat loving husband likes these. Makes a great summer meal, especially using onion rolls. I usually serve these with oven potatoes."

CARE OF FLOOR AND WOODWORK

Care of kitchen floor.

The best kitchen floor is of hard wood, oiled or varnished. If anything is spilled upon it, wipe or brush it up at once. Cover grease spots on wood or stone with flour, starch, or powdered chalk, which will absorb the grease. Cold water poured upon grease as soon as it is spilled will harden it; the greater part may then be scraped off. Sweep the kitchen floor thoroughly once a day. With care it will not need washing or scrubbing oftener than once a week.

How to sweep.

Before beginning to sweep, see that no food is left uncovered in the room. Sweep from the edges of the room toward the center. Sweep with short strokes, keeping the broom close to the floor. Turn it edgewise to clean cracks. When the dust has been gathered at one spot, take it up with a short broom and a dustpan, and if possible, burn it at once. Never sweep dust from one room into another. Always sweep a floor before washing or scrubbing it.

How to scrub a floor.

Softwood floors must be scrubbed. Provide two pails of cold or lukewarm water, a stiff scrubbing-brush, a large, soft, but not linty cloth, and soft soap and sand, or sand-soap. Dip the brush in water, then in soap, and lastly in sand. Look for grease-spots and take them out first. After the floor has become wet you cannot see where they are. Scrub with the grain of the wood, doing a few square feet at a time. Dip the cloth in clean water, and wash the part that has been scrubbed. Use no more water than you need. Wet the cloth again, wring it as dry as you can, and wipe the floor. Proceed in this way until the whole floor has been cleaned.

Care of hardwood floor.

On a hardwood floor use little water or none at all. Wipe it with a cloth moistened with a very little kerosene, - a teaspoonful or two to begin with, and as much more when that has evaporated. Rub hard with another cloth until the wood is perfectly dry. Windowsills and all hardwood finish may be cleaned in the same way.

Care of oilcloth.

Wash oilcloth with warm water and milk, - one cupful of skim milk to one gallon of water, - and wipe dry with a clean cloth.

* Cleaning paint. - To clean paint, provide whiting, two basins or pails of water, and three clean, soft cloths, - woolen is best. Take a little whiting on a damp cloth, and rub it on the surface to be cleaned. Do not let drops of water trickle down the paint. Wash off with a second cloth and clean water. Wipe dry with a third cloth. Clean a little at a time, leaving the cleaned part dry before going on.

Dusting.

After sweeping a room dust the woodwork, furniture, and movable articles with a soft cotton cloth. Spread the cloth out and gather the dust into it, folding it in as you work. Shake it frequently out of the window. In the kitchen where there are no delicate articles to be injured by moisture, use a damp cloth. To have it just damp enough, wet a part of it, wring this out, fold the damp part and the dry together, and squeeze them. When the room has been dusted, wash the cloth and hang it to dry.

Elements of the Theory and Practice of Cookery. A textbook copyrighted in 1901 and reprinted several times with the most recent one being in 1913.

You need the proper equipment to care for your kitchen.

BREADS

Old Boone Mercantile

The town of Boone was named for the frontiersman Daniel Boone, who maintained a hunting cabin in the area in the late 1700s. Before the name Boone was bestowed on the town it was known as Councill's Store, a landmark that was along a trading route that lay at the foot of Howard's Knob. The town was incorporated in 1871 (or 1872 depending upon your source) and is the county seat of Watauga County (Watauga is a Native American word meaning "beautiful waters").

As a side note, Valle Crucis was also considered for the location of the county seat, as well as a possible home for Appalachian State University. Jordan Councill and Ransom Hayes donated 25 acres each in Boone to locate the courthouse there.

The building housing Mast Store's Old Boone Mercantile has a varied history. Part of it was constructed in 1913 and part of it was built four years later in 1917. It once housed the People's Bank, which was closed down by the government in the Depression. In 1936 or so, the building housed a department store and a 5¢ & 10¢ store. Upstairs during this period, the area's first radio station was operated.

Guy Hunt opened his department store in the larger part of the building around 1940. Hunt's would remain a downtown fixture until 1987 when John and

Faye Cooper purchased the building to move in the Mast Store. The store has maintained much of the same atmosphere that attracted shoppers to Hunt's including old light fixtures, a "y'd" staircase, the creaking floorboards, and the neighborly service.

The Hunt's building is now Mast Store's Old Boone Mercantile. This picture was taken in the 1950s.

BANANA BREAD

3 cups sugar
1 cup oil
4 eggs
2 cups mashed bananas
1 teaspoon vanilla
3 cups plain flour
1 teaspoon baking soda
1 teaspoon baking powder
1/2 teaspoon salt
1 cup chopped black walnuts

Beat together sugar, oil and eggs. Stir in bananas and vanilla. Mix in the flour, soda, baking powder and salt. Mix well. Add nuts last. Divide mixture into two regular size loaf pans. Bake in preheated 350° oven for 1 hour or until cake tester inserted in center comes out clean. Turn pans over to remove breads.

Joyce M. Crandall
Hendersonville

"This recipe was given to me by a friend who worked at the Original Mast Store several years ago. It is so simple and so good."

A Crandall family get together.

Old Fashioned Cinnamon Loaf

1 package dry yeast
1/2 cup warm water
1 1/2 cups milk, scalded, cooled
1/2 cup mashed potatoes
1 cup sugar
7 1/2 cups plain flour
2 teaspoons salt
2 teaspoons cinnamon
1 teaspoon ground cloves
1/2 teaspoon nutmeg
2 tablespoons butter, melted

Dissolve yeast in warm water. In a large mixing bowl, combine yeast, milk, potatoes and sugar. In another bowl, mix together flour, salt, cinnamon, cloves and nutmeg. Gradually mix together flour and potato mixtures with butter. Make into a ball and knead 8 to 10 minutes. Place in an oiled bowl, cover and let rise. Punch down, cover and let rise again. Do this once more, then divide dough and shape into 2 loaves. Place into greased 9-inch loaf pans and brush tops with butter. Let rise. Bake in preheated 350° oven for 15 minutes. Increase temperature to 425° and cook until golden brown. Brush tops with butter. Cool.

Teresa Presnell
Original Store

GRAPE NUTS BREAD

1 cup grape nuts cereal
2 cups buttermilk
1 egg, well beaten
1 cup sugar
4 cups all-purpose flour
4 teaspoons baking powder
1 teaspoon salt
1 teaspoon baking soda

Soak cereal in milk for 20 minutes. Stir in egg and sugar. Add flour, baking powder, salt and soda. Pour batter in 2 greased 9-inch loaf pans. Bake in preheated 350° oven for about 40 minutes.

Kitty Rominger
Home Office

POPPY SEED BREAD

1 cup boiling water
2 tablespoons poppy seeds
1 box butter pecan cake mix
3 extra large eggs
1 (3.4-ounce) box coconut cream instant pudding mix
1/2 cup vegetable oil

Combine water and poppy seeds and let stand while mixing together other ingredients. In a large bowl, mix together by hand, cake mix, eggs, pudding mix and oil. Add poppy seed mix to batter. Pour batter into 2 loaf pans. Bake in preheated 350° oven for about 40 minutes. Cool on racks for 15 minutes. Then slice and serve.

April Trivette
Original Store

ZUCCHINI BREAD

3 eggs, beaten
2 cups sugar
1 cup vegetable oil
1 teaspoon vanilla
3 1/2 cups sifted all-purpose flour
1 teaspoon salt
1 teaspoon baking soda
1/4 teaspoon baking powder
3 teaspoons cinnamon
2 cups grated zucchini
1 cup chopped pecans or walnuts

Combine eggs, sugar, oil and vanilla; beat well. In another bowl mix flour, salt, soda, baking powder and cinnamon. Stir in zucchini and nuts. Pour into 2 well greased 9 x 5 x 3-inch loaf pans. Bake in preheated 350° oven for 1 hour or until well done. Cool in pans 5 minutes. Remove from pans and finish cooling on rack. Serve with butter or cream cheese.

Jill Meares
Asheville

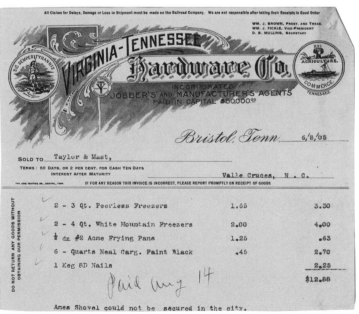

This invoice from 1905 shows one of the favorites we still carry in the store today - a White Mountain freezer for making ice cream.

LOW-FAT BRAN MUFFINS

1 cup all-purpose flour
1/3 cup brown sugar, firmly packed
1 1/2 teaspoons baking powder
1/2 teaspoon baking soda
1/2 teaspoon ground cinnamon
2 cups 100% bran cereal
1 1/4 cups skim milk
1/2 cup applesauce
1 egg

Mix flour, brown sugar, baking powder, soda and cinnamon in large bowl. In another bowl, mix cereal and milk; let stand for at least 5 minutes. Stir the applesauce and egg into cereal mixture. Add the cereal mixture to flour mixture; stir just until moistened (batter will be lumpy.) Spray a muffin pan with nonstick cooking spray. Fill each cup 2/3 full. Bake in preheated 400° oven for 18 to 20 minutes or until golden brown. Serve warm. These freeze well.

Jill Meares
Asheville

EASY HOMEMADE BISCUITS

2 cups self-rising flour
1/2 cup shortening
1 cup milk
1 stick butter or margarine, as needed

Put flour in a medium mixing bowl. Cut in shortening. Add milk and mix with a fork. Add additional flour until dough is stiff and not sticky. Turn dough out onto a lightly floured surface. Knead slightly and form into a ball. Use rolling pin to roll out dough to about 5/8 inch thick. Cut biscuits. Take remaining dough and repeat the process until all is used. You'll have just a little left. Roll it up in a ball, flatten it a little and put it on your cookie sheet, too. (This is a cathead, which is my favorite biscuit of all.) Cut a thin sliver of butter to put on top of each biscuit. Bake in preheated 450° oven for about 15 minutes, until tops are yellow-brown and bottoms are golden.

Sheri Moretz
Home Office

Sheri Moretz singing Christmas carols in 1967.

APPLE CINNAMON BISCUITS

2 cups self-rising flour
1 teaspoon ground cinnamon
1/2 cup shortening
1/2 cup finely chopped apples
2/3 to 3/4 cup milk

Mix flour and cinnamon together. Cut in shortening until crumbly. Stir
in apples and milk. Turn dough onto lightly floured surface. Knead
dough 10 times gently. Roll or pat dough 3/4 inch thick. Cut dough
with floured 2-inch biscuit cutter. Place about 1 inch apart on ungreased
cookie sheet. Bake in preheated 450° oven 12 to 15 minutes or until
light golden brown.

Glaze:
1 cup powdered sugar
4 to 6 teaspoons water

In a small bowl, combine powdered sugar and water until smooth. Pour
over cooled biscuits.

Catherine L. Main
Original Store

How to Have Good Coffee.

1. Buy freshly roasted, unground coffee, and grind it at home as needed; or
buy it freshly ground every two or three days. The longer it is kept after
roasting, particularly if ground, the more of its aroma does it lose.
2. Keep in an airtight can or jar.
3. Use an enameled or earthen coffeepot that is scoured clean, not omitting
the spout, after each using.
4. Either filter the coffee, or boil it not longer than three minutes.
5. Have coffee powdered for filtering finely ground for boiling.
6. Serve with hot, but not scalded, milk.

*Elements of the Theory and Practice of Cookery. A textbook copyrighted in 1901
and reprinted several times with the most recent one being in 1913.*

ANGEL BISCUITS

1 package dry yeast
1/4 cup warm water
5 cups plain flour
1/2 cup sugar
1 teaspoon baking soda
2 teaspoons salt
3 teaspoons baking powder
1 cup shortening
1 1/2 cups buttermilk

Dissolve yeast in warm water. Sift the flour, sugar, soda, salt and baking powder together in a large mixing bowl. Add the shortening; blend until crumbly. Add buttermilk, then dissolved yeast mixture; stir well. Cover bowl and chill. Make biscuits as needed. Place biscuits on a baking sheet and brush with melted butter. Cover and let rise in a warm place for 2 hours. Bake in preheated 400° oven for 15 minutes or until lightly brown. Dough will keep in refrigerator for 3 to 5 days, or make biscuits and freeze. Thaw and let rise, then bake.

Rebecca A. Fry
Boone Store

"Good for a crowd or weekend guests. I sometimes add 1 tablespoon chopped parsley and 1/2 cup finely grated cheddar cheese. Drop by tablespoons on a baking sheet, let rise 1 hour and bake as usual. They taste as good as restaurant biscuits."

CHRISTMAS ANGEL BISCUITS

1 package dry yeast
2 tablespoons warm water
1/4 teaspoon sugar
5 cups self-rising flour
1 cup shortening
2 cups buttermilk

Dissolve yeast in warm water. Stir sugar into flour and cut in shortening until mixture resembles fine crumbs. Stir in buttermilk and yeast. Dough should be soft and sticky. Turn dough onto generously floured board; roll in flour and shape into a ball. Knead 25 to 30 times, adding flour as needed. Place dough into greased bowl. Cover and refrigerate at least 3 hours, but no longer than 3 days. Use as needed. Roll dough 1/2 inch thick and cut with floured biscuit cutter. Place on ungreased cookie sheet. Let rise until doubled. Bake in preheated 400° oven until golden brown, 12 to 14 minutes. Remove immediately from baking sheet.

Jill Meares
Asheville

"After Henry and I had children, Christmas was at our house. To keep little ones from getting too hungry and filling up on stocking candy, we decided to open stockings, enjoy what we found there and play with the gifts from Santa. While this was happening, the angel biscuits, which had been prepared the day before, were removed from the refrigerator, allowed to rise, and placed in the oven to bake. Sometime between midnight and the fire being lighted on Christmas morning, jams, jellies, juice, plates, cups, etc. were set on the table. Just as the youngest one tired of Santa's gifts, breakfast was ready. After breakfast, Dad (Henry) handed out gifts. We let one person open their gift before going on to the next one so everyone had a chance to see and exclaim over each gift. It takes a long time to do it this way, but we enjoy the leisurely morning."

Rolls

1 package dry yeast
2 cups warm water
4 cups self-rising flour
1/2 cup sugar
3/4 cup oil
1 egg

Dissolve yeast in warm water and add to flour, sugar, oil and egg. Mix well; batter should pour easily. Grease muffin tins and fill 3/4 full with batter. Bake in preheated 400° oven for 25 minutes. Batter will keep in refrigerator for a week to 10 days. Keep well covered.

Lucy Mast Olsen
Valle Crucis

Grandma's #1 Rolls

1 yeast cake or 2 packages dry yeast
1/2 cup lukewarm water
1/2 cup butter or margarine
1/2 cup sugar
1 tablespoon salt
1 cup boiling water
1 cup cold water
2 eggs, well beaten
8 1/2 cups sifted all-purpose flour

Dissolve yeast in 1/2 cup lukewarm water. Place butter, broken into small pieces, sugar and salt in a large bowl. Add 1 cup boiling water. When the butter has melted, add 1 cup cold water, eggs and yeast mixture. Stir in sifted flour. Place in a greased bowl, cover and store in the refrigerator. Make rolls as needed and bake in a preheated 400° oven for about 20 minutes.

William and Anne Wilson
Home Office

QUICK GARLIC-PARMESAN ROLLS

2 cups self-rising flour
4 tablespoons mayonnaise
1 cup milk
6 tablespoons grated parmesan cheese
1 clove garlic, pressed
Garlic flavored cooking oil spray

Mix together flour, mayonnaise, milk, cheese and garlic. Spray muffin tins with garlic spray. Fill muffin tins 3/4 full. Bake in preheated 450° oven for 10 minutes or until golden. Spray tins after each batch.

Allen Mast
Original Store

"I prefer the mini-muffin pans because they give the rolls crunchier edges."

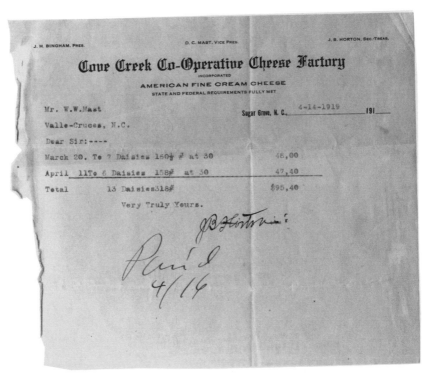

Cove Creek, a community just across Mast Gap, had a small cheese factory. D.C. Mast was the Vice President - he was related to the W.W. Mast family.

Herb French Bread

6 tablespoons butter, softened
1 to 2 garlic cloves, minced
2 teaspoons dried parsley flakes
1/2 teaspoon dried oregano
1/2 teaspoon dill weed
1 teaspoon parmesan cheese
1 loaf French bread, sliced

In medium bowl, combine butter, garlic, parsley, oregano, dill and cheese. Mix well. Spread on bread slices. Wrap in foil and bake in preheated 350° oven for 20 minutes.

Melanee Lester
Waynesville

Corn Fritter Bread

2 (8 1/2-ounce) boxes corn muffin mix
2 eggs, beaten
1 (14 3/4-ounce) can cream corn
1 (29-ounce) can whole kernel sweet corn, drained
1 (8-ounce) carton sour cream
1 stick butter or margarine, melted

Blend together muffin mixes, eggs, cream corn, whole kernel corn, sour cream and butter. Grease a 9 x 13-inch baking dish with margarine and pour in batter. Bake in preheated 350° oven for 30 to 40 minutes or until top is golden brown. Serve warm.

Greta Hollar
Home Office

"Low fat sour cream and egg substitute may be used."

CRACKLING CORN BREAD

2 cups cornmeal
3/4 cup flour
1 tablespoon sugar
1 cup milk
Water, if needed to thin mixture
Oil
1 cup cracklings

Mix and sift together cornmeal, flour and sugar. Add milk and water. Pour in heavy skillet with hot oil in it. Sprinkle cracklings over top and press them into mixture. Bake in preheated 375° oven for 30 minutes or until brown on top.

Debe Jones
Home Office

"I grew up on a farm below Tater Hill in Silverstone, North Carolina. We always raised a pig which we killed in the fall. We would take the fat strips from the pig and cook it down for the lard. The pieces that were left are called cracklings. Mom would make crackling corn bread for supper. My brother, Doug, loved it so much he thought he was in hog heaven when Mom made it. Crackling corn bread is really good with tenderloin, mashed potatoes and shelly beans."

Sweet Cornbread

1 cup yellow cornmeal
1 cup flour
2 tablespoons sugar
4 teaspoons baking powder
1/2 teaspoon salt
1 cup milk
1 egg
1/4 cup shortening

Blend together cornmeal, flour, sugar, baking powder, salt, milk, egg and shortening for about 20 seconds. Beat vigorously for 1 minute. Pour into greased 9 x 9 x 2-inch pan. Bake in preheated 425° oven for 20 to 25 minutes or until golden brown.

Jill Meares
Asheville

"Note: I melt the shortening in my cast iron frying pan and stir the melted shortening into the cornmeal mixture. Then I pour the mixture into the cast iron pan and bake."

Bottle cap checkers by the pot-bellied stove at the Original Store in Valle Crucis.

Homemade Crackers

3 cups quick-cooking oats, uncooked
2 cups unbleached flour
1 cup wheat germ
3 tablespoons sugar
1 teaspoon salt
3/4 cup canola oil
1 cup water

Combine oats, flour, wheat germ, sugar and salt in large bowl. Mix well. Add oil and water, stirring until dry ingredients are moistened. Divide mixture onto 2 ungreased cookie sheets. Roll mixture directly on cookie sheet to about 1/8 inch thickness. Cut into 2-inch squares or diamonds. Bake in preheated 350° oven for 20 to 25 minutes. Separate crackers and let cool on wire rack or counter. Store in tightly covered container.

Mary Getchell
Asheville

"Crisp and delicious!"

Pineapple Stuffing

1/2 cup butter or margarine
1 cup sugar
4 eggs, beaten
1 (20-ounce) can crushed pineapple
5 slices of bread, cubed

Cream butter and sugar; add eggs. Fold in pineapple and bread cubes; mix well. Turn into a well greased 1-quart baking dish and bake in preheated 350° oven for 1 hour.

Janet Bright
Hendersonville

CHEESE STRAWS

1 (10-ounce) package cheddar cheese, grated
3 sticks margarine
4 cups all-purpose flour
1/2 teaspoon dry mustard
1/4 teaspoon paprika
Cayenne or red pepper, to taste

Combine cheese, margarine, flour, mustard, paprika and pepper together in a food processor. Process until all ingredients are mixed together thoroughly. Use a pastry bag to pipe into desired shape. Bake in preheated 400° oven for 12 minutes. Yield: 60 or more depending on size.

Jeanne Norris
Home Office

SPECIAL GUEST CHEESE STRAWS

1/4 cup salted butter
1 pound extra sharp cheddar cheese, grated
1/2 teaspoon salt
1/2 teaspoon ground red pepper
1 3/4 cups plain flour

Cream butter; add cheese, salt and pepper. Add flour. Put into cookie press or roll thin into narrow strips. Arrange on cookie sheets and bake in a preheated 350° oven for 20 minutes or until golden brown.

Fred Martin
Home Office

SUNDAY MORNING PANCAKES

1 cup flour
1/4 cup wheat germ
1 teaspoon baking soda
1/2 teaspoon salt
1 egg
1 egg white (beaten with whole egg)
1/4 cup canola oil
1/4 cup honey
2 cups buttermilk

Whisk together flour, wheat germ, soda and salt. In another bowl combine eggs, oil, honey and buttermilk. Mix together dry and wet ingredients. Thin batter with water if necessary. Pour batter on preheated griddle at medium heat; turn when the pancakes start bubbling. Remove from griddle when lightly browned, top with maple syrup.

Mary Gretchell
Asheville

"With left-over batter make very large pancakes. When done, spread with butter and sprinkle with brown sugar. Roll up, wrap and save for later. 'Pancake Rollups' are a great version of trail food!"

Lucy's Spoon Bread

2 cups milk
1/2 cup cornmeal
1 tablespoon butter
2 eggs, separated

Heat milk and cornmeal in a pan until thickened. Add butter, then cool. Beat egg yolks and add to mixture. Beat egg whites and fold into mixture. Pour into greased glass casserole and bake in preheated 350° oven for 35 minutes.

Lucy Mast Olsen
Valle Crucis

Lucy's Other Spoon Bread

1 cup boiling water
1/4 cup cornmeal
1 tablespoon butter
2 eggs, separated
1/2 cup milk

To boiling water, slowly add cornmeal and stir for 1 minute. Remove from heat and add butter. Beat well; cool. Beat egg yolks and stir into mixture. Add milk; mix well. Fold in beaten egg whites. Pour into greased baking dish and bake in preheated 400° oven for 35 minutes.

Lucy Mast Olsen
Valle Crucis

ENTREES

Waynesville

The town of Waynesville was incorporated in 1810. First mentions of the newly named town in law documents were in 1811 (it was called Mount Prospect). Colonel Robert Love offered the name of Waynesville to honor the

Downtown Waynesville around the turn of the century. Photo courtesy of the Enterprise Mountaineer.

memory of General "Mad" Anthony Wayne whom he served under in the Revolutionary War. The town also has the distinction of being the last place in North Carolina where shots were fired during the Civil War.

Downtown Waynesville, circa 1971. Photo courtesy of the Enterprise Mountaineer.

The Mast Store in Waynesville was built during the 1930s as "The Toggery." It was a fine clothier carrying men's and ladies' fashions along with a shoe department. The mezzanine at that time was a combination of storage and office area. They engineered a unique way to send messages from the office area to the sales floor by rigging a pulley system to facilitate the exchange of information.

In 1991, this store opened for business as a part of the Mast Store organization. Many of the fixtures are from the turn of the century and came from a store located just outside of Spartanburg, South Carolina. The pressed tin ceiling is original to the building.

The Mast Store in Waynesville is located on Main Street.

Chicken a la Maria

3/4 cup fine Italian-seasoned bread crumbs
1/4 cup grated parmesean cheese
6 whole chicken breasts, skinned, split and boned
1/2 cup sliced green onion
2 tablespoons butter
2 tablespoons all-purpose flour
1 cup milk
1 (10-ounce) package frozen chopped spinach,
  thawed and drained
1 (4-ounce) package boiled ham slices, diced

Combine bread crumbs and cheese. Dip the chicken halves in mixture, coating lightly. Arrange in baking dish. Set aside remaining crumb mixture. In saucepan cook onion in butter until tender. Blend in flour and stir in milk all at once. Cook and stir till bubbly; then stir 1 minute more. Stir in spinach and ham. Spoon mixture over chicken and sprinkle with remaining crumb mixture. Bake uncovered in preheated 350° oven for 40 to 45 minutes.

Pamela Biemiller
Waynesville

CHICKEN PARMESAN

1/2 cup corn flake crumbs or bread crumbs
1/2 cup grated parmesan cheese
1/2 teaspoon dried thyme
1/2 teaspoon dried oregano
1/2 teaspoon pakrika
1/4 teaspoon salt
2 egg whites, lightly beaten
4 chicken breast halves, boned and skinned
2 tablespoons butter or margarine, melted
1 (1-pint) jar spaghetti sauce

In pie plate combine crumbs, cheese, thyme, oregano, paprika and salt. Pour beaten egg whites into second pie plate. Dip chicken into egg whites, then into crumb-cheese mixture, coating evenly. Place chicken in greased shallow 1-quart baking dish. Drizzle butter over chicken. Bake uncovered in preheated 350° oven for 20 to 25 minutes or until chicken is no longer pink in center. Heat spaghetti sauce and spoon over chicken when ready to serve. Good with noodles.

Jill Meares
Asheville

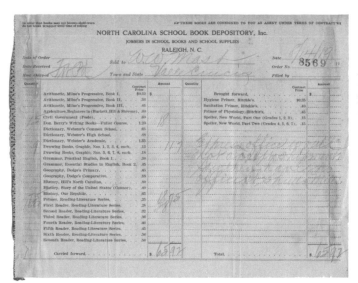

The Mast Store had goods for every aspect of life. In the early years of public education students had to purchase their own books, which would often be passed to younger children in the family as the older ones moved to more difficult lessons.

CHICKEN GOURMET

4 or 5 whole chicken breasts
Salt, to taste
1 carrot, sliced
2 celery tops
1 onion, quartered
1 (10 3/4-ounce) can cream of mushroom soup
2 cups sour cream
1/2 cup sauterne
1 (7-ounce) bag herb-seasoned stuffing mix
1 stick butter

Simmer chicken breasts in salted water with carrot, celery tops and onion, until done. Cool in broth. Pull meat off bones into fairly large pieces and place in bottom of shallow baking dish. Mix soup with sour cream and wine, and pour over chicken. Heat a cup of chicken broth and melt butter in broth. Toss into stuffing, mix lightly with fork; sprinkle over chicken. Bake uncovered in preheated 350° oven for 1 hour.

Pamela Biemiller
Waynesville

Chicken Divan

2 (10-ounce) packages frozen chopped broccoli
2 cups diced cooked chicken
1 cup mayonnaise
1 teaspoon lemon juice
1/2 teaspoon curry powder
2 (10 3/4-ounce) cans cream of chicken soup
1 tablespoon butter
1/2 cup bread crumbs
1/2 cup shredded cheese

Place broccoli in 8 x 10-inch pan which has been coated with vegetable cooking spray. Cover broccoli with chicken. Mix mayonnaise, lemon juice, curry powder and soup. Pour over top of chicken. Melt butter and toss well with bread crumbs. Spread crumbs and cheese evenly on top. Bake in preheated 375° oven for 20 to 25 minutes.

Faye Cooper
Home Office

"Note: when you pour sauce on chicken and broccoli, use a spatula along side and up and down to get into casserole. This recipe is good served with oranges, carrots, rolls and butter."

Recipe booklets were often used as promotions. Judging from the inside copy, we think this one was published by Purina. They say "Ask for Purina Flavor-Fed Domestic Rabbit."

CRUMB CHICKEN

1 roll of round butter crackers, crushed
1/2 cup grated parmesan cheese
8 to 10 chicken tenders
1 stick margarine, melted
Salt and pepper, to taste

Mix crushed crackers and parmesan cheese in a zip-top plastic bag. Dip chicken tenders in the melted margarine. Put them in the plastic bag one at a time and shake until well covered. Place chicken in a deep casserole dish and sprinkle with the leftover cracker and cheese mixture. Salt and pepper to taste. Pour the remainder of the butter over the chicken. Bake in preheated 350° oven for about 30 minutes or until top is golden brown.

Jessica Kirton
Home Office

ITALIAN PARMESAN CHICKEN

4 chicken breast halves
1 (8-ounce) bottle Italian salad dressing
2 cups grated parmesan cheese

Remove skin from chicken, rinse and pat dry. Place chicken in deep container and cover with Italian dressing. Cover container and place in refrigerator overnight. Remove chicken from marinade; roll in parmesan cheese. Place on baking sheet and bake in preheated 350° oven for 20 minutes or until chicken is golden brown and juices run clear when pierced with a fork.

Kelly Mast
Boone and Original Store

BAKED CHICKEN WITH GRAVY

2 pounds chicken pieces
1 (10 3/4-ounce) can cream of chicken soup
1/4 cup water
Pepper, to taste

In a greased 13 x 9-inch baking pan, arrange chicken pieces skin up. Mix together soup and water; pour over chicken. Sprinkle with pepper. Bake in preheated 350° oven for about an hour, or until tender.

Janet Bright
Hendersonville

"Mixed with chicken juices, this makes a good gravy. Serve with rice or mashed potatoes. Easy, easy! For more gravy, use another can of soup with 1/4 cup of water."

SESAME CHICKEN

4 chicken breasts halves
1 (12-ounce) can evaporated milk
1/3 cup plain bread crumbs
1/3 cup grated parmesan cheese
1/3 cup sesame seeds
1/2 teaspoon salt
1/4 teaspoon pepper
1 egg, beaten
3 tablespoons olive oil

In a large bowl, combine chicken and evaporated milk; refrigerate 1 hour. Combine bread crumbs, parmesan cheese, sesame seeds, salt and pepper. Dip chicken in egg, then coat with bread mixture. Place skin side up in a baking dish and drizzle with olive oil. Bake in preheated 350° oven for 1 hour or until chicken is done.

Connie Gioscio
Home Office

ZESTY LEMON CHICKEN

6 whole boneless, skinless chicken breasts
2 cups lemon juice (9 to 10 lemons)
1 cup flour
1 teaspoon salt
2 teaspoons paprika
1/4 teaspoon pepper
1/2 cup canola oil
1/3 cup packed light brown sugar
2 tablespoons grated lemon rind, zest only
1/4 cup chicken broth
2 lemons, sliced
Chopped parsley

Lay chicken in a casserole dish. Pour lemon juice over each piece. Cover and refrigerate overnight or slightly longer. Remove chicken from marinade and pat dry. Reserve 2 tablespoons of marinade. Mix flour, salt, paprika and pepper. Dredge chicken to coat evenly. Heat oil in large skillet and fry breasts a few at a time until well browned, about 10 minutes. Arrange chicken in single layer in a large baking dish. Spoon brown sugar on chicken and press down slightly. Sprinkle on lemon zest. Mix broth with 2 tablespoons of reserved marinade. Pour around chicken. Bake in preheated 350° oven about 30 minutes or until tender. Before serving, top with lemon slices and chopped parsley.

Gabrielle Wheeler
Hendersonville

"I use chicken bouillon cubes to make the broth."

CHICKEN LIVERS AND RICE-A-RONI

1 box Rice-A-Roni
1 container chicken livers
1 (10 3/4-ounce) can cream of mushroom soup
1/2 can milk

Cook Rice-A-Roni as directed on package. Brown livers. Combine rice, livers, soup and milk. Bake in casserole dish in preheated 350° oven for 30 minutes.

Mary Hazel Mast
Valle Crucis

CHICKEN LIVERS MONTREAL

4 strips bacon, cut in half
1 large onion, halved and sliced
1 bell pepper, seeded and sliced
1 pound chicken livers
1 (10 1/2-ounce) can beef broth, plus 1/2 can water
2 tablespoons cornstarch dissolved in 1/4 cup water
1/4 teaspoon black pepper
Salt, to taste

Cook bacon until just crispy, set aside. In bacon grease, saute onions until half done, then add peppers. When done, remove from pan and saute chicken livers. Drain livers and vegetables on paper towels. Clean pan of all bacon grease and add beef broth and water. While simmering, thicken with cornstarch mixture. Return chicken livers, onions, peppers and seasoning to gravy and heat through. Serve over rice and garnish with bacon.

Janet Bright
Hendersonville

"This is my version of a dish we ate in Montreal."

CHICKEN CHIMICHANGAS

1 pound chicken breasts, cooked and shredded
1/2 cup sliced green onion
1/4 teaspoon cumin
1/2 teaspoon oregano
Salt to taste
1 (16-ounce) jar salsa, divided
8 flour tortillas
1 (8-ounce) package shredded monterey jack or cheddar cheese
Sour Cream

Combine chicken, onion, cumin, oregano and salt in a large sauce pan. Stir in 3/4's of salsa. Cover and cook over medium heat for 5 minutes, stirring often. Spoon 2 tablespoons or more of chicken in the center of each tortilla. Sprinkle with cheese and add sour cream to taste. Fold sides to partially enclose filling, then fold top and bottom edges to make a square. Put folded side down in a lightly-greased baking dish. Bake in preheated 475° oven for 13 to 15 minutes. Top with remaining salsa and sour cream before serving.

Eron Schell
Annex

Chicken Enchiladas

1 pound boneless, skinless chicken breasts
1 can chopped green chilies
1 (10-3/4 ounce) can cream of mushroom soup
1/4 cup chopped green onion
1 cup sour cream
Flour tortillas
Taco sauce
1 cup shredded Monterey Jack cheese

Boil chicken, cool and hand shred. Combine chicken, chilies, soup, onion and sour cream. Spoon onto tortillas and roll up. Place rolled tortillas in a baking dish and top with taco sauce. Cover, bake in preheated 350° oven for 20 minutes. Uncover, sprinkle with cheese and return to oven until cheese is melted.

Eron Schell
Annex

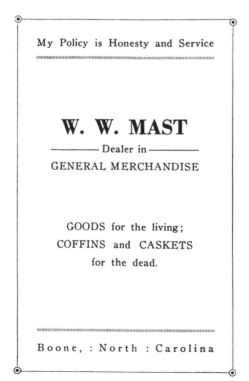

An actual ad from the 1923 Appalachian State University Yearbook.

JAMBALAYA

1/2 cup chopped onion
1/2 cup chopped green pepper
2 carrots, sliced
1 clove garlic, minced
1 tablespoon olive oil
3 to 4 (14-ounce) cans diced tomatoes
1 teaspoon oregano
1 teaspoon basil
Salt and pepper, to taste
1/2 teaspoon paprika
1/4 teaspoon red pepper flakes
2 cups cooked rice
3 to 4 chicken thighs, cooked and shredded (optional)
1 pound raw shrimp, shelled and de-veined

Saute onion, peppers, carrots and garlic in oil in large pot. Add tomatoes, oregano, basil, salt, pepper, paprika and red pepper flakes. Bring to a slight boil, then lower heat to a medium-low setting, stirring occasionally. Simmer for 15 to 20 minutes or longer. Add rice and chicken to jambalaya. Add shrimp about 5 minutes before serving and cook until shrimp turns pink.

Eron Schell
Annex

"I usually serve with a spoonful of sour cream added to each bowl."

Burgundy Pepper Steak

1/2 cup red wine
1/2 teaspoon ground black pepper
1 clove garlic, pressed
2 teaspoons soy sauce
2 steaks

Combine wine, pepper, garlic and soy sauce in a gallon zip-top plastic bag. Shake well to mix. Add steaks to bag and shake well to coat. Marinate in refrigerator for 18 to 24 hours. To cook, put steaks in a non-stick pan with 2 teaspoons of marinade. Throw away rest of marinade. Cover pan with lid and turn burner to medium. Cook for 3 minutes. Leave lid on pan and turn heat to low. Cook for an additional 12 minutes or until done to your liking.

Allen Mast
Original Store

Corned Beef Venison

5 teaspoons tender-quick salt
2 teaspoons brown sugar
1 teaspoon ground black pepper
1 teaspoon ground paprika
1/2 teaspoon ground allspice
1 teaspoon garlic powder
Vension roast

Mix salt, sugar, pepper, paprika, allspice and garlic in bowl. Rub well into roast, using all spice mix. Place roast in large zip-top plastic bag. Cure in refrigerator 10 days, turning roast every day. At the end of 10 days, place roast in pot, with water to cover only. Bring to boil, reduce temperature and simmer 3 to 4 hours.

Mary Getchell
Asheville

Szechwan Beef

2 tablespoons cooking sherry
4 to 5 shakes Tamari sauce
Szechwan sauce
1/2 pound flank steak, thinly sliced
2 cloves garlic, minced
2 tablespoons cooking oil
1 medium onion, cut in strips
2 to 3 stalks celery, cut in strips
2 to 3 carrots, cut in strips
1 cup broccoli florets

In a measuring cup mix sherry and Tamari sauce. Add enough Szechwan sauce to make a 1/4 cup. Pour over beef. Marinate beef in sauce for at least 30 minutes. In wok, stir fry garlic in cooking oil. Crush garlic. Add onion, celery and carrots. Stir fry for 3 to 4 minutes. Add beef and marinade mix. Stir fry until done. Add broccoli and heat thoroughly. Serve over rice.

Sean Finneron
Home Office

Baked Beef Stew

2 pounds cubed beef
1 large onion, sliced
Celery, carrots and potatoes, to taste
Salt and pepper, to taste
1 tablespoon sugar
3 tablespoons tapioca
1 (28-ounce) can tomatoes or tomato juice

Place beef in bottom of roaster. Cover with sliced onion, celery, carrots and potatoes. Sprinkle with salt and pepper, sugar and tapioca. Pour tomatoes and juice over all. Cover and bake in preheated 325° oven for 3 to 4 hours.

Mary Getchell
Asheville

Minorcan Shrimp Pilare

2 pounds raw shrimp
1/2 pound bacon
1 (8-ounce) can tomatoes, chopped
4 medium onions, chopped
1 small red or green pepper, chopped
Salt, to taste
3 1/2 cups water
2 cups rice

Wash and de-vein shrimp; cut each in half. Dice bacon and cook over low heat until crisp. Remove half of bacon from pan and add tomatoes, onion, peppers and salt. Cook until thick and browned. Add shrimp. Cook about 5 minutes, then add water. Put mixture in a heavy pot and bring to a boil. Add rice and again bring to a quick boil. Add remaining bacon. Turn heat to low and cook, tightly covered, until rice is tender and has absorbed all the moisture. Stir occasionally while cooking.

Melanee Lester
Waynesville

"Medium sized shrimp have the best flavor. Thyme, marjoram (up to 1 tablespoon) and garlic may be added with the onion."

Melanee Lester's family homestead in Mandarin, Florida (above) and Melanee in 1964 (right).

Shrimp with Garlic and Plum Tomatoes

2 to 3 garlic cloves, minced
1/4 cup olive oil
5 to 6 plum tomatoes, chopped
Dash of white wine
1 teaspoon parsley, or to taste
1 teaspoon basil, or to taste
1 1/2 pounds raw shrimp, peeled
Linguini pasta, cooked, served hot
Parmesan cheese, grated, to taste

Saute garlic in olive oil until fragrant. Add tomatoes, wine, parsley and basil. Add shrimp and cook until shrimp are pink. Serve on hot linguini and top with parmesan cheese.

Eron Schell
Annex

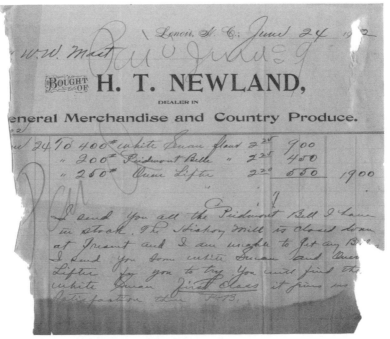

Sometimes our vendors would run short on items we ordered. Here a personal note in beautiful penmanship explains the situation.

SHRIMP AND WILD RICE

1/2 cup chopped onion
1/3 cup chopped green pepper
1/4 cup margarine
1 (28-ounce) can tomatoes, cut up
1 3/4 cups water
1/2 teaspoon salt
1/4 teaspoon pepper
1/4 teaspoon garlic salt
1/4 teaspoon dried rosemary, crushed
1/4 teaspoon paprika
1 (6-ounce) package long grain and wild rice mix
1 pound shrimp, peeled and cleaned

In 3-quart saucepan cook onion and green pepper in margarine for about 5 minutes. Add undrained tomatoes, water, salt, pepper, garlic salt, rosemary and paprika. Stir in both packets from rice mix. Cover and simmer 20 minutes. Add shrimp; cover and simmer 10 minutes more. Serves 6.

Pamela Biemiller
Waynesville

"Pass the hot pepper sauce with this recipe!"

ALMOST FRIED LOW-FAT CATFISH

2 catfish fillets
1 egg, beaten
1 cup herb-seasoned breadcrumbs

Wash fillets and dip in egg. Coat with breadcrumbs and spray baking sheet with vegetable cooking spray. Bake in preheated 400° oven for 10 minutes; turn over and cook 5 to 10 minutes more, until cooked through.

Lisa Martin
Home Office

CRAB APPLE CREEK GINGER GLAZED RAINBOW TROUT

3 trout, dressed, deboned and split (butterflied)
1/4 cup soy sauce
1/4 cup cream sherry
2 teaspoons sugar
1 tablespoon grated fresh ginger
2 garlic cloves, finely chopped
1 1/2 tablespoons olive oil
6 lemon wedges

Place prepared fish in pan. Combine soy sauce, sherry and sugar in a small saucepan and heat until sugar is dissolved. Add ginger and garlic and pour over fish. Marinate in refrigerator for 1 to 2 hours or at room temperature for 30 minutes. Remove fish from marinade, brush oil on both sides. Grill flesh side down first, basting with marinade. Turn and grill skin side down, basting again; do not overcook. Any leftover marinade may be served with fish. Garnish with lemon wedges.

Fred Martin
Home Office

"Salmon can be substituted for trout."

CHEESEBURGER PIE

1 pound lean ground beef
1 teaspoon salt
1/4 teaspoon pepper
1/4 cup chopped onion
1/4 cup chopped green pepper
1/2 cup fine dry bread crumbs
1/2 (8-ounce) can tomato sauce
1 unbaked pie crust

Brown ground beef and drain. Combine beef, salt, pepper, onion, green pepper, bread crumbs and tomato sauce. Pour into pie crust.

Topping:
1 (8-ounce) package grated cheddar cheese
1 egg, beaten
1/4 cup milk
1/2 teaspoon Worcestershire sauce
1/2 teaspoon dry mustard
1/2 teaspoon salt

Mix cheese, egg, milk, Worcestershire sauce, mustard and salt. Pour over pie. Bake in preheated 350° oven for 30 minutes. Serve in wedges with remaining tomato sauce.

Susan Benson
Home Office

"Back in the days when I was a poor college student, this was a dish that my roommates would request. With a salad and rolls, it made a great meal."

Ham and Egg Quiche

4 eggs, hard boiled, peeled and diced
1 deep-dish pie crust, baked
1/2 pound ham, ground or diced
1 cup shredded swiss cheese
1 cup shredded cheddar cheese
3 eggs, beaten
1 1/2 cups light cream
3/4 teaspoon salt
1/3 teaspoon pepper

Sprinkle hard boiled eggs in bottom of pie crust. Top with ham and cheese. Combine eggs, cream, salt and pepper; pour over filling. Bake on cookie sheet in preheated 350° oven for about 35 minutes, or until mixture is set. Let stand before serving.

Barbara Murdock
Home Office

"You can substitute 1/2 pound cooked and drained pork sausage for the ham."

How to Break Eggs

To break an egg, hold it in the left hand and crack the shell by striking it sharply with a knife; then put your thumbs together at the crack, and gently break the shell apart.

Elements of the Theory and Practice of Cookery. A textbook copyrighted in 1901 and reprinted several times with the most recent one being in 1913.

Melt in Your Mouth Chicken Pie

2 1/2 to 3 pounds chicken
2 cups chicken broth
1 (10 3/4-ounce) can cream of chicken soup
1 stick margarine, melted
1 3/4 cups self-rising flour
1 3/4 cups milk

Cook chicken and cool; remove skin and bones and cut chicken into pieces. Place pieces in a 2-quart casserole dish. Mix together broth and soup; pour over chicken. In a medium bowl, mix margarine, flour and milk. Pour over chicken and bake in preheated 350° oven for 35 to 40 minutes.

Lucy Mast Olson
Valle Crucis

Trading Chickens

General stores were marketing and distribution agencies for local area farmers. The stores would take produce, roots and herbs, and chickens in return for credit to the barterers. The items taken in trade from the farmers would then be sold to folks from the "city." The funds garnered from these sales would buy the goods to stock the store. Sometimes tokens, or "due bills," were used as currency when trading produce for goods. A local name for the "due bills" was "Doobaloos" or "Doogaloos."

There's a story told around the valley about trading chickens. Mr. Farthing at the Valle Crucis Company (the Annex), just like the folks at the Mast Store, took chickens and other items in trade. The chickens were weighed and their worth in trade determined before they were taken out to the coop around back of the store. Some enterprising youngsters in the Valle Crucis area watched this happening and came up with a plan to get more than what they bargained for.

They took some chickens to Mr. Farthing to trade and waited for him to put them in the coop. When they were sure he wasn't looking, they crept back to the chicken coop, unlatched the door, grabbed their chickens, and hightailed it across the creek and the field to the Mast Store to trade them again. Shenanigans such as these are perhaps one of the reasons that the chicken coop at the Mast Store is below the floor.

QUICHE LORRAINE TARTS

2 pie crust sticks
1 tablespoon poppy seeds
1 1/3 cups coarsely grated Swiss cheese
2/3 cup chopped salami
1/3 cup sliced green onions
4 eggs, slightly beaten
1 1/3 cups sour cream
1 teaspoon salt
1 teaspoon Worcestershire sauce

Prepare pastry for 2 pie crusts as directed, adding the poppy seeds into the crumbled dry mixture. Roll pastry to 1/16 inch thickness on lightly floured surface; cut into 3 inch rounds. Place rounds into 2 1/2-inch muffin pans. Combine cheese, salami and onions; spoon into pastry lined muffin pans. Stir together eggs, sour cream, salt and Worcestershire sauce; pour about 1 tablespoon of the egg and sour cream mixture into each muffin pan. Bake in preheated 375° oven for 20 to 25 minutes or until lightly browned. Allow tarts to cool in pans for 5 minutes before serving.

Tarts may be baked in advance, cooled, wrapped in foil, and refrigerated or frozen. At serving time, heat in oven at 350° for 10 minutes.

Jill Meares
Asheville

VEGGIE PIZZA

2 (8-ounce) packages cream cheese
1 cup mayonnaise
1 package ranch dressing mix
1 package refrigerated crescent rolls
Fresh broccoli, chopped
Radishes, chopped
Fresh cauliflower, chopped
1 onion, chopped
1 green pepper, chopped
1 (8-ounce) package shredded cheddar cheese

Combine cream cheese, mayonnaise and dressing mix in a medium bowl. Spread two crescent rolls out on cookie sheet and press seams together. Bake as directed. Let cool and spread cream cheese mixture on rolls. Sprinkle broccoli, radishes, cauliflower, onion and green pepper over entire surface of pizza, then sprinkle with cheese. Slice and enjoy.

Eric Baich
Home Office

"You can use other fresh vegetables, olives or bacon bits - whatever you like."

TUNA SWISS PIE

1 unbaked pastry shell
1 (12 1/2-ounce) can tuna, drained
1 cup (4-ounce) shredded swiss cheese
1/2 cup sliced green onion
3 eggs
1 cup mayonnaise
1/2 cup milk

Pierce pastry throughly with fork. Bake in preheated 375° oven for 10 minutes. In large bowl, toss together tuna, cheese and onion; spoon into pastry. In bowl, stir together eggs, mayonnaise and milk. Slowly pour over tuna mixture. Bake in preheated 375° oven 50 minutes, or until knife comes out clean.

The Old Mast Store Deli
Valle Crucis

CORN CHIP PIE

1 pound ground beef or turkey
1 small onion, chopped
1 (1-ounce) package taco seasoning
Lettuce, torn into small pieces
1 bag corn chips
Grated cheddar cheese
Sour cream
Salsa
Sliced black olives

Brown ground meat and onion; drain. Add taco seasoning and cook according to package directions. Cover bottom of soup plate or lunch plate with lettuce. Add a layer of corn chips, 1/4 of the meat mixture, and garnish with cheese, sour cream, salsa and olives.

Janet Bright
Hendersonville

DEELIGHTFULLY DEELICIOUS DUMPLINGS

1 pound ground beef, pork or chicken
6 cups blanched fresh spinach
1 (7 or 8-ounce) can corn
2 green onions, finely chopped
1 (10-ounce) jar roasted red peppers, chopped
2 tablespoons oyster sauce
2 teaspoons chili sauce
1/4 cup fresh chopped cilantro
2 garlic cloves, finely chopped
1 egg
1 package small wonton skins
Oil
3/4 cup salsa

Mix meat, spinach, corn, onion, peppers, oyster sauce, chili sauce, cilantro, garlic and egg. Add 2 teaspoons of mixture to each wonton skin. Crimp edges by dampening. Add 1 teaspoon oil to nonstick pan. Saute until bottoms are brown. Pour salsa around dumplings. Add 1/2 cup water, cover and steam about 15 minutes.

Mary Getchell
Asheville

"These are SOOOO good and worth the effort!"

SPAGHETTI SAUCE

1/2 bushel tomatoes, run through food mill
12 medium onions, chopped
2 large green peppers, chopped
48 ounces tomato paste
1 1/2 cups sugar
1/2 cup salt
6 bay leaves
2 tablespoons basil
2 tablespoons parsley
2 tablespoons garlic
2 tablespoons oregano

Mix tomatoes, onions and green peppers in a large pot. Cook 1 hour, stirring occasionally. Add remaining ingredients and let simmer 1 hour. Pour in prepared canning jars, seal. Process 10 minutes on 10 pounds pressure in pressure cooker.

Teresa Presnell
Original Store

This picture was taken by W.R. Trivett, a "pictureman." He was a farmer living in Watauga County (1894-1966) who just happened to supplement his income by taking portraits of neighbors and others in the Appalachian region.

These "picturemen" would travel to a family's home with all that they needed to take the picture - backdrop, glass plates, camera, tripods, etc. When he arrived the family might have an idea of the pose they wanted taken - it was their chance to show themselves as they wanted to be known not as the stereotypes of the time depicted. They might show a family gathering or strike a pose they saw in a picture show or newspaper. Contrary to popular notion, the people of the mountains were quite comfortable with modern technology.

The photos in our cookbook come to us via a circuitous route - the original glass plates were found stored in a barn loft. When they were developed, despite a few scratches and other signs of aging, they convey a story left untold by many authors and historians; they tell the story of what it means to be from Appalachia.

Many thanks to Ralph Lentz, a local historian and decendent of W.R. Trivett, for allowing us to use these photographs and to Bill Barrett, who developed them "the old-fashioned way."

Welsh Rarebit

Before beginning to cook the cheese: Chop 2 onions and soak in enough cider vinegar to cover onions.

1 pound sharp or extra sharp cheese
2 tablespoons cornstarch
2 eggs
3 tablespoons Worcestershire sauce
1 (12-ounce) bottle dark or lager beer or ale
1 pinch red pepper
1 teaspoon dry mustard

Chop cheese into small chunks and melt in top of a double boiler. Make a thickening of cornstarch and water. Beat eggs with Worcestershire sauce. Add cornstarch, eggs, beer, pepper and mustard to melted cheese. It will look really yucky. Beat with mixer constantly until creamy smooth. Serve over saltine crackers and top with chopped onions which have been soaked in vinegar. The Welsh way is to toast brown, black or pumpernickel bread so that it is crisp. Crumble bread and spoon rarebit over bread and top with onions.

Source: Ophelia (Mimi) McDonough
Tom McDonough
Home Office

"This is the dish that is probably the most famous McDonough family identifiable ethnic recipe known. It is one of the first entertainment dishes that I can remember as a child (the other was Mimi's corn pudding). This recipe was given to Mimi by an English couple in Richmond, Kentucky, sometime in the late 1920s right after Daddy Mac reported there for his new job at Eastern State Teacher's College. The couple's name was Cecil and Florry Way. I can't remember whether they were exiled from England or came over on their own. He was always playing tricks on people while being very much the Englishman.

"Mimi was just a young bride when she arrived and didn't know what to serve at her first dinner party for Daddy Mac's new boss, the President of Eastern State Teacher's College. Cecil Way insisted that she serve a famous continental treat for the occasion. Only after a very successful dinner did Cecil inform Mimi of the true origin of this treat called Welsh Rarebit. I'm not sure if she ever forgave Cecil, but she used it on many occasions to entertain.

"The traditional name for this dish is really Welsh Rabbit, presumably a joking reference to the fact that cheese was often available during hard times when the very poor Welsh could not afford or catch a rabbit. Also it was used over the stale dark bread to soften it rather than throw it away. Leftover ale or beer that was going stale was used for the same reason. It is easy to see why Cecil, an Englishman who traditionally looked down on the poor Welsh, playfully suggested this recipe to Mimi.

"I only know of two of the possible Irish origins of this recipe. The first is that it is one of the dishes that the early Irish settlers of what is now Wales brought with them from Ireland in the sixth and seventh centuries. Settling in the southern part of the British Isles, they found themselves harassed by their northern neighbors and suffered severe economic hardships. When hunting was scarce in the winter, they had to settle for cheese as a main dish since it could be preserved easily in those days.

"The second Irish connection was from a much later time. Some say that the recipe made its way to Ireland during the time of the Reformation when the Welsh were being persecuted for their Catholic beliefs. Many fled across the sea from Wales to Ireland where they blended many of their cultural ways into their new homeland.

"Either way we can confidently say that Welsh Rarebit has an Irish origin deep in its past, and it really doesn't matter since it is such an enjoyable feast.

"The only time that I can remember someone not finishing Mimi's Welsh Rarebit was when Uncle Will and Aunt Ida were visiting in Richmond and Mimi entertained them at our brand new home on Barnes Mill Pike. We had a full-time maid, Katherine, who took care of Bobby and me because Mimi was still recovering from her paralysis. Everyone was about to finish their plate when I asked if I could help Katherine stir in the beer for the second batch so we could all have seconds. Uncle Will and Aunt Ida did not touch another bite and never commented on the food from that point on. They were, needless to say, very staunch Methodists who were strict teetotallers! I also caught it royally after they left.

"Preparing Welsh Rarebit is both an art and an enjoyable event. Preparing it is half the enjoyment so make a production out of it, whether entertaining or just cooking for two. This is a good meal for a party in the kitchen with plenty of cold beer. First some notes:

1. Always buy the sharpest cheese you can find.

2. Always buy the darkest and strongest beer or ale you can find. Heineken Special Dark Beer has become my beer of choice for this recipe. Buy an extra bottle or two to drink while you are cooking.

3. Dry mustard is better than paste types. You need to experiment to suit your taste buds here.

4. Use a small hand held electric mixer to beat the mixture continuously while it is cooking. This will keep it from being grainy.

5. For a delightful change, try toasted dark bread cut into chunks or cubes instead of crackers.

6. Wine is not the best choice to serve with the meal but if you do, be sure to taste test one that will not be offended by the vinegar in the onions. A lite beer is better since it is not as filling and will allow you more room for the Welsh Rarebit.

"Serve with a light salad, lite beer and a lite lemony dessert. Enjoy, enjoy, enjoy!"

Tom and Mimi McDonough.

Vegetables/
Side Dishes

Hendersonville

Hendersonville, as well as Henderson County, is named for Leonard Henderson, who was the Chief Justice of North Carolina from 1829 until 1833. The town became known as "Little Charleston" in the mid 1800s because of the number of Charlestonians who had summer homes in area.

The Hendersonville store circa 1910.

Christopher Memminger, the first Secretary of the Treasury for the Confederacy, was one of the Charlestonians who had a summer home in these cool Blue Ridge Mountains.

Several famous folk traveled to Hendersonville in the late 1800s and early 1900s - including Thomas Edison doing research for his new light bulbs, Henry Ford, Harvey Firestone, and George Vanderbilt, who stayed a local hotel while the Biltmore House was being constructed.

The interior of our Hendersonville location when it was Maxwell's Grocery.

The Mast Store in Hendersonville was constructed in 1905 and was known then as the Syndicate Building. During its retail lifetime, it has been home to Maxwell Brown's Fancy Grocery Store, one of the first Winn-Dixie grocery stores, a "dime store," and a clothing store. The second floor served as offices for the "Pine Grove in the Supreme Forest" of the Woodmen of the World Society. We have heard that there were sometimes turkey shoots on the second floor. And they also had a "turkey drop" from the second floor windows.

The facade is typical of the high Victorian period and is well preserved as is the pressed tin ceiling throughout the first floor. The Hendersonville Store became a part of the Mast Store organization in 1995.

Mashed Potatoes

8 to 10 medium potatoes
1/2 stick margarine
1/3 cup milk
Salt and pepper, to taste

Peel and wash potatoes. Cut into pieces and place in a pot with cold salted water. Boil potatoes until they are tender, then pour off salted water and rinse with cold water; drain. Over low heat, slowly beat in margarine and milk; continue until potatoes are creamy. Add salt and pepper to taste.

Judy Phillips
Original Store

"Any left over mashed potatoes can be made into potato pancakes. To cold mashed potatoes, add 1 egg, 2 tablespoons flour, and chopped green peppers and/or onions. Mix well and make into patties. Brown both sides of potato patties in hot oil in a skillet."

Eron's Oven Potatoes

Red potatoes, washed (2 to 3 per person)
Olive oil
Salt and pepper, to taste
Paprika
Butter

Slice potatoes to about 1/4 to 1/2 inch thick and spread in a shallow glass 9 x 13-inch baking dish. Drizzle with olive oil and sprinkle with salt, pepper and paprika. Dot pieces of butter around potatoes in dish. Bake in preheated 400° oven for about 45 minutes. Pierce with fork about half way through cooking time.

Eron Schell
Annex

"I sometimes use Italian seasoning or dry mustard instead of paprika."

DOUBLE BAKED POTATOES

4 large baked potatoes
1/2 cup milk
2 tablespoons margarine
1 teaspoon salt
Dash of pepper
2 1/2 cups shredded cheddar cheese, divided
1/4 cup chopped onion
4 slices bacon, cooked crisp

Split each potato down the middle. Scoop out centers leaving 1/8-inch shell. Mash potato centers adding milk, margarine, salt and pepper. Beat until fluffy. Stir in 2 cups cheese and onion. Fill shells; top with crumbled bacon. Place potatoes on ungreased cookie sheet and bake in preheated 400° oven for 20 minutes. Remove from oven, top with remaining cheese and continue to bake until cheese begins to melt.

Debbie Matheson
Home Office

FAMOUS POTATO DISH

Potatoes, chunked
Green peppers, chopped
Onion, chopped
1 stick butter
Salt and pepper, to taste

Fill a 9 x 13-inch baking dish with chunked potato pieces, chopped green pepper and onion to cover. Dot with butter. Salt and pepper to taste. Bake in oven until potatoes are tender.

Mary Getchell
Asheville

"Optional: When done, sprinkle with favorite shredded cheese and heat for a few more minutes. This recipe can also be double-wrapped in foil and baked in the oven or cooked on a grill."

GERMAN POTATO SALAD

5 pounds red potatoes
1 pound bacon, cut into bite-sized pieces
1 large onion, diced
3/4 cup vinegar
3/4 cup sugar
1/4 cup chopped fresh parsley
Salt and pepper, to taste

Boil potatoes until tender, but firm; drain and cut into pieces. In skillet, fry bacon until almost done, add onions and saute until transparent. Add vinegar, sugar and parsley to skillet and cook until hot; stir. Pour dressing over potatoes, stir and keep warm. Salt and pepper to taste.

Mary Getchell
Asheville

"*Optional: add sliced green onions, black olives or radishes after salad is made.*"

ULTIMATE RICE PILAF

Small handful of vermicelli
2 tablespoons butter or margarine
1 (10 1/2-ounce) can beef or chicken broth
2 1/2 cups water
2 cups uncooked rice
Salt and pepper, to taste
Garlic powder, to taste
1 (4-ounce) can mushrooms, drained

Cook vermicelli in butter in large skillet until slightly brown. Pour broth and water over vermicelli and bring to a boil. Pour in the rice. Season with salt, pepper and garlic. Bring to a boil. Pour in can of mushrooms and stir. Cover and set on low. Let cook about 25 minutes.

Sarah Morgan Ernst
Original Store

Baked Tomatoes

Butter, melted
White bread, torn into small pieces
Fresh tomatoes, as many as needed
Salt and pepper, to taste
Brown sugar
Fresh basil, chopped
Sharp cheddar cheese, coarsely grated

Melt butter (1 tablespoon for each slice of bread) in a small frying pan. Add bread pieces and saute until bread is light brown. Set aside. Slice the tomatoes a little less than 1/2 inch thick. Place tomatoes closely together on a foil-lined baking sheet. Sprinkle tomatoes with salt, pepper, brown sugar (heavy on the sugar) and basil. Cover generously with the buttered crumbs. Sprinkle with grated cheese and bake in preheated 400° oven for 20 minutes.

Melanee Lester
Waynesville

"Cracker crumbs may be substituted for bread."

A young Melanee Lester.

BAKED BEANS

2 (28-ounce) cans pork and beans
3/4 cup packed brown sugar
1/2 cup molasses
1/2 cup chopped onion
3/4 cup ketchup
Bacon strips (optional)

Mix together pork and beans, brown sugar, molasses, onion and ketchup in a greased baking dish. Top with bacon strips. Bake in preheated 350° oven for 30 to 45 minutes.

Greta Hollar
Home Office

"You may substitute 3/4 to 1 cup of brown sugar for 1/2 cup brown sugar and molasses, if molasses is not available."

BAKED MACARONI AND CHEESE

2 tablespoons cornstarch
1 teaspoon salt
1/2 teaspoon dry mustard
1/4 teaspoon pepper
2 1/2 cups milk
2 tablespoons butter
8 ounces cheddar cheese, shredded, divided
8 ounces macaroni elbows, cooked 6 minutes, drained

In medium saucepan, combine cornstarch, salt, mustard and pepper; stir in milk until smooth. Add butter, and stirring constantly, bring to a boil over medium-high heat; boil 1 minute. Remove from heat. Reserve 1/4 cup cheese for topping; stir in remaining cheese until melted. Add macaroni, pour into greased 2-quart casserole. Sprinkle with reserved cheese. Bake uncovered in preheated 375° oven 25 minutes or until hot and bubbly.

Melanee Lester
Waynesville

Baked Carrots

4 cups peeled and diced carrots
1/3 cup butter, softened
1/4 cup sugar
1/4 cup light brown sugar
1 tablespoon salt
1/4 teaspoon cinnamon
1/3 cup boiling water

Spread diced carrots in casserole dish. In a bowl, cream together butter, sugar, brown sugar, salt and cinnamon. Add water and blend. Pour over carrots and bake in preheated 350° oven for 1 1/2 hours.

Allen Mast
Original Store

Green Beans with Almonds

2 pounds fresh string beans
Water
2 teaspoons salt, divided
1/4 cup butter or margarine
1 1/2 cups almonds
1 teaspoon pepper

Wash and break beans. Put in large covered sauce pan with enough water to cover top of beans. Cook in boiling water with 1 teaspoon salt for 20 minutes or until tender. Drain beans. In skillet, melt butter; saute almonds for 1 minute on medium heat. Add beans, 1 teaspoon salt and pepper to skillet. Heat through.

Allen Mast
Original Store

"Water chestnuts can be used in place of almonds."

GREEN BEAN CASSEROLE

2 (14 1/2-ounce) cans french-style green beans, drained
1 (10 3/4-ounce) can cream of mushroom soup
1/2 cup milk
1/2 teaspoon salt
1 teaspoon pepper
1 (6-ounce) can french fried onions

Mix beans, soup, milk, salt and pepper; pour into buttered 2-quart casserole. Top with onions and bake in preheated 350° oven for 30 minutes.

Judy Phillips
Original Store

COPPER PENNIES

6 carrots
1 medium red onion
2 celery stalks
1 medium green pepper
1 (10-3/4 ounce) can tomato soup
1 teaspoon salt
1 tablespoon Worcestershire sauce
1 teaspoon black pepper
1 cup sugar
1/2 cup salad oil
3/4 cup vinegar
1 teaspoon prepared mustard

Slice carrots, onion, celery and green pepper. Place them into a large container with a lid. In a separate bowl, mix together soup, salt, Worcestershire sauce, pepper, sugar, oil, vinegar and mustard. Pour over vegetables. Marinate overnight.

Susan Benson
Home Office

MUSHROOMS AND CASHEWS

1/2 pound fresh mushrooms
1/2 cup unsalted cashews
2 tablespoons soy sauce
1 clove garlic, pressed

Clean mushrooms and cut into quarters. Put into saucepan with cashews, soy sauce and garlic. Cover and cook on medium heat for 3 minutes. Turn heat down to low and simmer for 15 minutes, stirring occasionally.

Allen Mast
Original Store

ZUCCHINI AND MUSHROOMS

1 pound zucchini
8 ounces mushrooms
1 tablespoon cornstarch
1 tablespoon cold water
1/4 cup vegetable oil
1 medium onion, thinly sliced
2 cloves garlic, finely chopped
1/2 teaspoon salt
2 tablespoons dark soy sauce
1/4 cup chicken broth

Cut zucchini lengthwise into halves, then into diagonal 1/4 inch slices. Quarter mushrooms. Mix cornstarch and water and set aside. Pour enough water into a frying pan to cover the bottom of the pan. Heat until water bubbles. Add oil. Stir in onion and garlic. Stir fry until garlic is light brown. Add zucchini, mushrooms and salt. Stir fry for 2 minutes. Stir in soy sauce and then chicken broth. Heat to a boil. Add cornstarch mixture. Cook until thickened, about 10 to 15 seconds. Cool and serve.

April Trivette
Original Store

UNCLE ERNIE'S ROOT PIE

"Dice up as many roots as you can find: carrots, onion, red potatoes, turnips, rutabagas, beets, yams, etc. Place pie crust in bottom of baking dish and poke with fork a couple of times. Put diced and tossed roots in to about the top. Place 5 or 6 pats of butter or margarine on top; salt and pepper. Place second pie crust on top, crimp edges and poke top for steam to escape. Bake about 40 minutes. (Poke around inside to make sure the rootie items are the softness you like.) If you wrap a 1 1/2 to 2 inch-strip of aluminum foil around the edge for the first 30 minutes, the edge won't burn. When done, let cool a few minutes. Before serving, pour a dollop of Tiger Sauce on the plate and place the slice of pie on top of that. Great with a salad or any kind of meat, sausage or eggs. Simple, but man-that's good eatin'!"

Paul Saint Clair
Asheville

General Rules for Cooking Vegetables

1. Cook vegetables whole when practicable. When not practicable, cut them into as large pieces as are convenient. If the cooking water is to be served with the vegetable, the pieces may be smaller than would otherwise be desirable.
2. Use only as much water as is necessary to cover the vegetable. For small or cut-up vegetables that can be stirred, use just enough to keep them from burning, adding more as this cooks away.
3. Use the cooking water, if palatable, in sauces, soup-stock, cream-of-vegetable soups, etc. It contains much nutritive matter dissolved from the vegetables.
4. For vegetables cooked whole or in large pieces, keep the water boiling, that they may cook in the shortest possible time. Peas, beans, and any vegetables served in the cooking water are better simmered.
5. Green vegetables keep their color better if cooked uncovered. The reason for this is not known. Cook onions and cabbage uncovered; their odor is less noticeable when allowed to pass off continually than when escaping occasionally in bursts of steam.
6. The time required to cook any given vegetable depends upon its size, age, and freshness. Old beets may be so woody that they cannot be cooked tender. Dried or wilted vegetables cook more quickly if first soaked in cold water. Think of the part water plays in cooking starch, and explain why this is so.

Elements of the Theory and Practice of Cookery. A textbook copyrighted in 1901 and reprinted several times with the most recent one being in 1913.

Mama's Onion Pie

8 medium onions
4 tablespoons olive oil, divided
2 (9-inch) deep dish ready-made pie crusts
1 teaspoon salt
1/2 teaspoon pepper
1/4 cup grated parmesan cheese
2 small eggs, beaten
1/2 teaspoon chopped basil (optional)

Peel and coarsely slice onions. Heat 2 tablespoons olive oil in an 8-quart cooking pot at medium-low temperature. When oil is hot, add onions and approximately 2 more tablespoons of olive oil; stir until onions are coated with oil. Cook, stirring occasionally, over medium-low temperature until onions are soft and transparent; set aside to cool. Fill pie crust with onions using a slotted spoon so that any excess oil will drain off. Combine salt, pepper, parmesan cheese, eggs and basil in a bowl and mix well. Sprinkle over onions. Cover with top pie crust; crimp and seal edges, and make several slits in top of pie crust. Bake in a preheated 350° oven for approximately 40 minutes or until crust is golden brown. Cool. Serve warm or at room temperature. Can also be served cold out of the refrigerator.

William Butler
Hendersonville

A seven course "Mast Store Country Lunch" enjoyed by several of Watauga County's leaders. Photo courtesy of Watauga Democrat, March 30, 1972.

Roasted Red Pepper Sauce with Penne Pasta

3 red peppers or 1 (6-ounce) jar roasted peppers
2 1/2 tablespoons olive oil (use good quality)
3 garlic cloves, minced
1/2 cup chicken broth
2 tablespoons unsalted butter
1 (16-ounce) box penne pasta, cooked, served hot
Parsley, chopped, for garnish

Prepare roasted red peppers: cut tops off peppers, wash out seeds, and pat dry. Place in pan 6 inches from broiler - turn frequently for about 15 minutes or until skin is charred (can be roasted over grill). Cut peppers into 1/2-inch wide strips; set aside. In medium skillet, heat olive oil at medium heat; add garlic and cook while stirring without letting it brown (30 to 45 seconds). Add peppers (reserving a few for garnish) and broth; cook covered for only 2 to 3 minutes. Scrape into food processor, process until almost smooth, but still slightly chunky. For a rich finish, stir in butter as you turn over hot pasta. Serve at once, garnishing with roasted red pepper strips and chopped parsley.

Fred Martin
Home Office

Mast Store Country Lunch
as served in 1972

Longhorn Cheese • Brown Sugar • Vienna Sausages
Pork and Beans • Saltines
RC Cola • Moon Pies

The typical combinations are longhorn cheese atop a saltine cracker, brown sugar, then another saltine. Add to this a sardine or Vienna Sausage. For dessert, a Southern classic Moon Pie. The drink of preference is an RC Cola.

Kentucky Coleslaw

1 medium head cabbage, shredded
1 1/2 large carrots, grated
1 medium green pepper, chopped
1 1/2 cups sugar
3/4 cup white vinegar
3/4 teaspoon salt
3/4 tablespoon celery seed
3/4 teaspoon mustard seed

Combine cabbage, carrots and green pepper in a large bowl; set aside. Combine sugar, vinegar and salt in a sauce pan and bring to a boil for 2 to 3 minutes. Let cool and stir in the celery seeds and mustard seeds. Pour over the cabbage mixture. Cover and refrigerate for 24 hours. Makes about 2 1/2 quarts.

Diana Cogdill
Waynesville

Seasoning Vegetables

Use two teaspoonfuls of salt to one quart of water. To one pint of small, cooked vegetables, - beans, peas, onions, etc., - or to one pint of mashed or cubed turnips, potatoes, etc., use two tablespoonfuls of butter, one-half teaspoonful of salt, and one-eighth teaspoonful of white pepper.

Elements of the Theory and Practice of Cookery. A textbook copyrighted in 1901 and reprinted several times with the most recent one being in 1913.

Blue Bird Slaw

2 heads firm white cabbage (not green)
4 bell peppers, preferably red and green
1 quart yellow mustard
1 pint water
3 tablespoons salt
1 tablespoon white pepper

Use a wood block to do your cutting. Cut cabbage in two and cut out the center stem. Use a heavy knife to cut the cabbage in small parts, about the size of small buttons. Cut the bell peppers in two, removing the seeds and innards, and cut the same as cabbage, in small pieces. (Do not use a grinder as a subsitute for cutting with a knife.) In large bowl add mustard, water, salt and pepper to the cabbage and peppers. Mix all ingredients together using your hands. After mixing, jar the slaw and refrigerate until ready for use - it will keep for 3 to 4 months.

Faye Cooper
Home Office

"This is a great slaw to serve with hamburgers, hot dogs and barbeque. It was used by the Blue Bird Drive Inn in Winter Haven, Florida in the 1940s, 50s and 60s."

APPLE-WALNUT SLAW

4 cups thinly sliced green cabbage
1 cup coarsely shredded carrots
3/4 cup coarsely chopped toasted walnuts
1/2 cup light mayonnaise
1/2 cup 1% buttermilk
1/2 cup dark raisins
1/4 cup minced red onions
2 tablespoons sugar
1 tablespoon lemon juice
1/2 teaspoon salt
1/4 teaspoon pepper
2 apples, cored, quartered, and cut in thin wedges

Mix the cabbage, carrots, walnuts, mayonnaise, buttermilk, raisins, onions, sugar, lemon juice, salt and pepper together. Gently fold in apples, taking care not to break them. Refrigerate before serving.

Gabrielle Wheeler
Hendersonville

"To toast walnuts, spread on a cookie sheet and bake at 350° for 8 minutes, stirring occasionally."

How to Cook Vegetables

People are not agreed on what are the best ways of cooking vegetables. Too many cooks think only of getting them soft, without regard to retaining their juices and salts. Vegetables cooked in water lose a large proportion of their foodstuffs. In carrots this loss may amount to 20 per cent of their whole value when they are cut into large pieces, to 30 percent when they are cut small. Cabbage loses about one-third of its food value. Until we have more accurate knowledge, we can only try to make each vegetable palatable, endeavoring at the same time to keep it as nutritious as possible.

Elements of the Theory and Practice of Cookery. A textbook copyrighted in 1901 and reprinted several times with the most recent one being in 1913.

RICHARD'S FAMOUS DEVILED EGGS

18 large, hard-boiled eggs, shelled
3/4 cup mayonnaise-type salad dressing
1 tablespoon yellow mustard
1 tablespoon apple cider vinegar
1/4 cup sugar, or to taste
1/2 teaspoon salt
1/4 teaspoon pepper
Paprika
Lettuce leaves

Cut eggs in half lengthwise. Scoop out yolks of eggs and put in small mixing bowl. Mix yolks with salad dressing, mustard, vinegar, sugar, salt and pepper until smooth. The mixture should be the consistency of soft butter. If too dry, add small amount of salad dressing or vinegar. Be sure to taste test as you go along for sweet or vinegar taste. Make sure the whites of the eggs are clean; then fill with the egg mixture. Sprinkle paprika on tops. Arrange deviled eggs on lettuce leaves.

Richard Crandall
Hendersonville

"When we have gatherings at Christmas, birthdays, family picnics, etc., Richard has to take his deviled eggs. Always requested by the staff of the Mast General Store for covered dish meals!"

Richard Crandall with grandsons Thackston and Wyatt.

The '40 Flood

The aftermath of the 1940 flood. The Annex is to the left.

The mere mention of "The '40 Flood" conjures up many memories for those who lived through it. Over eight inches of rain fell in a 48-hour period on August 13, 1940. Normally small streams were transformed into raging torrents rumbling down the mountainsides. Devastation in Valle Crucis and throughout Watauga County was widespread. Some said that "it looked as if the mountains were alive" because of the landslides that occurred. Several lost their lives.

Mary Farthing Mast recounts her father R. A. Farthing working in the Valle Crucis Company store (now the Annex) to make sure items stayed dry. He put all kinds of items that usually occupied the floor up to higher shelves - those items included chop, which was used to feed cattle, sugar, and nail kegs. Even snakes were trying to escape the rising water (one found a nice dry spot in a nail keg). She watched her dad make his way back to their home and held her breath when his horse stumbled coming through the rushing water.

The water reached the first shelf in the Farthing Store - about 3 feet from the floor. The storm waters were so swift and had accumulated so much debris that the Methodist Church, just across from the Annex, was moved several feet from its foundation and the bridge was washed out. H. Mast remembers that his grandfather, W. W. Mast, who had been in Boone at a Northwestern Bank meeting, had to borrow an ax from the Valle Crucis Bank to cut down a sycamore tree to be used as a bridge to get across the creek and get home. The next day another tree had to be felled - the one from the previous evening had washed away.

More flood damage in Valle Crucis. To the left is the Valle Crucis Bank. To the right is the 1907 School House in its original location near the Valle Crucis Methodist Church.

Others in the valley were not as fortunate to arrive home safely. Two residents were swept over Dutch Creek Falls and carried to their deaths. One was found in a sand bar around the Watauga River Bridge. His body was brought to the Mast Store where he was outfitted in a suit and placed in a casket upstairs in the middle room.

CASSEROLES

Asheville

Asheville has been a town in the Blue Ridge Mountains since April 1793. It was first given the name of Morristown, and its town square lay at the intersection of two ancient trails used by both animals and Native Americans to travel through this remote area. These two trails are basically where Broadway/Biltmore Avenue and Patton Avenue are today. The landscape has changed greatly since those early days

Fain's was a popular shopping destination in the 1950s. Photo courtesy of N.C. Collection, Pack Memorial Library, Asheville, N.C.

as a frontier town, but Asheville has maintained a sense of natural beauty even as it developed into a city.

In the late 1880s, George Vanderbilt visited the area and stayed at the old Battery Park Hotel. During his stay, he was impressed with the beauty of the city and its surrounding forested land. Vanderbilt began buying land in 1889, some of it heavily logged and eroded, but because of his background and interest in agriculture and forestry it would soon be saved. America's largest private home opened its doors for a family gathering at Christmas 1895.

The Mast Store in Asheville was constructed in the mid 1940s for Fain's Department Store, a favorite shopping venue for locals. Several folks have told us that they remember their moms taking them downstairs for a hot dog at the

The Asheville Mast Store at 15 Biltmore Avenue.

cafeteria and then riding the nickel-operated pony while she shopped. Several features are left over from the Fain's era that are readily apparent to visitors include the "Fain's" name inlaid in terrazzo tile on the front doorstep and the intricate system of vacuum tubes that were used for sending communication and change from place to place.

Before the present day building was constructed, the Meares Brothers had a general store on the premises. It was built in the late 1800s. If you look closely while visiting the store, we have some of the old ads posted on the walls. The Mast General Store in Asheville is the largest store in the organization. It became a part of the "Mast Family" in 1999.

CHICKEN CASSEROLE

1 whole chicken
1 (10 3/4-ounce) can cream of mushroom soup
1 (10 3/4-ounce) can cream of chicken soup
1 soup can of milk
1 onion, chopped
3 cups of broth
1 (7-ounce) bag herb-seasoned stuffing mix
Margarine

In a large pot filled with water, boil chicken; debone. Save broth. Cut chicken in bite-sized pieces and spread in greased 13 x 9-inch baking pan. Mix mushroom and chicken soup with milk and pour over chicken. Saute onion in a little broth. Mix onion and 3 cups of broth together. Pour over casserole. Sprinkle stuffing mix over top. Dot with margarine. Bake in preheated 350° oven for 30 minutes or until bubbly.

Jennifer Kytta
Asheville

EASY CHICKEN CASSEROLE

4 chicken breasts
2 (6-ounce) boxes stuffing mix
1 (10 3/4-ounce) cream of chicken soup
1/2 cup water

Cook chicken until done. Remove meat from bones, place in a casserole dish. Prepare stuffing mixes as directed on box. Mix 1/2 of stuffing, soup and water with chicken. Spread remaining stuffing over the top. Bake in preheated 350° oven for 45 minutes.

Teresa Presnell
Original Store

SWISS TURKEY HAM BAKE

1/2 cup chopped onions
2 tablespoons butter or margarine
1 (10 3/4-ounce) can cream of mushroom soup
1/2 teaspoon salt
Pepper, to taste
1/2 cup milk
2 tablespoons sherry
2 cups cooked turkey, sliced
1 cup cooked ham, sliced
1/2 cup shredded Swiss cheese
1 1/2 cups soft bread crumbs
3 tablespoons butter or margarine, melted

Cook onion in the 2 tablespoons of butter until tender but not brown. Blend in soup, salt, pepper, milk and sherry; cook and stir until well mixed. Add turkey and ham. Pour into 1 1/2-quart casserole, top with cheese. Mix bread crumbs and melted butter; sprinkle around edge of casserole. Bake in preheated 400° oven for 25 minutes or until lightly browned. Serve over rice, noodles, or toast points.

Jill Meares
Asheville

"This recipe works great with chicken substituted for the turkey."

SUMMER-WINTER CASSEROLE

2 tablespoons oil
1/4 cup chopped onion
1/4 cup chopped green pepper
1 pound ground beef
1 (32-ounce) can whole tomatoes
2 tablespoons cornstarch
1 bay leaf
1/2 cup light or dark corn syrup
Salt and pepper, to taste
2 cups cooked macaroni
Parmesan cheese, grated

Heat oil in frying pan. Add onion, green peppers and beef. Cook until meat is browned; drain. Reserving 1/4 cup liquid from tomatoes, add tomatoes to beef and mix in, cutting into smaller pieces. Simmer for 10 minutes. Add cornstarch to reserved tomato juice and blend well. Pour into beef and tomato mixture. Add bay leaf, corn syrup, salt and pepper; stir well. Simmer 15 minutes. Mix beef mixture and cooked macaroni in a 2-quart casserole dish and sprinkle with grated cheese. Bake in preheated 350° oven for 1 1/2 hours.

Nancy Donnelly
Hendersonville

SAUSAGE RICE CASSEROLE

1 pound sausage
1 onion, chopped
1 green pepper, chopped
1 cup rice, uncooked
1 (10 1/2-ounce) can beef consomme
Water, enough when combined with consomme to make 2 cups
1 cup grated cheddar cheese, divided

In a large pan brown sausage, onion and pepper; drain excess grease. Add rice, consomme, water and 3/4 cup cheese to sausage mixture. Put into a 2-quart casserole dish. Sprinkle top with remaining cheese. Bake in preheated 350° oven for 1 hour. Serves 6 to 8.

Jill Meares
Asheville

"I sometimes serve this for breakfast. Just prepare, put in casserole and refrigerate. The next morning, just bake."

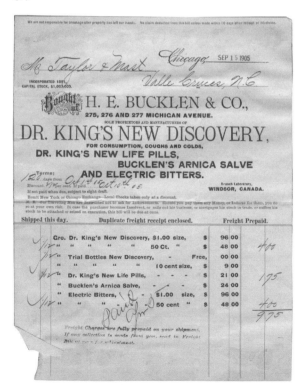

Some invoices just make good reading - especially when you add just a bit of imagination.

Cabbage, Beef and Rice Casserole

1 pound ground beef
1 onion, chopped
1 tablespoon oil
1 cup rice, uncooked
2 (5.5-ounce) cans tomato-vegetable juice
1 (8-ounce) can tomato sauce
Salt and pepper, to taste
1 medium head cabbage, coarsely chopped
1 tablespoons lemon juice

Brown beef and onion in oil; drain. Add rice to meat in skillet. Add one can tomato-vegetable juice, tomato sauce, salt and pepper. In casserole dish, layer cabbage, then meat mixture alternately, ending with meat mixture on top. Pour remaining tomato-vegetable juice and lemon juice over all. Bake in 350° oven in tightly covered casserole dish for 1 1/2 hours.

Sarah Morgan Ernst
Original Store

"This recipe was given to me by a friend in south Louisiana. Tastes great with cornbread!"

CABBAGE CASSEROLE

1 large head of cabbage, shredded
1 onion, chopped
6 tablespoons butter, divided
1 can cream of mushroom soup
1 (8-ounce) processed cheese loaf, cubed
Salt and pepper, to taste
1/4 cup dry bread crumbs

Cook cabbage in boiling salted water until tender; drain thoroughly. In a large skillet, saute onion in 3 tablespoons of butter until tender. Add soup and mix well. Add cheese; heat and stir until melted. Remove from heat. Stir in cabbage, salt and pepper. Transfer to an ungreased 2-quart baking dish. In a small skillet, melt remaining butter. Cook and stir bread crumbs in butter until lightly browned. Sprinkle over casserole. Bake uncovered in preheated 350° oven for 20 to 30 minutes or until heated through.

Melanee Lester
Waynesville

HASH BROWN POTATO CASSEROLE

2 pounds frozen hash brown potatoes
3/4 cup butter, melted, divided
1 1/2 teaspoon salt
1/2 teaspoon pepper
1 (10 3/4-ounce) can cream of chicken soup
1 (1-pint) carton sour cream
1 (10-ounce) package grated sharp cheddar cheese
1 cup crushed corn flakes

Mix potatoes, 1/2 cup butter, salt, pepper, soup, sour cream and cheese together in a large bowl. Pour into greased 9 x 13-inch casserole. Sprinkle with corn flakes and 1/4 cup melted butter. Bake in preheated 350° oven for 30 minutes.

Lucy Mast Olsen
Valle Crucis

LOVE HOLLAR VIDALIA ONION CASSEROLE

2 large sweet onions, cut into 1/2 inch thick rings
1 (10 3/4-ounce) can cream of mushroom soup
1/2 cup grated extra sharp cheddar cheese
Chopped roasted almonds

Spread onions in 9-inch casserole dish; cover with soup. Sprinkle cheese over soup, then sprinkle almonds over all. Cover and bake in preheated 350° oven for 20 minutes, then 10 minutes uncovered. Remove from oven and let stand for 10 minutes before serving.

Fred Martin
Home Office

"A good variation is to add chunks of cooked ham."

ITALIAN PASTA CASSEROLE

1 pound ground beef
4 cups twist noodles, cooked, drained
1 (30-ounce) jar tomato and basil spaghetti sauce
3/4 cup (3-ounces) grated parmesan cheese, divided
6 ounces mozzarella cheese, shredded
2 ounces cheddar cheese, shredded

Brown meat in large skillet, drain. Stir in pasta, spaghetti sauce and 1/2 cup parmesan cheese. Spoon into greased 13 x 9-inch baking dish. Top with mozarella, cheddar, and remaining parmesan cheese. Bake in preheated 375° oven for 20 minutes.

Sylvia Bryan
Home Office

"Any favorite spaghetti sauce can be substituted for the tomato and basil sauce listed."

SAUCY TWIST PORK DISH

1 (4-ounce) box corkscrew-shaped macaroni
1/2 cup chopped onion
1/3 cup chopped green pepper
1 tablespoon margarine
1 (12-ounce) can pork luncheon meat, cut in cubes
1 (10 1/2-ounce) can cream of mushroom soup
1/2 cup ketchup
1/3 cup shredded cheddar cheese

Cook macaroni according to package directions and drain. In large skillet, cook onion and green pepper in margarine until tender. Stir in macaroni, luncheon meat, soup, ketchup and cheese. Pour into ungreased 1 1/2-quart casserole. Cover and bake in preheated 400° oven for 30 minutes.

Susan Benson
Home Office

"This was a favorite with my college roommates. We ate it with a green salad, dinner rolls and gallons of iced tea!"

A Mast Store calendar plate dating back to 1909. Brenda Binning's aunt passed this beautiful piece of memorabilia on to her.

MEXICAN LASAGNA

1 pound ground beef or turkey
1 large onion, chopped
1 package taco seasoning
6 small flour tortillas
4 ounces low-fat sour cream
1 (24-ounce) jar salsa
2 (4-ounce) cans chopped green chilies
6 ounces grated cheddar cheese

Brown ground meat with onion; pour off grease. Add taco seasoning and cook according to directions. In 1 1/2-quart greased casserole, spread enough meat mixture to just cover bottom. Place 2 tortillas on top, spread 1/3 of the sour cream, then 1/3 meat mixture, salsa to taste, 1/3 of the chilies and 1/3 of the cheese. Repeat twice, adding extra cheese on top. Bake in preheated 350° oven for about 25 to 30 minutes, or until bubbly. Let sit for a few minutes before cutting into squares.

Janet Bright
Hendersonville

"This was concocted by my daughter, Lisa. It's easy to make, and you can double the recipe with larger size tortillas and an extra layer or two in a larger casserole. Leftovers warm up nicely in the microwave."

BACON SPAGHETTI

1/2 pound bacon
1/2 pound package of spaghetti (thin)
1 (15-ounce) can stewed tomatoes, chopped
1 tablespoon bacon drippings
2 cups shredded cheddar cheese, divided
Salt and pepper, to taste

Cook bacon until crisp; crumble and set aside. Cook spaghetti until tender, drain and put in a 9 x 13-inch baking dish. Add the stewed tomatoes, crumbled bacon, bacon drippings, 1 cup shredded cheese, salt and pepper. Mix well. Top with remaining 1 cup cheddar cheese and bake in preheated 350° oven for 25 minutes.

Della Goulter
Waynesville

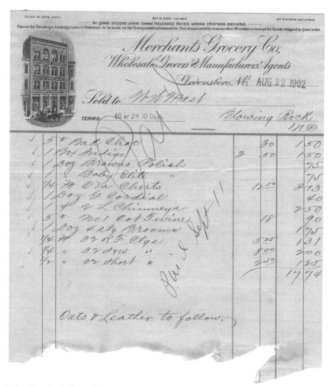

We often find that old invoices make good reading and provide insight into the needs and wants of the Valle Crucis residents. The prices are great, too!

CHICKEN SPAGHETTI

1 whole chicken
1 pound ground beef
1 stick butter
1 large onion
1 (8-ounce) can mushrooms, drained
1 clove garlic
1 quart tomatoes and juice
1 (15-ounce) can tomato sauce
Salt to taste
Vermicelli
Extra sharp cheese, grated
1 (6-ounce) can french fried onions

Boil chicken. When cooled, skin, bone and cut into small pieces; save a quart of stock. Brown ground beef in large skillet, drain. Add chicken and stock, butter, onion, mushrooms, garlic, canned tomatoes with juice, tomato sauce and salt. Cook on low heat about three hours. Boil desired amount of vermicelli. About 10 minutes before being ready, add vermicelli to chicken mixture. Sprinkle cheese on top. Spread french fried onions over all. Spaghetti is ready when cheese is melted.

Sarah Morgan Ernst
Original Store

SPAGHETTI CASSEROLE

1 1/2 pounds lean ground beef
1/2 cup chopped onion
1 clove garlic, minced
1 (30-ounce) jar chunky spaghetti sauce
1 (14 1/2-ounce) can diced tomatoes
1 tablespoon sugar
1 teaspoon salt
1/4 teaspoon pepper
1/4 teaspoon basil
1 (8-ounce) package spaghetti, broken, cooked, and drained
1 cup shredded mozzarella cheese
1 cup grated parmesan cheese

Brown beef, onion and garlic in large pan. Add spaghetti sauce, tomatoes, sugar, salt, pepper and basil. Bring to a boil. Turn down heat and simmer for 15 minutes, stirring often. Fold in the cooked spaghetti and the mozzarella cheese. Pour into a greased (I use a vegetable cooking spray) 9 x 13-inch pan. Sprinkle with parmesan cheese. Bake in preheated 325° oven for 30 minutes.

Joyce Crandall
Hendersonville

"This has become our families favorite dish when we gather together. With salad and garlic bread and usually a simple fruit salad for dessert."

SPAGHETTI PIE

6 ounces spaghetti
1/3 cup parmesan cheese
2 eggs, beaten
1 cup cottage cheese
1/2 cup onion
1 pound ground beef
1 (6-ounce) can tomato paste
1 (14-ounce) can stewed tomatoes
1 teaspoon sugar
1 teaspoon oregano
1/2 teaspoon salt
1/2 cup shredded mozzarella cheese

Cook spaghetti, drain and add parmesan cheese and eggs. Put in 9-inch glass baking dish to form crust. Put cottage cheese on top of crust. Brown onion and ground beef; drain and stir in tomato paste, stewed tomatoes, sugar, oregano and salt. Put on top of cottage cheese. Bake in preheated 350° oven for 20 minutes. Top with mozzarella cheese and bake until cheese is melted.

Jeanne Norris
Home Office

Jeanne and Ted Norris in the Boone Christmas Parade on the Mast Store Tinker Wagon.

Spinach Ziti

1 (16-ounce) package ziti
1 (16-ounce) carton cottage cheese
1/4 cup grated parmesan cheese
8 ounces mozzarella cheese, grated
1 tablespoon parsley
2 eggs
1 (10-ounce) package frozen spinach, thawed
1 (48-ounce) jar spaghetti sauce

Cook ziti 7 to 10 minutes; drain and rinse. While ziti is cooking, mix together cottage cheese, parmesan cheese and mozzarella cheese (reserving 2 tablespoons each of parmesan and mozzarella for top.) Add to that the parsley, eggs and spinach (make sure to squeeze out all of the water.) In a casserole dish, layer 1/4 of the spaghetti sauce, 1/2 of ziti, cheese mixture, then the other half of ziti. Top with remaining sauce. Bake in preheated 350° oven for 30 minutes, then top with remaining cheese. Bake for 10 more minutes or until cheese is melted.

Faye Cooper
Home Office

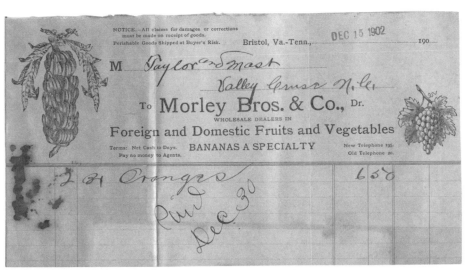

This invoice for 2 boxes of oranges is dated December 15, 1902. Oranges were a real treat at Christmastime. Many a child woke Christmas morning to find an orange and a few pieces of candy in his or her stocking. Also note the telephone number change from two to three digits.

BAKED PENNE

1 cup low-fat cottage cheese
1/2 cup low-fat ricotta cheese
3 tablespoons parmesan cheese
2 egg whites
2 teaspoons dried basil
1/4 cup chopped parsley
2 1/2 cups dry penne pasta
1 1/2 (26-ounce) jars prepared pasta sauce, divided

Combine cottage cheese, ricotta, parmesan, egg whites, basil and parsley. Cook penne pasta following package directions until slightly firm. Drain. Spread 1/2 jar of sauce on bottom of 12 x 8-inch baking dish. Layer pasta over sauce. Spread cheese mix over pasta and top with the remaining full jar of sauce. Cover with foil and bake in preheated 375° oven for 45 minutes. Uncover and bake another 10 minutes.

Sean Finneron
Home Office

"We usually serve this with salad and garlic bread."

Deluxe Macaroni and Cheese

1 (8-ounce) box small elbow macaroni
2 cups large-curd cottage cheese
1 cup sour cream
1 egg lightly beaten
3/4 teaspoon black pepper
2 teaspoons prepared mustard
2 1/2 cups grated extra sharp cheddar cheese, divided

Cook macaroni according to package directions. Mix cottage cheese, sour cream, egg, pepper, mustard and 2 cups cheddar cheese in a large bowl. Drain macaroni and toss with cheese mixture in bowl. Turn evenly into baking dish. Top with remaining cheese and bake uncovered in preheated 400° oven for 30 to 35 minutes. If top browns too quickly cover with foil after 20 minutes of baking.

Sarah Morgan Ernst
Original Store

Birdshot Theft Deterrent

Burglar alarms in the early 20th century weren't quite as sophisticated as they are today. Most might have consisted of an elaborate system of bells and strings if they existed at all. Mr. Farthing had occasion to utilize his own theft deterrent system.

He found that someone had decided they liked shopping after hours instead of when the store was regularly open. So, one night he decided that he would wait to see if there was a purchase he could help them with, and he brought along a very capable assistant - a shotgun filled with birdshot. The night grew dark, and he became more and more comfortable on his perch on the shelves near the rolling ladder at the Annex. Eventually, he fell asleep.

As the night wore on, Mr. Farthing moved just a little bit too much and dropped his gun, which immediately went off leaving a small, tightly grouped pattern of birdshot above the door entering the Annex. If the "shopper" had plans of visiting in the future, after hearing of the new assistant, he decided to take his business elsewhere.

MACARONI SOUFFLE

1 cup macaroni
1 1/2 cups milk
1 1/2 sticks butter
1 (10 3/4-ounce) can cream of mushroom soup
1 1/2 cups grated cheese
2 eggs, beaten
2 pimentos, chopped
1 tablespoon grated onion
1 tablespoon chopped green peppers
1 1/2 cups bread crumbs

Cook macaroni according to package directions, drain. Combine milk, butter, soup and cheese in saucepan; stir as it heats, then add to macaroni. Add eggs, pimentos, onion and peppers, stirring until cheese is melted. Pour into greased 1-quart casserole and sprinkle bread crumbs on top. Bake in preheated 350° oven for 30 minutes or until done.

Barbara Murdock
Home Office

"You may substitute 1 can cheese soup for grated cheese."

Hamburger Casserole

1 pound ground beef
3 medium potatoes, sliced
2 medium onions, chopped
Salt and pepper
1 (15 1/2-ounce) can kidney beans, drained
1 (10 3/4-ounce) can tomato soup

Place ground beef in the bottom of a casserole dish. Top with sliced potatoes. Add a layer of onions; salt and pepper to taste. Combine beans and soup, then layer over onions. Bake in preheated 350° oven for 1 hour covered and 30 minutes uncovered.

Jennifer Presnell
Home Office

Bean Casserole

1/2 pound bacon
2 to 3 small onions, chopped
1 cup brown sugar
1/2 cup vinegar
1 (15-ounce) can kidney beans, drained
1 (15-ounce) can lima beans, drained
1 (15-ounce) can butter beans, drained
1 (15-ounce) can pork and beans in molasses (not drained)

Chop and brown bacon in a large frying pan or Dutch oven. Add onions and cook until wilted. Add sugar and vinegar. Simmer about 20 minutes. Add kidney beans, lima beans, butter beans and pork and beans. Pour into a 2-quart casserole dish and bake in preheated 350° oven for 1 1/2 hours.

Sarah Morgan Ernst
Original Store

Bean Pot

1 (16-ounce) can pinto beans
1 (16-ounce) can kidney beans
1 (16-ounce) can lima beans
1 medium onion, chopped
3 tablespoons crisp, crumbled bacon
1/2 cup ketchup
1/4 teaspoon pepper
1 teaspoon dry mustard
3 tablespoons brown sugar

Mix undrained beans with onion, bacon, ketchup, pepper, mustard and sugar. Pour in a 2-quart casserole dish or bean pot. Bake in preheated 350° oven for 45 minutes.

Teresa Presnell
Original Store

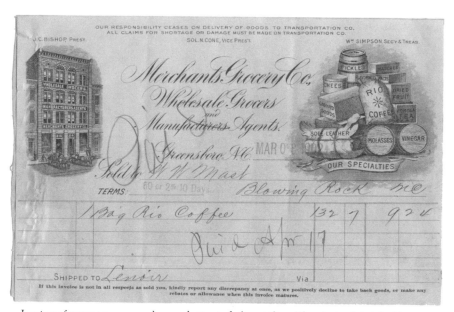

Invoices of yesteryear were used as marketing tools for suppliers. They depicted their buildings and the items they sold.

BLACK BEANS

2 cups dried black beans
Water
6 cloves garlic, minced
3 to 4 teaspoons cumin
1 1/2 tablespoons paprika
1/4 to 1/2 teaspoon cayenne pepper
2 teaspoons sage
2 teaspoons salt
Black pepper, to taste
1 bay leaf
1 tablespoon cilantro
2 teaspoons basil
1 (15-ounce) can diced tomatoes

Soak black beans overnight, rinse and put in large pot and cover with cold water.
Bring beans to a boil, then lower temperature. Add garlic, cumin, paprika, cayenne
pepper, sage, salt, pepper and bay leaf. Cook beans until tender; at least 3 hours.
Add additional water as needed. When beans are tender, add cilantro, basil and
chopped tomatoes. Simmer for 30 minutes. Serve over rice.

Della Goulter
Waynesville

Boston Baked Beans

2 pounds pea beans
1/4 pound salt pork (can be omitted for low-fat diet)
1 cup molasses
2 teaspoons salt
1 teaspoon dry mustard
2 tablespoons brown sugar

Carefully wash pea beans, watching for stones. Place in pot, cover with water, and bring to a boil quickly. Turn heat off and let peas soak for 1 hour. Turn heat on and cook until skins burst. Drain, keeping water. Cut salt pork into 2 pieces. Put 1 on bottom of baking pot; add beans. Mix molasses, salt, mustard and sugar. Pour over beans; add enough water to cover. Place the remaining salt pork on top of beans, rind side up. Bake in preheated 200° oven 6 to 7 hours. Uncover last 30 minutes.

Jill Meares
Asheville

"This is a dish that we have during the Christmas holidays, usually around December 22 or 23. We often serve cole slaw, smoked sausage (for those who have to have meat every meal) and steamed brown bread with butter or cream cheese."

BROCCOLI EGG PUFF

1 pound frozen chopped broccoli
2 tablespoons all-purpose flour
1/2 teaspoon baking powder
5 eggs, beaten
1 cup cream-style cottage cheese
4 slices bacon, cooked crisp, drained and crumbled
1/2 cup shredded cheddar cheese

Cook broccoli according to package directions. Drain and set aside. In a large mixing bowl, stir together flour and baking powder. Beat together eggs and flour mixture. Stir in cottage cheese and bacon. Evenly spread broccoli in bottom of a greased 10 x 6 x 2-inch baking dish. Pour egg mixture over broccoli. Bake uncovered in preheated 350° oven for 20 minutes. Sprinkle with cheese and bake 3 minutes, or until center is almost set and cheese is melted.

Sarah Morgan Ernst
Original Store

BROCCOLI CASSEROLE

1 package frozen chopped broccoli, cooked, drained
1/2 cup mayonnaise
1/2 (10 3/4-ounce) can cream of mushroom soup
1/2 to 3/4 cup grated sharp cheddar cheese
1 small onion, chopped
1 large egg, well beaten
Salt and pepper, to taste
Cracker crumbs
Margarine

Combine broccoli, mayonnaise, soup, cheese, onion, egg, salt and pepper. Mix well. Pour into a 9 x 13-inch casserole dish. Sprinkle cracker crumbs over top and dot with margarine. Bake in preheated 375° oven for 30 minutes.

Susan Benson
Home Office

Squash Casserole

2 pounds fresh squash (or 1-quart canned)
1 medium onion, chopped
1 tablespoon sugar
1 teaspoon salt
Pepper, to taste
1 egg, beaten
1 stick margarine, melted
2 cups corn bread crumbs
1 (10 3/4-ounce) can cream of celery, cream of chicken
  or cheddar cheese soup, undiluted

Cook squash until tender; drain. Add onion, sugar, salt and pepper. Stir in beaten egg. In a separate bowl, pour margarine over bread crumbs and mix well. Add 1/2 of bread crumbs to the squash mixture. Stir in the soup. Pour mixture into a 9 x 13-inch casserole dish. Sprinkle remaining crumbs over top of casserole. Bake in preheated 400° oven for 30 minutes.

Barbara Murdock
Home Office

Quick Squash Casserole

3 or 4 large yellow squash, sliced
1 large onion, chopped
Grated cheddar cheese
Captain's wafer crackers, crushed
1 egg
Milk

Cook squash and onion until tender. Layer in casserole dish. Add layer of cheese and cracker crumbs. Continue until layers reach top of casserole dish. Beat egg and add enough milk to make 1 cup. Pour over casserole. Bake in preheated 350° oven about 15 minutes or until cheese is melted.

Susan Benson
Home Office

CRUNCHY SQUASH CASSEROLE

2 pounds squash, sliced
1 medium onion, chopped
1 (10 3/4-ounce) can cream of chicken soup
1/2 teaspoon salt
1 (8-ounce) carton sour cream
1/2 cup butter, melted
1 (8-ounce) package herb or cornbread stuffing mix

Cook squash and onion in small amount of water until tender; drain. Add soup, salt and sour cream. Mix butter and stuffing mix. Put 1/2 stuffing mix in baking dish; add squash mixture. Cover with remaining stuffing. Bake in preheated 350° oven for 30 minutes.

Jill Meares
Asheville

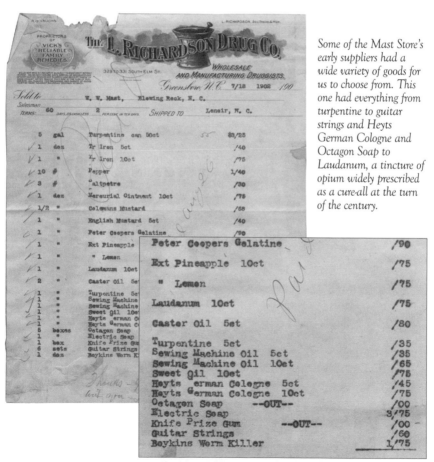

Some of the Mast Store's early suppliers had a wide variety of goods for us to choose from. This one had everything from turpentine to guitar strings and Heyts German Cologne and Octagon Soap to Laudanum, a tincture of opium widely prescribed as a cure-all at the turn of the century.

TACO CASSEROLE

1 pound ground beef
1/4 cup chopped onion
1 (10-ounce) can mild enchilada sauce
1 (8-ounce) jar mild taco sauce
1 (10 3/4-ounce) can cream of chicken soup
1 (14 1/2-ounce) bag tortilla chips, crushed
1 (8-ounce) package shredded cheddar cheese
1 (8-ounce) package shredded mozzarella cheese

Brown meat and onion together; drain. In separate bowl, mix enchilada sauce, taco sauce and cream of chicken soup; add to meat mixture. Spray a 9 x 13-inch casserole dish with vegetable cooking spray. Layer bottom of dish with half of the crushed tortilla chips. Pour meat and sauce mixture over chips. Layer with cheddar and mozzarella cheeses. Top with remaining chips. Bake in preheated 350° oven for 20 to 25 minutes.

Debe Jones
Home Office

Tuna Casserole

1 (8-ounce) box elbow macaroni
1/2 cup milk
2 (6-ounce) cans tuna, drained
1 (10 3/4-ounce) can cream of mushroom soup
2 1/2 cups grated extra sharp cheddar cheese, divided
1 (6-ounce) can french fried onions
1 (12-ounce) can asparagus, drained
Parmesan cheese, grated

Cook macaroni according to package directions, drain. Mix together milk, tuna and cream of mushroom soup. Layer macaroni and half of the milk, tuna and mushroom soup mixture in casserole dish. Spread 1/2 can of french fried onions and 1 1/4 cups grated cheese over macaroni layer. Add remaining grated cheese and french fried onions to the reserved milk, tuna and mushroom soup mixture; pour over the first layer. Top with the asparagus and sprinkle with grated parmesan cheese. Bake in preheated 350° oven for 35 minutes. (It may need to be covered with foil while baking.) Cool for 7 to 10 minutes before serving.

Sarah Morgan Ernst
Original Store

The Mast Store Annex during the flood of 1995.

CONNIE'S SWEET POTATO CASSEROLE

2 (29-ounce) cans sweet potatoes, drained and mashed
1/2 cup sugar
1/2 teaspoon salt
2 eggs, well beaten
1/4 cup butter
1/2 cup milk
1 teaspoon vanilla

Topping:
1/2 cup coconut
1/3 cup flour
3/4 cup brown sugar
1/2 cup chopped nuts

Combine sweet potatoes, sugar, salt, eggs, butter, milk and vanilla. Place in a 9 x 13-inch baking dish. Combine coconut, flour, brown sugar and chopped nuts; sprinkle topping mixture over potatoes. Bake in pre-heated 350° oven for 30 minutes.

Connie Gioscio
Home Office

Jeanne's Sweet Potato Casserole

3 cups sweet potatoes, drained and mashed
1 teaspoon vanilla
1/3 cup margarine, melted
1 cup sugar
2 eggs, beaten
1/2 cup milk
Dash of nutmeg

Mix sweet potatoes, vanilla, margarine, sugar, eggs, milk and nutmeg together. Pour into a greased 9 x 13-inch casserole dish.

Topping:
1 cup brown sugar
1 cup chopped pecans
1/3 cup flour
1/2 stick margarine, softened

Mix brown sugar, pecans, flour and margarine together. Sprinkle topping mixture over sweet potatoes. Bake in preheated 350° oven for 45 minutes.

Jeanne Norris
Home Office

APR 1960

Jeanne Norris on top of a mailbox in March 1960. That year it snowed for four Wednesdays in a row, with some 60 inches or more falling in one month.

His Wife's Sweet Potato Casserole

4 or 5 medium sweet potatoes, cooked and mashed
1/2 stick margarine, melted
3/4 cup sugar
3 eggs
1/2 cup evaporated milk

Mix sweet potatoes, margarine, sugar, eggs and milk. Put into a 9 x 13-inch casserole dish.

Topping:
1 1/2 cups crushed cornflakes
1/2 cup brown sugar
1/2 cup chopped pecans
1/2 stick margarine, melted

Mix cornflakes, brown sugar, pecans and margarine; sprinkle over top. Bake in preheated 350° oven for 20 minutes.

Ronnie Shook
Home Office

"Ronnie brought us this great recipe, but we suspect it came from his wife, Teresa."

Baked Grits and Cheese Casserole

1 1/2 cups grits
6 cups boiling water
3 teaspoons savory salt
2 teaspoons salt
1 teaspoon paprika
Dash of hot pepper sauce
3 eggs
1 pound sharp cheddar cheese, grated
1 stick butter

Pour grits into boiling water, stirring constantly until completely mixed. Cook until thickened. Add savory salt and regular salt, paprika and hot pepper sauce. Mix thoroughly. In a bowl, beat eggs slightly. Add a small amount of hot grits to eggs. Stir constantly to prevent coagulation of eggs. Add remaining grits gradually. Add cheese and butter; mix well. Pour into a buttered 9 x 13-inch casserole dish. Bake in preheated 350° oven for 45 minutes.

Barbara Murdock
Home Office

The town of Lenoir is about 30 minutes or so from Boone but in 1904, the date of this invoice, it was a long and arduous journey down the Linville toll road and the Yonahlossee Trail.

EASY BREAKFAST CASSEROLE

1 pound sausage, cooked and drained
1 (8-count) package crescent rolls
4 eggs
Salt and pepper, to taste
1 (8-ounce) package shredded cheddar cheese
1 (8-ounce) package shredded mozzarella cheese

Spray a 9 x 13-inch casserole dish with vegetable cooking spray. Roll out cresent rolls in the bottom of the casserole dish. Sprinkle sausage over rolls. Beat eggs with salt and pepper and pour over sausage. Layer the shredded cheddar and mozzarella cheese on top of casserole. Cover and refrigerate overnight. Next morning bake in preheated 350° oven for 15 minutes or until brown.

Debe Jones
Home Office

COMPANY BREAKFAST CASSEROLE

2 pounds bulk sausage
12 eggs
3 cups milk
1 teaspoon salt
Pepper, to taste
1 teaspoon dry mustard
6 slices bread, cubed
1 small onion, chopped
3/4 cup chopped green pepper
1 cup shredded cheddar cheese

Brown sausage; drain and cool. Beat together eggs, milk, salt, pepper and mustard. Fold in bread cubes, onion, green pepper and sausage. Pour mixture into greased 9 x 18-inch pan and cover with foil. Refrigerate overnight. Take out of refrigerator 1/2 hour before baking, and top with cheese. Bake uncovered in preheated 325° oven for 45 minutes. Let stand 3 to 5 minutes before cutting.

Jill Meares
Asheville

GARLIC CHEESE GRITS

2 cups cooked grits
1 1/2 sticks butter or margarine
1 pound cheddar cheese, grated, divided
2 teaspoons finely chopped garlic
2 teaspoons chopped green onion tops
3 eggs

Cook grits according to directions. Remove from heat and add butter, 1/2 the grated cheese, garlic and onion, stirring until cheese melts. Beat eggs and fold into grits mixture. Pour into greased 1 1/2-quart casserole; top with remaining cheese and bake in preheated 350° oven for 1 hour.

Jill Meares
Asheville

ALLEN'S CORN PUDDING

1 (16-ounce) can creamed corn
1 (16-ounce) can whole kernel corn, drained
1 egg, slightly beaten
1/3 cup Italian bread crumbs
1/2 cup sour cream
1/2 teaspoon salt
1/2 teaspoon pepper

Mix creamed corn, whole kernel corn, egg, bread crumbs, sour cream, salt and pepper. Pour into 1 1/2-quart buttered casserole dish. Bake in preheated 350° for about 50 minutes or until firm.

Allen Mast
Original Store

CORN PUDDING

1 tablespoon flour
1 teaspoon salt
1/4 teaspoon pepper
2 eggs
3/4 cup milk
2 cups canned cream-style corn
  or fresh cooked corn
3/4 stick butter or margarine, melted
1/4 cup chopped red pepper or pimento
1/4 cup chopped green pepper
1 tablespoon finely chopped onion
2 teaspoons sugar (if fresh corn is used)

Mix flour with salt and pepper. Beat eggs and milk together and stir gradually into flour mixture to keep flour from lumping. Add corn, margarine, peppers, onion and sugar. Place in greased casserole dish and bake in preheated 375° oven for 30 minutes or until knife inserted in center comes out clean.

Jill Meares
Asheville

"This recipe has been a favorite at every Thanksgiving and Christmas at our house."

NOT MEAT LOAF

1 onion
2-4 cloves of garlic
2 cups mushrooms
2 cups cooked lentils
2 cups cooked brown rice
1/2 cup toasted walnuts, sunflower seeds, sesame seeds
    or any combination of seeds/nuts of your choice, chopped
1 cup grated carrots
1/2 teaspoon sage or thyme
1/2 teaspoon salt
Ground black pepper to taste

In a small sauce pan, saute onion, garlic, and mushrooms until tender, then put aside. In a large bowl, mix lentils, rice, nuts/seeds, carrots, sage/thyme, salt, and pepper. Add sauteed ingredients and mix well. Put aside.

2 eggs, beaten
1/2 cup vegetable broth or water
1/3 cup soy sauce
1 tablespoon olive oil
1 cup whole wheat bread crumbs
2 tablespoons whole wheat flour

Combine eggs, vegetable broth or water, soy sauce and olive oil and mix well. Add bread crumbs and stir, then add to large bowl of other ingredients. Sprinkle flour over contents and stir well. Spread into a greased (olive oil) baking dish. Top with either sesame seeds or ketchup as desired. Bake at 350° until done - approximately 45 minutes to 1 hour (test with a fork - should come out clean). Best to allow it to cool somewhat before cutting in slices to serve (cooling will make it come out in clean slices). Excellent served with Shitake Mushroom Gravy (next page).

Claire McGuire
Home Office

Shiitake Mushroom Gravy (to be served with Not Meat Loaf)

1 onion
1 cup shiitake mushrooms, trimmed and sliced
3 1/2 cups water
1/4 cup soy sauce
1/4 cup + 1 tablespoon whole wheat flour
1 tablespoon fresh or 1/4 tsp dried thyme
2 teaspoon fresh or 1/8 tsp dried sage, to taste

In a large saucepan, cook onion and mushrooms over medium heat in a small amount of olive oil or cooking spray until they begin to exude moisture stirring ocassionally (about 10 minutes). Add soy sauce and water. Once water is heated, thicken by sprinkling in whole wheat flour slowly while stirring constantly until smooth. Add thyme and sage to taste. Serve gravy over Not Meat Loaf. This gravy is also good over rice or whipped potatoes.

Claire McGuire
Home Office

The proper cookware always helps.

Practical Points about Feeding A Family

1. Brainworkers (teachers, students, clerks, etc.) need easily digestible food; muscle workers (workingmen, etc.) find coarser food better suited to their needs.

2. No one meal need be "balanced," that is, need contain proteins, carbohydrates, and fats in a certain proportion, but each day's dietary should approach the proportion of one part protein to five and a half parts carbohydrate.

3. Diet should be varied as well as mixed; for example, do not depend too much on potatoes for starch; have rice or macaroni sometimes instead.

4. When planning a meal, think what was served at the preceding one; if starchy foods chiefly, supply plenty of protein. Do not forget that butter, eggs, milk, etc., used in cooking count as food just as much as if served by themselves on the table. By planning meals, in part at least, for several days ahead, you will find it easier to provide varied and rightly balanced fare.

5. Food is not necessarily nutritious in proportion to its cost.

6. Remember that plant protein may take the place of animal protein; if you have but a small piece of meat, serve peas or beans with it rather than beets.

7. Familiarize yourself with the composition of common foods so that you may readily think of suitable combinations and know how to supply lack of one food by another of similar character.

Elements of the Theory and Practice of Cookery. A textbook copyrighted in 1901 and reprinted several times with the most recent one being in 1913.

WELCOME to the
VALE CRUCIS
COMMUNITY
The Vale of †the Cross

DESSERTS

THE JOHN AND FAYE STORY

Better roads and manufacturing jobs in nearby Boone resulted in the folks in the valley beginning to leave their traditional agrarian endeavors in favor of making shoes or saw blades or resistors. Such was the case across much of the country in the middle part of the 20th century - it just seems like it took a bit longer to make its way to Valle Crucis. Along with the valley residents' newfound jobs went some of their shopping time.

In 1979, the Mast General Store was in danger of becoming another gray visage of the not too distant past - an old friend that everyone wanted to help, but no one knew just how. The store was just too far off the main road, so who would want to come here?

John and Faye Cooper, a couple of native Floridians with mountain roots, had visited the store several times when they had been in the area. They were both captivated by the old advertising art on the walls, the history of the building, and the people of the community. When they heard the old building was available for purchase, they made their decision to take a leap of faith by committing to save this Western North Carolina landmark. Faye is often quoted, "We knew someone should save it. We just didn't know it would be us."

In 1980 with their new acquisition.

So, the Coopers, John, Faye, and their two children John John and Lisa, left Florida for a new life-style. They set about cleaning and stocking the store. Their new home was made as an apartment on the top two floors of the store, where they lived for over four years. Having a vision of what the old store was and what they thought it should be and combining it with a bit of retail experience from both of them along with John's advertising background, the doors were opened with new shopkeepers on June 6, 1980.

Several of their first sales representatives, mostly hardware and general item wholesalers, spent time with them helping to make prudent choices with their limited funds. They expanded their lines to include clothing - both traditional fashion and good old-fashioned workwear - and shoes as they could, but still kept to the ideal that the general store should not be compromised. In the process, they developed a close relationship with several of the "drummers" (an old-timey name for sales reps) who came to show their goods. A few of them still stay in the Coopers' home when they make their sales call with the Mast Store.

After the store opened under new ownership, one of the first contributions the Coopers were able to make to the community was being able to successfully bring back a Valle Crucis address by reopening the post office in the store. Many communities have fallen off the map as they lost their post offices; now Valle Crucis had its identity back.

By having a real heart for the community and joining a fledgling tourism promotional organization, North Carolina High Country Host, the Mast Store was soon enjoying an eclectic mix of farmers, other locals, and some tourists who indeed DID want to venture off the main road to experience something uncommon.

A few years later, the selection of goods began to grow again. Not wanting to compromise the integrity of the general store as the need for space for clothing and outdoor goods was crowding out the

John and Faye Cooper today.

more traditional wares, the offer of space in the old Farthing Store was quickly accepted. The Annex became a part of the Mast Store. The Coopers were able to move from their quarters above the store to a home in Valle Crucis.

In keeping with their bent for re-using old buildings, an old greenhouse operation in Valle Crucis was purchased to act as the "home office" for the organization. Here all of the accounting functions, purchasing, pricing and receiving, advertising, and more are housed in one location.

With the popularity of the store, other towns and locations began inquiring about having their own Mast Store. When an old department store in Boone closed in 1987 the community requested the Coopers consider making a Mast Store along its main street. The building, with its department store history, lent itself well to the Mast ideal and was restored in 1988. By recapturing the art of customer service and providing quality goods at fair prices, the Mast tradition was further established. The popularity of the High Country stores and their reputations spread. More main streets wanted their own Mast Store. Waynesville opened in 1991, Hendersonville in 1995, Asheville in 1999, and Greenville, SC in 2003.

Bavarian Rainbow Cake

Crust:
1 1/4 sticks margarine (room temperature)
1 1/4 cups flour
1 1/4 cups chopped pecans, divided

Mix margarine, flour and 1 cup pecans together (reserve 1/4 cup pecans for topping). Press into a 9 x 13-inch pan. Bake 20 minutes in low oven. Cool completely before going to next step.

First layer:
1 (8-ounce) package cream cheese
1 cup powdered sugar
1 cup frozen nondairy whipped topping

Mix cream cheese and sugar. Fold in thawed whipped topping. Pour into pie shell.

Second layer:
2 (3.4-ounce) boxes chocolate instant pudding mix
2 cups cold milk

Mix pudding and milk and pour over first layer.

Third layer:
2 (3.4-ounce) boxes vanilla instant pudding mix
2 cups cold milk

Mix pudding and milk, then pour over second layer. Top pie with whipped topping and remaining chopped pecans. Refrigerate.

Sarah Morgan Ernst
Original Store

CARROT CAKE

2 cups plain flour
2 1/2 teaspoons cinnamon
2 teaspoons baking soda
1 teaspoon salt
2 cups sugar
1 1/2 cups oil
4 eggs
3 (6-ounce) jars junior carrot baby food

Sift together flour, cinnamon, soda and salt. Add sugar, oil, eggs and baby food; mix well. Pour in a greased 9 x 13-inch pan and bake in preheated 350° oven for 40 to 45 minutes. Frost with cream cheese icing.

Jeanne Norris
Home Office

"A perennial favorite at covered dish dinners, birthdays, or for that matter, "no reason at all". We all love Jeanne's carrot cake! You won't be disappointed with this cake – yummee!"

An Anonymous Carrot Cake Fan

Jennifer (left) and Jason (third from left), Jeanne's children, enjoy some of her famous carrot cake along with their first cousins, Crystal and Mark Norris.

CHURCH MOUSE CAKE

1/2 cup shortening
1 cup white sugar
1 1/4 cups white flour (no need to sift)
1/2 teaspoon salt
4 heaping teaspoons cocoa
1/2 cup buttermilk
1 egg
1 teaspoon vanilla
1 teaspoon baking soda
1/4 cup boiling water

Cream shortening and sugar. Mix flour, salt and cocoa together and add alternately with buttermilk. Add egg and vanilla; mix. Last, add baking soda dissolved in boiling water; mix (do not beat!). Pour into greased and floured 8 x 8-inch, or 8 x 12-inch pan. Bake in preheated 350° oven for 30 minutes. This recipe makes a one layer cake. For two layers, double recipe.

Duane Woolbright
Home Office

Duane's mom, Letha Woolbright, sent him this recipe with the following notes: "This is an old Kuhler family recipe, probably from Germany. Many different ingredients can be used to make this cake. The name comes from the saying, 'as poor as a church mouse.' Possible substitutions: in place of buttermilk, I use plain sour milk and have had good results using plain yogurt; for shortening I use vegetable shortening, but have used mayonnaise, lard or bacon drippings. Sour milk recipe: add 1 teaspoon vinegar or lemon juice to 1/2 cup sweet milk."

Coconut Cake

1 white cake mix
1 1/3 cups water
2 tablespoons oil
3 large egg whites
1 1/2 cups milk
1/2 cup sugar
1/2 (7-ounce) bag coconut
1 (8-ounce) carton frozen nondairy whipped topping

Blend cake mix, water, oil and egg whites in large bowl at low speed until moistened, about 30 seconds. Beat at medium speed for 2 minutes. Pour in greased sheet pan; bake in preheated 350° oven until done. Remove from oven and punch holes with large meat fork. Combine milk, sugar and coconut in pan and boil for 1 minute. Cool slightly and spread evenly over cake. When cool, spread whipped topping over top and sprinkle with a little more coconut. Keep refrigerated.

The Old Mast Store Deli
Valle Crucis

Easy Multi-Layer Chocolate Cake

2 boxes yellow cake mix
6 eggs
2/3 cup oil
2 cups water
1/2 teaspoon walnut flavoring
1/2 teaspoon rum flavoring
2 (16-ounce) cans dark chocolate icing

Stir together cake mixes, eggs, oil and water. Add walnut and rum flavoring. Melt one can icing in microwave. Cover bottoms of 9-inch baking pans with a thin layer of cake mixture. Bake in preheated 325° oven for 10 to 12 minutes or until done. Repeat this procedure 13 to 16 times. Layers of cake should be iced with melted icing as soon as they are taken out of oven and turned onto plate. After all layers have been done, frost the cake with the other can of unmelted chocolate icing.

Barbara Murdock
Home Office

German Chocolate Upside Down Cake

1 (8-ounce) package coconut
1 1/2 cups chopped pecans
1 German chocolate cake mix
1 1/3 cups water
1/2 cup vegetable oil
3 eggs
1 (16-ounce) box powdered sugar
1 (8-ounce) package cream cheese
1 stick margarine

Grease and flour 9 x 13-inch cake pan. Layer coconut and pecans in bottom of pan. Beat cake mix, water, oil and eggs in large bowl, scraping bowl constantly. Pour over coconut and pecans. Mix sugar, cream cheese and margarine with mixer. Drop with spoon over cake mix; don't stir. Bake in preheated 350° oven for 45 to 50 minutes.

Gail Ward
Original Store

MISSISSIPPI MUD CAKE

2 cups sugar
1 cup shortening
4 eggs
1/4 teaspoon salt
1 1/2 cups plain flour
1/2 cup nuts
3 teaspoons vanilla
1/3 cup cocoa
1 (5-ounce) bag small marshmallows

Cream sugar and shortening. By hand, blend eggs, salt, flour, nuts, vanilla and cocoa into sugar mixture. Pour into greased and floured 9 x 13-inch pan. Bake in preheated 300° oven for 30 minutes. Remove from oven and sprinkle marshmallows evenly over top of cake. Return to 350° oven for 5 minutes. Let cool before icing.

Icing:
1 (16-ounce) box powdered sugar
1 stick margarine
1/3 cup evaporated milk
1 teaspoon vanilla

Mix powdered sugar, margarine, milk and vanilla well. Spread on cake.

Cindy Presnell
Home Office

Mocha Pudding Flip

3/4 cup sugar
1 cup plain flour
1/4 teaspoon salt
2 teaspoons baking powder
1/2 cup butter
1 square unsweetened baking chocolate
1/2 cup milk
1 tablespoon vanilla

Sift sugar, flour, salt and baking powder together. Melt butter and baking chocolate over low heat. Add to sifted dry ingredients. Add milk and vanilla. Mix until smooth and well blended. Spread in 1 1/2-quart round baking dish.

Topping:
3/4 cup sugar
1/2 cup brown sugar
1/4 cup cocoa
1 cup warm black coffee

Mix sugar, brown sugar and cocoa. Sprinkle over top of cake in baking dish. Slowly pour warm coffee over top. Bake in preheated 350° oven for 40 minutes. Serve warm. Cake comes to top and thick pudding forms in bottom as they flip over during baking.

Rebecca A. Fry
Boone

"Great quick dessert."

ORANGE CAKE

1/2 cup brown sugar
Juice of 1 orange
1 cup sugar
1/2 cup shortening
2 eggs
2 cups flour
1/2 teaspoon baking soda
1/2 teaspoon salt
1/2 teaspoon baking powder
1 cup sour milk
1 cup ground raisins
1 orange rind, grated

Combine brown sugar and orange juice; set aside. Cream sugar and shortening with a mixer. Add eggs and beat well. Sift flour in another bowl. Add soda, salt and baking powder; sift again. Add alternately with milk to sugar, shortening and egg mixture. Add raisins and orange rind; mix well. Bake in sheet cake pan in preheated 350° oven until straw inserted in center comes out clean. Pour sugar and juice mixture over cake.

Lucy Mast Olsen
Valle Crucis

PEACH CAKE

1 box white or yellow cake mix
3 eggs
1 (16-ounce) can peaches, undrained
1/2 cup brown sugar
1 stick butter
1/2 cup sugar
1/2 cup sweetened condensed milk

Combine cake mix, eggs and can of peaches, with juice. Pour in greased and floured
9 x 13-inch pan. Sprinkle with brown sugar. Bake in preheated 350° oven about 35
minutes or until done. While cake is baking, boil butter, sugar and milk. When
cake comes out of oven, pour boiled ingredients over cake. Let it sit a few minutes.
Serve warm or cold.

The Old Mast Store Deli
Valle Crucis

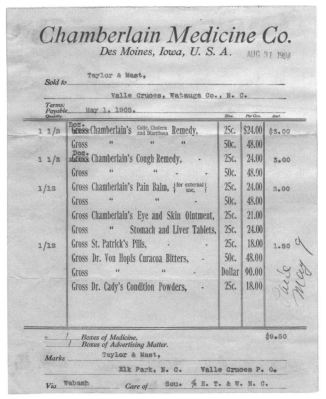

Aside from the interesting products sold by the Chamberlain Medicine Co., this invoice has some interesting shipping information. The goods were sent to the then Taylor and Mast Store via the ET & WNC Railroad. Locals had an endearing name for the engine and accompanying rolling stock - they called her Tweetsie (although some had a little fun with the initials - thus Eat Taters and Wear No Clothes). The railway eventually reached Boone in 1918, but in 1905, the closest stop to Valle Crucis was Elk Park.

PERFECT PICNIC CAKE

6 tablespoons cocoa
2 sticks unsalted butter or margarine
1 cup water
2 cups flour
2 cups sugar
2 teaspoons baking soda
1/2 teaspoon salt
2 eggs
1/2 cup sour cream

Combine cocoa, butter and water in saucepan and bring to gentle boil. Cook and stir for 2 minutes; set aside to cool. In large bowl blend flour, sugar, soda and salt. Combine this with liquid mixture and stir lightly. Add eggs and sour cream. Blend entire mixture well. Bake in greased pan(s) in preheated 350° oven until center of cake springs back when touched.

Mary Getchell
Asheville

"One square bittersweet chocolate plus 2 tablespoons cocoa can be substituted for the 6 tablespoons of cocoa."

PLUM CAKE

3 eggs
2 cups sugar
1 cup vegetable oil
1 teaspoon cinnamon
1 teaspoon cloves
2 (6-ounce) jars junior baby food plums
2 cups self-rising flour

Mix together eggs, sugar, oil, cinnamon, cloves and plums. Gradually add flour and mix well. Pour into greased and floured bundt pan and bake in preheated 350° oven about 45 minutes. Cool in pan 10 minutes before removing cake.

Lemon Glaze:
3 tablespoons butter
1 cup confectioners sugar
1 1/2 to 2 tablespoons lemon juice

In microwave, melt butter in glass bowl. Blend in confectioners sugar, and gradually add lemon juice until the right consistency. Add water a few drops at a time, if necessary. Drizzle lemon glaze over cake.

Janet Bright
Hendersonville

"This moist, easy to make cake was a favorite of my friend, Audrey."

Pumpkin Cake

1 1/2 cups oil
2 cups sugar
2 cups pumpkin, mashed
4 eggs
2 teaspoons vanilla
1 cup raisins
1 (8-ounce) can crushed pineapple
2 cups plain flour
1 teaspoon baking powder
2 teaspoons baking soda
1 teaspoon salt
1 teaspoon allspice
3 teaspoons cinnamon

Mix oil and sugar together in large bowl. Add pumpkin, eggs, vanilla, raisins and pineapple. In separate bowl combine flour, baking powder, soda, salt, allspice and cinnamon. Add to oil and sugar mixture; mix well. Pour into greased and floured cake pans and bake in preheated 325° oven for 1 hour.

Lucy Mast Olsen
Valle Crucis

QUICK APPLE CAKE

3 eggs
3/4 cup oil
1 teaspoon vanilla
1 3/4 cups sugar
2 cups plain flour
1 teaspoon salt
1 teaspoon baking soda
1 teaspoon cinnamon
1 teaspoon baking powder
4 cups chopped apples
1 cup chopped pecans
1 (6-ounce) package butterscotch chips

Mix eggs, oil and vanilla in large bowl. Add sugar, flour, salt, soda, cinnamon and baking powder. Mix well. Fold in apples and nuts. Mixture will be thick. Spread in 9 x 13-inch pan. Sprinkle chips over top. Bake in preheated 350° oven for 30 minutes.

Lucy Mast Olson
Valle Crucis

Spicy Southern Gingerbread

3/4 cup oil
3/4 cup brown sugar
3/4 cup molasses
2 eggs
2 1/2 cups self-rising flour
1/2 teaspoon baking soda
1 1/2 teaspoons ginger
1 teaspoon cinnamon
1/4 teaspoon nutmeg
1 cup hot water

Combine oil, sugar and molasses. Stir in eggs. In a separate bowl combine flour, soda, ginger, cinnamon and nutmeg. Add the dry ingredients to the oil mixture, adding water as needed to keep batter moist. Mix well. Pour into greased cake pan and bake in preheated 350° oven for 45 minutes.

The Old Mast Store Deli
Valle Crucis

Directions for Measuring

1. Sift, or shake up lightly with a spoon, all dry materials (flour, baking powder, etc.) before measuring them. Always sift mustard.
2. All measures are to be taken level unless otherwise directed.
3. To measure a cupful of dry material, fill the cup with a spoon or scoop, and level off with a case knife. To measure a teaspoon or tablespoon of dry material, fill the spoon by dipping it into the material, lift it, and level off with a case knife. To measure a half spoonful, divide a spoon lengthwise with the knife. Divide a half-spoonful crosswise to measure a quarter, and a quarter-spoonful crosswise to measure an eighth. Less than an eighth of a teaspoon is called "a few grains."
4. A cupful of liquid is all the cup will hold; a spoonful of liquid is all the spoon will hold. A heaping spoonful of dry material is all the spoon will hold. A scant cupful is measured by filling the cup to within one-eighth of an inch of the brim.

Elements of the Theory and Practice of Cookery. A textbook copyrighted in 1901 and reprinted several times with the most recent one being in 1913.

STRAWBERRY CAKE

1 (3-ounce) box strawberry flavored gelatin
1/2 cup very hot water (or juice from berries)
1 cup oil
4 eggs
1 box white cake mix
1/2 cup strawberries

In large mixing bowl, dissolve gelatin in water, cool. Add oil and eggs, one at a time, beating after each. Add cake mix and strawberries. Pour in greased cake pan and bake in preheated 350° oven until done.

Icing:
1 stick butter, softened
1 box powdered sugar
1/2 cup strawberries

Cream together butter and sugar, add strawberries. Frost cooled cake.

The Old Mast Store Deli
Valle Crucis

Measuring is the key to any baking recipes. From "Elements of the Theory and Practice of Cookery."

TURTLE CAKE

1 German chocolate cake mix
1 (12-ounce) can evaporated milk, divided
3/4 cup melted butter
1 (7-ounce) package caramels
1 (12-ounce) package chocolate chips
1 cup pecan pieces

Mix cake mix with 2/3 cup evaporated milk and 3/4 cup melted butter. Pour half of the cake batter into a greased 9 x 13-inch pan and bake in preheated 375° oven for 10 minutes. Melt caramels with 1/3 cup evaporated milk and pour on top of the baked portion of the cake; sprinkle chocolate chips and nuts over caramel. Then pour on the remaining cake mix and bake for another 20 minutes at 375°.

The Old Mast Store Deli
Valle Crucis

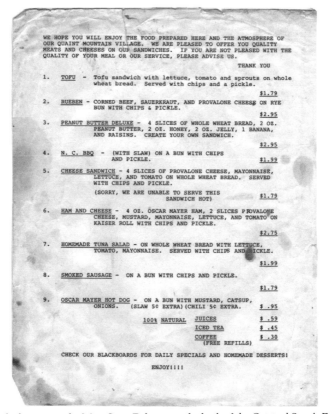

In the beginning, the Mast Store Deli was in the back of the Original Store's Front Room - and Faye Cooper was the principal cook. This is one of the first menus.

BLACK WALNUT POUND CAKE

2 sticks margarine
1/2 cup shortening
3 cups sugar
5 eggs
1 cup sour cream
3 cups flour
1/2 teaspoon baking powder
1/2 teaspoon salt
1/2 cup milk
1 teaspoon vanilla
1 teaspoon black walnut flavoring
1 cup chopped black walnuts

In a large mixing bowl, blend margarine, shortening and sugar. Add eggs one at a time, mixing well. Add sour cream. In another bowl, sift together flour, baking powder and salt. Add to first bowl, alternately with milk. Add vanilla, black walnut flavoring and nuts. Pour into greased tube pan and bake in preheated 325° oven for 1 hour. Reduce to 300° and bake for 30 minutes. Cool and frost with cream cheese icing.

Jeanne Norris
Home Office

"This is absolutely, without a doubt, the richest, most delicious cake I've ever eaten!"
An Anonymous Black Walnut Cake Lover

BROWN SUGAR POUND CAKE

1 cup butter, softened
1/2 cup butter-flavored shortening
1 (16-ounce) package light brown sugar
1 cup sugar
5 large eggs
1/2 teaspoon salt
1 teaspoon baking powder
1 1/2 teaspoons vanilla
3 cups plain flour, sifted
1 cup milk

In a large mixing bowl, cream butter and shortening together. Beat in brown sugar and granulated sugar. Add eggs one at a time, beating well after each. Beat in salt, baking powder and vanilla. Add flour and milk, alternating ingredients. Beat well. Pour into greased and floured tube pan. Bake in preheated 325° oven 1 hour and 45 minutes. Remove from pan and glaze while hot.

Glaze:
1 cup sifted confectioners sugar
1 1/2 tablespoons butter, softened
3 tablespoons milk
1/2 teaspoon vanilla

Beat sugar, butter, milk and vanilla well. Brush on cake while still warm. Cool and serve.

Della Goulter
Waynesville

CARAMEL POUND CAKE

1 cup (2 sticks) butter or margarine
1/2 cup vegetable shortening
1 (16-ounce) box light brown sugar
1 cup white sugar
5 large eggs
3 cups plain flour
1/2 teaspoon salt
1/2 teaspoon baking powder
1 cup milk
1 tablespoon vanilla

Cream butter and shortening with a mixer. Add brown sugar and white sugar a little at a time; beat until light and fluffy. Add eggs 1 at a time; beat 3 minutes. Sift flour with salt and baking powder. Add to beaten mixture, alternately with milk. Blend in vanilla. Pour into greased and floured tube pan. Bake in preheated 350° oven for 1 1/2 hours.

Icing:
1/2 cup (1 stick) butter or margarine
1 cup brown sugar
1/4 cup warm milk
2 cups powdered sugar
1 cup chopped nuts (optional)

In a sauce pan, over medium heat, mix margarine and sugar, stirring constantly. As soon as the mixture begins to boil, remove it from heat and let cool. Stir in milk. Mix in powdered sugar and nuts. Spread over cooled cake.

Lucy Mast Olsen
Valle Crucis

CINNAMON POUND CAKE

1 box yellow cake mix
1/2 cup sugar
1/2 teaspoon vanilla
3/4 cup vegetable oil
1 pint sour cream
4 eggs

Nut mixture:
3 teaspoons cinnamon
6 tablespoons brown sugar
1 1/2 cups nuts

By hand, stir together cake mix, sugar, vanilla, oil, sour cream and eggs until well mixed. Mix together cinnamon, brown sugar and nuts. In a well-buttered tube pan put a layer of nut mixture, then add a layer of cake batter. Pour three layers of each. Bake in preheated 325° oven for 1 hour.

Barbara Murdock
Home Office

CREAM CHEESE POUND CAKE

3 sticks margarine
1 (8-ounce) package cream cheese
3 cups sugar
Dash of salt
1 1/2 teaspoons vanilla
6 large eggs
3 cups sifted cake flour

Cream margarine, cream cheese and sugar until light and fluffy. Add salt and vanilla and beat well. Add eggs one at a time. Beat well after each addition. Add flour to mixture beating at low speed. Spoon mixture into greased and floured tube pan. Bake in preheated 300° oven for 2 hours or until cake tester comes out clean.

Melissa Edmisten
Home Office

CREAM CHEESE ICING

1 (8-ounce) package cream cheese, softened
2/3 stick margarine, softened
1 (16-ounce) box powdered sugar
1 teaspoon vanilla
1 cup pecans, chopped

Combine cream cheese and margarine. Add powdered sugar, vanilla and pecans. Mix to spreading consistency.

Jeanne Norris
Home Office

"You may substitute 1 teaspoon of black walnut flavoring for vanilla and 1 cup of black walnuts for pecans."

NANNY'S PORK CAKE

1 pound pork sausage
1 pound raisins
1 pound currants
4 cups brown sugar
2 cups boiling water
1 tablespoon cinnamon
1 teaspoon cloves
1/2 teaspoon nutmeg
1 teaspoon salt
1 tablespoon baking soda
1 cup English walnuts
5 1/2 cups flour

Mix together sausage, raisins, currants and sugar. Pour boiling water over mixture, then allow to cool. Add cinnamon, cloves, nutmeg, salt, soda and nuts. Gradually add flour. Divide between 2 greased loaf pans. Bake in preheated 350° oven for 1 to 1 1/4 hours. If large mold is used, bake 2 hours.

Janet Bright
Hendersonville

"This is a great substitute for the 'dreaded fruitcake.' Personal note from my mother, Jackie: 'Joe's mother (born 1880) has had this recipe in the family for years, and it is suprisingly good. When I cannot find currants, I substitute raisins.'"

OLD SOUTH FRUITCAKE

1/2 pound flour
1 teaspoon cinnamon
1 teaspoon ground cloves
1 teaspoon allspice
1/2 pound butter
1/2 pound sugar
6 eggs
1 pound raisins
1/2 pound green candied pineapple
1/2 pound mixed candied citron
1/2 pound almonds, chopped
1/2 pound pecans, chopped
1/2 pound English walnuts, chopped
1/2 pound Brazil nuts, chopped
1 pound crystalized red cherries
1 pound thick strawberry preserves

Sift flour and spices together. Remove 1/2 cup of flour and spice mix and set aside. Cream butter and sugar. Add one egg at a time, mixing well after each addition. Add flour and spice mix to make a thick batter. In a very large bowl, mix together raisins, pineapple, citron, almonds, pecans, walnuts, Brazil nuts and cherries. Sift flour that was reserved over the fruits and nuts and mix well. Pour cake batter over dredged fruits and nuts. Add strawberry preserves. Mix well with two spoons or with hands. Line loaf pans with foil. Pour batter into pans. Decorate tops with red and green fruits. Cover completely with foil and bake in preheated 250* oven for 3 hours. Then uncover and bake at 325° for 1 hour. Let cakes cool in pans for 30 minutes. Remove from pans and store in a cool space for up to one month.

Rebecca A. Fry
Boone

"My mother has used this recipe all my life. My godmother shared it with her from the Civil War times. My godmother died at 98 years old in 1961. Mom and I have carried this recipe on and we bake it just after Thanksgiving. We give as gifts or share with the family. It's moist and good - better than any I've ever tasted. This recipe makes 15 pounds of cake (1 large tube pan and 2 regular loaf pans, or 6 regular loaf pans.)"

CHEESE CRUMB-TOPPED APPLE PIE

Pastry for single crust 9-inch pie
1/3 cup packed brown sugar
1/3 cup granulated sugar
2 tablespoons all-purpose flour
1/2 teaspoon ground cinnamon
1/8 teaspoon ground nutmeg
1/8 teaspoon salt
4 1/2 cups peeled, thinly sliced Granny Smith apples

Place pastry in a 9-inch pie plate. Combine sugars, flour, cinnamon, nutmeg and salt in a large bowl. Add apples; toss gently to coat. Pour into pie crust.

Crumb Topping:
1/3 cup all-purpose flour
1/3 cup sugar
2 tablespoons rolled oats
1/2 teaspoon ground cinnamon
1/8 teaspoon ground nutmeg
1/2 cup grated sharp cheddar cheese, softened
3 tablespoons butter or margarine, softened

Combine flour, sugar, oats, cinnamon and nutmeg in a medium bowl. Add cheese and butter. Using a fork, blend until the mixture resembles coarse crumbs. Sprinkle crumb mixture over apples. Cover pastry edge with foil to prevent over browning. Bake in preheated 375° oven for 25 minutes; remove foil. Bake 20 to 25 minutes longer or until top is golden brown. Cool on wire rack.

Jill Meares
Asheville

"You may sprinkle 1/3 cup chopped pecans over apple mixture before adding topping or omit cheese from crumb topping mixture."

CHOCOLATE CHESS PIE

4 tablespoons butter
4 tablespoons cocoa
1 1/2 cups sugar
Dash of salt
1 teaspoon vanilla
2 eggs, beaten
1 (5-ounce) can evaporated milk
1 pie shell

Melt butter. Mix in cocoa, sugar and salt. Stir in vanilla and eggs. Add milk and mix well. Pour into pie shell and bake in preheated 350° oven for 45 minutes. Remove and let stand until it cools to room temperature.

Anne and William Wilson
Home Office

CHOCOLATETOWN PIE

1/2 cup butter or margarine, softened
2 eggs, beaten
2 teaspoons vanilla extract, or 2 tablespoons bourbon
1 cup sugar
1/2 cup all-purpose flour
1 cup chocolate chips
1 cup chopped pecans or walnuts
1 (9-inch) pastry shell

In small mixing, bowl cream butter, add eggs and vanilla or bourbon. Combine sugar and flour, add to creamed mixture. Stir in chocolate chips and nuts. Pour in pastry shell and bake in preheated 350° oven for 45 to 50 minutes or until golden. Cool about 1 hour.

The Old Mast Store Deli
Valle Crucis

PINEAPPLE PIE

1 (14-ounce) can sweetened condensed milk
1/3 cup fresh lemon juice
1 teaspoon vanilla
1 (12-ounce) carton frozen nondairy whipped topping
1 (20-ounce) can crushed pineapple, drained
2/3 cup chopped pecans
2 graham cracker pie crusts

Pour sweetened condensed milk into a medium bowl; gradually fold in lemon juice, vanilla and whipped topping. Add pineapple and nuts and pour into pie crusts. Chill several hours before serving.

Jill Meares
Asheville

EASY PINEAPPLE PIE

1 (14-ounce) can sweetened condensed milk
1/4 cup lemon juice
1 (8-ounce) can crushed pineapple, drained
1 cup chopped pecans
1/2 (8-ounce) carton frozen nondairy whipped topping
1 graham cracker pie crust

Mix sweetened condensed milk, lemon juice, pineapple and pecans. Fold in whipped topping, then pour into graham cracker pie crust. Refrigerate overnight.

Susan Benson
Home Office

GRANDMA'S CHESS PIE

2 cups packed light brown sugar
1/2 stick butter, softened
2 eggs, slightly beaten
2 tablespoons flour
1/2 cup milk
1 teaspoon vanilla
1 unbaked 9-inch pie shell

Combine sugar and butter in a mixing bowl. Add eggs, flour, milk and vanilla. Beat until well mixed. Pour into 9-inch unbaked pie shell. Bake in preheated 450° oven for 15 minutes. Turn oven down to 350° and bake for an additional 30 minutes.

Rebecca A. Fry
Boone

"I often add 3/4 cup finely chopped pecans to top before baking. I've used this recipe for 40 years. It's perfect every time. It was given to me by my mother's mother."

ICE CREAM PIE

1/2 gallon vanilla ice cream, softened
1 (6-ounce) can frozen lemonade, softened
2 (8-inch) graham cracker pie crusts

Mix ice cream and lemonade. Pour in graham cracker pie crusts and freeze.

Myrna Newkirk
Hendersonville

Key Lime Pie

1 (14-ounce) can sweetened condensed milk
4 egg yolks
1/2 cup lime juice
4 egg whites, divided
1/2 teaspoon cream of tartar
6 tablespoons sugar
1 pie shell, baked according to directions,
  pricking bottom before baking

Mix milk, egg yolks and lime juice. Beat 1 egg white stiff. Fold into milk mixture. Pour into pie shell. Beat remaining 3 egg whites, adding cream of tartar and gradually adding the sugar, until stiff. Spread to edges of pie and bake in preheated 350° oven until meringue is golden brown.

Janet Bright
Hendersonville

Easy Key Lime Pie

1/2 cup lime juice
1 (14-ounce) can fat-free sweetened condensed milk
1 (8-ounce) carton frozen nondairy whipped topping, softened
1 graham cracker pie shell

Stir lime juice and milk to blend. Slowly fold in whipped topping. Pour into pie shell. Refrigerate overnight or until firm.

Sylvia Bryan
Home Office

"Tip: if you pierce the limes then put in the microwave for 30 seconds, you get more juice."

Lemon Chess Pie

3 eggs, beaten
Juice of 2 lemons (about 6 tablespoons)
1 cup sugar
1/2 cup butter or margarine, melted
1 pie shell, unbaked

Mix eggs, lemon juice, sugar and melted butter together. Pour into pie shell and bake in preheated 400° oven for 35 minutes.

Janet Bright
Hendersonville

"Quick and simple!"

Lemon Cake Pie

1 1/2 cups sugar
1 tablespoon flour
3 eggs, separated
3 tablespoons butter, melted
3 tablespoons milk
3 tablespoons lemon juice
3 tablespoons grated lemon rind
1 (9-inch) unbaked pie shell

Mix sugar and flour together and slowly add to slightly beaten egg yolks. Add the melted butter, milk, lemon juice and grated lemon rind. Beat egg whites until stiff, and fold into lemon mixture. Place in unbaked pie shell and bake in preheated 375° oven for 35 to 40 minutes.

Jill Meares
Asheville

MOM'S LEMON MERINGUE PIE

1 1/4 cups sugar
1/4 cup cornstarch
1 1/2 cups cold water
1/4 cup lemon juice
Grated peel of 2 lemons
1 tablespoon butter
3 eggs, separated
1 baked 9-inch pie crust
1/3 cup sugar

In top of double boiler combine sugar and cornstarch, stirring and adding water gradually. Place over bottom of double boiler and cook over medium heat. Stir until mixture thickens, then add lemon juice, peel and butter. Spoon some of the mixture into slightly beaten egg yolks. Add egg yolks to mixture in double boiler. Stir continuously as it thickens. Remove from heat and pour into pie crust.

Meringue:
Beat egg whites with an electric beater until they form stiff peaks. Still beating at high speed, add 1 tablespoon of sugar at a time until meringue forms peaks. Spread meringue over top of pie, sealing edges. Bake in preheated 350° oven for 15 to 20 minutes or until golden brown. Cool before cutting pie.

Rebecca A. Fry
Boone

NANNY'S SOUR CREAM PIE

1/2 cup butter or margarine
2 cups sugar
4 eggs, separated
Pinch of salt
1 tablespoon flour
2 cups sour cream
2 tablespoons cinnamon
Juice of 1 lemon (about 3 tablespoons)
2 unbaked pie shells

Cream butter, sugar, egg yolks, salt and flour; add sour cream. In a separate bowl, beat egg whites until stiff, and gradually add cinnamon. Fold sour cream mixture into egg whites; add lemon juice. Pour into 2 unbaked pie shells. Cover crust edges with foil for the first 20 minutes. Bake in preheated 400° oven for first 10 minutes, then reduce temperature to 375° and bake for an additional 40 to 45 minutes. Do not overbake, or outer edges of filling will be hard after pie cools.

Janet Bright
Hendersonville

"Personal note: My grandmother Zellah was born in 1880. This was her recipe from the early 1900s, and I've never seen another like it. It's very easy to make."

Nanny Zellah, Mike, Lisa and Janet Bright in 1968.

PECAN CHIFFON PIE

1 cup coarsely chopped toasted pecans
1 cup dark brown sugar, packed
1 1/3 cups water
4 tablespoons cornstarch
1/4 cup cold water
2/3 cup egg whites, room temperature
1/4 cup sugar
2 (8 or 9-inch) pie crusts, baked
Whipped cream or topping

Toast pecans in preheated 325° oven until they barely begin to turn brown, watching carefully so they won't burn. Combine brown sugar and water in a saucepan; bring to a boil. Mix cornstarch and cold water thoroughly. Add to boiling brown sugar mixture; cook until it becomes clear and consistency of thick pudding. Remove from heat. Beat egg whites until peaks form. Slowly add the 1/4 cup sugar and beat until peaks are stiff. Fold hot cooked mixture into egg whites. Add nuts. Put into pie crusts. Top each with 1 cup whipped topping and sprinkle with a few additional nuts.

Lucy Mast Olsen
Valle Crucis

PUMPKIN CREAM PIE

1 (4.6-ounce) box vanilla instant pudding mix
2 cups cold milk
1 cup canned pumpkin
1 teaspoon pumpkin pie spice
1 cup frozen nondairy whipped topping, thawed
1 baked pie shell

Mix pudding mix with milk; stir in pumpkin until smooth. Add spice, then whipped topping. Beat on low 1 minute. Pour into pie shell. Chill until set, at least 3 hours. Garnish with whipped topping and chopped pecans or 1/2 sliced cherry.

The Old Mast Store Deli
Valle Crucis

PEANUT BUTTER PIE

1 1/2 cups confectioners sugar
1 (8-ounce) package light cream cheese, softened
2/3 cup milk
8 tablespoons peanut butter
1 (12-ounce) carton light frozen nondairy whipped topping
2 graham cracker pie crusts
Chocolate syrup and crushed peanuts for topping, optional

Cream together sugar and cream cheese. Add milk and continue to mix. Add peanut butter and whip until smooth. Reduce speed of mixer and slowly add whipped topping until well blended. Pour mixture into crusts and place in freezer. Remove from freezer about 15 minutes before serving. Drizzle with chocolate syrup and crushed peanuts, if desired.

Barbara Murdock
Home Office

EASY PEANUT BUTTER COOKIES

1 cup peanut butter
1 teaspoon baking soda
1 egg
1 cup sugar

Mix peanut butter, soda, egg and sugar. Roll dough into 1 inch balls and place on cookie sheet one inch apart. Bake in preheated 325° oven for 8 minutes. Do not let them brown.

Catherine L. Main
Original Store

SECRET PEANUT BUTTER PIE

1 cup powdered sugar
1/2 cup peanut butter
1 baked pie shell
1 (4.6-ounce) box vanilla cooked pudding mix
3 cups milk
4 egg whites
6 tablespoons sugar

Blend powdered sugar and peanut butter with a pastry blender until it has the consistency of tiny peas. Put all but 1/4 cup of mixture in the bottom of the baked pie shell. Combine pudding mix and milk and cook as directed on box. Pour the hot mixture over peanut mixture in pie shell. Let cool for 30 minutes. Prepare egg whites by beating with mixer on high until stiff, adding sugar during beating process. Spread meringue over pie, sealing edges well. Sprinkle 1/4 cup reserved peanut butter mixture over meringue. Put in oven on broil and brown for 3 to 4 minutes. Watch closely.

Joyce M. Crandall
Hendersonville

"I promised not to give this recipe to anyone. But that was 23 years ago, and it's time to share this great recipe! I always double the recipe and bake 2 pies at once."

Peanut Butter Cookies

1 cup (2 sticks) margarine
1 cup brown sugar
1 cup white sugar
2 eggs
1 cup peanut butter
1 teaspoon vanilla
3 1/4 cups flour
2 teaspoons baking soda
1/2 teaspoon salt

Mix together margarine, brown sugar and white sugar. Add eggs, peanut butter and vanilla. Combine flour, soda and salt in another bowl, then add to peanut butter mixture. This should make a stiff dough. Shape into balls and place on a cookie sheet. Criss-cross the top of each cookie with a fork while pressing down to flatten the cookie. Bake in preheated 350° oven for 15 minutes. Cookies will be very soft when taken from oven. Let cookies cool completely before removing from cookie sheet.

Jeanne Norris
Home Office

"This recipe is my mother's and her secret is not to overbake cookies. Always use margarine in stick form when making cookies. If you use a spread, your cookies won't turn out right. I prefer using an air-bake cookie sheet, because I think the cookies come out better."

Peanut Butter Filling

1/2 cup peanut butter
1 teaspoon vanilla
4 tablespoons milk
3 cups powdered sugar

Mix peanut butter, vanilla, milk and sugar together until creamy.

Teresa Presnell
Original Store

"This is very good spread between peanut butter cookies."

Pecan Balls

1 cup butter, softened
1/2 cup sugar
1/4 teaspoon salt
1 teaspoon vanilla
2 1/4 cups self-rising flour
1 cup chopped pecans
Confectioners sugar

Cream butter, sugar, salt and vanilla together until fluffy. Mix in flour and pecans. Chill dough until firm. Roll into 1 inch balls. Place on ungreased baking sheet and bake in preheated 350° oven for 10 to 12 minutes until set but not browned. While still warm, roll in confectioners sugar; cool, then roll again.

Judy Phillips
Original Store

"I prefer to shake cooked balls in a bag with the confectioners sugar - about 6 at a time."

PECAN CRESCENTS

4 heaping tablespoons powdered sugar
3/4 cup butter
2 cups flour
1 cup finely chopped nuts
1 teaspoon vanilla

Mix sugar, butter, flour, nuts and vanilla together in medium bowl. Shape by hand into crescent shapes and place on cookie sheet. Bake in a preheated slow oven (250° to 300°) for 45 minutes. Do not brown. Roll in powdered sugar.

Lucy Mast Olsen
Valle Crucis

NO BAKE COOKIES

1 stick margarine
2 cups sugar
1/2 cup milk
3 cups oatmeal
1/2 cup peanut butter
4 tablespoons cocoa
1 teaspoon vanilla

Put margarine, sugar and milk in a large sauce pan. Bring to a boil over medium heat; let boil 2 to 3 minutes. Take off heat and add oatmeal, peanut butter, cocoa and vanilla. Mix well and drop from teaspoon onto waxed paper. Let cool.

Cindy Presnell
Home Office

JOLLY GINGERBREAD MEN

1/2 cup butter or margarine
1/2 cup shortening
1 cup granulated sugar
1/3 cup brown sugar
1 egg
1/4 cup light molasses
3 1/2 cups flour
2 teaspoons baking soda
2 teaspoons cinnamon
1 teaspoon ground ginger
1/2 teaspoon ground cloves
Red cinnamon candies
Raisins

Thoroughly cream together butter, shortening, sugars, egg and molasses. In a separate bowl, sift together flour, soda, cinnamon, ginger and cloves. Stir into creamed mixture. Chill well. On lightly floured surface, roll dough to 1/4 inch thickness. Cut with gingerbread boy cookie cutter. Place 1 inch apart on ungreased cookie sheet. Decorate with cinnamon candies or raisins. Bake in preheated 375° oven for 7 to 8 minutes. Cool slightly; remove to rack and cool.

Jill Meares
Asheville

"This is a recipe that I began using the first Christmas after Henry and I were married. We gave the gingerbread boys to friends in our neighborhood. When our children came along, they helped with the preparation and gave out cookies to their friends and teachers. Today, some of our grandchildren help their moms and dads carry on this tradition. Of course, I still try to make a batch of gingerbread men every year."

Congo Bars

2/3 cup shortening, melted
2 1/2 cups dark brown sugar
2 eggs
2 3/4 cups flour
2 teaspoons baking powder
1/2 teaspoon salt
1 teaspoon vanilla
1 (6-ounce) bag chocolate chips

Combine shortening and brown sugar, let cool. Add eggs, flour, baking powder, salt and vanilla. Mix well. Stir in chocolate chips. Spread dough into oblong cake pan. Bake in preheated 350° oven for 25 to 30 minutes.

Mary Getchell
Asheville

Munchie Bars

1 stick margarine, melted
3 eggs, divided
1 box cake mix, any kind
1 cup pecans, chopped
1 (16-ounce) box powdered sugar
1 (8-ounce) package cream cheese

Mix margarine, 1 egg and cake mix. Dough will be stiff. Spread in greased and floured 13 x 9-inch pan. Sprinkle pecans over mixture. Mix sugar, 2 eggs and cream cheese. Pour over pecans. Bake in preheated 350° oven for 40 to 45 minutes.

Barbara Murdock
Home Office

"I prefer to use yellow cake mix in this recipe."

Raisin Bars

1 cup raisins
1 cup water
1 cup sugar
1/2 cup oil
1 3/4 cups plain flour
1/4 teaspoon salt
1 teaspoon baking soda
1 teaspoon cinnamon
1 teaspoon nutmeg
1 teaspoon allspice
1/2 teaspoon ground cloves
1 egg, slightly beaten
1/2 cup chopped walnuts

Combine raisins and water in 2-quart pot and bring to a boil. Remove from heat. Add sugar and oil. Cool to lukewarm. Sift together flour, salt, soda, cinnamon, nutmeg, allspice and cloves. Add gradually to raisin mixture. Add egg; stir in walnuts. Pour into greased 13 x 9 x 2-inch baking pan. Bake in preheated 375° oven for 20 minutes. Cool on rack. Dust with powdered sugar and cut into bars.

Rebecca A. Fry
Boone

"These will keep for several days and are great for gift giving and shipping."

Berry Cobbler

1/2 stick butter
1 cup sugar
1 cup self-rising flour
1 cup milk
1 to 2 cups berries

Melt butter in 9 x 9-inch pan. In small bowl, mix sugar, flour and milk. Pour on top of melted butter. Sprinkle berries over all. Bake in preheated 350° oven for 30 minutes.

Jennifer Presnell
Home Office

Blueberry Yum Yum

2 cups graham cracker crumbs
1 stick of butter or margarine, melted
1 tablespoon sugar
1 (3-ounce) package cream cheese, softened
1 cup sugar
2 1/2 teaspoons vanilla, divided
1 package whipped topping mix
1/2 cup cold milk
1 (15-ounce) can blueberry pie filling

Mix graham cracker crumbs, margarine and 1 tablespoon of sugar together. Spread 1/2 of mixture in bottom of a 9 x 13-inch baking dish. In a bowl, combine cream cheese, 1 cup of sugar, and 2 teaspoons vanilla. Make whipped topping according to package directions. Fold whipped topping into cream cheese mixture. Pour half of the cream cheese mixture over graham cracker crust. Pour blueberry pie filling over cream cheese layer. Spread rest of cream cheese mixture over pie filling; sprinkle with remaining graham cracker crumb mixture. Cover and refrigerate overnight.

Debbie Matheson
Home Office

CHOCOLATE ECLAIR

2 (3.4-ounce) boxes French Vanilla instant pudding mix
3 cups milk
1 (8-ounce) carton frozen nondairy whipped topping
1 box graham crackers

Combine pudding and milk; mix well. Fold in whipped topping and beat 2 minutes at medium speed. Butter long glass dish. Layer graham crackers, then pudding mixture. Add layer of crackers, then pudding, then crackers.

Topping:
1/4 cup milk
1/3 cup cocoa
1 cup powdered sugar
1/8 teaspoon salt
1/4 stick margarine
1 teaspoon vanilla

Combine milk, cocoa, sugar and salt in saucepan. Bring to a boil and cook for 1 minute. Remove from heat and add margarine and vanilla. Mix well. Let cool and pour over top of graham crackers.

Kim Edmisten
Home Office

CHOCOLATE PIZZA

1/2 cup sour cream
1 teaspoon baking soda
2 sticks margarine
1 cup water
4 tablespoons cocoa
2 cups all-purpose flour
2 cups sugar
2 eggs
1/2 teaspoon salt

In a small bowl, mix sour cream and soda; set aside. In a sauce pan, bring to a boil margarine, water and cocoa. Combine flour, sugar, eggs and salt in a large bowl. Add sour cream mixture to the flour. Add liquid mixture; stir well. Pour into greased pizza pan. Bake in preheated 350° oven for 20 to 25 minutes.

Icing for Chocolate Pizza:
1 stick margarine, melted
5 tablespoons milk
4 tablespoons cocoa
1 (16-ounce) box powdered sugar
1 teaspoon vanilla
1 cup chopped pecans or walnuts

Melt margarine in a sauce pan. Add milk and cocoa and bring to a boil. Remove from heat and add powdered sugar and vanilla. Stir until thickened. Add nuts and quickly pour on pizza. Smooth icing out to edges. Cool.

Joyce Crandall
Hendersonville

"My children called this 'the pizza cake' because it was made in a pizza pan. It will look like a big pan of fudge after the icing is spread on."

LEMON LUSH

1 cup flour
1 stick margarine, melted
1/2 cup walnut pieces
1 (16-ounce) carton frozen nondairy whipped topping, divided
1 (8-ounce) package cream cheese, softened
1/2 cup confectioners sugar
2 cups milk
2 (3.4-ounce) boxes lemon instant pudding mix

Crust:
Mix together flour, margarine and walnut pieces. Press into bottom of 9 x 12-inch pan. Bake in preheated 425° oven for 10 to 15 minutes or until brown.

Filling:
Beat together 1/2 of whipped topping, cream cheese and confectioners sugar. Spoon into cooled crust. Mix milk with lemon pudding. Beat at low speed for 2 minutes. Spoon onto top of pie. Spread remaining whipped topping over pudding layer. Refrigerate 1 hour before serving.

George Brudzinski
Sales Consultant
Blue Horse Promotions

LEMON SQUARES

2 sticks butter (or 1 stick each butter and margarine)
2 cups flour
1/2 cup powdered sugar
4 eggs, slightly beaten
2 cups sugar
6 tablespoons lemon juice with grated rind
1 tablespoon flour
1/2 tablespoon baking powder

Mix butter, flour and powdered sugar together by hand. Press into 10 x 14-inch baking dish. Bake in preheated 325° oven for 15 minutes. Mix eggs, sugar, lemon juice, rind, flour and baking powder together in a medium bowl. Pour over pastry in baking dish, then bake at 325° for 45 minutes.

Lucy Mast Olsen
Valle Crucis

Sugars-Candies

Sugar a valuable food. - Sugar is not only a food pleasing to the taste, but is one of the best of heat givers and force producers. This is why children, naturally more active than grown people, are more eager for sugar.

Common sense in the use of sugar. - Because sugar dissolves readily, small quantities of it are easily digested; but if more than a little is taken at once, some of it is likely to ferment in the stomach, causing distress, and interfering with the digestion of other foods. It may ferment in the mouth and make the teeth decay.

Do not eat sweets just before meals; they will take away your appetite for more substantial food. Use sugar sparingly on oatmeal and in beverages; a little tastes as sweet as more to one who has not blunted his taste by using too much. Do not be tempted by sweets in the bakeshop; they are bad for teeth, complexion, and health.

Elements of the Theory and Practice of Cookery. A textbook copyrighted in 1901 and reprinted several times with the most recent one being in 1913.

CHOCOLATE CHIP CHEESECAKE

Chocolate Crumb Crust:
1 1/2 cups graham cracker crumbs
1/3 cup cocoa
1/2 cup confectioners sugar
1/3 cup butter or margarine, melted

Combine graham cracker crumbs, cocoa, sugar and butter. Mix until moistened. Press crumb mixture in bottom of a 9-inch spring form pan.

Cheesecake Filling:
3 (8-ounce) packages cream cheese, softened
1 (14-ounce) can sweetened condensed milk
3 eggs
2 teaspoons vanilla extract
1 cup semi-sweet chocolate chips, divided
1 teaspoon flour

Beat cream cheese until fluffy. Add condensed milk. Beat until smooth. Add eggs and vanilla. Toss 3/4 cups of chocolate chips in flour, then add to mixture. Pour over crust in spring form pan and sprinkle with rest of chocolate chips. Bake in preheated 300° oven for 1 hour or until center is set. Cool and refrigerate.

William Whitaker
Home Office

CHOCOLATE TURTLE CHEESECAKE

1 (7-ounce) package caramels
1/4 cup evaporated milk
3/4 cup chopped pecans, divided
1 (9-inch) chocolate crumb pie crust
2 (3-ounce) packages cream cheese, softened
1/2 cup sour cream
1 1/4 cups milk
1 (3.4-ounce) box chocolate instant pudding mix
1/2 cup fudge topping

Place caramels and evaporated milk in a heavy saucepan. Heat on medium low heat, stirring until smooth, about 5 minutes. Stir in 1/2 cup pecans. Pour into pie crust. Combine cream cheese, sour cream and milk in a blender, until smooth. Add pudding mix, process for about 30 seconds longer. Pour pudding mixture over caramel layer; chill, loosely covered, until set, about 15 minutes. Drizzle fudge topping over pudding in a decorative pattern. Sprinkle top of cake with remaining pecans. Chill until serving time.

Barbara Murdock
Home Office

NO BAKE CHEESECAKE

1 (8-ounce) package cream cheese, room temperature
1/3 cup lemon juice
1 (14-ounce) can sweetened condensed milk
1 teaspoon vanilla
1 graham cracker pie crust

Mix cream cheese, lemon juice, condensed milk and vanilla. Whip until smooth. Pour into crust and chill. Top with your favorite fruit.

Debbie Matheson
Home Office

MILLIE'S APPLE PUDDING

1 stick margarine
1 cup sugar
1 egg
1 cup flour
1 teaspoon baking soda
1/2 teaspoon cinnamon
1/2 teaspoon nutmeg
3 or 4 apples, chopped

Cream margarine and sugar with a mixer. Mix in egg. In another bowl, sift together flour, soda, cinnamon and nutmeg. Add dry ingredients to the mixer. Stir in apples. Mix well. Pour into greased 1-quart baking dish and bake in preheated 350° oven for 45 minutes.

Lucy Mast Olsen
Valle Crucis

MILLIE'S LEMON PUDDING

2 tablespoons butter
1/2 cup sugar
3 eggs, separated
1/4 cup flour
1 large lemon
1 1/2 to 2 cups milk

Cream butter and sugar with mixer. Beat egg yokes, and add with milk and flour to butter mixture. Beat until smooth. Grate lemon rind and extract juice from lemon; add to mixture. Beat egg whites and fold into pudding. Pour into glass baking dish and place in pan of hot water. Bake in preheated 350° oven until set.

Lucy Mast Olsen
Valle Crucis

Pumpkin Roll

3 eggs
1 cup sugar
2/3 cup cooked pumpkin
3/4 cup self-rising flour
1 teaspoon cinnamon
1 teaspoon nutmeg
1/2 teaspoon ginger
1/2 cup powdered sugar

Beat eggs for 5 minutes. Gradually add sugar. Mix in pumpkin. In a separate bowl sift together flour, cinnamon, nutmeg and ginger. Add to mixture, pour in greased 15 x 10 x 1-inch pan. Bake in preheated 375° oven for 15 minutes. Sprinkle hand towel with powdered sugar. Turn cake out on towel and roll up. Let cool.

Filling:
1 (8-ounce) package cream cheese
1 cup powdered sugar
1 stick margarine
1/2 teaspoon vanilla

Mix cream cheese, powdered sugar, margarine and vanilla. Unroll cake and spread filling on cooled cake. Roll up and place in refrigerator to chill. The longer it sets the better it gets. Slice to serve.

Melissa Edmisten
Home Office

BROWNIES

2 cups self-rising flour
2 cups sugar
8 tablespoons cocoa
2 teaspoons vanilla
1 cup oil
4 eggs
1/2 cup nuts

Using mixer, combine flour, sugar, cocoa, vanilla, oil and eggs. Stir in nuts by hand. Pour in greased 9 x 13-inch pan and bake in preheated 350° oven for 25 to 30 minutes.

Cindy Presnell
Home Office

APPLESAUCE CHOCOLATE BROWNIES

1/2 cup shortening
1 cup sugar
2 eggs
1 teaspoon vanilla
1/2 cup cocoa
1 cup flour
1/2 teaspoon baking soda
1/2 teaspoon baking powder
1/8 teaspoon salt
1/2 cup sweet applesauce
1/2 cup black walnuts or pecans

Cream shortening and sugar; add eggs and vanilla. In separate bowl, combine cocoa, flour, soda, baking powder and salt. Mix dry ingredients with shortening mixture; add applesauce then nuts. Pour into cake pan and bake in preheated 350° oven for 25 minutes.

The Old Mast Store Deli
Valle Crucis

CARAMEL BROWNIES

        1 (5-ounce) can evaporated milk, divided
        3/4 cup margarine, melted
        1 box German chocolate cake mix
        1 (14 or 15-ounce) bag caramels
        1 (6-ounce) package semi-sweet chocolate morsels
        1 cup chopped pecans

Add 1/2 can milk and margarine to cake mix. Pour 1/2 of mix into greased 9 x 13-inch pan. Bake in preheated 350° oven for 6 minutes. Sprinkle chocolate chips and pecans over cake. In saucepan, melt caramels with 1/2 can evaporated milk; pour on top. Spread rest of cake mix over all; bake for 20 minutes.

Kitty Rominger
Home Office

"You can substitute candy coated chocolate pieces or chocolate covered toffee pieces for the pecans."

COCOA BROWNIES

        3/4 cup sifted all-purpose flour
        1/4 teaspoon salt
        1/2 cup margarine
        1 teaspoon vanilla
        1 cup sugar
        1/4 cup cocoa
        2 eggs
        1/2 cup nuts, chopped

Combine flour, salt, margarine, vanilla, sugar, cocoa and eggs. Mix on medium speed with electric mixer for two minutes. Add nuts. Bake in greased 8 x 8 x 2-inch baking pan in preheated 350° oven for 20 to 25 minutes.

Jeanne Norris
Home Office

Blueberry Buckle

1/4 cup shortening or margarine
1/2 cup sugar
1 egg
1 cup plain flour
1 1/2 teaspoons baking powder
1/2 teaspoon salt
1 cup milk
1 pint blueberries

Cream together shortening and sugar; add egg. Sift together flour, baking powder and salt. Add dry ingredients and milk alternately into sugar mixture. Mix well, pour into 8 x 10-inch greased pan; sprinkle with blueberries.

Crumb Topping:
1/3 cup flour
1/2 cup brown sugar
1/2 teaspoon cinnamon
1/4 teaspoon nutmeg

Combine flour, brown sugar, cinnamon and nutmeg; sprinkle over blueberries and dot with butter. Bake in preheated 350° oven for 30 to 35 minutes.

The Old Mast Store Deli
Valle Crucis
Via Dr. Richard Reeser

BLACK BOTTOMS

1 (8-ounce) package cream cheese
1 egg
1 1/3 cups sugar, divided
1/2 teaspoon salt
1 cup chocolate chips
1 1/2 cups flour
1/4 cup baking cocoa
1 teaspoon baking soda
1 cup water
1/3 cup oil
1 tablespoon white vinegar
1 teaspoon vanilla

Mix cream cheese and egg until smooth. Stir in 1/3 cup sugar, salt and chocolate chips; set aside. In a separate bowl, mix flour, 1 cup sugar, cocoa, soda, water, oil, vinegar and vanilla. Fill pastry cups half full with cocoa mixture. Top with 1 teaspoon of the cream cheese mixture. Bake in preheated 350° oven for 15 to 20 minutes.

Susan Hopkins
Asheville

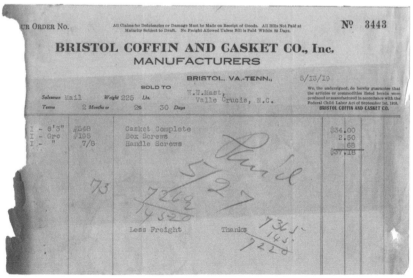

A general store's inventory had most everything you would need - including the final need. Caskets could come complete or pieces could be ordered for those who built their own.

CHOCOLATE COVERED CHERRIES

3 tablespoons butter, softened
3 tablespoons white corn syrup
2 cups powdered sugar
4 or 5 jars of cherries with stems, drained
1 (12-ounce) package semi-sweet chocolate chips

Mix butter and corn syrup. Blend in powdered sugar with a fork. Wash cherries and pat dry with a paper towel. Powder hands with powdered sugar. Pinch off 1 teaspoon of butter mixture. Make a patty and wrap it around a cherry. Continue until all cherries are covered with butter mixture. Refrigerate overnight, or for at least 2 hours. Melt chocolate chips in a double boiler. (If chocolate is too thin, add 1 to 2 teaspoons of vegetable shortening.) Dip cherries and place on a cookie sheet. Refrigerate.

Ashleigh Bishop
Hendersonville

NO COOK BON BONS

3/4 cup peanut butter
2 sticks margarine
2 1/2 to 3 cups graham cracker crumbs
1 (3 1/2-ounce) can coconut
1 (16-ounce) box powdered sugar
1 cup chopped pecans
2 teaspoons vanilla
6 to 12-ounces semi-sweet chocolate morsels
1/2 block of paraffin wax

Melt peanut butter and margarine in microwave. Add graham cracker crumbs, coconut, powdered sugar, pecans and vanilla; mix well. Shape into small balls. Melt chocolate morsels and paraffin wax in a double boiler. Dip each ball in chocolate and place on waxed paper to cool.

Teresa Presnell
Original Store

Homemade Fruit Ice Cream

2 pints fresh fruit (peaches or strawberries)
1 pint half and half
1 lemon freshly squeezed, or 2 tablespoons lemon juice
1 1/2 cups sugar
1 quart milk

Blend mashed fruit, half and half, and lemon juice. Add sugar then milk. Pour into ice cream freezer can to within 2 inches of the top; if necessary add more milk. Put into freezer securing lid. Pack with ice and coarse salt. Churn until firm.

Jill Meares
Asheville

Homemade Vanilla Ice Cream

2 (14-ounce) cans sweetened condensed milk
1/4 cup sugar
Milk

Combine sweetened condensed milk and sugar. Add enough milk to bring mixture to the fill line on a 4-quart freezer can. Freeze as directed for the ice cream maker.

Variations:
Banana: Add 5 to 6 ripe mashed bananas before freezing
Peach: Add 4 cups pureed peaches before freezing
Strawberry: Add 4 cups pureed strawberries before freezing
Chocolate: Add 16-ounce can chocolate syrup before freezing

Melissa Edmisten
Home Office

STICKIES

1/2 cup shortening
2 cups self-rising flour
1 cup milk
1 stick butter or margarine, as needed
Ground cinnamon
Brown sugar

In medium size bowl, cut shortening into flour. Add milk and mix with a fork. Add additional flour until dough is stiff and not sticky. Pinch off enough dough to form a 1 1/2 inch to 2 inch ball. Knead slightly on a floured surface. Using a rolling pin, roll dough into an oval about 1/4 inch thick. Cut slivers of butter and spread in the middle of the oval. Sprinkle one heaping tablespoon or more of brown sugar over butter. Then sprinkle a dash of cinnamon over sugar. Bring edges together length-wise and pinch across the top. Put on baking sheet. Repeat with remaining dough. Bake in preheated 450° oven for about 15 minutes or until tops are golden brown.

Sheri Moretz
Home Office

"These were always a treat when Mom made them as I was growing up."

BANANA NUT DESSERT

1 (3.4-ounce) box vanilla cooked pudding mix
2 cups milk
2 medium bananas, sliced
1/2 teaspoon vanilla extract
1/4 cup chopped pecans or walnuts
3 tablespoons sour cream
Crushed cookies (optional)

Make pudding as directed on box. Let cool for 5 minutes. Transfer pudding to serving bowl. Mix in bananas, vanilla, nuts and sour cream. Top with crushed cookies. Chill 30 minutes before serving.

Allen Mast
Original Store
218 Desserts

MICROWAVE FUDGE

   1 cup butter
   1 (12-ounce) can evaporated milk
   4 cups sugar
   1 (7-ounce) jar marshmallow creme
   1 (12-ounce) package semi-sweet chocolate morsels

Mix butter, evaporated milk, sugar and marshmallow creme in a deep bowl. Microwave on high for 22 minutes. Stir in chocolate morsels and pour into buttered dish.

Jimmy Tucker
Woolrich representative

"To make peanut butter fudge, substitute 1 (7-ounce) jar chunky peanut butter for chocolate."

PEANUT BUTTER FUDGE

   2 cups firmly packed light brown sugar
   2 cups granulated sugar
   1 cup milk
   1/4 teaspoon salt
   1/4 teaspoon cream of tartar
   2 teaspoons vanilla
   1/2 cup crunchy peanut butter

Butter the sides and bottom of an 8-inch square pan. Stir together the sugars, milk, salt and cream of tartar in saucepan. Cook over medium heat, stirring until the sugars dissolve and the mixture boils. Continue cooking until temperature reaches 234° on candy thermometer. Remove from heat. Add vanilla and peanut butter, but do not stir it in. Cool mixture until temperature drops to 115° (may take an hour). Beat mixture until it thickens and turns lighter in color (about 3 minutes). While the fudge can still flow from the saucepan, pour it into buttered pan. Cool. Cut into squares.

Jill Meares
Asheville

PEACH DELIGHT

2 cups self-rising flour
2 sticks margarine, melted
1 cup chopped pecans
1 (8-ounce) package cream cheese
2 1/2 cups confectioners sugar
1 (8-ounce) carton frozen nondairy whipped topping
4 cups peaches, diced (canned or fresh)
1 cup sugar
4 tablespoons flour
4 tablespoons peach flavored gelatin
1 cup water

Mix flour, margarine and pecans. Press in a 9 x 12-inch pan. Bake in a preheated 375° oven for 15 minutes; let cool. Mix cream cheese, confectioners sugar and whipped topping together. Spread this over first layer; refrigerate while preparing third layer. Spread peaches over second layer. Mix sugar, flour and gelatin in a medium sauce pan; stir in water. Cook over medium heat until mixture is thick and clear. Cool completely and pour over peaches. Refrigerate overnight.

Debe Jones
Home Office

PINEAPPLE ORANGE FLUFF

1 (8-ounce) carton light frozen nondairy whipped topping
1 (2.1-ounce) box pistachio sugar-free instant pudding mix
1 (15-ounce) can mandarin oranges, drained
1 (15-ounce) can crushed pineapple, drained
3/4 cup mini marshmallows

Combine the whipped topping and pistachio pudding, mixing well. Fold in the mandarin oranges, pineapple and marshmallows. Chill and serve.

Della Goulter
Waynesville

WHITE TRASH

1 stick butter
1 (12-ounce) bag chocolate chips
1 (18-ounce) jar creamy peanut butter
1 (12-ounce) box crispy cereal squares
1 (6 1/2-ounce) can salted peanuts
1 (9 to 12-ounce) bag mini pretzels
1 (10 1/2-ounce) bag miniature marshmallows
1 (15-ounce) box raisins (optional)
1 1/2 (16-ounce) boxes confectioners sugar

Melt butter and chocolate in microwave and stir in peanut butter. Put cereal, peanuts, pretzels, marshmallows and raisins in "doubled" paper bags. Pour chocolate mixture over ingredients in bag and shake until well coated. Open bag and stir to insure even coating. Pour mixture into clean "doubled" bags and add confectioners sugar. Shake to coat. Store in airtight containers.

Melanee Lester
Waynesville

"Requires a whole lot of shaking, but worth the effort!"

GRAHAM CRACKER PIE CRUST

1 package graham crackers
1/4 cup sugar
1 stick margarine

Crush graham crackers into fine crumbs. Mix crumbs with sugar. Melt margarine in 1-quart pan. Add crumbs to margarine and mix until they are dampened. Pour into pie pan and press to sides with a tablespoon. Put in the freezer while you prepare filling.

Barbara Murdock
Home Office

Quick and Easy Pastry Mix

7 cups plain flour
1 tablespoon salt
2 cups shortening

Combine flour, salt and shortening in large bowl. Cut with pastry blender until mixture forms into fine crumbs. Store in air tight container. Use 1 1/2 cups of mix and add 3 to 4 tablespoons of cold water. Shape as desired. Prick crust with fork. Bake in preheated 425° oven.

Rebecca A. Fry
Boone

"I keep this pastry mix on hand all the time. It will make 5 single pie crusts. I've used this recipe for at least 25 years."

Fat as Food

Fat as food; no diet well balanced without it. - Knowing fat to be a heat giver, we can understand why we like, in winter, foods containing more fat than we care for in summer, and why arctic explorers come to like whale-blubber and walrus fat. But when we learn that the natives of even tropic India pour melted butter over their rice, we perceive that in any climate, and under all conditions, men need to eat some fat. In a body poorly supplied with this, its proper fuel, protein has to take its place. But protein is costly, is needed for tissue building, and besides, is worth less than half what fat is as a heat giver. So that in burning protein to keep up our bodily heat, we are like people who, stormbound on the prairies and out of firewood, feed their stoves with furniture and even with grain; that is, we use for fuel, material intended and needed for other purposes, and which we can still afford to burn. Girls often dislike fat, particularly the thin, delicate ones who most need it. If possible it should be offered to them in tempting and digestible forms, cream salads dressed with oil, and crisp, fat bacon. But all kinds of fat can be so prepared as to be unobjectionable. Some ways of using it, however, are harmful to health. To see why this is we must understand something about the digestion of fats.

Elements of the Theory and Practice of Cookery. A textbook copyrighted in 1901 and reprinted several times with the most recent one being in 1913.

THIS AND THAT

The School House

The Little Red School House was one of the county's finest when it was built in 1907. It was erected and used by the people of Valle Crucis and was called the Valle Crucis Academy. Unlike other school houses around the county, the Academy was built to allow for one, two, or three rooms, and it housed grades one through high school. Remember, at that time high school would have been grades eight and possibly nine.

The School House was originally located near the Methodist Church in Valle Crucis on the banks of Dutch Creek. Blanche Greer remembers going to school there and students bringing lunch in buckets that were put in the creek to stay cool.

When the new elementary school was built,

Students at the Valle Crucis School in 1930.

the old school house was moved to a location behind the rock structure. It was used as a gymnasium and as a lunch room. In the 1960s, the school system sold the old school, and two Valle Crucis residents wanted it - Frank Mast and Frank Taylor. A coin toss was used to determine the buyer, who was Mr. Taylor. He moved the school house for a second time and used it as a tobacco barn.

The Valle Crucis School House as it appears today.

In 1989, John and Faye Cooper bought the school house and moved it to its current location behind the Original Store. Several former students have visited the school since it has been a part of the Mast Store. One commented that he remembered the floor having holes drilled in it to allow the water and mud to drain out from the flood in 1940.

WASSAIL

1 stick of cinnamon
1 tablespoon whole cloves
2 quarts sweet apple cider
1 (46-ounce) can pineapple juice
2 cups orange juice
1 cup lemon juice
1/2 (14-ounce) package red hot cinnamon candy

Tie up cinnamon and cloves in spice bag (or cheese cloth) for easy removal. Mix the cider, pineapple juice, orange juice, lemon juice and cinnamon candy together in a large sauce pan. Add spice bag and bring to a boil. Reduce to a simmer for about 15 minutes. Remove spice bag and serve. Can be kept hot in crock pot.

Janet Bright
Hendersonville

"Great for holiday parties!"

EVERGREEN PUNCH

1 cup sugar
1 quart hot water
2 packages unsweetened lime flavored drink mix powder
1 (46-ounce) can pineapple juice
2 large bottles ginger ale
1 pint Gold Label Rum (optional)

Dissolve sugar in hot water; cool. Mix powdered drink, pineapple juice and sugar water. Pour into containers or molds and freeze. Before serving, place frozen molds in punch bowl and pour ginger ale over them. Break up molds, and add rum. Serve punch when it is an icy consistency.

Jill Meares
Asheville

BLANCHE'S GINGER TEA

1 cup water
1 teaspoon ginger (or a smidgen more)
Sugar, to taste
2 tablespoons whiskey (bourbon)

Bring water, ginger and sugar to a boil. Let boil for one minute. Put the mixture in a cup and let it cool a bit, then add whiskey and stir well. This tea is good for colds and flu...and upset stomach (without whiskey). Consume tea and go immediately to bed, cover up, and sweat your cold away. Be sure not to drink the tea too hot!

Sheri Moretz
Home Office

HOT CHOCOLATE MIX

1 (16-ounce) box powdered sugar
6 ounces powdered nondairy coffee creamer
1 (16-ounce) box powdered cocoa
12 cups powdered milk
1 teaspoon salt

Mix sugar, creamer, cocoa, milk and salt in a gallon container and keep tightly covered. To serve: mix approximately 2 tablespoons with a cup of hot water.

Jill Meares
Asheville

INSTANT RUSSIAN TEA

2 1/4 cups instant orange flavored breakfast drink mix
1 cup sugar
1/2 cup instant tea, regular flavor
1 teaspoon cinnamon
1/2 teaspoon ground cloves
1 package lemon flavored drink mix powder

Mix orange drink mix, sugar, tea, cinnamon, cloves and lemon drink mix. Keep in covered jar. To serve: stir 2 teaspoons into a cup of hot water.

Jill Meares
Asheville

"This is a great winter-time drink, and makes a super gift when given in small decorative jars."

MOCHA MIX

2 cups instant hot chocolate powder
2 cups powdered nondairy creamer
1 cup instant coffee granules
1 teaspoon cinnamon
1/2 teaspoon nutmeg
1 1/4 cups sugar

Blend the hot chocolate powder, nondairy creamer, coffee granules, cinnamon, nutmeg and sugar together until well blended. Store in a covered jar. To serve: add 2 teaspoons of mix to a cup of boiling water.

Mary Jane Matthews
Waynesville

LOW-FAT VANILLA MILKSHAKE

4 cups nonfat frozen vanilla yogurt
1 3/4 cups skim milk
1/2 teaspoon vanilla extract

Combine frozen yogurt, skim milk and vanilla extract. Process in blender until smooth. Serve immediately.

Catherine L. Main
Original Store

CURRIED FRUIT

3/4 stick butter or margarine
1 cup firmly packed brown sugar
1 teaspoon curry powder
1 (15-ounce) can pear halves
1 (15-ounce) can peach slices
1 (20-ounce) can pineapple slices
1 (15-ounce) jar spiced apple rings
1 (6-ounce) jar maraschino cherries

Combine butter, sugar and curry powder in a sauce pan and bring to a boil. Drain fruit and arrange in a 2-quart baking dish. Pour sauce (while hot) over fruit. Garnish with cherries. Bake in preheated 325° oven for about 40 minutes.

Jill Meares
Asheville

BROILED GRAPEFRUIT

Grapefruit (1/2 grapefruit per person)
Brown sugar
Butter
Maraschino cherries with stems

Halve each grapefruit and sprinkle top of each with brown sugar. Dot with butter. Place on a cookie sheet or in a baking dish and broil in oven for 3 to 5 minutes, or until tops are slightly brown. Remove from oven and top each with a maraschino cherry.

Joyce Crandall
Hendersonville

"These are great served for brunch or with dinner, and are very simple to make."

LEMON BUTTER

1/4 cup butter (do not use substitute)
2 cups sugar
4 eggs
8 tablespoons lemon juice

Mix butter, sugar, eggs and lemon juice in double boiler and cook over medium heat until the consistency of honey. Stir constantly with a wooden spoon. Pour into a jar with a cover and refrigerate. Spread on biscuits, toast, etc.

Janet Bright
Hendersonville

"One of my mother-in-law Harriet's favorites! Be sure to mix ingredients exactly in order given. Lemon butter will keep in the refrigerator a long time."

RHUBARB-PINEAPPLE CONSERVE

5 cups diced rhubarb
4 cups sugar
1 cup crushed canned pineapple, drained
1 (6-ounce) box wild strawberry flavored gelatin

Combine rhubarb, sugar and pineapple in a pan and cook for 10 minutes. Remove from heat and add gelatin; mix well. Pour into jars and seal with paraffin.

Lucy Mast Olsen
Valle Crucis

SAWMILL GRAVY

1/4 cup cornmeal
3 tablespoons bacon grease
2 cups milk

Brown cornmeal in hot bacon grease. Add milk, stir on medium heat until gravy thickens. Serve over corn bread.

Debe Jones
Home Office

"I remember my mother making this for supper when I was growing up. My father helped a neighbor run a sawmill, so we called it 'Sawmill Gravy'."

CHOCOLATE GRAVY

1/2 cup sugar
Dash of salt
2 tablespoons cornstarch
2 tablespoons cocoa
1 1/2 cups milk
1 tablespoon margarine

Mix sugar, salt, cornstarch and cocoa. Add milk and margarine. Cook over low heat, stirring constantly until thickened. Serve over hot biscuits.

Jeanne Norris
Home Office

CAJUN STYLE MEAT SEASONING

1/2 cup salt
1/4 cup granulated garlic
1/4 cup black pepper
1 tablespoon cumin
1 tablespoon cayenne pepper
1 tablespoon white pepper

Combine salt, garlic, pepper, cumin, cayenne pepper and white pepper; mix thoroughly. Store in glass jar in cool, dry place. Rub into meat before cooking.

Allen Mast
Original Store

"Great on any kind of meat."

Bar-Be-Que Sauce

1 medium onion, chopped
1/2 cup water
2 tablespoons margarine
2 tablespoons vinegar
4 tablespoons lemon juice
1 cup ketchup
2 tablespoons brown sugar
1/2 teaspoon prepared mustard
3 tablespoons Worcestershire sauce
Salt and pepper, to taste
Cayenne pepper, to taste

Combine onion, water, margarine, vinegar, lemon juice, ketchup, brown sugar, mustard, Worcestershire sauce, salt, pepper and cayenne pepper in a sauce pan and simmer for 30 minutes.

Barbara Murdock
Home Office

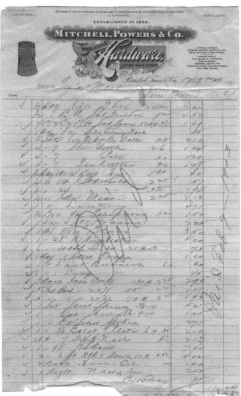

This invoice is from the very early 1900s. Mitchell Powers Hardware is still one of the Mast Store's suppliers.

CHILI SAUCE

2 quarts ripe tomatoes
1 cup chopped onion
1 cup chopped celery
4 sweet peppers
1 hot pepper (if desired)
1 pint apples, peeled and cored
1 1/2 cups vinegar
2 3/4 cups sugar
1 1/2 tablespoons cinnamon
2 tablespoons mustard seed
1/2 tablespoon ground cloves
2 teaspoons salt

Cook tomatoes, onions, celery, peppers, and apples after putting through a grinder (this saves time and continual stirring). Add vinegar, sugar, cinnamon, mustard seed, cloves and salt. Boil until "proper" consistency, stirring frequently while cooking. Seal in jars while hot. Good on burgers, hot dogs, etc.

Janet Bright
Hendersonville

"This recipe comes from my husband John's Grandma Bright."

BLUE CHEESE DRESSING

1 (1-pint) carton sour cream
1 cup mayonnaise
2 cloves garlic, grated
3 tablespoons dill pickle juice
1 cup crumbled bleu cheese
Dash salt
1/4 teaspoon ground black pepper

Combine sour cream, mayonnaise, garlic, pickle juice, bleu cheese, salt and pepper. Chill in refrigerator overnight.

Jill Meares
Asheville

ALFALFA SPROUTS

In a wide-mouth canning jar, add 2 1/2 teaspoons of alfalfa seeds. Cover with water and let sit overnight. Cover the top of the jar with a "store-bought" sprout screen topper or make your own top out of fine gauge screen. Rinse the sprouts twice a day for about 3-4 days. Refrigerate.

The Old Mast Store Deli
Valle Crucis

DAD'S COUGH SYRUP

2 tablespoons whiskey/bourbon
(or White Lightening if you can get it)
Splash of lemon juice
1 teaspoon honey
Dash of ginger

Mix whiskey, lemon juice, honey and ginger in a small glass. Fill a bowl with hot water (bowl must be big enough to hold the glass). Put the glass in the water and stir its contents until warm. Drink and go to bed.

Sheri Moretz
Home Office

RECIPE FOR A GOOD LIFE

1 cup good thoughts
1 cup kind deeds
1 cup consideration for others
2 handfuls generosity
3 cups sacrifice for others
3 cups forgiveness
2 cups well-beaten faults
1 lifetime of service

Mix these thoroughly and add tears of joy and sorrow and sympathy for others. Flavor with little gifts of love. Fold in 4 cups of prayer and faith to lighten other ingredients and raise the texture to great heights of Godly living. After pouring all of this into your daily living, bake well with the heat of human kindness. Serve with a smile.

Debe Jones
Home Office

BAKED OATMEAL

3 cups oatmeal
1 cup brown sugar
2 teaspoons baking powder
1 teaspoon salt
1 teaspoon cinnamon
1/2 cup margarine, melted
2 eggs, beaten
1 cup milk

Mix oatmeal, sugar, baking powder, salt and cinnamon in a mixing bowl. Add margarine, eggs and milk. Mix thoroughly and pour into a buttered 8 x 8-inch pan. Bake in preheated 350° oven for 40 to 60 minutes.

Barbara Murdock
Home Office

"My family likes their baked oatmeal with milk and applesauce."

INDEX

Mast Store Has Handmade "Cures" for Gout and Gray Hair

It used to be roots and herbs and crops and chickens that folks brought to the Mast General Store in historic Valle Crucis for trade. Today, the items "traded" are more along the lines of baskets, birdhouses, bread, homemade butter, and hand-turned bowls. Although the products may have changed, the intent is still the same - the Mast Store provides a marketplace for local and regional residents and artists to present the fruits of their efforts.

"Crafting is quite a productive cottage industry in the mountains," said Sheri Moretz, a life-long resident of Watauga County and publicist for the Mast Store. "Recently, the spotlight on crafts has shone even brighter through the work of *Handmade in America*. We really have some talented people practicing skills and making goods that can't be found just anywhere."

A Mast Store customer demonstrates a gout rocker on the back porch of the Original Store.

One of those items you can find at any of the Mast General Stores, but probably not anywhere else, is a Gout Rocker, made by Cove Creek resident Pat Reece. It was once the prescribed treatment for a painful foot ailment, but now it is a popular addition to any rocking chair as well as an interesting conversation piece. Consisting of two rockers on curvaceous legs and a thin upholstered cross-piece, the rocker looks something like a child's rocking chair that was left unfinished.

"The idea initially came from Harllee Rothenberger, who worked in the Mast Store mercantile area. She used to see 'gout rockers' come to the Mast Store, but they were a little chunkier than the ones you'll see today. Harllee took the design and incorporated a few dressier elements to make an improved piece," said Pat from her Cove Creek home.

Not much is known about the actual origin of the gout rocker. Harllee grew up in plantation country and heard of them as a child and Harlee's father, who was a pharmacist, spoke of them. It just seemed like a natural progression to move from a stool to a rocker because it's just that much more comfortable when sitting in your rocking chair and having your feet rock along with you.

"Much of what we did was trial and error in the beginning," said Pat with a grin. "We experimented with everything - even a stain concocted of Varsol compounds and walnut hulls for coloring. Once we tried filling an order with a new kind of wood. We tried every way imaginable to dry the wood out - including zapping it in the microwave. As it turned out, we had to buy a whole new shipment of wood to complete the order."

From its humble beginnings using common hand tools, the ladies added pieces of equipment to make their job a little easier. But that didn't mean sacrificing quality or wasting materials.

"I'm a fanatic for craftsmanship. If I don't feel like it's put together well and will stand up to usage, I won't let it out of my shop," explained Pat. Her shop includes a number of "jigs" and templates used to speed up the process, but even with these time-saving apparatuses, each rocker has its own unique character and look. "No two gout rockers are exactly alike."

Harllee passed on a few years ago, a victim of cancer, but Pat points out, "Everyone that we encounter leaves a part of themselves with us. Harllee left me a great gift in these rockers and her friendship." This could also be said of craftspeople, who pass on a little of themselves in every piece of art they make.

Pat, who lives with her family and her father in Cove Creek, North Carolina, is a teaching assistant at Watauga High School in the Vocational Arts area.

Gout rockers are not the only product that Mast Store carries with a little bit of local history. Traditional sun bonnets - those like Caroline Ingalls wore on the television show Little House on the Prairie - have been made for the Mast Store by a member of the same family for four decades.

Reba Townsend said, "I remember my grandma Coffey tellin' me 'git something on your head. If you'd jest wear a bonnet or somethin', your hair won't turn gray.' I guess she was right, 'cause when she died, she didn't have hardly a gray hair on her head." Reba took some of her grandmother's words to heart - but not necessarily the wearin' of a bonnet, as her gray hair can attest. She has been making bonnets for the Mast Store for some 10 to 12 years using patterns that are at least 50 years old.

"I got into making bonnets when Mack's mother, Clemmie, came to stay with us after a spell in the hospital. She had some already started, and I helped her finish them up." Clemmie Townsend made bonnets for the Mast Store for probably 25 years and dealt with Howard Mast. After one time helping Clemmie, she and Reba started making them together.

Reba recalled that she started sewing when her mother sat her down with some quilt scraps and got her started. "She also tried to teach me how to make bedspread lace, but it kinda bugged me. I stuck to sewing." (However, she has been known to tie a few

The Creekside Deli owner dons one of Reba's bonnets

lengths of bedspread lace, too.)

Reba and her husband Mack are both natives of the area. She was born on Dutch Creek in April, 1924, not too far from her present-day home and went to school on Dutch Creek before graduating from the Mission School (now the Valle Crucis Conference Center). Mack was born on Clarks Creek in October, 1924 and went to school in the original Valle Crucis School (located behind the Original Mast Store in Valle Crucis and now housing Beaumont Pottery).

She hopes to pass along the bonnet-making business to her granddaughters, who live just a hop, skip, and a jump up Dutch Creek and to get them interested in her and her husband's other mountain crafts.

The Mast Store has many stories to tell of crafters, history, and heritage. It carries on the tradition of general stores marketing locally produced goods.

Greenville, SC

The city of Greenville springs from humble beginnings. In 1797, land was donated by Lemuel Alston for a jail and a courthouse, and the small hamlet was dubbed "Pleasantburg." Though appropriately named, Pleasantburg never caught on among the populous. It became known as Greenville Courthouse, named for Revolutionary War general Nathanael Greene.

Being nestled in the upstate of South Carolina between the mountains of the Smokies and the stretches of the piedmont, Greenville and its surrounding area became a resort destination particularly popular with Charlestonians. The Mansion House, a hotel built in 1824, stood at the same location as the Westin Poinsett does today. The city's location near ample water resources also allowed industry, especially textiles, to flourish.

The Mast Store in Greenville was constructed in 1898 as a dry goods and shoe store. Over the years, part of the building has served as a theatre and as a Civil Defense fallout shelter. The location is best known to long-time Greenvillians as the old "Meyers-Arnold," a locally-owned department store carrying everything from housewares and lingerie to small appliances and men's shoes.

Meyers-Arnold occupied the location from 1903 until 1971.

In March of 2003, it opened as a part of the Mast Store family of stores. Old employees and family members were impressed with the restoration work once again exposing the pressed tin ceiling and warm maple flooring.

The Greenville store circa 1962.

INDEX

Notes_____

Notes

Notes

Notes

MAST STORE COOKS
From Potluck Dinners to the Potbelly Stove

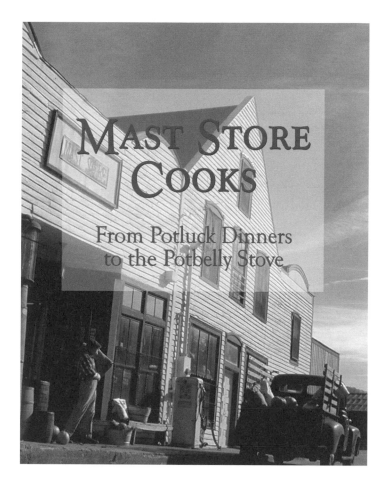

Makes a great gift for newlyweds, housewarmings, history lovers,
and those who like to cook.

Order a copy and have it shipped directly to friends and family by calling
Mast Store's toll-free number — 866-FOR MAST (866-367-6278) or visit
online at MastStoreOnline.com. Of course, we'd love to see you at one of
our locations in North Carolina, including Valle Crucis, Boone, Waynesville,
Hendersonville, and Asheville; South Carolina, including Greenville and
Columbia; and Knoxville, Tennessee.